THE HENRY L. STIMSON LECTURES SERIES

OUR DOLLAR, YOUR PROBLEM

An Insider's View of Seven Turbulent Decades
of Global Finance, and the Road Ahead

Kenneth Rogoff

Yale
UNIVERSITY PRESS
NEW HAVEN AND LONDON

The Henry L. Stimson Lectures at the Whitney and Betty MacMillan Center
for International and Area Studies at Yale.

Published with assistance from the foundation established
in memory of Amasa Stone Mather of the Class of 1907, Yale College.

Copyright © 2025 by Kenneth Rogoff.
All rights reserved.
This book may not be reproduced, in whole or in part,
including illustrations, in any form (beyond that copying permitted
by Sections 107 and 108 of the U.S. Copyright Law and except by
reviewers for the public press), without written permission
from the publishers.

Yale University Press books may be purchased in quantity
for educational, business, or promotional use. For information, please e-mail
sales.press@yale.edu (U.S. office) or sales@yaleup.co.uk (U.K. office).

Set in Yale and Alternate Gothic No2 type by Integrated Publishing Solutions.

Printed in the United States of America.

Library of Congress Control Number: 2024947017
ISBN 978-0-300-27531-5 (hardcover : alk. paper)

A catalogue record for this book is available from the British Library.

This paper meets the requirements of ANSI/NISO Z39.48–1992
(Permanence of Paper).

Authorized Representative in the EU: Easy Access System Europe, Mustamäe
tee 50, 10621 Tallinn, Estonia, gpsr.requests@easproject.com.

10 9 8 7 6 5 4 3 2

To Natasha Lance Rogoff

CONTENTS

Preface ix

Chapter 1. Introduction: The Making of a Dominant Currency 1

PART I. PAST CHALLENGERS TO DOLLAR DOMINANCE

Chapter 2. The Soviet Challenge 13
Chapter 3. Japan and the Yen 25
Chapter 4. The Single Currency in Europe 42

PART II. CHINA: THE PRESENT-DAY CHALLENGER

Chapter 5.   This Time Is Different 65
Chapter 6.   Zhu Rongji's Uncanny Forecasts 74
Chapter 7.   The People's Bank of China 82
Chapter 8.   Prelude to Crisis 91
Chapter 9.   The End of High Growth 96
Chapter 10. The Inevitability of Dollar Decoupling 110

PART III. EVERYONE ELSE'S PROBLEM: LIVING WITH THE DOLLAR

Chapter 11. The Lure of Fixed Exchange Rates 117
Chapter 12. Hyperinflation 126

CONTENTS

Chapter 13. When Exchange Rate Pegs Outlive Their Shelf Life   134
Chapter 14. Lebanon and Argentina: Unique or Prototypical?   145
Chapter 15. The Tokyo Consensus   154
Chapter 16. Fixed Exchange Rates Redux   161

PART IV. ALTERNATIVE CURRENCIES

Chapter 17. Global Currencies   173
Chapter 18. Cryptocurrencies and the Future of Money   182
Chapter 19. Central Bank Digital Currencies   199

PART V. THE PERKS AND BURDENS OF BEING THE DOMINANT CURRENCY

Chapter 20. Perks of Currency Dominance   211
Chapter 21. Exorbitant Privilege or Taxation Without Representation?   219
Chapter 22. Small Ways the United States Helps Countries Deal with Dollar Dominance   229
Chapter 23. Costs of Being a Dominant Currency   236

PART VI. PEAK DOLLAR DOMINANCE

Chapter 24. Central Bank Independence: The Bulwark of Currency Dominance   247
Chapter 25. Debtor's Empire: The United States' Achilles' Heel   262
Chapter 26. The Siren Call of "Lower Forever" Interest Rates   273
Chapter 27. The End of the Pax Dollar Era?   289

Notes   293
Acknowledgments   333
Index   335

PREFACE

One never ceases to be amazed at the blasé complacency of modern-day perspectives on international macroeconomic and financial issues. It is not that I ever believed my ironically titled 2009 tome *This Time Is Different* (co-authored with Carmen Reinhart), which was seven years in the making, would permanently awaken the world to the risks of debt-fueled financial and spending excess. Countless readers enjoyed the book, and it became extremely well known, but that is a far cry from changing habits deeply rooted in human behavior. Still, it was surprising how quickly new "this time is different" stories replaced ones that had just crashed and burned in the global financial crisis: Now that economists understand inflation, it will never again be a concern. The speculative real estate boom in China is different thanks to superior state competence and booming growth, and so forth.

Academic economists also came up with one theory after another on why real (inflation-adjusted) interest rates will remain ultra-low forever, giving governments the green light to ignore any risks arising from very high debt. Anyone who doesn't believe that very high debt is a free lunch must be in favor of austerity. With cryptocurrencies, the nuttiness goes in both directions, including those who think they will supplant the dollar and those who think Bitcoin is a scam. Although for many years my own work pushing back on such ideas (and

PREFACE

others) continued to be prominently published in the very top academic journals, my views were very much in the minority. That is perhaps a bit less so today.

Still, U.S. policymakers and smug economic commentators take on blind faith that we are in a pax dollar era that everyone should be grateful for and that can be relied on to produce stability and growth for the indefinite future. Most of the world, even America's friends, do not necessarily share this perspective, which will eventually be a problem, especially given the challenges that the United States faces in keeping its own macroeconomic house in order.

The title of this book is an allusion to the oft-cited retort of Treasury Secretary John Connally. In 1963, Connally, then the governor of Texas, was seriously wounded while riding in the presidential limousine when John F. Kennedy was assassinated. And he might have been most remembered for that but for a meeting in Rome in 1971, shortly after President Richard Nixon suspended the convertibility of U.S. dollars to gold. By then the Treasury secretary, Connally was confronted by furious European leaders whose countries were holding vast stores of U.S. Treasury bills. Even more importantly, they had built their entire post-war monetary and financial systems on the premise that the dollar was as good as gold. "Our dollar, your problem," Connally famously told them. As the reader of this book will come to understand, Connally was only half right. The inflation that Europeans feared would savage their dollar reserves was not very good for Americans either, a lesson that was painfully relearned in the early 2020s.

Today, the global financial system is at a critical inflection point not seen since the early 1970s, when the Bretton Woods fixed exchange rate system collapsed, or the late 1980s, when the Berlin Wall fell and China's meteoric rise began to accelerate. The United States no longer guarantees foreign central banks that they can exchange their dollars for gold. Instead, it promises to maintain low inflation and thereby preserve the purchasing power of the dollar, which is what the European finance ministers really cared about. The problem is that in a world in which the United States always looks out first and foremost for its own self-interests, that promise is getting harder to deliver on. The U.S. Federal Reserve, which manages America's monetary policy, is a great institution. Unfortunately, it is difficult to stand as an island of technocratic competence in a sea of political turmoil, both domestic and international. Delivering

PREFACE

low inflation year in and year out in a world of burgeoning political and fiscal pressures is no simple task, especially when the occasional burst of inflation is the safety valve of first resort to avoid sudden excessive austerity, heavy-handed financial controls, or default. This will be particularly so if the world experiences a sustained period where investors demand higher inflation-adjusted interest rates and suddenly debt starts looking a lot less like the free lunch that many have thought it to be, especially since the 2008–2009 global financial crisis. And such a scenario may already be upon us.

Indeed, there are ample reasons to believe that over the coming decade, the world will experience higher interest rates and inflation than policymakers have gotten used to and that the dollar's unique borrowing privilege might be considerably less amid a considerably more fragmented global financial system. (Of course, interest rates will still be lower in recessions.) The era in which the dollar was utterly dominant and reliably stable may have passed its peak. The likely result will be a global rise in the number and intensity of debt, inflation, financial, and exchange rate crises—these won't happen all the time, but a lot more often than the world has gotten used to—especially when you look at the decade before the pandemic.

The prospect of rising instability may come as a surprise to those who have imbibed the "end of history" philosophy that permeates modern economics, whereby economists think they have it all (mostly) solved but for some refinements. In fact, an important part of the vaunted stability seemingly engineered by central banks over the last half century is an artifact of a period in which trade and financial globalization were rapidly increasing, great power conflict had faded, and populism had been suppressed. Needless to say, all these trends may be reversing.

Over the course of my five decades as a professional economist, I have observed that, although the financial system usually evolves glacially, the occasional dramatic turn is to be expected. Political upheavals, technological disruptions, wars, and other kinds of extreme duress have happened in the past, and they will happen again. The notion that we will almost always live in a world of ultra-low inflation and interest rates, and stable major currency exchange rates, is wishful thinking.

To put the remarkable evolution of today's dollar-centric global currency

PREFACE

system in historical perspective, as well as to give the underlying analytical discussion texture and color, this book will frequently bring in my own professional and policy experiences. Perhaps reviewing real-time uncertainty about past changes and episodes will also provide a frame of reference for just how much uncertainty we face going forward right now and why the scenarios I will discuss later in the book, though perhaps outside the consensus, are hardly unrealistic.

It is true that the dollar has remained on top even though the United States has repeatedly been the epicenter of worldwide crises and recessions. Indeed, the 2008–2009 global financial crisis, much like the Great Depression of the 1930s, had its roots in U.S. policy blunders, yet it was the rest of the world that suffered the most. Ironically, the U.S. dollar emerged from that episode more dominant than ever. Don't count on that happening again, especially given U.S. political dysfunction and debt problems and China's zeal to break away from the dollar bloc. Although the dollar will likely stay on top for some time to come, its global footprint may shrink after decades of continual expansion; if so, the shift could further exacerbate the difficult fiscal adjustment the United States already faces.

If the United States wants to keep the dollar from dropping to a lower orbit, and encourage adherence to dollar rule, Americans need to appreciate that the rest of the world, even our friends, have mixed feeling about U.S. hegemony. As a teenager representing the United States in high-level chess tournaments across Europe in the late 1960s and early 1970s, I was constantly confronted with this paradox. People were steeped in American music and film. Inside at a crowded seedy bar in Sarajevo, the Jefferson Airplane song "White Rabbit" was booming out from the radio. It was stunning to hear half the people belting out every word even though almost none of them spoke English. It was embarrassing not to know the words myself as the lone American, and doubly so when I later learned that back in the states, my close and far cooler friend Kim Commons had been giving chess lessons to that band's lead singer, Grace Slick. Sometimes even the thinly disguised KGB agents who would accompany the Russian chess players couldn't hide their fascination with American culture. One "escort" I met couldn't stop talking (in perfect KGB English) about U.S. basketball star Wilt Chamberlain. Yet many of these same people would sit across

PREFACE

from you at dinner and matter-of-factly denigrate the United States as a racist, war-mongering society.

These tensions and contradictions very much still exist today. The United States' allies and competitors alike enjoy the convenience of a quasi-global currency, much as English provides the common language of international trade and diplomacy. They bristle, however, at how exposed their economies are to the vicissitudes of self-absorbed U.S. macroeconomic policy. American financial officials typically pay little more than lip service to foreign concerns, sometimes leaving their foreign counterparts pining for Connally's directness so that they would at least know where things stand. Looking at the periodic financial turmoil of the past seventy-five years and the extreme divisiveness of the U.S. political situation today, not to mention the rise of China, the rest of the world is right to worry about what all of this implies for global macroeconomic stability in the coming decades.

CHAPTER 1

INTRODUCTION

The Making of a Dominant Currency

Before we dive into the odyssey of the dollar, and a bit of my own journey in trying to understand it, it is helpful to set the stage with a few key facts. Perhaps the single most important thing to know is that the mantle of the world's dominant currency does not change hands very often. One to two centuries is the norm, and the transition is typically marked by the co-existence of both the old dominant currency and the eventual new champion. In this sense, the era of dollar dominance, having lasted just over a century, may be regarded as late middle-aged. Conflict typically plays a major role in the changing of the guard, although innovation can also be a factor as, for example, in the case of the Dutch. The Netherlands held the mantle of dominant currency in the seventeenth century, thanks in no small part to the innovation of having silver-coin-backed bank paper notes, called "florin," circulating alongside Dutch guilder coins.[1]

Although the financial press regularly features articles about foreign leaders or Silicon Valley innovators who bluster about replacing the dollar, in reality the greenback rules the global financial system today like no currency before it — not the Spanish "pieces of eight" of the sixteenth century, or the Dutch guilder that came next, or even the British pound sterling at its peak from the end of the Napoleonic Wars through World War I, when the sun never set on the British

INTRODUCTION

Empire. The dollar is the undisputed lingua franca of today's highly globalized trade and financial markets. Indeed, what it means to be the dominant world currency has considerably expanded as the world has globalized and as the financial system has evolved; the Spanish peseta was of little significance in sixteenth-century India and China, whereas the dollar plays a central role throughout Asia—at least for now.

From the perspective of the rest of the world, the least attractive feature of the current regime is that although countries mostly trust the United States not to default (don't ask Russia or China), it still has wide berth to use inflation to decrease the real value of its debt. An unexpected burst of inflation is, after all, tantamount to partial default since the government gets to repay its debt in dollars that buy much less than originally expected when the debt was issued. This is exactly what happened in the 1970s, when European central banks saw the value of their dollar reserves wilt away. And, of course, the purchasing power of the dollar fell suddenly again after the pandemic.

For bond holders, inflation is the scourge of modern government-issued money. And the risk of high inflation remains the Achilles' heel of the system. Sure, the U.S. central bank—the Federal Reserve—can promise never to allow inflation to spike. If the Federal Reserve's inflation targets are treated as sacrosanct, however, what then is the safety valve for unsustainable debt or unexpected costs in the future (say, for emergency defense needs, the green transition, or a presidential administration gone off the rails)? Austerity? Financial repression (forced holdings of debt at low interest rates)? Outright default?

Mind you, there was inflation before the printing press; it was just much harder to do. When coins were made of precious metals, a government wanting to decrease the value of its currency—that is, to inflate—would have to call in its coins and then re-issue new ones with less silver content. Sometimes the old coins were just clipped and recirculated. Such debasement can be readily observed in exhibits at modern numismatic museums, such as those in Tokyo, Jerusalem, and Dresden: when one lines up a nation's coins over the decades and centuries, the shrinkage is typically manifest.

Henry VIII of England is famous for beheading two of his six wives: "divorced, beheaded, and died; divorced, beheaded, survived" is the old rhyme that English schoolchildren learn and that was most recently featured in the clever

INTRODUCTION

Broadway musical *SIX*.² In monetary economics, however, Henry VIII is just as famous for decapitating the United Kingdom's coinage: the silver content of the sterling shrunk by 50 percent in 1551.³ Of course, Henry VIII was a piker next to Robert Mugabe of Zimbabwe or Nicolás Maduro of Venezuela, who achieved hyperinflation this century with the aid of the modern printing press, as we shall come to later.

It was in part by not overindulging in shrinkage that Spain managed to have the dominant global currency in the 1500s. Spain was helped immensely by an influx of precious metals from mines in the New World, which were manned by native labor working under harsh conditions. Using mountains of silver plundered from the Potosí mines in the eastern Andes and the Zacatecas mines in Mexico, Spain was able to man armies, build ships, and deploy weapons on a scale far beyond its poorer European rivals; it became the foremost economic and military power of the sixteenth century. And when spoils from the colonies were not enough to satisfy the ambitions of the Spanish crown, Spain borrowed promiscuously, so much so that it defaulted on debt to foreign creditors six times from 1557 to 1647.⁴ The 1557 "Trinity Default," in particular, marks one of the most significant global financial crises in history, with nearly simultaneous defaults in Spain, France, and the Netherlands.⁵

The Sea Hawk is a classic film that captures the ethos of the time from an unabashedly biased British American perspective. Set in the 1580s, the film stars Errol Flynn as the swashbuckling English privateer who had to overcome countless obstacles to warn England's Queen Elizabeth that a huge fleet was being readied by Spain's King Philip II for a surprise attack on England. The movie makes much of the fact that British captives were relegated to galley slaves in Spanish ships, whereas Flynn's character, upon seizing a Spanish ship, gives its surviving crew free run of his own pirate vessel, save for the weapons cache. The sinking of the invincible Spanish Armada, which was partly due to bad weather, was a turning point in dominant-currency history. By the nineteenth century, the pound sterling, and with it the U.K. banking system, had established the kind of global reach that King Philip II could scarcely have dreamed of.

The twentieth-century transition from the pound to the dollar also arose from conflict, even though the United States and United Kingdom fought as allies. As a result of two devastating world wars, the United Kingdom had ex-

INTRODUCTION

hausted a great deal of its wealth and lost part of its industrial base; it could no longer even hold on to its colonies. The United States, although suffering mightily, each time lost much less. After an interwar period in which the sterling and the dollar were co-dominant, the mantle passed definitively to the United States.

The global economic supremacy of the United States after World War II was breathtaking; in 1950, the U.S. economy accounted for an astounding 36 percent of global GDP.[6] The post-war system of fixed exchange rates, hammered out in 1944 in Bretton Woods, New Hampshire, not only placed the U.S. dollar at the center but also gave the dollar extraordinary privileges by design.[7] All other participating countries were required to fix their exchange rates to the dollar, and it was each country's responsibility to keep enough dollars on hand to achieve that end, subject to allowances for small fluctuations. The United States, on the other hand, was free to pursue whatever interest-rate and inflation-rate policy it wanted, with the main proviso that, in theory, the U.S. government had to stand ready to exchange dollars for gold for any government that wished to do so.

Thanks to network effects, international currency usage is a natural monopoly. So it should not be surprising that once a currency establishes itself in international transactions, the use of most other currencies falls by the wayside. Today, there are over 150 currencies in the world;[8] world trade and finance would be a Tower of Babel if they were all used. A remarkable 90 percent of all foreign exchange transactions involve the dollar on one side or the other.[9] That's because the market for most currency trades is so thin that it's cheaper to use the dollar as a "vehicle currency" for, say, converting Canadian dollars to Australian dollars than to swap the two directly. The transaction costs of the two trades (Canadian to U.S. dollars, then U.S. to Aussie dollars) are less than those of the direct trade. A mind-blowing fact is that the dollar, not the euro, is the dominant vehicle currency even for trades involving countries that border the eurozone (e.g., a trade from Turkish lira to Bulgarian lev).[10]

The dollar's position atop the currency food chain shows up across many quantitative metrics. For example, although the United States accounts for roughly a quarter of global output (measured at 2024 market exchange rates), almost 60 percent of foreign exchange reserves are held in U.S. dollars.[11]

INTRODUCTION

The dollar also plays a central role in the pricing of international goods and financial assets. The share of the global oil trade priced in dollars remains around 80 percent, despite China's recent efforts to promote the renminbi; most other commodity trades are similarly dominated by dollar pricing.[12] Over 40 percent of global goods trade is priced in dollars, and that is an understatement because it counts trade between eurozone members as international trade. The dollar's share would be far higher otherwise; for example, over 85 percent of India's trade is in dollars.[13] Global bond markets are even more dollar-centric.

Figure 1 offers perhaps the best and most nuanced summary measure of dollar dominance for the year 2019, before the pandemic.[14] The map shows which countries' central banks either stabilize their currencies against the dollar or implicitly use the dollar as their main reference currency. Darkened areas show countries that have joined the dollar bloc since 1999. China, a charter member of the modern dollar bloc, is highlighted with striped lines because it has allowed a bit more exchange rate flexibility, especially since 2015. However, it is a borderline case, with the renminbi-dollar exchange rate in 2024 only slightly weaker than the exchange rate before the global financial crisis, and China could just as well have been included as a full member of the dollar bloc. Russia was forced to become less dollar-centric after the full-scale invasion of Ukraine in 2022, and the eastern former Soviet states followed in its wake. Nevertheless, the greenback remains in widespread circulation.

It is hardly surprising that so many of the world's central banks, especially in developing and emerging-market economies, care about stabilizing their dollar exchange rates given that such a large fraction of trade, and often a similarly large proportion of their international debt, is in dollars.[15] In general, one can think of the exchange rate regime as a portmanteau measure of all the different ways the dollar matters for a country, since the central bank must take all of these into account in determining its exchange rate regime. If the central bank views the economy as highly sensitive to movements in the dollar exchange rate, it will be careful not to let that exchange rate move too much too fast.

A major factor in favor of the dollar is that the U.S. economy is the world's largest. Although its size advantage has been decreasing over time, this has happened far more slowly than most experts had predicted. Since 1950, the U.S. share of global GDP, measured at market exchange rates, has dropped to about

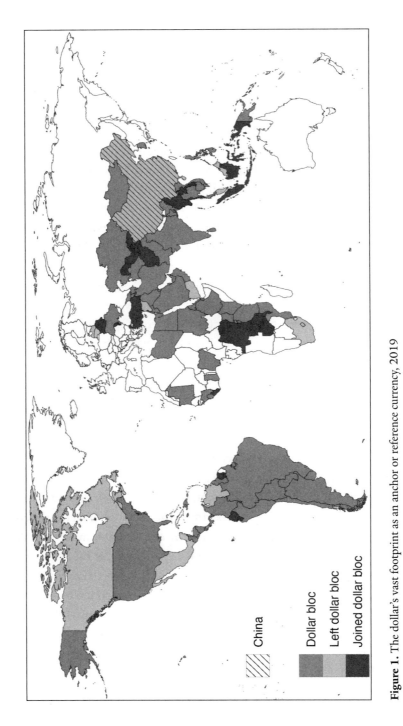

Figure 1. The dollar's vast footprint as an anchor or reference currency, 2019

Source: Updated from Ilzetzki, Reinhart, and Rogoff, *Quarterly Journal of Economics*, 2019.

INTRODUCTION

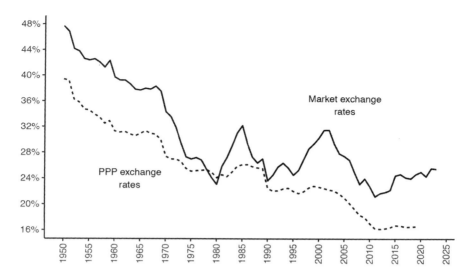

Figure 2. U.S. share of global GDP, 1950–2023
Data Source: Total Economy Database (market rates); Penn World Tables (PPP rates).

25 percent (as shown in figure 2).[16] The decline came in two spurts: the first as the economies of Europe and Japan rebuilt from World War II; the second when China hit its peak growth period in the early 2000s.

Figure 2 also shows a second way to measure the size of the U.S. economy. That method uses artificially constructed purchasing power parity (PPP) exchange rates, which attempt to use a common set of prices to better compare living standards. The United States' decline is sharper by the PPP living-standard measure: under that measure, the U.S. share of global GDP has fallen to under 17 percent. However, for the purposes of understanding international trade and financial power, the market measure is more meaningful; a country cannot buy oil or Patriot missiles with PPP dollars.

In 2000, the economy of the European Union was roughly the same size as the U.S. economy and seemed on track to achieve co-equal status. Now it, too, has been left in the dust by the U.S. economy, mainly because of the technology sector. The Chinese juggernaut is impressive, but if one compares economies using market exchange rates to convert income to dollars, the Chinese economy

INTRODUCTION

is still two-thirds as large, despite the fact that China has four times as many people.[17]

Size matters but isn't everything. Importantly, the U.S. economy is also the most open of any large economy, but that status is under assault. In 2018, President Donald Trump instituted significant tariffs that his successor Joe Biden maintained and amplified through a muscular industrial policy with strong made-in-America requirements to tap new green transition subsidies. During the 2024 election campaign, Donald Trump proposed instituting average tariff rates above those of India and Brazil, the two most protectionist major economies in the world. And it very likely gained him votes.

The size of U.S. financial markets, which remain disproportionately large relative to U.S. income, is also extremely important to the dollar's position atop the currency food chain, and indeed plays an increasingly large role in dollar dominance. For now, U.S. financial markets remain very open to foreign investors; periodic proposals to tax financial transactions have not taken root. Above all, the United States has an established rule of law that is more favorable to creditors than the laws in most countries, even in Europe.

The U.S. university system has long been welcoming to foreign students, providing yet another incentive for their parents to accumulate dollar assets. More generally, the United States remains the largest and most important destination for immigrants, even if policy in recent years has become more erratic, and at times incomprehensible. As of 2019, the United States had more than fifty million immigrants, over three times as many as the next country, Germany.[18]

In sum, the dollar's dominance is the product of many factors that reinforce each other. The size and depth of U.S. markets still far surpass those of any other currency. Also, the dollar having started out in an undeniably privileged position after the destruction of World Wars I and II, network effects have set in that make using the dollar extremely convenient for private markets, even if other governments chafe at the advantages they perceive that the dollar gives the United States. Critically, despite recent protectionist turns, the United States remains very open to trade and even more so to finance. The rule of law still reigns, and foreign investors generally enjoy far greater protection than in most of the world. Of course, as we shall see over the course of this book, it would be folly to assume that the dollar's current lofty status is immutable. Both internal

INTRODUCTION

and external forces currently at play could both shrink and destabilize the dollar's status sooner than most realize.

Issuing the global currency is great. Being the country that has just lost global currency status, not so much. After World War II, given the conflict between growing social demands, the need to rebuild factories and infrastructure, and the United Kingdom's desire to continue to project colonial power, not to mention the fact that its post-war debt exceeded 240 percent of GDP, it is little wonder that the United Kingdom ran into recurrent financial problems. The United Kingdom was forced to go, hat in hand, to the International Monetary Fund for bailout funding no less than three times — in 1956, 1967, and 1976 — and it had several other smaller programs besides these.[19] The pound's glory days as the global currency became a distant memory.

The U.S. dollar is several bad turns away from any such fate; the dominant dollar might be late middle-aged, but it is still in good health. Nevertheless, before turning to the challenges ahead (discussed in the last part of this book), one must understand how the world came to this place of dollar dominance, including why past challengers have failed, why the present challenger China has a tough mountain to climb, and how the rest of the world deals with dollar dominance. All the while, one must not be confused by thinking of the past evolution of the system as the inevitable and only possible outcome. There have been moments when things could have gone quite differently, at least in the sense of leading to a much less dollar-centric world, and this may help us understand why that is a distinct possibility in the future.

Table 1. A timeline of the global safe asset

Period	Asset used	Exchange rate practices and arrangements in major financial centers
1509–1598	Spain: *juros*	Spanish dollar, or piece of eight, with fixed silver content becomes international standard. A gold escudo is issued in 1537.
1599–1702	Dutch province of Holland: *renten*	Mainly silver standard. Dutch florins and guilders with fixed silver content, as well as Dutch bills of exchange (backed by florins), circulate as the international medium of exchange. Spanish dollars still circulate widely internationally.
1717–1815	British consol	Silver standard, except in England, which is effectively on a gold standard.
1816–1907		Pound-gold standard. Britain officially adopts the gold standard, with the pound fixed in price to gold. Sterling notes are widely accepted outside Britain.
1908–1913	German Imperial 3% bond	
1914–1918	British consol	
1919–1939	U.S. Treasury debt and British consol	Frequent instability with competitive devaluations and hyperinflations. Gold standard is the most common de jure arrangement.
1943–1947	U.S. long-term Treasury bond (11.5-year maturity)	
1948–1973	U.S. 10-year Treasury bond	Gold-dollar standard. Bretton Woods.
1973–2025	U.S. 10-year Treasury bond	Dollar standard. Bretton Woods fixed-rate system collapses, leading to high inflation and hyperinflation in the 1970s-1990s. Eventually, the dollar loses Europe but gains much of Asia, the Middle East, and Africa.

Sources: Based on Ethan Ilzetzki, Carmen M. Reinhart, and Kenneth S. Rogoff, "Rethinking Exchange Rate Regimes," in *Handbook of International Economics*, vol. 6, ed. Gita Gopinath, Elhanan Helpman, and Kenneth Rogoff (Amsterdam: Elsevier, 2022), 99. Safe-asset epoch dates are from Paul Schmelzing, *Global Real Rates: 1311–2023* (New Haven, Conn.: Yale University Press, forthcoming).

PART I

PAST CHALLENGERS TO DOLLAR DOMINANCE

CHAPTER 2

THE SOVIET CHALLENGE

We now know that the Soviet Union's economy was never going to catch up to the United States' economy. Nor would the inconvertible Russian ruble take a significant role outside the Soviet bloc, beyond occupied Eastern Europe and a few small communist states such as Cuba and Albania. The limitations of central planning, including how it fosters corruption and stifles economic incentives, are now clear. However, to say that everyone *knew* this in the 1950s, 1960s, or even into the 1970s is nonsense. Indeed, a number of leading economists believed that parity — or near parity — between the Soviet Union and the United States was not only likely but inevitable. To this day, I remain convinced that giving the "wrong" answer to a question on the great promise of the Soviet economy, posed by a prominent New York financier, got me bounced at my Rhodes Scholarship interview in 1974 — that or my discount-rack electric-blue polyester suit, which looked quite out of place among the dark-blue or gray banker suits others wore. Still, one wants to avoid getting trapped in the mindset of thinking that United States–Soviet competition could have ended only one way and that better policy choices by the Kremlin at critical junctures might not have produced a somewhat more balanced outcome.

During the first decades after the Second World War, the Soviet Union set about building steel plants, cement factories, roads, and railroads — not to mention nuclear missiles and aircraft carriers — at an impressive clip. Indeed, Moscow's sparkling and well-maintained metro system put New York's depressing and crime-ridden one to shame. The Soviet system delivered cutting-edge sophistication in many critical areas, not least including space travel. When Yuri Gagarin became the first person in space in 1961, the United States went into a tizzy.

It should have been no surprise; Soviet mathematicians, engineers, and physicists long ranked among the best in the world. Russia's excellence in sports and culture was equally breathtaking; its classical musicians, ballet dancers, and Olympic athletes were world-class, not to mention its longtime dominance in chess. The Soviet Union was in no way, shape, or form a developing nation. It was a formidable superpower capable of focusing huge resources to modernize its economy, and even innovating at the highest level in some areas.

Other than weapons, the Soviet Union's main exports consisted of commodities, though it also produced manufactures for satellite states in Eastern Europe. Soviet consumer goods were drab and dull; one had to be a visitor from North Korea to think Moscow's Red Square GUM department store a shopper's paradise. The USSR was particularly poor at producing consumer goods, and scarcities were rampant. Anyone who has spent any time in a communist country (or in a modern socialist paradise such as Cuba or Venezuela) is familiar with the endless queues. Citizens of Moscow knew that anytime they saw a queue, they should just jump in, no questions asked. More than likely, the line signified that some hard-to-come-by commodity such as meat was in stock.

In the 1961 edition of his best-selling undergraduate text, Paul Samuelson, one of the great economists of the twentieth century, argued that although the Soviet economy was only half the size of the United States', it would likely catch up because it was growing so much faster.[1] Samuelson gave a wide berth to the exact catch-up date, putting it between 1984 and 1997, but he betrayed little doubt that it would ultimately happen. Soviet growth in the 1960s was disappointing compared with growth in the 1950s, but the Soviet economy was still growing faster than the U.S. economy, at least according to the best available data at the time. Over the next couple of decades, Samuelson kept recalibrating the inflection points, but he stuck to his core logic.

Samuelson's text was required reading in my freshman economics course at

THE SOVIET CHALLENGE

Yale in the 1970s, as it was at numerous other universities. Samuelson's claim should have given me pause. Before entering college, I traveled extensively in Europe playing chess professionally, and spent eight months in the former Yugoslavia, playing in international tournaments in Zagreb, Belgrade, and Sarajevo. These cities are now situated in separate countries—Croatia, Serbia, and Bosnia and Herzegovina, respectively; back then the strongman Josip Broz Tito held them all together. Yugoslavia supposedly enjoyed a better standard of living than Russia thanks to its slightly more flexible interpretation of communism. Nevertheless, living conditions clearly lagged those in the United States by a very wide margin. The dormitories at the University of Zagreb, for example, had very crude plumbing, to say the least.

Ordinary people did not seem particularly elated about their lives in the workers' paradise—certainly not compared with the muscular proletariat depicted everywhere in street posters and cast-iron statues. This was especially true in Serbia, where communist repression felt the most acute.

On occasion, when chess friends invited me to their modest apartments, typically a minuscule space with dull concrete walls, they clearly felt privileged to have their own space. The biting tone of the Beatles' song "Back in the USSR" seemed to capture the reality of the Soviet bloc far better than a book full of impressive growth statistics; it was ironic when one of my hosts had a bootlegged copy to play for me. John Lennon and Paul McCartney's sarcastic admonition to young Soviets about how lucky they are to live in the USSR makes me laugh to this day.

Samuelson was hardly alone in his belief that rapid Soviet economic growth posed a significant threat to the United States. The legendary Soviet economics specialist Abram Bergson similarly warned his Harvard students that catch-up was likely.[2] The former Harvard professor (and later senator) Daniel Patrick Moynihan noted that the mantra of the Soviets significantly closing the economic gap with the United States dominated White House strategic thinking in the 1960s and 1970s.[3]

Another leading economist who was deeply concerned about the USSR's growth was Walt Rostow of the University of Texas, who was influential during the 1960s in both the Kennedy and Johnson administrations. Rostow is best known in academic circles for his 1960 work on the stages of economic growth, for which Stalin's industrialization policies provided an important inspiration.[4] Rostow, to be fair, believed that the real problem was that even if the Soviet Union's economy did not fully catch up to the United States', it would still grow fast enough to allow the Soviet Union to build a comparable or superior military and to seed mischief around the developing world, advancing its worldwide trade network and perhaps in due time the ruble.

The Samuelson-Rostow view was by no means universally held among economists. Chicago's Milton Friedman, also one of the great economists of the twentieth century, was deeply skeptical. Friedman doubted that a socially planned economy, no matter how well run, could ever compete with a market economy. His writings were rather persuasive, though because he was considered an ultraconservative, we were taught at Yale to treat his claims of market supremacy with a healthy dose of suspicion. Over time, Friedman's views on economics became much more mainstream, though now, with Keynesianism resurgent and much more focus on inequality, they are less so. It is a fair bet, however, that as a new generation of scholars refines Friedman's ideas, and as some new-age government-heavy solutions prove to work less well in practice than on paper, the pendulum could eventually swing back the other way.

At Yale, there was a small cadre of professors who specialized in Russia and the Soviet bloc; as a joint economics and Russian-studies major, I naturally took their classes. It quickly became apparent that the biggest puzzle in the field was not why the Soviet system worked so badly but rather why it seemed to work so well. In market economies, prices move to bring demand and supply in line; in the old Soviet Union, almost everything was done by command and control. It was an iterative process whereby the central government planners would allocate inputs across firms and industries, generally starting with what had been needed the previous year. The Kremlin planners then absorbed feedback on where the imbalances were and tried again, typically going through the process several times. This kind of planning is hard enough to do in a simple agrarian economy, where one still has to allocate land, labor, seeds, fertilizer, water, and plows. In a modern industrial economy, central planning is exponentially more complicated. Yet, across the Soviet bloc, it worked, sort of. A big part of the reason why the Soviet-bloc consumer enjoyed such a narrow variety of goods was precisely because uniformity made the planning process easier. If most men's suits are made from the same drab gray cloth, the decision of which material to ship to the clothing factories becomes that much simpler, and there is no need to forecast which material will be most popular. Indeed, when I took my discount-rack electric-blue suit to play in a high-level chess tournament in communist Poland in 1975 — the same suit that was so out of place at my Rhodes Scholarship interview — everyone seemed to love it. Did all Americans have such great suits?

One of my favorite professors at Yale, J. Michael Montias, established conditions under which the Soviets' iterative planning system could replicate a market system in which prices did all the work of signaling shortages.[5] Montias's conditions were not terribly realistic, but the approach was still very elegant and clever. Another, Martin Weitzman, wrote a paper demonstrating that the slowdown in Soviet growth from the 1950s and 1960s had partly been because output was responding only very slowly to increases in capital spending.[6] It should be said that both professors later studied other topics: Weitzman did absolutely seminal work on environmental economics, and Montias is famous in the art world for having written the foundational book on the economics of art.[7]

Just how successful was the Soviet economy actually? Back in the 1960s and 1970s, it was very hard to get a handle on exactly what the Soviet Union's growth numbers were, all the more so because it did not use prices to allocate goods. After all, the key measure of output economists use to measure a country's economic capacity is gross domestic output, calculated by summing *market prices* across goods (netting out intermediate goods to avoid double counting). Moreover, the Soviet Union's output mix was so different from that of the United States that it would have been difficult to make meaningful comparisons even with the best of data. What was relatively scarce in one country (say, computers in Russia and steel in the United States) was sometimes plentiful in the other. As a result, it flattered Soviet output to use U.S. prices, which attached a high relative price to the Soviet Union's abundant steel output. By contrast, computers were relatively scarce in the Soviet Union and had very high value, making the relative size of the U.S. economy, which was much better at producing computers, look relatively larger using Soviet prices.

The Soviet Union did publish books giving details on its output and production, but it was hard to know how far these publications could be trusted, and again there were no prices. The Soviet propaganda machine desperately wanted to exaggerate the country's achievements compared with those of the bourgeois Americans even if, by the end of the 1960s, it had become apparent that the capitalist system would not fall of its own accord as Karl Marx had predicted.

Elsewhere, at Harvard, it was common for a student writing a Ph.D. dissertation on the USSR's economy to spend years trying to calculate a meaningful estimate of Soviet output for a single year. (When I chose to go to graduate school at MIT, a couple of my Russia-specialist Yale professors were disappointed that I did not pursue this path.) At the same time, an entire industry of economists at the CIA and the Department of Defense were also trying to figure out Soviet GDP; they were particularly interested in whether Russia could keep up with the United States in military spending. According to the celebrated economic historian Angus Maddison, the Soviet Union was spending an average of 12 percent of GDP on its military in the period 1953–1965.[8]

Maddison's overall assessment of how to calibrate Soviet growth and its future trajectory was somewhere between Samuelson's Panglossian projections and Friedman's deep skepticism. In his 1969 book assessing Russia's and Japan's post-war growth experiences, Maddison acknowledged that between 1953 and 1965, the USSR had been one of the world's fastest-growing countries. Moreover, by his calculations, the Soviet Union was clearly the world's second-largest economy at the time. Nevertheless, Maddison sided squarely with Friedman on the question of long-run economic growth. Despite the Soviet Union's immense natural resources, Maddison thought the Soviet system simply too inflexible to go toe to toe with a market economy when it came to innovation — especially an economy like that of the United States, which was also rich in natural resources. Nevertheless, the Soviet Union industrial complex was quite capable of competing militarily, as least for a time.

By the early 1970s, it was clear that this time was coming to an end. The Kremlin concluded that to keep up with the United States' superior innovation, it would have to make a determined effort to steal U.S. technology. There was no other way to keep up militarily, or to produce sufficient civilian goods to project wealth and success to the Russian people and to the world. Taking advantage of President Richard Nixon's policy of détente, the Russians were able to send to the United States numerous delegations heavily laced with KGB operatives, who spearheaded a large and evidently quite successful effort to pirate industrial information, helped of course by other methods and sources. The popular television series *The Americans*, about a married pair of KGB spies living undercover in Virginia in the 1980s, is a fictional depiction of the tail end of this effort.

In real life, a major turning point came when French intelligence was able to turn one of Moscow's agents in the early 1980s. This not only led to information about the specific embassy personnel and methods behind Moscow's operations but also gave the United States the opportunity to feed fake blueprints and designs for circuitry and equipment to the USSR. These fakes led Soviet engineers down rabbit holes, taking up resources and leaving Russia even further behind.[9] When President Ronald Reagan announced the United States "Star Wars" program in 1983 to double down on the United States' technology advantage, the Kremlin knew it was in deep trouble.[10]

For the Soviet Union to keep growing its economy and supporting its outsize military, its only other strategy would have been to keep increasing investment, and that approach was running out of steam. The boom years of Russian growth were fueled by massive infrastructure projects that could be directed efficiently by command and control, especially in an economy rich in natural resources. Eventually, however, the payoff from adding yet another railway, cement factory, or power plant began to decline.

A third challenge was the corruption fostered by the command-and-control system. With rampant scarcities, a culture of bribes and payoffs was inevitable. Corruption was hardly new for Russia, tracing back at least to the Mongol occupation of the thirteenth to fifteenth centuries. That said, communism certainly did not help. More recently Russia's initial failures in its February 2022 full-scale invasion of Ukraine, despite years of massive military investment, also appear to have had their roots in corruption, with huge sums wasted and embezzled.

In the early 1990s, after the breakup of the Soviet Union, economists began rethinking its growth experience. One conclusion was that the USSR was probably never doing as well as once thought; output was lower, and repressed ruble inflation much higher, than conventional Western estimates had suggested.

Although Samuelson and Rostow proved way off the mark in their optimistic extrapolations, Milton Friedman was probably too dismissive, and in particular he could have given the Soviet Union much more credit for some of its genuine accomplishments. In a short time, it took a large, uneducated agrarian population and produced a workforce that had a high general level of education, and not just at the very top. Far too little of all this ingenuity found its way into civilian use, but in a parallel universe, it might have.

For a few years after Leonid Brezhnev and Alexei Kosygin deposed Nikita Khrushchev and assumed power in 1964, there was some real energy behind reform efforts to try to rationalize the system and to bring in some elements of markets and the price mechanism.[11] Had such reforms been implemented, they might have given the Soviet Union some of the success that China's more flexible implementation of socialism brought after Deng Xiaoping came to power, and perhaps the Soviet Union's rapid growth might have maintained momentum.

If the Soviet Union had been able to adapt and continue growing rapidly, might the ruble have ever been considered a major global currency, even if an unconventional one? It certainly would have represented a much larger economic bloc. To go further, and to give the ruble real meaning outside the Soviet bloc, the Soviet Union would have had to introduce market-oriented reforms, as China later did, so that prices could play a more significant role in the economy. Eventually, the Soviet Union would have had to allow the ruble to become a convertible currency—that is, one people could freely buy and sell without huge fees or taxes on the transaction. This, in turn, would have considerably facilitated trade expansion. With a price mechanism, members of the Soviet bloc could have used the ruble for trade, just as eurozone countries use the euro, without the complex machinations required to match the value of exports and imports between countries in a way that was fair, or at least transparent.

The ultimate breakup of the Soviet Union in the 1990s led to a period of desperation and destitution, as the old regime no longer worked and the new market-oriented economy had not yet taken root. Russia, along with the former Soviet republics, experienced brutal hyperinflation, or near hyperinflation, that took years to stabilize. Because of the empire's ignominious collapse, the suggestion that the Soviet Union might ever have competed with the United States economically now sounds laughable. But be sure, in the first few decades after World War II, it was no laughing matter.

THE SOVIET CHALLENGE

My own travels to Russia began only after the fall of the Soviet Union. During my chess years, Americans were rarely invited to Soviet chess events. Soviet authorities did not know how to handle the Russian public's adoration of the American grand master Bobby Fischer, whom many still consider the greatest player of all time. In 1971, Soviet fans once paralyzed Moscow's phone system in their excitement to hear news of Fischer's unprecedented string of victories. Finally, at one point, the operators, who had to make connections manually back then, would simply pick up the line and say "shest nol" (six nothing), and then hang up.[12] That was the final score of Fischer's best-of-ten world championship semifinal match with the Danish grand master Bent Larsen. It was a bit like pitching a perfect game in the World Series of baseball, and Fischer had done it to two world-class opponents in a row.

Soviet authorities lauded Russia's chess supremacy as a demonstration of their superior system and culture. When Fischer captured the world championship from the Russian grand master Boris Spassky in a historic match in Reykjavík, Iceland, in 1972, the event made the front pages of major newspapers all over the world for six weeks. PBS Television in the United States covered the event live for several hours each day. I was the guest commentator for game thirteen, which Fischer won after surprising Spassky with the rare Alekhine's defense, in which Black answers White's king-pawn advance by bringing out his king-side knight instead of moving one of his own pawns forward, thereby immediately conceding space in hopes of finding counterattacking possibilities. Modern computers have now shown this to be an inferior opening for Black, and even back then it was considered a bit sketchy. However, in a game between two humans, the surprise element is worth a lot. The loss of the world chess title was a huge psychological blow to the Kremlin. When I finally received an invitation in 1977 to play in Russia's most elite grand master tournament in Moscow, it felt like being invited to the Tchaikovsky competition (where the American concert pianist Van Cliburn won gold at the height of the Cold War in 1958), although I would have struggled to win as many games as I lost. By then, unfortunately, I had psychologically committed to focus on economics research, and with great anguish had to decline.

My first trip to Moscow did not come until May 1995, when I visited my American-born fiancée, Natasha, who was the lead producer (what nowadays in television would be called the showrunner) for *Ulitsa Sezam*. It was to be an original Russian version of *Sesame Street*, with its own set, characters, and music, and was being produced by the not-for-profit Children's Television Workshop in New York. It was strange how composed Natasha appeared despite the violence all around her, including serial assassinations of her Russian broadcast partners and a car bomb that almost killed a major sponsor.

It was useless trying to persuade her to leave; she believed that there was too much at stake for post-Soviet children, who had little to cheer them up, and wanted to offer a kinder, gentler version of what post-Soviet society might look like. In addition, her team of several hundred actors, musicians, directors, set designers, painters, and others were themselves taking great risks. These artists represented virtually every region and nationality of the former Soviet Union—Ukrainians, Armenians, Georgians, Uzbeks, and so on. Those I met were clearly struggling to survive; the production was a lifeline for a Soviet film and television industry in complete collapse. Sadly, today, many of these creatives are in exile; a few probably in prison. Although the show no longer airs, starting in 1996 it was initially carried in prime time six nights a week across the eleven time zones of the former Soviet Union, and stayed on the air for almost ten years, well into the Putin era.[13]

I traveled to Russia again in 2003, this time as the International Monetary Fund's chief economist. The economic situation had dramatically stabilized; this was during the early Putin years, when technocrats were still allowed to play a big role in economic policy. In 2001, with the implementation of a flat 13 percent tax on personal income and a unified social tax to replace a mélange of social-support taxes, the Putin administration energized the Russian economy and initiated a period of healthy growth.[14] Indeed, this is one occasion when the Laffer curve—which claims that cutting tax rates can boost growth so much that government tax revenue rises instead of falls—actually worked. According to the International Monetary Fund, Russian tax revenues actually rose by 26 percent the year after the flat tax was implemented. Even Putin's most ardent critics generally admit that from a narrow economic point of view, the flat tax was an unqualified success. Then again, the tax simplification might have been the last really good economic policy Putin ever implemented.

Despite the relative health of the economy in 2003, it was clear from one press interaction after another that media repression was already quite severe. One prominent radio personality, a colorful character with a large Moscow audience, told me in a nervous voice just before our interview that he doubted his show would be allowed to air much longer. It was pretty jarring. I did my best to keep my composure as it sunk in how much danger this bright, pleasant man might be in.

My IMF colleagues insisted that I meet the person they universally agreed was the best economic mind in the Russian government, Arkady Dvorkovich, who also apparently had Putin's ear at the time, at least when it came to how to improve the economy. At Arkady's capacious office inside the Kremlin, there were shelves of books and documents, a magnificent desk, a large couch, and chairs. In the middle of all of that, a chess board had been set up with an endgame position from a game I had played in Lone Pine, California, in 1978 against the legendary Samuel Reshevsky. I learned that Arkady's father was the renowned chess arbiter Vladimir Dvorkovich.

It was a bit stunning to see how young Arkady was (evidently thirty years old) given that he commanded so much influence. The conversation did not disappoint, and although of course it is essential to take anything you are told inside the Kremlin with a large grain of salt, it is also important to hear other perspectives. Arkady's candid and concise explanations of Russia's economic strengths and weaknesses were remarkably insightful—for example, the difficulties of maintaining basic medical care in an economy in which trained physicians could earn more driving a taxicab. He did not shy away from any topic and even addressed how difficult it was back then to fight corruption in the military and the police given low pay and the desperate problems faced by many of their families. If you give Makarov pistols to hundreds of thousands of police and Kalashnikov rifles to over a million young Russian soldiers, it is going to be difficult to stop them from ever extracting bribes. That rang true and backed up Natasha's seeming paranoia about having our car commit the slightest traffic violation for fear of getting shaken down for bribes.[15]

I did make a few further short trips to Russia over the years to give academic lectures and to speak at conferences. In 2006, I presented lectures at the New Economic School in Moscow in honor of the Lithuanian-born Harvard economist Zvi Griliches. My host was the internationally respected economist Sergei

PAST CHALLENGERS TO DOLLAR DOMINANCE

Guriev, today a prominent critic of Putin's and dean of the London Business School. Sergei took me by subway from Domodedovo International Airport into the city. He explained that not only was traffic terrible in Moscow but, with Putin in town, there was also a chance that the streets could be impassable. Evidently, anytime Putin decides to leave the Kremlin, his security team shuts down all the streets and everyone has to wait until he is gone. As Sergei explained on a later occasion, Putin is a "grand master of personal security." That was even more apparent on my next trip in 2012. Although I was an invited speaker at the Russia Forum, and had all kinds of identification to prove it, it was almost impossible to get past the sea of brusque guards to watch a discussion in which Putin was appearing on stage with a panel that included the star economists Raghuram Rajan and Paul Krugman. I eventually gave up and watched the congenial discussion on a television monitor.

In January 2020, I spoke at the Gaidar Forum, one of the last remaining places where some measure of economic-policy dissent was still tolerated in Russia. Natasha also came. She hoped to do interviews for her *Muppets in Moscow* book and to revisit the giant Ostankino television studio where she had produced *Ulitsa Sezam* twenty-five years earlier. Natasha was worried that a 2016 film she had posted on YouTube entitled *Russian Millennials Speak Openly About America*, which had some 2.5 million views and was not terribly flattering to Putin, might get her blocked. Coming with me to the Gaidar Forum might fly under the radar, so I accepted an invitation. It worked.

In June 2022, the *New York Times* reported that the conference organizer, Professor Vladimir Mau, had been arrested, ostensibly for corruption. No doubt the real reason was to send a signal that even technocratic criticisms of economic policy are no longer tolerated in Putin's Russia. Mau's arrest sent shock waves through the country's academic and economic elite.[16] At this writing, things are only getting worse by the day.

The war in Ukraine has not helped the Russian economy either — even if Western sanctions have been less than effective, in no small part because most of the developing world prefers to remain neutral. In 2024 Russia's GDP was estimated to be $2.2 trillion, less than a tenth that of the United States, and the ruble is hardly a major currency. To say, however, that economists always knew that Russia's growth would fall so far short, is just wrong.

CHAPTER 3

JAPAN AND THE YEN

The rise and fall of Japan as an economic rival to the United States, and along with it the importance of the yen relative to the dollar, is one of the most disputed episodes in the modern history of international finance. Many believe that Japan's collapse happened because the United States forced Japan to drastically appreciate the yen in the mid-1980s, which crushed Japan's export engine. China's leaders have long bought into this view and have vowed never to submit to the same treatment. Much of the world agrees and views this as a prime example of the United States' willingness to let other economies do well, but not too well. I had long thought that this interpretation was wildly overblown given that the yen's appreciation had largely taken place by the end of 1988 but Japan's economic collapse did not start until 1992; in between, Japan's markets boomed.

Now I am not so confident. Sure, if Japan had had better financial market regulation when the boom came, its economy would never have overheated and then stalled as badly it did. On the other hand, it was U.S. pressure that forced Japan to adapt to a stronger yen faster than its politics, culture, and institutions could handle.

When I arrived at the Bank of Japan in the late spring of 1991 for twelve weeks as a visiting scholar, the Japanese financial system was starting to melt down, though either no one knew, or no one wanted to admit it because the party was too much fun. The Nikkei 225 stock index had fallen by more than a third from its peak in December 1989, but then it had more than tripled in the preceding five years. In any event, land values were seen as the true gold in the economy, and prices were still rising. With over 120 million people squeezed onto an island only 90 percent the size of California, the view was that land prices would never go down.

To understand what a consensus-driven society Japan is, one only has to spend a few days visiting the Bank of Japan cafeteria. I regularly ate lunch with my research department colleagues, following their helpful instructions since my determined efforts to learn basic Japanese had fallen short. The food was delicious, though the selection was quite narrow compared with what the Federal Reserve's cafeteria offered, which I knew well from working as a Fed economist in Washington in the 1980s. After a week or two of this, I noticed a second entrance to the cafeteria where there was also line of people, almost all women. What do they have there? Is it something different? "Oh, that line is for anyone who wants a smaller portion," I was told.[1]

It took me, and most of the world, many more years to figure out what was really going on in what was then the world's second-largest economy. When I arrived at the Bank of Japan, the country's income, its stock market, and its land values still seemed headed for the moon, even if equity prices had taken a detour. Paradoxically, the United States' attempt to contain Japan by forcing it to appreciate its currency had instead given Japan a huge short-term boost. The near doubling of the yen had not helped contain Japanese exports to the degree the United States had hoped, partly because Japan was becoming more efficient, partly because Japanese firms were moving up the value chain, and partly because firms could afford to absorb losses in order to preserve market share. On the other hand, the strong yen turned Japanese financial firms and investors into behemoths on the world market, able to soak up cheap dollar assets with their richly valued currency.

The Soviet Union might once have been a serious challenger to the United States militarily, but it never came close to being a serious challenger economically. In this sense, Japan was a much more formidable competitor in trade and finance. The fact that its population then was only half that of the United States was hardly disqualifying for achieving dominant-currency status. After all, being a relatively small nation certainly did not get in the way of the United Kingdom or the Netherlands before it.

Memories fade, but from the late 1970s to the early 1990s, there was a widespread view and fear that Japan would eventually overtake the United States as the world's predominant trading and economic power. Its superior manufacturing methods and culture seemed to be crushing the United States in one important industry after another. *The Competitive Advantage of Nations*, written in 1990 by the Harvard Business School professor Michael Porter, showcased Japan as a coming giant that would be difficult to fend off. Japan had a sophisticated financial system, good institutions (including a constitution written by the United States after World War II), and growing international competitiveness.[2]

In that same year, the *Harvard Business Review* published an influential article by the management professors C. K. Prahalad and Gary Hamel arguing that Japanese firms were more disciplined than U.S. firms and knew how to stick to their "core competencies."[3] Prahalad and Hamel contrasted the uncontrolled expansion of General Telephone and Electric (which years later merged with Bell Atlantic to form Verizon) with the disciplined focus of the Japanese firm National Electronics Corporation, which grew into a dominant force in semiconductors. And long before these authors, there was the sociologist Ezra Vogel's 1979 bestseller *Japan as Number One: Lessons for America*.[4] These authors were not alone; economic fear of Japan was pervasive.

If at first Japanese firms succeeded by imitating U.S. products and selling them to U.S. consumers at lower prices, over time the genuine innovation coming out of Japan in consumer goods became remarkable. For example, Sony's Walkman was the precursor to Apple's iPod, and for a time the Walkman was everywhere. Travelers to Japan always seemed to return with one amazing new consumer invention after another, such as electronic watches that doubled as calculators — things that may seem simple now but were absurdly innovative at the time. Canon ingeniously improved copy machines by making the toner cartridge replaceable, which reduced repair costs and opened the door to today's inexpensive, easy-to-maintain personal copiers. In the auto industry, Japan outcompeted Detroit on quality and price; U.S. cars certainly did not match up on *Consumer Reports* tests. It did not help when "the Boz," a college football superstar, boasted to *Sports Illustrated* that to deal with boredom at his summer job at a General Motors auto plant in Oklahoma City, co-workers taught him how to insert bolts in hard-to-reach places so that when they later came loose, their rattling would drive consumers crazy.[5] That remark was later recanted after the ensuing uproar; perhaps it would not have been so damaging if concerns over low quality hadn't resonated with many U.S. car owners.

The U.S. government tried many ways to push back, famously insisting, for example, that Japan "voluntarily" restrict its total exports of cars to the United States. In May 1981, Japan began restricting its auto exports to 1.68 million vehicles per year and continued doing so for many years thereafter. Although a postmortem in the mid-1990s by leading trade and industrial-organization economists suggested that the costs to American consumers, and the gains to American manufacturers, were not nearly as large as some believed,[6] the policy sent a broader message to Japan to be wary in the future. In any event, the restrictions also created scarcity that allowed Japanese firms to raise prices and pushed them to open plants in the United States.

Over time, American companies adopted many Japanese techniques, including teamwork and quality circles. That said, it is not clear even now that General Motors can make cars as well as Toyota, despite their now defunct joint venture, New United Motor Manufacturing.[7] Toyota still routinely ranks as the brand requiring the fewest and least-expensive repairs. Today, Japanese car companies as a group constitute both the largest seller and the largest employer in the automobile industry in the United States.[8]

Nowadays, economists write about the "China shock," but the "Japan shock" occurred long before it. Although Detroit is the most famous victim, my hometown of Rochester, New York, suffered just as much and received almost no attention from the U.S. government. The economy of Rochester was basically gutted by competition from Japan in the 1980s and 1990s, with giants like Kodak (cameras, film) and Xerox (copiers) cut to size by their Japanese competitors Fujiphotofilm and Canon (copiers, cameras, and medical devices), among others. One might argue that Kodak really failed because of internal management problems; it had trouble pivoting in a fast-moving global economy. To show how lost Kodak's management became: In January 2018, the company announced KodakCoin, a cryptocurrency, which initially led to a doubling of the company's stock price but ultimately failed.⁹ Xerox eventually entered a joint venture with Fuji to create Fuji Xerox (now Fujifilm). Whatever the reality, it is probably fair to say that Japanese competition accelerated Rochester's decline.

It was sad as many of my friends and neighbors from Rochester found their jobs downsized or eliminated. In the 1960s, Rochester ranked as one of the most affluent cities in America, with a major research hospital, a world-class golf course, and its own philharmonic orchestra. The Eastman School of Music, Strong Memorial Hospital, and the Oak Hill Country Club are all still there; indeed, Rochester hosted the PGA championship in 2022. However, the population of the city itself has shrunk by a third since 1960.[10] Bausch and Lomb (vision, optics) is still in Rochester, but with operations spread over a hundred countries it is no longer a major local employer. Although the city has reinvented itself with small health-care and ed-tech businesses, Rochester has gone from one of the richest cities in the country — a veritable 1960s Silicon Valley — to a depressed midsize town with a per capita income below the U.S. average. Hit by the exodus of jobs and tax revenues, the city's fortunes became so depressed that the inner-city high school I attended, East High School, with its highly diverse student body, was put into receivership.[11]

One has to understand that by the 1980s, Japan's economy seemed to be bearing down on the entire United States like an express train; Rochester and Detroit were just the early casualties. As Japan emerged from its bombed-out World War II shell, its growth rate was simply astounding. In barely more than a generation, per capita GDP rose from just over 20 percent to over 80 percent of U.S. levels, as measured using purchasing power parity weights.[12] If one instead uses market exchange rates (perhaps less meaningful for asking about the welfare of the average consumer), Japan's per capita income was briefly even above the United States'. These statistics do not even consider that Japan was spending less than 1 percent of its GDP on its military, whereas U.S. spending on defense as a share of GDP averaged over 7 percent during the 1980s.[13] The differential left that much more for Japan to invest in civilian infrastructure, manufacturing plants, and housing.

Although voluntary export restraints on autos might have had some impact, it was not nearly enough to tame Japan's trade surpluses. Japan's auto companies adjusted, and as Rochester would soon discover, other Japanese companies started conquering one industry after another. So the United States, together with Europe, decided to bludgeon Japan with a much bigger bat. Many policymakers and economists came to the conclusion that Japan was unfairly holding down the value of the yen, making its goods hypercompetitive, and the Reagan administration decided to do something about it.

Enter James A. Baker, a Texan who served as chief of staff to President Ronald Reagan in his first term in office and was then promoted to U.S. Treasury secretary in Reagan's second term.[14] Like his 1970s-era predecessor John Connally, Baker was known for his unapologetically muscular approach to maintaining the dollar's undisputed centrality in global finance. As relayed to me by a former MIT classmate who witnessed Baker in action at Group of Ten (G10) ministerial meetings, Baker had little tolerance for complaints about U.S. exchange rate policy. When a finance minister from a midsize European economy threatened to sell dollar reserves unless the United States paid more attention to Europe's exchange rate problems, Baker supposedly retorted, "My daddy taught me never to point a gun at someone unless you're prepared to pull the trigger."[15]

No country bore the brunt of U.S. bullying more brutally than Japan. In the famed Plaza Accord of September 1985, the Japanese contingent agreed to allow the yen to sharply appreciate and become more valuable relative to the dollar. The rationale was to make Japanese imports more expensive for American and world consumers. Evidently, the Reagan administration believed that the United States had played nice with Japan to help it recover from World War II for too long and that it was time to push back hard.[16]

What exactly happened? A decade later, in the mid-1990s, Baker came to give a small informal talk to faculty at the Princeton School of Public and International Affairs, where I was a professor at the time. We spoke one-on-one afterward. "How is it possible that the Japanese authorities had so much control over their exchange rate given that most other advanced economies seemed to have so little?" I asked.

I mentioned to Baker that in my first job out of graduate school, as an economist in the International Finance Division at the Federal Reserve Board in Washington, I was assigned to write a background research paper in the lead-up period to the Plaza Accord. Mind you, we peons had no idea what was afoot;

maybe no one did. My task was to address a nerdy technical question having to do with the effectiveness of "sterilized intervention," which is a way for central banks to intervene in foreign exchange markets without changing their money supplies, essentially by issuing domestic currency bonds to buy an equivalent value's worth of foreign-currency bonds.[17] To be honest, assessing the academic evidence at the time, I doubted that Japan could do much to radically push up the yen without substantially raising interest rates and thereby making the yen more attractive to international investors. And it would be hard to raise rates that much without reducing their money supply, which in turn would likely cause a deep recession.

Baker explained that he too had not been sure it was possible; nevertheless, the Japanese finance minister at the Plaza meeting insisted that his team could pull it off as long as the other central banks did not counter Japan's actions. However, the finance minister could not act on his own authority; in consensus-oriented Japan, he needed to go back to Tokyo to confer. To Baker's amazement—and to the amazement of a couple of Europeans present at the Plaza meeting whom I have also spoken to over the years—Japan delivered, and within a couple of weeks the yen was up more than 10 percent; Japan achieved the agreed-upon target with almost surgical precision. Smiling, Baker explained that once the yen started going up, the Ministry of Finance and the Bank of Japan had no clue how to stop it. As we shall see, what happened over the next few years, and who was to blame for the mess that followed, is a matter of some dispute.

The yen went from a value of 244 yen per dollar in September 1985 to 156 yen per dollar just a year later, and then fell further to 121 yen per dollar a year after that.[18] That is, the yen nearly doubled in value against the dollar. This took a toll on Japan's export engine but, as already noted, less of a toll than had been expected. In addition to cutting margins and moving up the quality ladder, Japanese auto companies adapted in part by moving plants to lower cost, newly industrializing Asian "tiger" economies, including Singapore, South Korea, Hong Kong, and Taiwan.

The surge in the yen inflated Japan's wealth in dollar terms, like a body builder on steroids. The American and European policymakers who had thought a stronger yen would hobble Japan had not counted on that.[19] By the end of 1989, the Nikkei 225 index had tripled from its 1985 value. And that is looking only at the yen value. Measured in dollars and incorporating the sharp appreciation of the yen, the Japanese stock market increased by a factor of five. Land prices increased even more; by September 1990, the urban land price index had peaked at almost four times its September 1985 value, and by seven times in dollar terms.[20]

Fueled by the high value of the yen as well as the vast wealth from high asset valuations, Japanese banks became some of the largest in the world and became correspondingly influential in global finance, providing financing for leveraged buyout firms, as famously portrayed in the book *Barbarians at the Gate* and the subsequent HBO film with the actor James Garner.[21]

Japanese buyers snatched up one trophy property after another in the United States, including, most famously, Rockefeller Center in New York and Pebble Beach Golf Links in Monterey, California. (Golf is enormously popular in Japan.) At one point Japanese investors held over 12 percent of the U.S. stock market.[22] It turned out that Japanese investors vastly overpaid in a number of cases and were later forced to sell at steep discounts.[23]

There are various hyperbolic metrics of just how overvalued Japanese stocks and real estate became—for example, the claim that land under the imperial palace in Tokyo (which in fact is not marketable) was worth more than all the land in California. Hyperbole aside, the hard metrics are still pretty sobering. As figures 3 and 4 illustrate,[24] the total market value of Japanese real estate far exceeded that of the United States for an extended period, and the total market capitalization of the Japanese stock market briefly surpassed that of the U.S. stock market. Put differently, the world market view was that Japanese companies were collectively worth as much as all U.S. companies, and its real estate far more.

Considering that Japan's land mass is less than 5 percent that of the United States and that its population in 1990 was half as large, those are stunning valuations. The 1980s optimists, which is to say much of the investing world, believed that these valuations made sense because "this time is different": Japan's continuing economic rise was inevitable given its extraordinarily high savings rate, strong work ethic, and hypercompetitive manufacturing firms.

During the 1990s, to help my students understand the scale of Japan's financial might, I showed them that if Japan and the United States were corporations

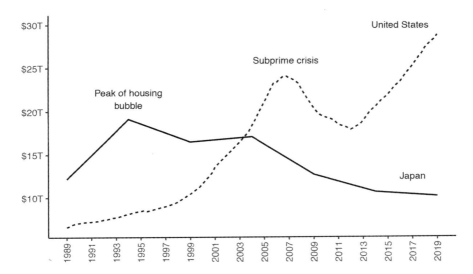

Figure 3. Market value of household real estate in Japan and the United States, 1989–2019
Data Source: Financial accounts of the United States (Federal Reserve Board); National survey of family income, consumption, and wealth (Statistics Bureau of Japan).

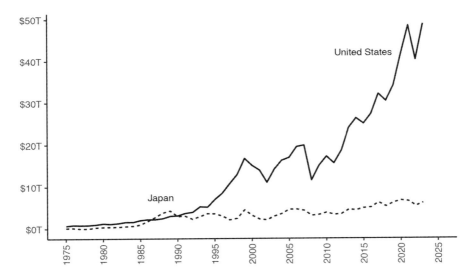

Figure 4. Total stock market capitalization in Japan and the United States, 1975–2023
Data Source: World Federation of Exchanges.

instead of countries, Japan would have been well positioned to execute a leveraged buyout of the United States. Japan could have pitched the deal to the market by arguing that it was going to do a much better job managing the assets. The reality, of course, is that Japan was experiencing a classic pre-financial-crisis asset bubble.

Perhaps you are old enough to have lived through this era and knew all along that the bubble would inevitably collapse. But it was not easy to call the timing. When I left my first job at the Federal Reserve to go teach at the University of Wisconsin in January 1985, it seemed to make sense to put my (very modest) rollover pension account into a mutual fund that held Japanese stocks. This was not based on any deep foresight that the Japanese stock market was about to triple; rather, it seemed like a sensible way to diversify since the rest of my portfolio was in U.S. stocks. In addition, my instinct was that the yen was badly undervalued against the dollar and that if one waited long enough, it would appreciate.

Half the reason why I received an offer to teach at Wisconsin was the budding academic influence of my work with Richard Meese.[25] Our paper showed that in practice, it is extremely difficult to systemically explain exchange rate changes after the fact, let alone predict what they are going to be in the future. A qualifier, though, was that if macroeconomic fundamentals fall far out of line, then at least over a period of several years the odds of an adjustment are significant. The Japanese yen seemed to be such a case in spades, particularly in light of measures of its purchasing power relative to the dollar. In 1985, the yen looked very cheap. How did my investment pan out? Let's just say that my Japanese stock purchase was a fantastic investment for several years and would have been amazing if I had pulled out in 1989 instead of 1996.

Which brings us back to where we started this chapter. Sometimes when you travel to a country, you learn a lot just in the process of getting there. The visa for my visiting-scholar position at the Bank of Japan in the summer of 1991 required me to produce a photocopy of my doctoral diploma, which happened to be buried in a box. Given that I was already a full professor at Berkeley, a position for which a Ph.D. is prerequisite, wasn't it enough to provide a letter from my department chair confirming my position? No, the Ministry of Justice had to see the doctoral diploma itself. Now I really understood why U.S. trade negotiators had complained for decades that the Japanese bureaucrats are masters of the invisible "non-tariff" barrier.

Finally arriving at the Bank of Japan and looking over shelves of recent statistical publications, which the Bank of Japan helpfully provided in English, revealed something quite startling.[26] While other advanced economies were still reining in inflation in 1991, Japan's wholesale price index showed that goods prices had been declining for a couple of years. The consumer price index, which also includes services, was still rising, so the economy was not yet in deflation. Falling consumer prices came later, but back then even a falling wholesale price index was surprising. Deflation became a common concern only a couple of decades later, after the global financial crisis, as a number of advanced economies experienced episodes of borderline price decline if not outright deflation. In the early 1990s, however, deflation was a singular rarity outside an occasional episode in the French franc zone in Africa. I wrote off the anomaly to the sharp appreciation of the yen post-September 1985, which reduced the yen cost of imports.

In any event, my colleagues at the Bank of Japan did not seem particularly concerned about it. Japan, like a number of other countries including the United Kingdom, had seen its inflation exceed 20 percent in the 1970s, after the Bretton Woods fixed exchange rate collapse. At the beginning of the 1990s, most central banks' view of inflation was that you can never have too little of it — their own version of the Duchess of Windsor's "You can never be too rich or too thin." No one yet realized the dangers.

I focused on the project I had originally proposed to work on. The Bank of Japan was interested in my research on the real exchange rate, which is the exchange rate between two currencies adjusted for relative price differences. The Bank recognized that if the yen had been undervalued before the Plaza Accord in 1985, it now seemed overvalued. Walking around Tokyo and looking at the prices, I found it hard to argue with the overvaluation thesis. After being converted to dollars, the yen prices for consumer goods in Japan's meticulously kept department stores seemed implausibly high, as did apartment rents, especially in the glamorous Aoyama district, where the Bank of Japan housed its visiting scholars. I was told that the Bank's comfortable but hardly ostentatious two-bedroom apartment where I was housed would rent for several times the rent on my similar-size Berkeley apartment, just across the bay from San Francisco. This was stunning given that, to my mind, San Francisco is the most beautiful city in the world and one of the United States' most expensive places to live. Riding the jam-packed Tokyo subway made the rent seem a little more plausible, especially at stations where "pushers" had been hired by the subway companies to literally stuff people into the cars. Some of my colleagues had commutes of over 90 minutes, although most of that commute was on somewhat nicer trains.

My research concluded that one possible explanation of the yen's appreciation was that during the 1970s and at least into the mid-1980s, Japan's productivity gains considerably outpaced those of its trading partners. As a consequence, Japanese consumers felt richer and thus bid up the price of non-traded goods (e.g., haircuts, restaurant meals) relative to traded goods (e.g., autos, electronics), which was accomplished through appreciation of the exchange rate. Although my paper did not state it outright, one simple way to alleviate domestic price pressures was to find a way to admit more immigrant workers, a long-standing challenge for Japan given its close-knit and relatively homogeneous society.

The exchange rate appreciation, though, is far from the entire story as to why Japan's economy suddenly slowed between the 1980s and the 1990s. Three other factors loomed large. First and foremost, Japan experienced a steady decrease in birth rates starting in the early 1970s: the total fertility rate dropped from 2.16 births per female of child-bearing age in 1970 to 1.30 in 2024. In advanced economies a rate of 2.1 is needed to maintain a stable population (in the absence of immigration).[27] As a result, starting in the late 1980s, Japan's labor force began to decline; even as many of the "young old" (those between 65 and 75) continue to work in second careers today, the prime-age labor force in Japan continues to shrink at roughly 0.5 percent per year.[28]

A second factor was the same "decreasing returns to investment" problem that the Soviet Union faced. In the early years of post-war reconstruction, there were huge returns from rebuilding cities and roads. Certainly, Japanese work culture played a role in the country's success, as did the institutions that developed after World War II. And as already noted, Japanese industry introduced many important innovations to the world, such as the Toyota production system and its "just in time" process. With the benefit of hindsight, though, it is now clear that the biggest factor in Japan's post-war growth spurt was indeed its exceedingly high level of investment in physical capital and education, which was funded in turn by the highest savings rate of any advanced economy. Japan's citizens were determined to build a better future for their children and were willing to sacrifice both leisure and consumption to do so. Unfortunately, as the economist Robert Solow famously demonstrated, there are limits to how long a country can enjoy exceedingly high growth thanks to investment alone. Inevitably, diminishing returns to scale set in, and eventually long-term output growth is governed by the economy's underlying rate of productivity and labor force growth.[29]

A third factor was the rise of the newly industrializing Asian economies, especially Korea, Taiwan, Hong Kong, and Singapore, whose individual populations are all significantly smaller than Japan's but which collectively (today) have roughly 70 percent as many people.[30] These countries followed Japan's model of emphasizing export-led growth to bring innovation and competition into their economies. Later on came China, a country that also built on the Japanese model. Although some of Japan's companies were able to thrive by moving jobs abroad, the dynamism of its domestic economy languished from the growing competition.

The combination of wildly overheated asset prices and suddenly slowing growth is a potent antecedent of a financial crisis. And Japan's came with a vengeance. By August 1992, the stock market was already 60 percent off its peak. The fall in land prices was more gradual but even more brutal; by 1999, they had fallen 80 percent from their peak.[31] Residential housing prices fell with a lag and by less, but still collapsed by over 35 percent in real terms, and unlike in the United States, where home prices rapidly fell by a similar amount after 2007, there was no significant bounce back in the ensuing decade (see figure 3). Japan's real growth rate collapsed to an average of 1 percent per annum in the 1990s, down from heady rates of 4 percent in the 1970s and 1980s and 9 percent in the 1960s, and stayed depressed for decades.[32]

The land, housing, and stock-price busts led to an acute stage of the simmering banking crisis, as several of Japan's largest firms defaulted on loans collateralized by land whose value collapsed; the decrease in land value was further amplified by fire sales from bankrupt firms. Some of the losses on these loans were borne by international bond markets, which larger Japanese firms had succeeded in tapping during the bubble years. Small and medium-size firms and developers, by contrast, had borrowed almost exclusively from Japanese banks, whose balance sheets became deeply compromised. This forced the banks to cut back on lending in other areas, thereby considerably amplifying the economic cost to the country as a whole.[33]

Carmen Reinhart and I discussed the Japanese experience in the context of other post-war financial crises in our 2009 book *This Time Is Different*. There is some debate among scholars about exactly when Japan's banking crisis started. The government and banks did their best to deal with their balance-sheet problems as quietly and as gradually as possible, so the full-blown crisis didn't peak until 1998. Most scholars, including Reinhart and I, peg the start of the crisis at 1992, when banks were forced to start reining in lending, which is the main macroeconomic concern from a financial crisis. There are a few scholars who date the start of the crisis at its apex in 1998,[34] though that seems like saying that Bernie Madoff's Ponzi scheme started only when he confessed to his sons in December 2008 and the fraud became public.

Regardless, if Japan once seemed a potential economic rival to the United States — certainly, world stock market and real estate investors thought so — it clearly is not anymore. Today, per capita GDP in Japan, measured at purchasing power parity exchange rates, is only 63 percent of U.S. per capita GDP,[35] a quantum fall from the over 80 percent level it once reached. By the end of 2023, real residential housing prices were still barely 70 percent of their peak,[36] though of course that can change as Japan's inflation picks up. Regardless, outside the main cities, empty houses are a growing problem, with millions of abandoned properties.[37] The abandoned-housing problem is partly related to Japan's stagnant population. Whereas in 1990 Japan's population was half that of the United States, today it is only a third.

Then there is the problem of Japan's government debt, which makes the country acutely vulnerable to a rise in real long-term interest rates. As I will discuss extensively toward the end of this book, long-term real rates have already risen significantly in the United States and Europe and on average, even if they fall temporarily during recessions. Although as of this writing, Japan has bucked the trend, this cannot last indefinitely in a world of open capital markets. With gross debt of 251 percent of GDP (in 2024), Japan's debt burden is far above that of any other major economy; by comparison, the U.S. debt-to-GDP ratio was "only" 121 percent.[38] Netting out Japan's trillion plus dollars in foreign exchange reserves and various intergovernmental holdings brings the debt-to-GDP ratio down somewhat. On the other hand, one needs to consider the massive unfunded liabilities inherent in the country's old-age benefits and medical-care programs, which tax payers must also absorb.

How did debt in Japan get so high? At first, it soared as Japan tried to use government spending stimulus to counter the effects of its growth and financial crisis. Debt also rose as the government, trying to make the old playbook work, attempted to keep growth rates up by continually expanding infrastructure. The problem is that during its growth heyday, the country had already extensively invested in infrastructure, and it became ever more difficult to find projects offering the same kind of growth returns as in the past. Building a bridge in the middle of nowhere is not necessarily going to pay off, nor is building yet another new school in a rural town that is already losing population.

There are some who assert that Japan is proof that very high government debt doesn't matter and deny any association between high debt and low growth. Really? No doubt during Japan's financial crisis, its debt accumulation helped cushion the country and made sense. However, the attempts since to fight productivity and population problems with aggregate-demand stimulus have created a long-term debt trap that has proved difficult to escape. As long as interest rates remained very low, the debt cost little to service. Now there are tremendous pressures for interest rates to rise. High interest rates elsewhere in the world have put enormous downward pressure on the yen. This makes imports very expensive compared with domestically produced Japanese goods, especially considering that inflation is much higher elsewhere. Although the pass-through of import prices to retail consumer prices in Japan has been modest in recent decades, the drop in the real value of the yen is so dramatic that inflation is still seeping through, putting enormous pressure on the Bank of Japan to raise rates. It was only at the end of July 2024 that the Bank of Japan finally raised its policy rate to 0.25 percent.

The Bank of Japan was understandably very slow to start raising interest rates. The country's extremely high public debt is overwhelmingly held by Japanese; foreigners hold only about 7 percent, compared with 23 percent for the

United States. As a result, the debt is stuffed into every crevice of the Japanese financial sector, including banks, insurance companies, pension funds, and especially the central bank. One would have to go to low-income developing countries to find any comparable example of government financial dominance. The implication is that any significant rise in interest rates will impose massive losses across the system, raising the specter of severe financial stress. At the same time, higher interest rates will constrain the ability of the government to solve problems with further stimulus given that debt is already extraordinarily high by any metric.

To be fair, in many ways the Japanese government has managed the end of the fast-growth era and the bubble that followed with admirable grace. Japanese society has not experienced the social upheavals that many Western countries have; unemployment never rose to the kinds of levels the United States and Europe have experienced. There has not been a second financial crisis — yet. Still, one wonders what might have happened if Japan had not been forced to allow the huge currency swing in the mid-1980s, which likely made the bubble much bigger than it would have been and the subsequent collapse much worse.

In recent years, the Japanese economy has been enjoying something of a renaissance, albeit from a fairly low base. At least its businesses have been having a good run, mainly by inserting themselves into high-value niches in the Asian supply chain. Although Japan no longer produces so many marquee international consumer brands, its intermediate products capture a significant share of value-added global supply chains. After all, as the UC San Diego professor Ulrike Schaede has observed, somehow for all its shortcomings, Japan today is still among the world's four largest economies, neck and neck with Germany for third place (although India is coming up fast).[39] Taking advantage of the country's cutting-edge technology — open a Patriot missile and you will see a lot of Japanese writing on the parts — Japanese corporations have managed to reinvent themselves as suppliers of high-tech component parts and programs.

Could the yen ever have become a challenger to the dollar? Remarkably, in the exchange rate classification I developed with Ethan Ilzetzki and Carmen Reinhart, which was used to construct the map in figure 1 (in chapter 1), not a single one of the 186+ countries in the world chooses to stabilize its exchange rate against the yen. The yen is regarded by most as a very safe currency, but it is not central to global trade and finance except as a vehicle for speculation.

If an Asian yen bloc was ever a theoretical possibility in the 1980s and 1990s, that moment is likely gone now that China's economy is more than four times the size of Japan's.[40] If a renminbi bloc were to gel, however, Japan's central bank would likely give the Chinese currency a much larger weight in its exchange rate management than it does currently, even if Japan does not join the bloc outright.

Lastly, American economic and political commentators sometimes relish how the U.S. economy ultimately crushed the challenge from Japan's economy, proving all the dollar pessimists wrong and that Japan will never be the economic superpower once feared. They shouldn't gloat so much. As the much larger and geopolitically ambitious Chinese economy emerges, the United States needs a strong Japan as a bulwark in Asia, just as Japan needs the United States for military protection. An ever-weaker Japan is not in the United States' interests. Today, a strategy of closing off the United States via tariffs and protectionism and pressing Japan to raise interest rates simply for the sake of making the yen appreciate against the dollar is deeply misguided. After all, Japan is likely to end up at the strategic border between any Chinese renminbi juggernaut and a shrinking dollar bloc. Needless to say, we will return to this theme in later chapters.

CHAPTER 4

THE SINGLE CURRENCY IN EUROPE

In early 2010, just as the Greek debt crisis was unfolding, an important continental European central banker popped by my Harvard office. "What kind of advanced economy doesn't pay their debt?" he asked. I pulled *This Time Is Different* off the shelf and turned to page 99, where it shows that Greece has been in a state of default for more than half its years since independence.

Back in the 1980s and 1990s, many American economists (including me) were deeply skeptical that the Europeans would pull off a merger of the legacy currencies of Europe, combining the French franc, the German deutsche mark, and the Italian lira, along with many others. When the euro's carefully designed transition plan spectacularly blew up in the early 1990s, it did not surprise me in the least. What was surprising, however, was the determination with which European policymakers and political leaders got back on the horse and made the euro happen anyway. In my book, the unification of currencies in Europe stands as perhaps the most remarkable example of regional macroeconomic policy coordination in modern history. Historically, when several countries have moved to a common currency, it is usually because one of them has conquered all the others.

This is not to say that the formation of the euro has proved an unqualified success; that proposition remains debatable even if one accepts the euro as a fait accompli. A big part of the appeal to the populations of Europe was the promise of enjoying the same kind of low inflation levels Germans had. My guess is that had each of their countries simply established independent central banks, designed to place a large weight on inflation stabilization, it would have done the job, or so my research in the early 1980s suggested.[1] The Harvard professor Martin Feldstein (who years later became my friend and colleague) was prepared to go much further than that. In 1997, he penned an article in *Foreign Affairs* arguing that rather than strengthen peace in Europe, the euro was just as likely to aggravate conflict.[2] Europeans were outraged that one of America's leading economists would suggest, even for a moment, that the euro would lead to war not peace. Of course, this is a crude overstatement of the conflict concerns expressed by Feldstein, who was then president of the esteemed National Bureau of Economic Research. Yet there was conflict. Any visitor to Athens in early 2010, just after the Greek mess became apparent, could see a city seething and ready to explode, and with immense anger toward Germany. My meeting at the Finance Ministry to discuss resolutions to the crisis (I favored a debt write-down) was canceled because the Finance Ministry employees were on strike. In any event, Feldstein's real point was that the straitjacket of the euro would prove antithetical to growth, which, nearly three decades later, is still looking rather prescient.

Other American economists, notably former IMF chief economist Maurice Obstfeld (a longtime friend and co-author), argued that it was going to be profoundly difficult for a currency union to deal with banking and financial crises without a clearly defined lender of last resort to stem panics. Princeton University's Peter Kenen argued that if the exchange rate could not be used to cushion cross-country shocks, there would need to be a mechanism for making fiscal transfers from winners to losers.[3] If Feldstein's critiques were exaggerated, Obstfeld's and Kenen's scholarly characterization of the problem proved an understatement.

To be sure, there were at least a couple of leading American economists—let's call them the Europhiles—who thought that the euro was the greatest thing since sliced bread. Not surprisingly, they were feted in conferences across Europe.

The main intellectual energy behind the euro movement, though, came from European economists and technocrats, who shared a faith-based conviction in the euro project. They were convinced that someday the economy of the European Union would surpass that of the United States and that the euro in turn would at least rival the dollar. Their rallying cry was an impressive monograph produced in 1990 by economists at the European Commission entitled *One Market, One Money: An Evaluation of the Potential Benefits and Costs of Forming an Economic and Monetary Union*.[4] The monograph seemed to think of everything and made a case that the gains could be large. By one calculation, if a tourist traveled across the countries of Europe, changing currency at each stop, they would be left with perhaps half of what they started with. Having traveled from the United Kingdom to Spain to France to Italy to Bosnia and then to Athens on one trip playing chess professionally as a teenager, I had seen that in action. (My East High School friends—a significant share of whom were of Italian descent—delighted in the "thousand-lira shoes" I had picked up at a train stop outside Venice for the equivalent of a few dollars.) Yet for most tourists going to only one or two countries, or for companies engaging in large transactions at wholesale rates, the costs were not so dramatic. The Commission's document also made much of the expense to multinational companies of keeping books in multiple currencies, although the monograph came out just as modern accounting software had greatly simplified that task. Brilliant as the Commission's piece was overall, it said little about what to do if there was a debt or financial crisis.

There were some impressive quantitative arguments on the Commission's side. Why shouldn't the euro rival the dollar? By the mid-1990s, the combined GDP of the European Union economies was roughly the same as that of the United States, as was the market capitalization of the European stock market, as shown in figure 5. Indeed Europe's stock markets stayed on par with the United States' until the mid-2010s.[5] At one point as the euro was coming into being, a leading European economist startled us at a conference at the Centre for Economic Policy Research in London by proudly declaring that there was now more euro-denominated government debt outstanding than dollar-denominated debt. Was that a sign that things were going well, or about to fall apart?

The idea of a single currency in Europe had been kicking around ever since the 1957 Treaty of Rome, which was aimed at trade integration and initially included Germany, France, Belgium, Italy, Luxembourg, and the Netherlands.

THE SINGLE CURRENCY IN EUROPE

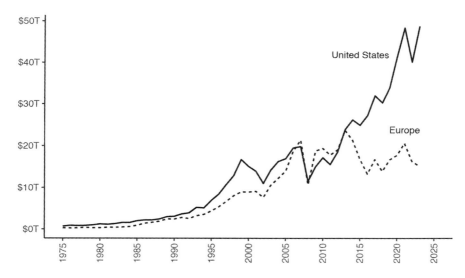

Figure 5. Total stock market capitalization in Europe and the United States, 1975–2023
Data Source: World Federation of Exchanges.

For France, the creation of a European rival to the dollar was enormously appealing, not only from a macroeconomic point of view but also as a way to project European (read: French) power. And if there were fringe benefits in terms of lower interest rates and greater market liquidity, that would be icing on the cake. Above all, the euro was to create an irreversible bond between countries that had fought two devastating world wars in the twentieth century. No wonder the Europeans were so incensed at Feldstein.

The single currency did not gain much traction early on. The dollar-centric post-war system of fixed exchange rates seemed to be working to Europe's benefit, helping countries rebuild their economies after the war. If individual European countries were already pegging to the dollar, and therefore indirectly pegging to each other (save for occasional modest realignments), what was left to be gained by having a unified currency?

That bubble burst when Nixon eliminated the convertibility of the dollar into gold in 1971, after which the Bretton Woods system soon collapsed and it was "game over" for Europe's dollar pegs. With any link to gold gone, and no alternative plan in place to stabilize prices, inflation in many European countries soared to even higher levels than in the United States (where it peaked at 14 percent). U.S. inflation over the course of the 1970s savaged the real value of Europe's dollar reserves, which had been the immediate concern of its finance ministers when the U.S. Treasury secretary John Connally made his famous put-down. Soon, this seemed like the least of Europe's problems. The process of getting from the monetary chaos of the 1970s and 1980s to the relative stability in Europe today is an important one, and is discussed in more detail in chapter 11. For now, suffice it to say that the merging of currencies did eventually work out, although the system wobbled along the way and even suffered a meltdown in 1992. Yet, each time, the Europeans found a way to keep pedaling forward.

The euro came into being on January 1, 1999, when its first group of members permanently and immutably fixed the cross exchange rates of their national currencies. The changeover became much more visceral to the public when, three years later, on January 1, 2002, euro paper currency notes and coins were introduced. The legacy national currencies were all phased out.[6] Today, twenty of the twenty-seven member countries in the European Union are members of the eurozone. The remaining seven (Bulgaria, the Czech Republic, Denmark, Hungary, Poland, Romania, and Sweden) are all eligible to join in due time. The United Kingdom would have been eligible as well, except that it dropped out of the European Union entirely in 2020, after the Brexit vote was finally implemented.

Before I turn to a broader assessment of how the euro has performed, and where it might go, it is worth pausing to remember just how remarkable it is that the euro is around at all. Merging the currencies of myriad complex developed economies with open capital markets and floating exchange rates, without causing a blowup, was extraordinary, perhaps akin to docking several high-speed orbiting spacecraft at the same time; one slight misstep and there will be a huge crash. European policymakers and technocrats may have expected that it would all go seamlessly, but given all the instability along the way, others were holding their breath.

There were other currency unions before Europe's.[7] The Central African Economic and Monetary Community, the West African Economic and Monetary Union, and the Eastern Caribbean Monetary Union had already been around for decades. These earlier currency unions, however, all revolved around hard pegs to a convertible currency and so were not true fiat currencies.[8] (A fiat currency is a government-issued money that is not backed by gold or any physical commodity, but only by trust in the issuing authority; we will come back to this topic in chapter 18 on cryptocurrencies.)

Today, the euro is easily the most important alternative to the dollar in international trade and finance. The overwhelming share of trade among the twenty-seven countries of the European Union is conducted in euros, as is most trade between the European Union and the post-Brexit United Kingdom. The euro is by far the second-most-important currency in central bank reserve holdings, constituting 20 percent of reserve holdings versus the dollar's 58 percent.[9] (Third after the euro is the yen at 6 percent and the British pound at 5 percent. The Chinese renminbi still accounts for only 2 percent of central bank reserve holdings.) Similar statistics hold across a range of metrics. Yet, as successful as the euro has been, it remains largely a regional currency. Figure 6 shows countries that either have the euro as their currency or use it as an anchor;[10] the contrast with the world map for the dollar shown in figure 1 (in chapter 1) is stunning. Outside Europe, only a few former French colonies that had once pegged to the franc—countries belonging to the aforementioned African currency unions—are now pegging to the euro. I am setting aside the large, darkened area at the top left center of the map, which is Greenland, an overseas territory of Denmark that is three times the size of Texas but whose population is only 57,000. Greenland uses the Danish krone, which itself closely mirrors the euro.

This is not to say that Europe has failed to take business from the dollar. Together, the European Union and the United Kingdom have a combined GDP of over $22 trillion, which means that 20 percent of global GDP focuses on the euro instead of the dollar for intra-bloc trade.[11] But the euro is not a global currency in the sense of being used extensively in trade between non-EU countries. In the economics jargon introduced in chapter 1, the dollar is a major vehicle currency and is routinely used as a common denominator to bridge exchange between non-dollar countries; the euro is also used but far less. In fact, the share of countries pegging (or loosely pegging) to the euro is more or less the same as the combined shares of the countries that were already pegging to the German deutsche mark or the French franc before 1999, when the European Central

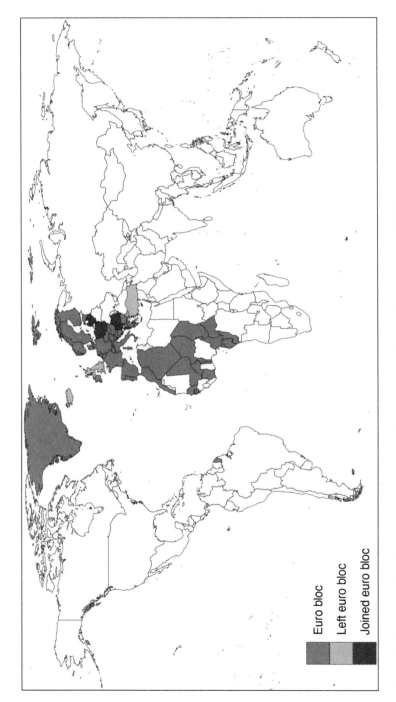

Figure 6. Countries with exchange rate regimes using the euro as the anchor or reference currency, 2019

Source: Updated from Ilzetzki, Reinhart, and Rogoff, *Quarterly Journal of Economics*, 2019.

Bank came into full operation.[12] That is, the euro has managed to hold the share that France and Germany had collectively, but not to increase it.

It is not difficult to find fault with the euro as a serious long-term competitor to the dollar. Eurozone government-debt markets are balkanized. Investors rightly do not yet regard German and Italian debt as the same thing; such debt is more akin to New York and California state debt than to U.S. Treasury bonds. During the pandemic, the European Union did begin to issue bonds that all countries jointly guaranteed; these EU bonds are more akin to U.S. Treasury debt, but so far these constitute only a modest fraction of total government debt. And it will be difficult to do much more given that there is no euro-wide fiscal authority with significant spending and taxation powers. A larger central government would be unsustainable if not accompanied by a much deeper political union, something a considerable majority of Europe's population finds anathema, although young people are more open to the idea. Europe does not need to converge into a United States of Europe; a somewhat looser confederation such as Canada's can work. All of this feeds into Europe's inability to provide for its own defense, not that the 1.3 percent of GDP that Canada devotes to defense is anything to write home about.

The lack of a strong fiscal authority is at the root of other major limitations in the euro—for example, the fact there is still no euro-wide deposit insurance scheme, a fundamental necessity for a fully developed banking union. Officially, the eurozone can claim to have a banking union in the sense that the European Central Bank gained power to supervise Europe's largest banks a decade ago. These same banks, however, as well as all smaller financial institutions, still need to report to national regulators as well, far more so than in the United States. Going beyond banks to financial markets more generally, the fact that each country has its own bankruptcy laws means that Europe is also nowhere near meeting the fundamental prerequisites for a capital market union. That is impossible if in different countries debt obligations mean completely different things. The lack of a capital market union or a more fully integrated banking system, together with the fragmented nature of European government debt, is a major handicap for the euro in competing with the dollar.

Correspondingly, Europe's growth in recent decades has not impressed. Feldstein was right about that. At the turn of the twenty-first century, after fifty

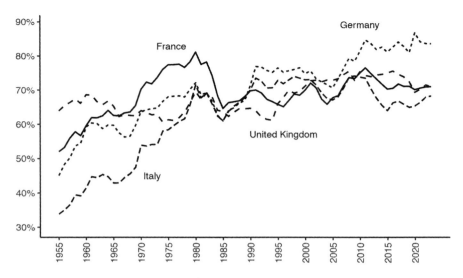

Figure 7. European per capita GDP relative to U.S. per capita GDP, 1955–2023
Data Source: Penn World Tables (to 2019); Total Economy Database (from 2020).

years of rebuilding and catch-up, the northern countries — Germany, France, Austria, Belgium, and the Netherlands — were doing quite well. Although none had fully caught up with the United States, they had reached levels in the range of 70 to 80 percent of U.S. per capita GDP, depending on what measure one uses. The progress has since stalled or worse, except for Germany. As figure 7 illustrates using purchasing power parity exchange rates, Germany's per capita GDP today is just over 80 percent of the United States', Italy's is below 70 percent, and France's just above 70 percent.[13] As to the poorer states of Europe, Greece's per capita GDP is only 40 percent of the United States' and Portugal's is only 45 percent.[14] In terms of global economic power, one must also factor in that the United States, thanks to higher immigration and birth rates, has also enjoyed considerably faster population growth than Europe.

The differences are even starker when one looks at total stock market capitalization. By mid-2024, Europe's stock market was worth well under half that of the United States, as illustrated earlier in figure 5. Because stock prices embody investor expectations about future growth, these drastic differences suggest that markets have vastly more optimism about future U.S. growth than about European growth. European leaders do not necessarily have to fully agree with the market (and part of the differential is attributable to the high value of the dollar relative to the euro), but it would be foolish indeed to ignore what the market is telling them.

The lack of European dynamism has many causes, including high taxation and a much larger welfare state. Its population is also far ahead of the United States on the aging curve.[15] It is not my purpose to evangelize one approach to government versus another; some have argued that, on balance, Europeans enjoy a higher level of overall welfare than Americans because of shorter working hours and more generous government support systems. In this sense, Europe is a lifestyle superpower. Unfortunately, as the 2024 Draghi report highlighted, over 70 percent of the gap with the United States is lower productivity, and Europe may struggle to maintain its lifestyle.

The euro does have some undeniable strengths that just might come to the fore in coming decades. For starters, the independence of the European Central Bank is etched into the Maastricht treaty of 1992. The U.S. Federal Reserve, by contrast, was founded in 1913 by an act of Congress. As a result, if it were Congress's will, the Federal Reserve could be closed down and absorbed back into the U.S. Treasury in a matter of weeks. It's not impossible, and as I will discuss in chapters 19 and 24, there are those on both the left and the right who would have the Fed effectively dismantled. Beyond the ECB's constitutional stature, its primary mandate is to maintain low inflation across the eurozone. Although its charter does not specify how it is to maintain low inflation, its narrow focus leaves less room for creative interpretation than does the Fed's dual mandate of maintaining stable prices and maximum employment, which by convention the Fed interprets as low inflation and full employment. The Fed is far more exposed to political pressure, for example, in what weight to attach to inflation as opposed to unemployment.[16]

The shared responsibility for governance of the European Central Bank also provides a measure of stability; the landslide election of an extreme left-wing or right-wing populist in a major European country will test the ECB but will not compromise its underlying structure. The U.S. Fed is more vulnerable.

Relatedly, the Maastricht treaty's inflexible rules on debt and deficits, although interpreted somewhat loosely in practice, do provide some checks and balances on spendthrift national politicians. The European Commission, charged with monitoring compliance with the Maastricht treaty's fiscal rules, often bends them, especially for the larger economies. Nevertheless, its decisions have bite. The United States has only the Congressional Budget Office (CBO), which produces well-respected long-term debt projections but otherwise has no real power—even to prevent Congress from gaming its forecasts. For example, a standard congressional trick for understating the true cost of a politically popular tax or spending bill is to include a "sunset provision" so that it will expire in, say, five years, when in reality everyone knows perfectly well that the tax or spending bill is nearly certain to be renewed. Thus, when the CBO is asked to tally the expected cost of a bill over, say, ten years, it is forced to completely ignore the later years.

The European Commission is far less constrained than the U.S. Congressional Budget Office with respect to the assumptions it can make in its forecasts. Given that ballooning debt burdens are a likely future source of political pressures on central banks, especially if the era of ultra-low interest rates does not return, the Maastricht treaty restrictions, which for years many liberal economists have argued are vastly too restrictive, will likely help protect the independence of the ECB, as they were intended to do. Very recently, in 2024, the European Council and Parliament produced a refinement of the fiscal rules that aims to provide more short-term flexibility while still stressing long-term debt sustainability. Whether this refinement will prove sufficient in a world in which real long-term interest rates have risen remains to be seen.[17]

When I first met Otmar Issing in 2002, he was renowned not only as a board member of the European Central Bank but also as its influential director of research, who substantially controlled the information the bank's other board members received. In central banking, economic information and staff analysis are the ultimate sources of power. One's view on where growth and inflation are headed dictates what should happen to interest rates. I had been chief economist at the International Monetary Fund for less than a year and was a complete policy novice compared with the seasoned and deeply respected Dr. Issing. He came to our meeting with a copy in hand of Stefan Zweig's classic short story "The Royal Game," which portrays a prisoner thrown into total isolation by the Gestapo. The prisoner survives by playing chess in his head against himself (this much I admit to doing all the time), eventually splitting into two personalities. I briefly wondered whether there was some other meaning to the book choice that I was supposed to appreciate; I am so often slow at such things. I eventually realized that it was just an extraordinarily generous and kind gesture. Issing knew that most American economists remained a bit skeptical about the euro in general, and the inflexibility of European policy in particular.

In 2003, at an IMF press conference on the global economy, after forecasting a resumption of strong growth in the United States but not for Europe, I quipped that "for now, if Europeans want to see a real recovery, they will have to watch it on TV."[18] The point was to suggest that more stimulus, including interest rate cuts from the ECB, was needed.

Issing suggested that to understand the importance to the ECB of maintaining strong anti-inflation credibility, one needed to understand the significance of the euro at a more visceral level. He explained that the proposal to share a currency with the likes of France and Italy was not an easy sell to the German people, who regarded their deutsche marks zealously and had great confidence in the Deutsche Bundesbank (the German central bank). The older generation, especially, deeply feared that monetary cohabitation with chronically inflating southern countries was a recipe for inflation disaster. (Recall my thousand-lira shoes.) They or their parents had lived through the post–World War I hyperinflation when inflation reached over a thousand percent per month. The Weimar Republic hyperinflation of 1921–1923 still scars the German psyche and has transformed Germans into the most staunchly anti-inflation populace in Europe, if not the world. And this was also a source of great national pride.

Issing explained that as a German traveling around Europe in the first decades after World War II, you pretty much knew that everyone hated you. Still, no matter how bitter their memories of the Nazis, no matter how they detested Germans, everyone still coveted the deutsche marks in their pockets; it was a thread of national dignity one could hang on to. Thanks to the Bundesbank, Germany had managed to re-establish monetary stability long before any other country in Europe, save for Switzerland. For Germans to exchange their beloved, trusted deutsche mark for the untested euro was the ultimate act of national sacrifice.

Issing's point that the euro was mainly a political project was something we could agree on. A decade earlier, in 1991, I was invited to give a presentation to the Board of Governors of the Federal Reserve System on the prospects for a single currency in Europe. The topic was being widely discussed after the European Commission's aforementioned seminal publication *One Market, One Money* in 1990.[19] The paper I prepared for the Board argued that by several of the criteria the Commission had stressed—for example, the co-movement of business cycles—a North American currency shared between the United States, Canada, and Mexico (which I christened the "NACho") would make just as much sense as the single currency in Europe.[20] Europe's common currency, for better or for worse, was first and foremost about politics.

In the heady early days of the single currency, few European policymakers or academics anticipated the disaster that was to come a decade later. The European debt crisis of 2010–2012, when Greece defaulted on its debt, and Spain, Italy, Ireland, and Portugal were forced to the brink, was a huge confidence setback, a near extinction-level event. How had these countries been painted into such a corner? After the euro launched in 1999, many investors took all European debts to be the same, as good as Germany's. European economists widely celebrated the huge flows of investment from the northern European countries (Germany, the Netherlands, France, Belgium) to the southern countries (Spain, Portugal, Italy, Greece); the economists Olivier Blanchard and Francesco Giavazzi suggested that the integration of Europe might have finally solved the famous puzzle posed by the economists Martin Feldstein and Charles Horioka, which argued that current account deficits—essentially trade imbalances—tend to be small relative to national savings and investment, at least among the advanced economies.[21] Feldstein and Horioka took this as evidence that international capital markets are much less integrated than economists had believed. In seminars and at conferences, MIT's Rudiger Dornbusch, a larger-than-life figure who was also my Ph.D. thesis adviser, often described this as "the mother of all international financial puzzles." A long literature followed trying to prove Feldstein and Horioka wrong. The piles of German and French money pouring into Portugal, Greece, and other southern European countries appeared to show that, at least within Europe, the famed Feldstein-Horioka puzzle had disappeared. Or had it?

In early March 2008, I was seated at a table with a group of European central bankers and regulators in the "Golden Room" at the Banque de France. With its breathtaking baroque decor consisting of ornate gold statues and columns surrounded by elaborate frescos on the walls and ceiling, it projects a feeling of majestic power and wealth. That power and wealth was about to be tested. The U.S. financial system had been coming under enormous pressure since the summer of 2007, and things were reaching a crescendo. On March 11, the venerable investment house Bear Stearns collapsed and had to be bailed out by the Fed.

At the time, only a few of us were suggesting that things were likely to get much worse. Nouriel "Dr. Doom" Roubini was famously predicting a crisis by piecing together a broad range of astute observations,[22] though at the time this view was still way outside the consensus among business economists. At the beginning of 2008, Carmen Reinhart and I presented a scholarly paper at the American Economic Association meetings in New Orleans in which we identified concrete quantitative markers for a financial crisis through an examination of prior systemic crises. We argued that the U.S. economy was exhibiting flashing bright red lights across the board, including debt-fueled run-ups in housing prices and the stock market, a large trade deficit, and especially slowing growth.[23] Our paper received widespread attention in the press,[24] but was generally viewed as far too alarmist. Yet there were so many other clues floating in the air that I later doubled down on our forecast, as the reader will see toward the end of the book.

The conversation in the Golden Room that evening was positively giddy, almost gleeful. European regulators had been arguing for years that U.S. and British financial regulators were too lax. Now, at last, Anglo-American sins were coming home to roost. Continental European policymakers felt supremely vindicated; the United States, with its ostensibly superior financial system, was about to get its comeuppance. This time it is "your dollar, your problem." Unfortunately, as astute as their insights about the U.S. economy were, the European policymakers were blithely unaware that if the United States had a financial earthquake of epic proportion, then as night follows day, a financial tsunami would come tearing across the Atlantic. And so it did, especially after the large and globally interconnected U.S.-based investment bank Lehman Brothers went bankrupt in September 2008. The worldwide housing bust hit particularly hard in Spain and Ireland, where banks collapsed under the weight of real estate loans gone bust and government debt followed suit thanks to explicit and implicit deposit insurance.[25] (Iceland's banking crisis hit full throttle slightly earlier, and for a while the gallows humor was, "What's the difference between Iceland and Ireland? One letter and a couple of months."[26]) The United States was not the only country with lax banking regulation.

Europe was already in deep trouble when investors learned in late 2009 that the Greek government had been grossly understating its deficit and that the country's debt problems were far worse than had theretofore been reported. If the euro had never come to pass, and Greece had been able to borrow in its own currency, it would have had the option of printing money to cover the losses, which quite likely would have led to painfully high inflation but would have avoided even more painful sovereign default. Of course, had Greece been borrowing in its own currency, investors might never have entrusted it with so much money in the first place. Other countries, including Portugal, Ireland, Italy, and Spain, all ran into trouble, one after another. At least in the case of Spain and Ireland, the problem was not so much conventionally measured debt but off-the-books fiscal expenditures arising from implicit guarantees to the banking sectors, a variant of what Reinhart and I term "hidden debt." Eventually, the European Union asked the International Monetary Fund to step in to help organize a program for Greece and help monitor the other debt-stressed periphery states.

It was quite a moment. For the three previous decades, only emerging markets or poor developing economies had called for help from the International Monetary Fund. (Greece, at least according to the European Union and the International Monetary Fund, was considered an advanced economy.)

The nightmare scenario, which some economists had long warned about, was unfolding. Without a powerful central fiscal authority capable of quickly backstopping a region-wide banking collapse, Europe was paralyzed. If the global financial crisis was bad for the dollar, it was disaster for the euro.

Because I had spent much of my career looking at debt and financial crises, it was clear to me that to avoid a severe and prolonged recession, there was little alternative to a massive bailout of the southern European countries. Ideally this would include a significant write-down of debt or large transfers from the north. Otherwise, any ultimate resolution would cost northern countries such as Germany even more in the long run, as I wrote in my *Project Syndicate* columns and elsewhere.[27] In early 2012, I made the case for closer fiscal union and debt relief in a meeting with the German finance minister Wolfgang Schäuble at the German Finance Ministry's offices at the Detlev Rohwedder Building in Berlin.

The Detlev Rohwedder Building was completed in 1936 as one of the prestige projects of the Nazi regime; it housed the Reich Air Ministry until the end of the war and was Hermann Göring's power center. In 2012, it still had the old East German elevators, which move slowly up and down between floors without ever stopping. You have to properly time your jump in and out of the open doors so as not to get maimed.

At our meeting, Schäuble reiterated his public position that Germany favored a move to closer European unification. He knew that I had been writing in favor of debt write-downs for southern Europe, but said that more time was needed to put in place safeguards so that a write-down of, say, Greek debt did not lead to an immediate stampede out of all southern European debt. He mentioned a short thought piece I had written with Carmen Reinhart in 2010 that argued that very high debt is associated with lower growth.[28] I said that although I believed that to be true as a very-long-run proposition, research on the topic was just beginning, and regardless, the gains from using debt as needed in a financial crisis surely outweighed the longer-term cost, as long as rates didn't spike.

After the meeting with the finance minister, I was to be taken to meet the German chancellor Angela Merkel in her offices at the Bundeskanzleramt, a much-newer-looking complex. I had met Merkel once before, a couple of years earlier, in a small meeting with some other economists at the World Economic Forum in Davos; she is enormously impressive. This particular meeting included just me, the chancellor, and her chief economist; it was initially scheduled for thirty minutes but lasted almost two hours.

Before I started my position as chief economist at the International Monetary Fund, Larry Summers—who had just left his position as Treasury secretary under President Clinton and was about to become president of Harvard—gave me an invaluable piece of advice: When speaking to high-level policymakers, one's inclination as an academic is to tell them what they should be worried about, and then give your view on how to solve it. That approach is wrong.

PAST CHALLENGERS TO DOLLAR DOMINANCE

Rather, you should listen carefully to what the policymakers are worried about and then do your best to address their concerns. Of course, that advice is easier to follow if you are Larry Summers and can proffer concise, brilliant thoughts on almost any topic.

The discussion with Chancellor Merkel was initially quite wide ranging, covering, among other things, the U.S. and Chinese economies. It quickly turned to Greece and the broader debt crisis Europe was facing, and I made the same case as I had before with Schäuble. Merkel forcefully emphasized that the German people had not been prepared for this eventuality when the euro was adopted; they had been promised no bailouts. They were emphatically told that the eurozone was not going to be a "transfer union." She also said that it was unclear whether the German Supreme Court would overrule any attempt to channel bailout funds to southern European countries. Leaders in the Netherlands (with whom I also discussed the issue) and Belgium saw their countries as painted into the same corner. As for allowing higher inflation to help both private and public debts—as I had been advocating since late 2008 and which did in fact relieve debt burdens after the 2020 pandemic—Merkel had already begun a previous meeting in Switzerland by noting that the German people cannot abide by inflation, so there was no point in bringing it up.[29] I did mention that there were more opaque ways of doing bailouts and suggested some options, including having the ECB buy up some of southern Europe's debt.

At the end of the meeting, the chancellor had our picture taken next to two massive lifelike chess pieces that she kept in her office, which she said were a gift from the German Forestry Association. Evidently, like many from the former East Germany, Merkel played chess growing up. In retrospect, the wooden sculptures almost looked like the giant king and queen that the fictional chess genius Beth Harmon (played with élan by the actress Anya Taylor-Joy) would visualize moving about on ceilings in the brilliant Netflix adaptation of Walter Tevis's book *The Queen's Gambit*. But in dealing with the European debt crisis, Merkel was playing a much more challenging game.

Of course, most European central bankers understood perfectly well that quantitative easing in the eurozone—when the European Central Bank issues very-short-term bank reserves to purchase the national debt of, say, Italy—is not at all the same thing as in the United States. (In private, a few were even willing to admit as much.) In conducting its open-market operations, the U.S. Federal Reserve buys U.S. federal-government debt, not the debt of Illinois or Rhode Island. In the eurozone, however, there is no unified fiscal authority. As a result, the cost of any reduction in the value of debt that the ECB holds, either through outright default or through high inflation, is spread around the eurozone's membership, in proportion to their share in the central bank. The gains, however, are concentrated on the country that issued the debt, which gets a lower interest rate. So, for example, a decade later, when there was unexpectedly high inflation during 2022 and 2023, the Italian government was a big beneficiary, whereas the ECB, which held a large slice of Italy's debt, was a big loser. Italy would be right to point out, however, that the consistent undershooting of the ECB's inflation target for a decade after the financial crisis likely cost the Italian treasury dearly. Just as unexpected high inflation helps debtors and hurts creditors, surprise low inflation does the opposite.

There is no question that what finally stemmed the crisis was the declaration by the head of the ECB, Mario Draghi, in a tense and emotional response to questions in July 2012, that he was ready to do "whatever it takes" to keep the weaker countries afloat. What this meant precisely was that the ECB would find ways to channel money to backstop Italy even if, from an actuarial point of view, this bordered on being a transfer outside the ECB's mandate. Draghi's bailout promise could not have been made without Germany's tacit approval: Merkel had finally relented when it had become absolutely clear that nothing else was working.

Draghi's line in the sand is of such fundamental historical importance, not only to the euro but also for central banking in general, that it is worth pausing to emphasize his precise wording, which was, "Within our mandate, the ECB is prepared to do whatever it takes to preserve the euro. And believe me, it will be enough."[30] The last phrase, not in his original written remarks, was delivered with strong emotion. Technically, Draghi did say "within our mandate" so that northern European politicians and economists could not accuse him of deliberately trespassing into fiscal policy, which of course was exactly what the ECB was doing. Markets heard only the impromptu emotional flourish at the end, which they took to mean that the European Central Bank would intervene decisively no matter what the institutional risks. In retrospect, the phrasing and theatric delivery was nothing short of masterful. Central bankers know that speaking to the markets is like talking to your dog: a dog is acutely sensitive to its owner's mood and tone of voice but probably does not fully understand every detail of what it is being told.

To say the least, the European debt crisis was a growing experience for the eurozone. A decade later, during the pandemic, northern European countries responded not only with loans but also with outright grants (which do not have to be repaid) under the banner "NextGenerationEU." This was much more in line with what I had advised during the debt crisis, although to be fair the case for large-scale transfers was far easier to agree on after a natural disaster than it had been during the earlier debt crisis, which mainly reflected problems of each country's own making. Still, for now, the pandemic response appears to have given investors confidence that Europeans will somehow rise to the occasion and find a way to make under-the-table transfers as needed to bail out weaker countries.

Nevertheless, markets appreciate that there are limits to what northern Europe is prepared to do, which is why interest rates still differ significantly across the eurozone. Of course, a portion of these differentials has to do with differences in the depth and liquidity of the markets, but surely this does not explain why Italy—which accounts for a third of all eurozone country debt—has long paid a significantly higher interest rate than Germany: as of August 5, 2024, the German ten-year government bond rate was 2.2 percent versus 3.7 percent for Italy; France was in between at 3.0 percent. The only way to cure this problem is to greatly strengthen the fiscal capacity of the central European government, a step Europeans have been deeply reluctant to take. They already pay far higher taxes than Americans and rightly worry that any expansion of the central government will sharply raise their already high overall tax bill, with power-seeking national governments not cutting taxes nearly as much as the central European government is raising them.

Moreover, Draghi's "whatever it takes" and the pandemic transfers from the "NextGenerationEU" loans took place in a global environment in which real interest rates on government debt were effectively zero, or even negative. Although there was much squabbling, the pandemic-era bailouts could be accomplished at relatively low cost. If, as discussed later in part VI, real interest rates have returned to more normal historical trends, the "free lunch" argument for the bailouts will be revealed to be specious, and the debates will become more contentious. That could destabilize the euro if further progress on integration is not made before the inevitable next euro crisis.

Europe's fiscal paralysis plays out in two other areas: military power (a topic we will return to in chapter 23 on the burdens of issuing a dominant currency) and, relatedly, tech. As Chris Miller has shown in his celebrated book *Chip Wars*, there is a symbiosis between military investment and cutting-edge technology, since innovative military applications often seed early-stage innovation.[31] And tech is critical to the development of financial infrastructure in the twenty-first century. Europe is a tremendous laggard in tech, trailing the United States, China, and perhaps even Japan. The United States has Facebook, Google, Microsoft, and Apple. Europe has LVMH, Hermès, and L'Oréal, although to be fair it also has Novo Nordisk, the Danish company behind the weight-loss drug Ozempic.

One should not totally dismiss the possibility that Europe's dynamic will change. In the near term, Europe faces the difficult prospect of having to spend much more on defense. Even if the United States also increases its defense expenditures, the Russian invasion of Ukraine has marked a major geopolitical shift, and the European polity is starting to wake up to the problem. The most likely outcome is that higher defense spending will lead to higher taxes and higher debt, neither of which is good for growth. But it is also possible that Europe's focus on defense will provide an incentive to try to create an environment in which tech development can flourish, even if at the moment that does not seem to be the case.

So where does all of this leave the euro going forward? It has been a huge success in some dimensions and has maintained the world market share of the individual European currencies it replaced, albeit mainly by monopolizing the European market rather than by becoming a global vehicle currency. Above all, if a country aspires to become or remain a dominant-currency issuer, it does not help to have a major debt crisis. The U.K. government's default on its debts to the U.S. government in 1931 was unquestionably an important step on the way to the passing of the baton from the pound sterling to the dollar.[32] Nor does it help to have a major war on Europe's eastern border.

PAST CHALLENGERS TO DOLLAR DOMINANCE

Still, even with the current dominance of the dollar, and the coming rise of the Chinese renminbi, one should not assume that it is all downhill from here for the euro. If the dollar falters—say, because a gridlocked U.S. Congress decides to create financial chaos by pushing the country into sustained technical default for months on end—no currency will benefit more than the euro. And just as Europe surprised many economists in pulling off the single currency, it may surprise again and achieve a far higher level of integration than most currently imagine.

All in all, though, the Chinese renminbi, to which we turn our attention next, would appear to be a far more potent threat to the dollar.

PART II

CHINA

The Present-Day Challenger

CHAPTER 5

THIS TIME IS DIFFERENT

For years, whenever anyone asked whether there was a quintessential "this time is different" story on the horizon — and they have asked this question a lot since the 2008–2009 global financial crisis — my answer was invariably, "China." The biggest meltdowns often happen precisely where no one is expecting it. When markets boom for years on end, optimists reign supreme. Regulators who try to enforce limits gradually get worn down, if not by seeming too alarmist year after year, then by politicians who overrule them. In the case of China, "this time is different" optimists long pointed to the undeniable competence of the country's technocrats, the country's stunningly high savings rate, the government's trillions of dollars in foreign exchange reserves, the Asian work ethic, and the creativity and dynamism of China's entrepreneurs, among other factors.

Granted, China was never likely to experience a Western-style financial blowup given the powerful central government's capacity to allocate losses at hyper-speed compared with the snail-like pace of Western courts. Moreover, if needed, the Chinese government can liberally disburse state funds to facilitate restructuring without having to reckon with legislative pushback. Nevertheless, state capacity does not make China immune to credit cycles; it just means that they play out differently. Falling housing and land prices weaken bank, firm, and household balance sheets just the same and lead to the same loss of credit activity and lower consumer demand. Although Japan repressed its financial crisis of the 1990s for many years, lending was still constrained by weak bank balance sheets, and growth still collapsed.

For many years, mine was not the conventional view on China, to say the least. Until quite recently, most prognosticators confidently predicted that China's fast-growing economy would continue apace. Many believed that within as little as two or three decades, the Chinese economy would eclipse that of the United States by any measure. Within due time, the renminbi would supplant the dollar. In 2020, when the IMF's Yuanchen Yang and I published a working paper entitled "Peak China Housing," no one much noticed.[1] Our paper strongly suggested that China's construction sector was likely running into sharply diminishing returns and that, even if there were no financial crisis, it would be difficult to reallocate resources away from that sector. If the tail end of the Japanese construction boom became famous for its "bridges to nowhere," in China it is shaping up as "high-speed railways with no riders" and "houses that no one lives in," especially in China's smaller and less prosperous "tier 3" cities (think of Cincinnati, Ohio; Rennes, France; or Liverpool, United Kingdom, home of the Beatles).

Although our working paper was an academic piece, it was still surprising that our rather compelling metrics on overbuilding in China drew so little interest. The few who did comment strongly disagreed, giving all kinds of reasons why China is different. A year later, though, in the summer of 2021, when the bankruptcy of Evergrande (the second-largest construction firm by sales in China at the time) brought the problem to the world's attention, our paper exploded across the world media. Meanwhile, investment analysts and policy institutes pored over details of the paper's two dozen figures and tables. There were still many who disagreed with our basic premise. In November 2021, the *Economist* published a piece suggesting that the whole problem was perhaps not nearly as bad as we had suggested, highlighting unpublished, much lower estimates from the Asian Development Bank that were later sharply revised upward.[2] The *Economist* entirely missed the key point that after decades of torrid investment in real estate and infrastructure, large regions of the country were becoming overbuilt, so comparisons to, say, India, which was just getting to speed on its annual infrastructure investment, were misplaced.

China's growth problems are only partly due to diminishing returns from investment.[3] There are numerous challenges on other fronts, including slowing productivity gains, increasing centralization of authority, deglobalization, and a steep demographic decline. Nowadays, the discussion has turned entirely, and the debate is much more about "peak China," not just "peak China housing."[4] We will come to a broader discussion of China's growth challenges later in this section; some of the arguments are quite speculative. The evidence on China's overbuilding in real estate and infrastructure is, however, quite concrete.

This is not to say that China has failed. It has been a spectacular success until recently; it is just not going to take over from the United States nearly as fast as many experts have long been breathlessly predicting.[5] And it may never do so. When the history of the world is told a hundred years from now, the transformation of China will still be the most important single economic event of the 1980–2020 period. China's meteoric rise is comparable to the rise of the United States in the second half of the nineteenth century, although China started from a lower base. China's per capita income relative to that of the United States (calculated using purchasing power parity exchange rates) rose almost fivefold, from 5 percent of U.S. per capita income in 1980 to 22 percent in 2019, as illustrated in figure 8.[6] And that is during a period when U.S. per capita GDP itself doubled. If one uses purchasing power parity weights, then, on the basis of overall GDP, China has already overtaken the United States as the world's largest economy. But if one uses market exchange rates, which as discussed make more sense when analyzing a country's global economic power, China's economy is still only two-thirds as large as the U.S. economy as of this writing. Unfortunately, if China's trend growth has slowed as sharply as I will argue here, China will have come up far short of other Asian economies such as Korea and Japan in terms of per capita income relative to the United States.

Even if China falls short of overtaking the U.S. economy, it can still be a huge threat militarily, as the economic historian Angus Madison had warned about Russia. And if the Chinese central bank were to ever fully cut the renminbi loose from the dollar, it could take a big chunk out of the dollar bloc that the United States dominates. At present, China's adherence to a dollar-centric exchange rate system helps promote the use of the dollar throughout the entire Asian supply chain. Asia as a whole constitutes over half of the dollar bloc, ex-

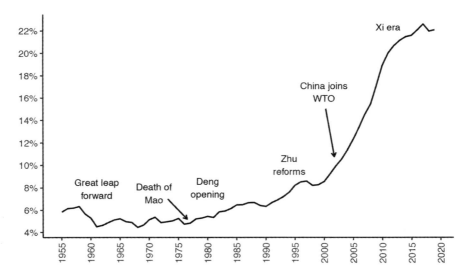

Figure 8. China's per capita GDP relative to U.S. per capita GDP, 1955–2023
Data Source: Penn World Tables.

cluding the United States, on a GDP-weighted basis.[7] Moreover, if the renminbi were to float against the dollar — say because the Chinese central bank's interest rate policy focused on stabilizing domestic inflation rather than the dollar exchange rate — it would likely take a number of other Asian supply chain partners with it. Given that Asia is still the fastest-growing region of the world economy, the potential impact on dollar demand could be far reaching, leading to a substantial shrinking of the dollar's domain.

The case of China is so important and so fundamental to thinking about the future of the global exchange rate system that it is worth stepping back and providing some perspective. The next few chapters will follow my own journey toward better understanding the Chinese economy, and only after that, return to a more analytical discussion of the renminbi versus the dollar.

Like everyone else at the time, I followed the remarkable events surrounding President Richard Nixon's historic trip to China in 1972, which built on small earlier steps, especially the U.S. table-tennis team's surprise visit in 1971. The celebrated novelist Gish Jen's book of short stories *Thank You, Mr. Nixon*, though fictional, eloquently captures the cognitive dissonance the typical Chinese person must have felt.[8] In the opening story, the American president visits a rural Chinese town and meets a young girl who has borne witness to the terrible cruelties of Chairman Mao's Cultural Revolution, but cannot understand it, much less dare to speak of it. Just a few years later, in 1978, after the death of Mao in 1976, Deng Xiaoping became president and China's new era of seemingly miraculous growth began. Unlike Mao, who dogmatically rejected capitalism, Deng famously quipped, "It does not matter if a cat is black or white as long as it catches mice."

The opening of China did not turn the world upside down overnight; China's exports grew quickly, but again from an extremely low level. In the early 1980s, the pandas that Mao had gifted to the National Zoo in Washington, D.C., were a highlight for locals and visitors alike. Contemporary Chinese artists started to be featured at the art galleries in Dupont Circle. Still, at the International Finance Division of the Federal Reserve Board, where I worked as an economist after graduate school, all the focus was on Japan and Germany; China was still a curiosity.

Over time, China's presence in the United States became increasingly noticeable. I moved from my job at the Federal Reserve Board in Washington to go teach at the University of Wisconsin–Madison in early January 1985. Let's just say that it gets very cold in Wisconsin—even for a Rochesterian—sometimes reaching minus 15 degrees Fahrenheit (minus 26 degrees Celsius) in the middle of the day. As a consumer, I was incredibly grateful that one could buy Chinese down ski jackets for a fraction of what a U.S. brand-name coat would cost. Sure, my super-insulated silver-colored coat was incredibly puffy and made me look like the Abominable Snowman, but it was very warm. Little did I realize that the economic gutting of Detroit and my hometown of Rochester (discussed in chapter 3 on Japan) would be repeated across a much larger swath of the United States, particularly after China's entry into the World Trade Organization in 2001.

That same year when China entered the World Trade Organization, I took public-service leave from Harvard University to serve as chief economist and director of research at the International Monetary Fund. By then China had already become an increasingly important economy, commanding increasing attention from the IMF for its growing global impact. There was considerable concern that despite the capital controls that insulated China during the Asian debt crisis in the 1990s, its fixed exchange rate regime would eventually lead to trouble, both for China and for everyone else.

Moreover, both the Europeans and the Americans believed that China's intervention in foreign exchange markets was artificially holding down the value of its currency. Indeed, by October 2002, China had amassed $265 billion in reserves by repeatedly selling its renminbi for dollars to keep its exchange rate from rising.[9] The IMF rules permit exchange rate intervention for the purpose of keeping the currency market stable, but consistent one-sided intervention for the purpose of gaining a competitive advantage is a violation; a central bank does not accumulate hundreds of billions of dollars in reserves through balanced purchases and sales of dollars.

For American policymakers and politicians, the fact that China was running a very large trade surplus year after year was proof positive that its intervention must be unfair. Lay people, and frankly even some policy economists, tend to think that trade deficits and surpluses are all about the competitiveness of a country's exchange rate; so do some American presidents. In fact, as those who have studied international economics well understand, what matters is the overall balance between a country's savings and investment. The exchange rate is only one of the factors that drive the current account deficit; other factors include productivity, interest rates, savings preferences, and business cycles.[10]

China's citizens and corporations had (and still have) a very high propensity to save compared with Americans. Between 2001 and 2008, China's savings rate averaged a staggering 48 percent of GDP; by comparison, the U.S. savings rate during this period was under 20 percent, and today it is lower still. Much of China's savings was being absorbed by the fast-growing country's need to fund new factories and infrastructure; between 2001 and 2008, investment (in real assets) averaged 41 percent of GDP. But that still left a large gap of unemployed savings that inevitably spilled overseas.[11]

In addition, China's policymakers believed that accumulating dollars was a way to help maintain broader financial stability. After all, even though China had held on to its fixed exchange rate, the country had experienced a raft of bankruptcies from the late 1980s up to the Asian financial crisis, particularly after China unified its exchange rate regime in 1994, stripping out trade subsidies and controls that had propped up some firms.

Although the IMF was reluctant to force China to stop its mostly one-way intervention, we still spent long hours debating the peg's merits with Chinese officials, trying to make the case for greater exchange rate flexibility from a purely Chinese perspective. We warned that although China was currently in a position of great strength with its large trade surpluses, the experience of other countries showed that things can turn quickly and painfully, typically resulting in a large depreciation of the currency. Introducing some two-sided flexibility into the exchange rate would prevent speculators from being assured of a one-way bet. Anyone who took a large stake against a currency would have to consider the possibility that it might strengthen instead of weakening. Might not it be better for China to move off the hard peg now, from a position of strength? we asked. The Chinese expressed confidence that their capital controls were reasonably watertight, though they did not have a good answer when asked about the large discrepancies between the export and import numbers China was reporting and the corresponding data being reported by its trade partners. These discrepancies suggested that companies were getting quite a bit of money in and out of the country using the time-honored accounting trick of under- and over-invoicing.

In one meeting, I commented that Europe had strong capital controls in the years after World War II. However, as trade grew those controls became easier to evade and Europe's fixed exchange rates against the dollar kept coming under attack. The Chinese were still unimpressed. Our final argument was that if China kept its exchange rate at an artificially low level for too long, the high cost of imports would shift demand toward non-traded goods (including construction and services), which would cause domestic inflation. To this, the Chinese officials answered something along the lines of, "If the day ever comes when we see a lot of inflation, we will phone you."

It was indeed puzzling that China was managing to avoid inflation without allowing its exchange rate to appreciate to reflect its rapid productivity growth. What were we missing? A good rule of thumb is that in fast-growing economies, the traded-goods sector tends to experience productivity growth at a much faster pace than the non-traded-goods sector, since the latter is not facing international competitive pressures. In time, the highly productive traded-goods sector starts siphoning workers from the rest of the economy, bidding up wages even for restaurant and hotel workers, who are mainly producing for the domestic market. With higher wage costs, and minimal offsetting productivity gains, restaurant meals get more expensive.[12]

By this standard, China had been quite an outlier. With a fixed exchange rate against the dollar, it was generally experiencing lower inflation than its main trading partners, including the United States. One-sided exchange market intervention could explain how China was able to temporarily make its goods more competitive, but over time inflationary forces should push up costs, undoing the central bank's efforts.

As the IMF Research Department dug deeper into the issue, we found an intriguing answer that even to this day is underappreciated by most economists and policymakers. Simply put, the Chinese government was able to hold down wages by taking advantage of differing rates of economic development in different parts of the country. Whereas cities on China's eastern coast (where Beijing and Shanghai are located) were experiencing rapid industrialization, the rest of country was not. Rural China—back then over half the population—was falling ever further behind. To help the rural population, and at the same time relieve upward wage pressure for firms on the eastern coast, the government orchestrated a mass migration from the underemployed agrarian sector to its cities, on the order of 10–15 million people per year.[13]

In most developing countries, the "Lewis transition" (named after the Nobel Prize–winning economist Arthur Lewis) is something that happens on its own, as poor rural farmers migrate to the city in search of better employment opportunities. The Chinese authorities, having witnessed how uncontrolled mass migration overran urban centers in places like India and Brazil, attempted to control the rate of urbanization. China's household registry, or "Hukou," system requires that rural migrants have official permission to go to the cities; otherwise they will not be able to receive publicly provided health care for their families or education for their children.

What China attempted to do, by and large quite successfully for many years, was to spread the migrants across different urban areas at a rate the cities' infrastructure and public services could handle, while still allowing the urban labor supply to grow fast enough to restrain wage pressures in the factories. As long as this process was in motion, inflation could be contained. That is what Western critics, including at the IMF, had been missing. Later, as we shall see, China's efforts to spread out its citizens, although quite successful in many respects, are also at the root of today's intractable real estate problems.

Parenthetically, such arguments did not sway U.S. authorities in the least. After eventually giving up on strong IMF action, the United States periodically threatened to declare China a "currency manipulator," which would have opened the door to trade sanctions. For years, the threat was never carried out. Over time, China's trade surplus waxed and waned; indeed, in 2015, after the Shanghai stock market fell by 30 percent in just a few weeks, investors who had been clamoring to get into China suddenly wanted to get out.[14] The Chinese central bank had to intervene to prevent the renminbi from *depreciating*. If China had been holding down its currency in the past, the case that it was still doing so suddenly become much thinner. This episode, however, did not stop the Trump administration from later pulling the trigger and formally declaring China a currency manipulator in August 2019. By then, China had become far too large to be bullied, and its policymakers certainly did not want to repeat what they viewed as the mistake of Japan in the mid-1980s, when it agreed to the Plaza Accord that James Baker had helped broker. And unlike Japan, China does not need U.S. military protection, so the United States does not have anywhere near the same degree of leverage. The fundamental connection between military power and currency dominance is one we will keep returning to.

CHAPTER 6

ZHU RONGJI'S UNCANNY FORECASTS

My first trip to China was in October 2002, to participate in a seminar hosted by the People's Bank of China entitled "Management of Short-Term Capital Movements and Capital Account Liberalization." The topic might not sound terribly sexy, but after the Asian financial crisis of 1997–1998, which brought Thailand, Indonesia, and Korea to their knees, understanding international capital flows was a very big deal to Asian policymakers. In fact, the issue was so sensitive that it was surprising that the Chinese felt comfortable having an open discussion with all the leading central bankers from Asia, who were also at the conference.

At the time, believe it or not, U.S. authorities wanted to see more capital flow into China. They reasoned that if U.S. companies were able to build more plants and equipment in China, buy up Chinese companies, and make loans to the Chinese government and businesses, the demand for renminbi assets would bid up the price of China's currency. This, in turn, would make U.S. goods more competitive with China's. Yes, that really was the thinking and how the strategy was sold; the powerful U.S. financial-sector lobby was a driving force, as were many companies eager to move production to low-cost China.

In preparing for my visit, I took advantage of conversations with my tall, overly modest, and deeply experienced IMF colleague David Robinson. David, who had once managed IMF missions to China, served as my deputy director in charge of supervising the World Economic Outlook Division. That division bears primary responsibility for producing the IMF's hugely influential global growth and inflation forecasts. My first encounter with David's deep understanding of China came near the start of my IMF tenure, in August 2001, as we were marking up the first round of forecasts for our September *World Economic Outlook* publication. Our big question then was whether, with the tech bubble bursting, the United States was likely to enter a recession.

"How can it be that we are still forecasting over 7 percent growth for China, in both 2001 and 2002, when we are projecting a recession for China's major trading partners?" I inquired. How can China be immune? David patiently explained that our forecasts would later be judged by how well we predicted the *official* numbers. Given that Premier Zhu Rongji had just given a speech in August 2001 calling for output growth to be 7.5 percent in 2001 and 7.1 percent in 2002, we probably should consider those estimates a very well-informed guess of where the official numbers would eventually land. As it turned out, the official 2001 number landed at 7.3 percent and the official 2002 number at 8 percent (which only became fully clear well into 2003). We (and the premier) were a little off, but in the very uncertain world of economic forecasting, this was still pretty close to a bullseye or, to be precise, where the Chinese government later decided to place the bullseye.

On another occasion, I asked David how China could possibly put together accurate numbers for real GDP growth — even after the fact — when much richer countries like the United States and the United Kingdom, armed with far more information and resources, struggle with deep conceptual problems such as how to account for new products and quality improvement. The numbers in many sectors — for example, financial services — are imputed with heroic statistical extrapolations after only a small sample of data has been collected. An expert at the Federal Reserve Bank of New York, who graduated a couple of years ahead of me at MIT, once quipped in a meeting that the methods for imputing financial-services output are "a dark art."

With almost 1.3 billion people, how can Chinese government statisticians possibly know what is happening in the smaller cities and rural villages? David explained that going back two thousand years, the emperors never really knew

THE PRESENT-DAY CHALLENGER

what was happening in the countryside and that even by 2002, the government basically had decent data only for the big cities and pretty much guessed at the rest. (Today, with China's formidable surveillance infrastructure, the central administration has vastly more information on the hinterlands, but still far less than for the major cities.)

In advance of my visit to Beijing, the IMF China Division prepared a brief, since the chief economist needed to be well informed about current issues, and especially any points of contention between the IMF and China. The brief emphasized IMF concerns that bad loans remaining in China's banking system could potentially hold back lending or, worse yet, be a sign of a festering financial crisis. The intensity of this debate between the IMF China Division and the Chinese authorities became clear only later during the course of my trip.

As we drove to the city from the Beijing airport, it was stunning to see the streets filled with so many bicycles and so few cars. The singer Katie Melua's song about Beijing, "Nine Million Bicycles," which was released a couple of years later, spoke to me when I heard it.[1] Today, of course, car traffic in Beijing is as bad as it is in any major city; the pollution is so awful that the government shuts down some of the outlying factories before foreign dignitaries visit.[2]

Making our way past the thousands of bicycles, we eventually arrived at the Diaoyutai State Guesthouse, a magnificent array of structures built in the late 1950s but looking as if they had been around forever.

In the spirit of the conference, my particular topic was "sequencing and pre-conditions of capital account liberalization." In non-jargon terms, the issue was when and how to make the transition from a typical developing economy in which the government keeps a tight lid on how much banks and companies can borrow from abroad, to a typical modern advanced economy in which there are reporting requirements but typically very few outright restrictions. The danger is that by liberalizing too fast, particularly in terms of allowing short-term dollar borrowing from abroad, countries open themselves up to the kinds of crises the Asian economies experienced in the late 1990s, when foreign funds, which had been pouring in, were quickly withdrawn. On the other hand, never opening up at all can stifle growth. (Nowadays, somewhat more can be said, thanks in part to the work of Gita Gopinath, who is the second-highest-ranking official at the IMF as well as a world-renowned scholar; Gita was my former colleague at Harvard and before that I was her Ph.D. thesis adviser at Princeton.) China's experience in many ways captures the challenges, since inevitably as a country develops it will want more open capital markets. For all the rhetoric about the huge dangers of international capital flows, all the advanced countries in the world are quite open, and none of them have sharply retreated for any sustained period of time.

After the conference, about ten to twelve of us were invited to meet with China's premier, Zhu Rongji, the second-most-powerful leader in China after the president. The other invitees were all finance ministers or heads of central banks; I felt quite fortunate to be included. Zhu was perhaps the most important architect of China's economic policy since Deng Xiaoping. I have had the great privilege of meeting many presidents and world leaders over the years; no other meeting was quite the same.

When we stepped off the bus at Zhu's residence, we were met by young women dressed in stunning blue silk robes. As they guided us to our seats in magnificently carved wooden chairs, it became apparent that these women were serving as Zhu's personal security guards. One kneeled beside each of us and assisted with serving tea. Sitting in Zhu's palatial garden outside a building that looked eons old, I felt as if I were in a James Bond movie. The fact that Zhu was already in his seventies (though he looked far younger) only amplified the effect. I suspect I was not alone in wondering what these women were really for. Then, very suddenly, as one of the guests turned around in his chair to view the grounds, he completely let go of his teacup and saucer. Faster than one could blink, the hand of the young woman kneeling next to him shot out and caught both, seemingly without spilling a drop. It was surreal. So much for wondering about how good the security was. I was reminded of a 1950s Japanese movie in which Toshiro Mifune, as a highly trained samurai, scares off a group of thugs surrounding his table by calmly using his chopsticks to catch flies, paying them no attention. When the thugs realize what Mifune is doing, they back off in terror.[3]

Zhu gave very short introductory remarks and then asked what we would like to speak about. Although the central bank governors and ministers constituted a very senior group, Zhu clearly viewed Andrew Crockett as the most important given his role as head of the Bank for International Settlements (BIS),

THE PRESENT-DAY CHALLENGER

a global international organization that most of the leading central banks belonged to. Crockett, who was British, was an incredibly gracious and distinguished man who played a huge role in restoring the BIS to its leading role today in coordinating ideas and policies across the world's central banks. He also had been my boss in an earlier incarnation in the 1980s, during my short first stint at the IMF. Crockett's questions were very diplomatic and included many compliments on how China had managed to navigate the 1997–1998 Asian financial crisis and maintain such consistent, strong growth for so many years. Zhu spoke excellent English but mostly answered through a translator, no doubt to be completely precise. The translator's ability to take in long answers without pause, and then convert them to perfect English while incorporating any emphasis the premier gave, was remarkable.

Most of the others were reluctant to speak, but as the IMF representative I believed it my responsibility to say something. So I raised my hand and explained who I was, though it soon became clear that Zhu was well aware of my debate, in June 2002, with the Nobel Prize winner and former World Bank economist Joseph Stiglitz, who had just published his widely discussed book *Globalization and Its Discontents*.[4] I agreed with some of the book's ideas—for example, that overly rapid financial market liberalization is ill advised. Indeed, I had published (jointly with the Stanford economist Jeremy Bulow) an even stronger view a decade earlier, arguing that foreign lenders should not be allowed to rely on New York courts to enforce loan contracts with sovereign borrowers and that these loans should instead be governed by developing-country courts, even if it makes it more difficult for some countries to borrow internationally.[5] (Stiglitz was the editor of the journal.) However, I disagreed with other elements. For example, the apparent suggestion that developing countries should fight off speculative exchange attacks by lowering interest rates appeared to me to be contrary to common sense and long experience. Normally, if money is fleeing the country, the central bank needs to raise interest rates to persuade investors to stay. Lowering the interest rate on a currency everyone is dumping is not going to cause it to suddenly sell like hotcakes, I argued.[6]

As soon as I introduced myself, Zhu jumped into answering the questions he suggested that I would have. He began by bluntly stating that he knew that the IMF was quite worried about the Chinese banking sector and that the IMF believed that the official Chinese figure for bad loans was much too low. The IMF bad-loans estimate was just wrong, Zhu said. With the benefit of hindsight, it is now clear that the IMF, along with most Western analysts, was indeed wrong and that Zhu was right. China grew so fast that even some of the weakest firms still turned out to be good credits. (Parenthetically, that was back during the heady days of 10 percent growth. Now, in 2025, it is going to be far more difficult for China to dig its way out of widespread financial problems.)

The premier continued, saying that he was well aware that the IMF had concerns about China's rigid exchange rate peg to the dollar given that many other countries had succumbed to speculative exchange rate attacks. I responded that of course China needed to act at the pace it thought best but that I hoped it was aware of the heightened risk of financial crisis and inflation that the fixed-rate policy, if carried on for too long, might produce. Zhu said that this was a concern but was manageable for now.

As others started to speak, the conversation turned to pan-Asian cooperation and other topics, and finally the premier inquired whether there were any further questions. Rather spontaneously, I said, "Forgive me for asking: What keeps you up at night?" Zhu laughed, looked away for a moment, and then repeated my question. His face turned quite pensive as he explained that what worried him most was social stability. As long as China was growing rapidly, and people believed that their lives were improving, the political, social, and economic fabric of China's society would hold together. If anything were to disrupt the growth process, however, it could also produce significant unrest, and the whole dynamic could be disrupted. The candor and clarity with which Zhu explained the core conundrum facing the Chinese Communist Party was startling and impressive. Needless to say, Zhu's insight remains central to the political economy of China even today.

Upon returning to the Diaoyutai State Guesthouse that evening, we were treated to a magnificent banquet hosted by Dai Xianglong, the governor of the People's Bank of China. The People's Bank has a staff of over 125,000 but was much larger at one time, before some of its activities were spun off. My deputy David Robinson had great respect for Dai from his years as IMF mission chief. I wanted to ask Dai more about China's growth numbers—how they could be so stable year after year, and how China managed to gather meaningful statistics across such a vast country. Unfortunately, back then Chinese banquets were invariably marked by so many toasts that it proved a less-than-propitious occasion for that kind of conversation. Such a discussion would have to wait until a later trip to Beijing. It should be mentioned that in recent years, since President Xi Jinping's anti-corruption campaign, official dinners have become more circumspect. Unless there are foreign guests, there is no alcohol, and the participants are more likely to get a box lunch than a feast.

The few of us who were not heavily drinking got into a long discussion about the global economy and the dollar. I had previously met some of the governors and ministers at the IMF's biannual meetings, where the chief economist has the task of opening the meetings with a presentation of the world economic outlook to an audience consisting more or less of all the heads of central banks and finance ministers from around the world.

The issue I had chosen to emphasize at the biannual IMF meeting in Washington just a few weeks earlier was the extraordinarily high value of the dollar. In 2002, the purchasing power of the U.S. dollar (the "real U.S. dollar") relative to the currencies of U.S. trading partners hit its highest peak since the mid-1980s and the United States had a deep trade deficit, not least because of China. When the dollar is too strong, it places huge pressure on the entire world economy, and particularly on countries whose firms have borrowed a lot in dollars but earn their revenues in local currency. The topic had to be discussed, even though a U.S. official came up to me beforehand and asked me not to say anything about it, opining that the high value of the dollar was just a sign of the world's huge confidence in the United States. Over the next few years, the dollar fell sharply.

As we discussed the dollar at the dinner, it was clear that many Asian policymakers considered the high value of the dollar a particularly acute problem, in part because a lot of their government and corporate borrowing was in dollars. They said that a fall in the dollar would actually be a relief, though easier to digest if it happened slowly. It was an interesting insight; my IMF colleague Carmen Reinhart had written a very influential, and now quite famous, paper with Guillermo Calvo emphasizing exactly this issue. The paper, entitled "Fear of Floating," argued that large movements in the exchange rate wreak havoc with balance sheets, especially for small open economies in which a large fraction of public and private borrowing is denominated in dollars.[7] Though it will be obvious to some readers, the title of their paper is an allusion to Erica Jong's risqué novel *Fear of Flying*, published in 1973. It is a great title because it provokes the reader to wonder where Calvo and Reinhart are going with it. Then again, it was probably not their intention for anyone to read too much into the title, given that one of their main points is that until countries can do more of their public and private international borrowing in their local currency instead of dollars, their central banks have good reason to fear large fluctuations in their currency's dollar exchange rate.

CHAPTER 7

THE PEOPLE'S BANK OF CHINA

By the summer of 2005, I had returned to Harvard from my public-service leave at the IMF. The IMF was an incredible experience in so many ways, but even with the freedom offered to the chief economist, it still felt too constraining. At the same time, I was very excited about my research project with Carmen Reinhart on eight centuries of debt, inflation, and financial crises — research that ultimately led to our 2009 book *This Time Is Different*, which improbably reached number 4 on Amazon, just behind the three books of *The Girl with the Dragon Tattoo* series; then again those books have sex and violence.

I had not been planning to go back to China anytime soon, but in 2005 one of my colleagues, Shing-Tung Yau (a 1982 Fields Medal winner in mathematics) contacted me about a trip to China that would include Yau as well as Harvard's longtime director of admissions, Bill Fitzsimmons. I was to give talks at institutes and universities in Beijing, Shanghai, and Xi'an. Importantly for me, my family was also able to get visas. Otherwise, I would not have been able to make a solo trip like this during the August school break, especially after having been away so much during my IMF years.

On our first evening in Beijing, while our children watched Chinese TV in the hotel, Natasha and I met with Robert, a thirty-something American who had been working in Beijing for the past few years and was a good friend of one of my graduate students at Harvard. The part of town where we met had an incredibly vibrant nightlife; Robert proudly explained that almost everything around us was new. One hears that often in Beijing, I imagined. The downside was that all too often, long-standing residents would get pushed out of their homes and businesses to make room for progress. At some point I asked, "Do you think this could have happened so fast if China were a democracy?" Robert, together with his friend who had since joined us, pushed back, noting that members of the Communist Party had quite a significant voice in how the country was run and that the leadership had to listen to them. On the one hand, he noted, only 6 percent of the population are party members; on the other hand, that is eighty million people. (One of my Chinese students once quipped that in her country, if you are "one in a million," it means that there are one thousand, four hundred people just like you.) Robert's provocative statement reminded me that in the very early days of the United States, there were states where only property owners could vote, and of course it wasn't until 1919 that women gained suffrage. And then there was slavery. Yet we are taught that the United States was always a democracy. To be clear, Robert was not trying to justify the Communist Party's monopoly rule; he was only making the point that its limited democracy was not the same thing as autocratic rule.

"What about all the corruption, though?" I protested. Yes, China was corrupt, Robert and his friend agreed; they knew well from having done business in China for several years. However, they argued, the bribes and side payments were more predictable and less crippling than, say, in Russia. Natasha, who knew a thing or two about dealing with Russian officials, agreed that it could not possibly be as bad. It is hard to know. In 2013, when Xi Jinping came to power as the president of China, the crackdown on corruption was one of his signature programs, absolutely one of the most popular, and no doubt badly needed by then.

On our second day in Beijing, I arrived at the main office of the People's Bank of China to give a seminar to the senior research staff. The deputy governor of the People's Bank, Madame Wu Xiaoling, greeted me as I was still seated by the guards' desk, waiting to be escorted to my seminar. At that time in China there were still many women in significant positions of power. Almost before saying hello, Madame Wu launched into a rather passionate explanation of why the IMF was being unfair in its criticisms of China's capital-control regime. She complained that the IMF was not giving China enough credit for all it had done to loosen capital controls, explaining that China had eliminated forty-eight of the sixty-five restrictions that the IMF had listed, or something of that order of magnitude. I was caught completely off guard. My initial reaction (which I kept to myself) was that her claim was meaningless. Obviously, what matters is not the number of controls but their pervasiveness and intensity. After all, it should take only a small number of controls to block most capital movements if the rules are sufficiently broad and enforced strictly enough. A country's proclamation that it had eliminated three out of five methods of capital punishment probably would not get it off human-rights watch lists.

Had I been quicker on my feet, I would have been more sympathetic. In their work on measuring capital controls, the economists Menzie Chinn and Hiro Ito argued that although of course what matters is the intensity of a country's capital controls, not just their number, very often the two are highly correlated.[1] Countries with intense capital controls need to have a wide range of restrictions to shut off every avenue of evasion.

And Madame Wu's assessment did align with what might be termed "de facto" measures of China's openness to foreigners wishing to invest in the country or, conversely, the ability of Chinese citizens to invest abroad. After all, the proof is in the pudding: If a lot of money is flowing in and out, then at least some measure of international capital market integration is taking place; it does not matter whether a country has myriad controls on paper if there are low-cost ways to get around them. Indeed, at the time, China's capital markets were more open than they appeared, as my own research with IMF colleagues had shown.[2]

In sum, I should have just emphatically told Madame Wu, "You are absolutely right," but instead I dull-wittingly said something more like, "I appreciate your telling me, and I will look very closely as soon I get back to my office at Harvard." The guards finally finished processing my entry, and I was escorted inside the building.

My seminar was being hosted by Governor Zhou Xiaochuan, who had taken over from Governor Dai in late 2002. I had already seen Zhou in action at a couple of IMF meetings and had been deeply impressed by both his understanding of economics and his forceful presence. To be honest, the first time I heard Zhou speak at length was in a small meeting of leading central bank governors, many of whom were probably hearing him speak for the first time too. As Zhou mesmerized the room, all I could think was, "This guy is incredibly good. Where did he come from?" Unfortunately, there wasn't a chance to speak with him on that occasion.[3]

My presentation focused on exchange rates and the current account, covering some of the same issues as in my aforementioned 2002 IMF presentation but in considerably more depth. My main focus was on the dollar, but of course China was becoming more and more prominent in any analysis of the U.S. dollar and U.S. trade. China's trade surpluses were growing hand in hand with U.S. trade deficits.

Having given many seminars at central banks all over the world for two decades already, I knew that the background of the participants can be quite diverse, which means that it is usually best to gloss over the technical details, even significant ones, that would be front and center in a presentation to an academic audience. As I entered the room to give the seminar, all signs suggested that they were expecting a serious presentation. For one thing, most of the participants were seated around a long table; others were in chairs along the walls. In this setup, everyone can see everyone. Had they wanted me to give a less technical presentation in the form of a speech, they would have held the talk in a large hall, with me at a podium and the audience seated in rows of chairs. I also could not help but notice that a few attendees were holding English editions of my 1996 book with the Berkeley professor Maurice Obstfeld, *Foundations of International Macroeconomics*, which my students had nicknamed "Barney" thanks to its distinctive purple and white cover. (Barney is a large purple anthropomorphic dinosaur from the children's television show *Barney & Friends*.) Replete with mathematical equations, Barney the book is not for the faint of heart.

My talk was frequently interrupted with sharp, penetrating questions from the audience, almost all in excellent English. I could have been at the University of Chicago, famous for the tough grilling they give speakers. At the end, Governor Zhou thanked me for my views on the United States but wondered whether I had any policy advice for the People's Bank of China. "Well, since you ask, I do have a couple of thoughts." First, although China did not share information about the currency composition of its reserves, my very strong presumption was that the overwhelming share was mostly in dollars. Would it not be a good idea to diversify into other currencies like the euro, I suggested, pointing to how much China had lost over the preceding few years on the dollar (which had indeed fallen by almost 20 percent against other major currencies since my September 2002 IMF annual meetings talk had warned of this risk). I also asked why China did not hold more gold to give it some resilience against any games the U.S. and European monetary authorities might play. Advanced economies had decided some years earlier to start winding down their gold stocks in an effort to fully demonetize gold, but it had not worked as planned. Why then should China follow suit? Governor Zhou sat poker-faced, but the nervous reaction of his staff suggested that I had hit on a sensitive topic.[4]

I then tackled the elephant in the room, China's exchange rate peg to the dollar: Shouldn't a large country like China have greater monetary independence? At the time, I did not fully appreciate what a reformer Zhou was. I later learned that he had been arguing internally for a more flexible exchange rate system. Again, however, he sat poker-faced.

After the seminar, Governor Zhou took me to lunch with two of his top researchers. Zhou spoke English quite decently, and the lunch was an opportunity to ask the question that I had wanted to ask Governor Dai at the 2002 banquet: How do you have any idea what national income is? We are constantly revising our numbers in the United States, and sometimes the statisticians go back and do major "baseline" revisions, with very significant changes. I noted that once, some years earlier, a governor of the Bank of England told me that he viewed baseline estimates of the U.K.'s national income, now about $3.4 trillion, as having at least a 10 percent margin of error. Zhou explained, with surprising candor, that constructing national income was especially difficult in China given that a lot of the staff at the National Bureau of Statistics had been trained as Marxists. Although they were used to summing quantities of physical production, the concept of creating a single aggregate measure weighing each sector's output by its market price was thoroughly alien to most of them; China's bean counters did not yet understand how market economies functioned. The process was incredibly difficult, and the official figures were at best very crude approximations. With over half the population living in rural China, and with the local officials often having little information themselves, of course it was difficult to know what was going on.

I gave several other academic talks on this trip, including at Peking University, where I met Professor Justin Lin for the first time. Lin, who had been a military officer in Taiwan's army, swam four miles from the Kinmen Islands to Chinese-controlled Xiamen, where he sought asylum. To make a long story short, Lin eventually became one of the top academic economists in China, with considerable policy influence. He also later became chief economist at the World Bank, the first from a developing economy.

The meetings with Professor Lin and his colleagues were extremely interesting and helped me considerably in my later research on Chinese housing and infrastructure, which we will come to later in this section. I learned, for example, that China imposed national standards on construction to a far greater extent than did the United States. No matter how far-flung and poor a province, if a highway was built, it had to be solid enough to handle a landing by a large passenger jet.

Perhaps my most unusual seminar on this trip was for the Chinese Executive Leadership Academy Pudong in Shanghai. It was unusual in part because the academy was housed in a building unlike anything I had ever seen — a 750,000-square-foot art installation. Almost flat on top and with large slats below on either side, the academy, my hosts explained, was designed to resemble an ancient painter's table, which was used to teach painting and calligraphy. The painter's table is an image that plays an important role in Chinese culture and is meant to simultaneously capture stability and change.[5] Painted in spectacular red, and with cavernous spaces where the spires came down to represent the legs, the academy's grandeur and scale evoked the Golden Gate Bridge in San Francisco. Except that it represented something very different.

The leadership academy is a kind of Harvard Business School executive-education program for top party officials aimed at teaching officials new ideas as well as giving them an opportunity to network. Officials are often invited to attend when they are being considered for promotion, say, from mayor of a small city to mayor of a large city, or to a high-level position in the provincial government. I was told that periodic attendance was required for all but the very-highest-ranking officials.

At my lecture on exchange rates, participants asked questions both in English and through a translator. What shocked me was the participants' willingness to throw out questions quite critical of China's exchange rate policy, a pillar of its macroeconomic policy regime. Later the director of the academy, himself a very powerful official for his role in advising on promotions, explained to me that inside the closed walls of the academy, students and faculty were encouraged to have extremely open dialogue, with nothing off limits. The irony of writing about free speech in the Chinese leadership academy of 2005 and comparing it with the uneasy relationship with free speech that American universities struggle with today is not lost on me. Of course, China today is also very different.

Before leaving Beijing, we were informed that our small group was being invited to Beidaihe, a seaside retreat that hosts the most important meeting of the Chinese leaders each year. There we were to meet with the former Chinese president Jiang Zemin, who had just stepped down in 2003 after ten years in office, the last five of which Zhu Rongji was his powerful premier. The meeting was not completely unexpected; we had known it was a possibility. My mathematician colleague Yau is a huge celebrity in China, his work having helped open important doors in theoretical physics. Moreover, a book about how to get your child into Harvard was a massive bestseller in China, making the Harvard director of admissions a big celebrity as well.

However, what was completely unexpected is that the two of us with families on the trip were invited to bring them. For Natasha and me, this included our son, Gabriel, who was about to turn nine, and our daughter, Juliana, who was seven. This set us into a bit of a panic. Although it seemed extremely unlikely that they would be invited to meet the president, there did seem an outside chance that he might greet them before they were shunted off. And Gabriel had nothing but T-shirts and jeans; Juliana not much better. We raced around the city to rectify the situation. I thought I knew but was still shocked that prices were about 25 percent of U.S. prices, and that was for full-price items at perhaps the most expensive stores in Beijing. No wonder the Chinese are eating our lunch in world exports. We found Gabriel a dark suit, white shirt, and tie that all sort of fit, and Juliana a dress. Juliana insisted on carrying a small fan that a store clerk had given her, saying that fans are used in China as a sign of respect.

Jiang's economic legacy included ten years of epic growth in China and the halving of rural poverty rates; hundreds of millions of people were lifted out of abject poverty.[6] China's per capita income today is still nowhere near U.S. income levels, no matter how one adjusts for price differences and exchange rates in comparing incomes. Still, perhaps 500 million of China's 1.4 billion people have joined the global middle class, and perhaps a quarter of those would be considered upper-middle class. Indeed, by some measures, China now has as many billionaires as the United States (about 800 at the end 2023).[7] That still leaves 900 million people who are lower-middle class or poorer, but China is still a far cry from where it was at the outset of its economic liberalization, when per capita income was 3 percent of U.S. levels. Of course, economic prosperity is only one measure of a society's well-being, and critics rightly point to injustices and human-rights violations.

The grounds at Beidaihe were spectacular; though perhaps modest compared with the sprawling imperial palaces in Beijing, they were still overwhelming. As we exited the bus that had taken us there, I hoped that Natasha would get to meet the president, but I was shocked when told that he had extended an invitation to Natasha, Gabriel, and Juliana to sit in and listen. As President Jiang greeted Natasha, he said, "Dobro pozhalovat, Tovarich" (Welcome, comrade) in perfect Russian. She responded (also in perfect Russian), "Greetings, it is a great honor to meet you. I understand that you, too, studied in the Motherland." Jiang laughed heartily; in the 1950s, he had gone to Moscow to work and learn at the Stalin automobile works.

Inside a giant hall, big enough to comfortably seat a couple hundred people, our small group was seated in a large semicircle around President Jiang, with the Western guests on one side. Jiang's staff and interpreters sat on the other, as did Governor Zhou, who had arrived separately and sat next to the president. At one point, Governor Zhou introduced me and explained that I had given a talk at the central bank the day before on exchange rates and international trade imbalances. The president said, "I trained as an engineer, not as an economist." Governor Zhou then suggested that perhaps I should say something about the global economy.

I said that the world was in an extraordinarily strong growth period thanks in part to what China had accomplished during his decade as president. In fact, global growth had been rising for some time. Nevertheless, there were worrisome imbalances that could lead to a financial crisis later on in the West, in China, or in both. I pointed to the high level of consumption in the United States, partly financed by consumers borrowing against their homes. Correspondingly, it seemed that the level of consumption in China was extraordinarily low, even by the standards of Asian economies. That was helping to produce a large flow of funds from China to the United States. That inflow, in turn, was contributing to very low interest rates in the United States, not only for the government but also for households, as well as a massive run-up in equity and housing prices. Near term, the risks were greater for the United States. However, China's fixed exchange rate regime posed its own risks of inflation and crisis, and if there were ever a problem, the IMF would not have nearly enough resources to deal with it. The president responded that he was well aware of these issues, but that the current system had worked well so far.

After perhaps ninety minutes of conversation, President Jiang smiled warmly and said, "I see I have bored one of my guests." Our seven-year-old daughter, Juliana, had fallen asleep in her chair.

CHAPTER 8

PRELUDE TO CRISIS

In economics, things take longer to happen than you think they will, and then they happen faster than you thought they could.
— RUDIGER DORNBUSCH

The exact timing of when an economic crisis will strike is extremely difficult to get right. There are important markers to look for, such as a rapid rise in borrowing and asset prices, especially housing prices. In general, however, it is far easier to forecast how the aftermath of a financial crisis will unfold than the timing of when it will hit. The issue occurs in science and medicine as well. For example, although physicians can identify factors that increase the risk of a heart attack, very-high-risk patients can live long lives without experiencing one, and low-risk patients who have just gotten a clean bill of health at the doctor's office can experience one the next day.

Over time, I became increasingly convinced that China's growth model was going to start running into difficulties, if not immediately then certainly within five to ten years. Starting in 2014, almost a decade after my meeting with President Jiang Zemin, I began to emphatically highlight the risks of a Chinese growth and financial crisis in my articles, in my talks, and in media appearances. I warned that China's growth rate was likely to fall significantly within the coming decade, a warning captured in headlines such as "Ken Rogoff Warns That China Is the Next Bubble to Burst."[1] I was told by insiders that Chinese authorities were well aware of my research and that these concerns were sometimes referenced in high-level meetings. The crisis did eventually happen, but it took somewhat longer than I expected.

The first signs of real pressure came in 2015, when capital began exiting China on a massive scale; there was no way to gloss over the problems with minor administrative adjustments. A slowdown in growth and a stock market slump so unnerved speculators, normally pushing to get their money into China, that they started pushing to get out. The run accelerated when the central bank allowed a small depreciation of the renminbi against the dollar; it was only 1.9 percent, but the markets immediately became concerned that there was more to come. The government responded by selling dollars and buying renminbi to bid up the price of the renminbi — exactly the opposite of what it had been doing for most of the preceding three decades. Before this intervention in the foreign exchange markets was over, the government had thrown $1 trillion of its $4 trillion of foreign exchange reserves into the battle.[2] Just as China had smashed all previous records in the speed with which it poured cement, there had never before been a foreign exchange intervention on this scale. It was still not enough, and by then journalists and policymakers elsewhere started to ask what warning signs they had missed.[3] But as calamitous and costly as the episode was, China was not ready to back down from its dollar exchange rate regime just yet. The authorities finally prevailed by sharply tightening restrictions on capital flows, both formally by cracking down on over- and under-invoicing by firms, and informally by erecting all kinds of administrative barriers for individuals seeking dollars for education or travel. It was an impressive show of competence and will on the part of the Chinese authorities.

There were costs. The episode greatly set back plans for financial liberalization. The retreat from financial market openness quelled, for a time, talk about the renminbi soon becoming an international currency, given that a very basic requirement is convertibility. (Such talk has very much returned since.) And although the controls temporarily propped up the imbalances that remained across China's economy, they did little to solve the underlying issues. A few prominent Chinese economists voiced concerns about the sustainability of China's exchange rate system — or to be precise, were allowed to openly express such thoughts[4] — but the majority of Western economists and investors were as bullish as ever. One billionaire investor, a founder of a highly successful private-equity firm, told me that he liked his investments in the United States but loved his investments in China. That investor was not alone.

Each year in March, the Chinese government holds the country's marquee international policy conference in Beijing, under the auspices of the China Development Research Foundation. The premier and the country's top financial and economic officials participate, as do many of the world's top business and financial leaders and a small handful of academics. Held shortly after the Communist Party sets the course of the economy for the year ahead, the China Development Forum offers party leaders and technocrats an opportunity to listen to ideas and suggestions from outside experts; this does not mean that they take them, however. (There have certainly been occasions — for example, during the early days of the 2008–2009 global financial crisis — when U.S. authorities would have done well to take in suggestions from foreign experts, especially those who had experience navigating a banking crisis.) Because the government makes clear that the event is an important one, invitations cannot be lightly refused by business leaders whose companies take large profits out of China or have significant production there. And this remains true today, even with heightened tensions between the United States and China.

Given my well-known views on China, it was something of a surprise when Lu Mai, the powerful secretary-general of the China Development Research Foundation, extended an invitation to its 2016 forum. Moreover, the invitation was to speak at the main opening event that all the participants typically attend. My invitation emphasized that this particular meeting was being held just as China was setting the parameters of its thirteenth five-year plan for 2016–2020, which gave the forum special significance to the officials and technocrats in attendance. Notably, the forum asked that my remarks be submitted in writing in advance "to help the translators." No good academic speaker wants to read from a script, much less be censored, so I decided to comply by sending a thoroughly anodyne version of what I was actually intending to say.

My panel was to deal with the global economy, and since I was a former chief economist at the IMF, my hosts presumably expected me to give a concise tour covering the United States, Japan, Europe, and emerging markets, and to leave China to others. What, though, would be the point of ignoring the economy facing the biggest crisis risks?

THE PRESENT-DAY CHALLENGER

As the car I was picked up in made its way to Beijing from the airport, the contrast between the nine million bicycles of 2002 and the perhaps five million cars of 2016 was stunning. I don't know the exact number, but the official Xinhua News Agency reported at the end of 2022 that China had 415 million motor vehicles.[5] Indeed, Facebook founder Mark Zuckerberg, who also attended the conference, posted photos of his smog-choked jog through Tiananmen Square, somewhat embarrassing his hosts, but delighting his huge millennial fan base back in the United States.[6] Facebook, of course, has been blocked in China since 2009, so unlike the throngs of other top CEOs, Zuckerberg perhaps believed he had little to lose.

The venue for the opening panel was again the Diaoyutai State Guesthouse, this time in a vast yawning hall packed with official attendees, with our panel seated on stage. A couple of the speakers, including another Western academic, took the opportunity to criticize the United States, stressing how it fostered inequality, a sure-fire recipe for pleasing the hosts in most socialist countries around the world. The other safe strategy was to praise how China's remarkable growth trajectory had lifted hundreds of millions of people out of poverty, without mentioning all the others who were left behind.

It is notable that a few years later, in 2020, China's premier, Li Keqiang, apparently stepped out of bounds when he candidly admitted that six hundred million people in China still earned less than $141 per month. To put that figure in perspective, note that the U.S. Census Bureau considers an American family of four earning ten times that amount to be at the poverty line.[7] Such honesty probably did not sit will with President Xi. Li Keqiang was replaced as prime minster at the party congress in March 2023, and when he passed away later that year, the absence of the usual ceremony surrounding the death of such an important leader was widely commented on in the foreign press.

When it came my turn to speak, I began by briefly discussing growth prospects and risks in the United States, Europe, and emerging markets, and then turned to China's future prospects. I noted that China's growth had already been slowing down for some time, and I presented six reasons why growth over the next couple decades was likely to be much lower still.

First, China's growth model depended heavily on investment, which would eventually run into diminishing returns, as it had everywhere else in Asia and in

Europe. Second, China could not expect to keep increasing exports at the same rate as in the past, given that it already commanded a high share of the world market across many goods and that its main export destinations, the United States and Europe, were not growing nearly as fast as China. Third, I doubted whether China could depend on consumption to make up for slowing investment and exports; until the social safety net was greatly expanded to cover health, education, and retirement, consumers would continue to save large amounts. Fourth, China was facing severe demographic problems, partly the legacy of its one-child policy, which began in the early 1980s and had only just been relaxed in January 2016.[8] Fifth, with China already reaching the technology frontier in many areas, the ability to get very fast growth through adapting Western technology was declining. Even though China was producing many innovations of its own, this was almost invariably a much slower process.

Before getting to the sixth and final point, I paused to take a breath, knowing that my hosts might not want to hear it. I went on to express concern over the extent to which China's economic decision-making had become more and more centralized in recent years. To a Western-trained economist, this did not seem like a recipe for efficiency and growth, especially considering that in the past so much of China's growth had come from the private sector. (Mind you, even today, there are many top officials in China still convinced that the government does everything better, as one recently deposed technocrat explained to me.)

When the session was over, a couple of leading officials in the audience came up to me, and each said how much they appreciated my comments. I wondered: Had my remarks been translated correctly? Or is that what they say just before having you arrested?

CHAPTER 9

THE END OF HIGH GROWTH

How spectacular, exactly, has China's growth been? According to official numbers, average real growth over the period 1980 to 2012 was 9.9 percent and slowed down to a still brisk 7.0 percent for the period 2012 to 2019, or 6.1 percent if one includes the Covid years and extends through 2023.[1] The pace looks a bit less otherworldly using the latest version of the Penn World Tables, which attempt to measure growth using international prices (that is, at purchasing power parity exchange rates). The Penn World Tables data suggest 7.1 percent growth from 1980 to 2012 and 3.5 percent growth from 2013 to 2019.[2] (At present, the data only go through 2019, since producing PPP calculations requires a major research effort.)

There really isn't much argument among economists that China's growth rate has to slow down at some point, and probably all the way down to advanced-economy growth levels, which currently average 1 to 2 percent per year. The question is when: Within a decade or two? Or not until the end of the century? The debate for some time has been whether China would be able to escape "the middle-income trap" that has plagued so many large developing economies — for example, Mexico, Brazil, and Indonesia. These countries experienced fast growth for an extended period until financial crises derailed progress and left per capita income levels stuck far below those of the typical advanced economy, let alone the United States. The middle-income trap is a key reason why country income levels have remained so stratified despite the powerful forces of convergence that should favor middle-income countries catching up to richer ones, such as a rising capital stock and moving up the value chain. One cannot really look to post-war Europe or Japan as models. Those countries already had the institutions, the culture, and the human capital required to be able to rebuild quickly. Once rich, it is far easier to become rich again. The exceptions to the middle-income trap are few; they include small island nations such as Singapore and Hong Kong, and perhaps most notably Korea.

There are many rationales for the middle-income trap. Perhaps the leading one is that as a fast-developing country becomes richer, populist pressures for redistribution will derail growth one way or the other, regardless of the form of the government. Often the result is a financial crisis. In the typical case, as growth slows and the government looks for ways to sustain it, financial deregulation, including borrowing abroad, can be a powerful short-term fix. A fresh jolt of foreign funds can juice up any economy, for a time at least. If nascent government institutions are weak—and usually such institutions take generations to develop—the surge in borrowing may easily end up being channeled into low-productivity investments that do not, in the end, produce the growth needed to justify them. The borrowing may work as a short-term fix, but inevitably growth will slow again, making it apparent that the accumulated debts are unsustainable. Financial pressures and banking weaknesses mount, sometimes for years, and at some point, it all implodes. If there has been heavy borrowing from abroad, foreign lenders flee, and as they do, the country's exchange rate plunges and the financial burden of paying off dollar debt with local currency earnings goes sky high. The result is a deep financial crisis.

The government will invariably step in, but the weak value of its currency amplifies the costs of bailing out the banks and firms that have borrowed from abroad in dollars; the high cost of imports pushes up inflation sharply. On top of all of this, the local stock market collapses. In the worst cases—and there are many—a once fast-growing country simultaneously has to face a financial crisis, a government-debt crisis, an exchange rate crisis, a stock market crash, and galloping inflation. Political instability follows, and the situation takes many years to sort out.[3]

THE PRESENT-DAY CHALLENGER

China's officials have long been acutely aware of the risks of both social and financial crises and have taken great pains to adopt policies so that if a slowdown happens, it will unfold at a manageable pace that, most importantly, leaves the Communist Party firmly in power. Zhu Rongji had been quite candid about this. China's technocrats have been extremely cautious about financial liberalization, not just of international capital flows but of the domestic banking system as well. Even today, there remains a raft of regulations on what interest rates banks can pay depositors, and what rate they can charge borrowers. Regulators have allowed private banks and wealth-management funds, but the large state-owned banks, which are under the direct control of the Communist Party, still control the vast bulk of lending resources. The problem is that state-directed lending does not necessarily go to the most dynamic firms, which makes it harder to produce organic growth. (The same issue will come up again in chapter 19 in discussing progressive economists' proposals for how a central bank digital currency should be structured.)

For years, the Chinese government has tried to compensate by promoting a very large real estate sector, turbocharged by massive investments in infrastructure. This approach has also been a vehicle for trying to fight inequality by improving housing, roads, and sewage pipes in the poorer provinces in China's northern and western regions. Unfortunately, such a strategy leads to very lopsided growth that cannot go on indefinitely.

The speed at which China builds infrastructure is legendary. There is the apocryphal story of the Chinese tourist group that came to New York and visited the construction site of the new Second Avenue subway line, which looked to be far along. When the group's translator asked how much longer it would take to complete, their American tour guide cheerfully said, "Just two more years." After huddling with the group, the translator came back to the tour guide and said, "The group thinks perhaps I misunderstood; you must have meant two more *months*, right?"[4]

The view that China might be running into sharply diminishing returns in real estate and infrastructure has now become mainstream, but it certainly wasn't when my co-author Yuanchen Yang and I began researching the topic in 2018. After all, price appreciation in Chinese housing, at least as officially reported, had continued to be breathtaking. Before the financial crisis began in

2008, U.S. housing prices had doubled in less than a decade in some states. In China, over the three decades through 2022, prices had gone up by a factor of ten. Was it a bubble? Most thought not, the usual argument being that cities in China would one day be fully on par with the West. Why shouldn't housing prices in Shenzhen be the same as in San Francisco, prices in Beijing be the same as in Washington, or prices in Shanghai be the same as in New York? The problem with this logic is that China may be getting rich, but it is not rich yet—far from it. If one assumes that growth will be 7 percent a year, then yes, China will catch up soon enough. But is that realistic? This logic never made sense to me, and my skepticism underpinned a 2015 paper I wrote on why China was likely to be the next major country to experience debt and financial problems, as well as my speech at the 2016 China Development Forum.[5]

However, until meeting Yuanchen in October 2018, I lacked the capacity to access microeconomic evidence needed to convincingly make the case to skeptics, that is to say, most other economists and analysts. Yuanchen was a Ph.D. economics student at Tsinghua University in China who, although still improbably young, had supported herself through university and graduate school as a research assistant for Chinese policy institutes. Her work brought her into contact with many technocrats at the National Bureau of Statistics and helped her gain a deep knowledge of China's economic statistics. She knew of my interest in China's real estate challenges and had thought deeply about the problem, believing it to be much more severe than commonly appreciated.

There had been a few academic papers on the topic of Chinese real estate already, including one co-written by my superstar Harvard colleagues Ed Glaeser and Andrei Shleifer. However, their paper was based on data ending in 2011, and although they recognized that the price spiral was predicated on continuing high growth, they were cautious on the risks of a collapse.[6] Other papers written by Chinese scholars were even more circumspect.[7] With the notable exception of a couple of perma-bears who did not provide much hard data to support their views, the investment community was by and large willing to believe Chinese authorities that everything was fine. (The reader is invited to read statements by Federal Reserve officials in the run-up to the catastrophic 2008–2009 financial crisis that were similarly sanguine.[8])

Yuanchen had two major points. First, the half-dozen years since the earlier papers were a lifetime in the world of Chinese growth. Just as the nine million bicycles had suddenly turned into five million cars in the mere decade between two of my trips to Beijing, China's housing market could similarly turn. A housing boom anywhere can turn into a bubble very quickly. After all, back in 1999, who would have thought that housing prices in many U.S. metropolitan areas would double and then collapse within just a decade? Second, along with the accelerating housing bubble, many other areas of vulnerability had been shooting up, including especially debt that local governments were taking on to finance real estate–related infrastructure. In addition to her cogent analysis, I was struck by Yuanchen's willingness to disagree with the assessment of much more senior Chinese scholars on the topic, something one does not often see.

Our collaboration took a couple of years to bring to fruition, as serious academic papers usually do, especially when they require massive processing of city-level data across such a vast country. As the paper progressed, we circulated drafts seeking comments from the major scholars in the area, including authors whose work we were building on. Finally in August 2020, we issued a working paper entitled "Peak China Housing." In general, the feedback we received was that although there may be concerns, any serious problem must be far off. We must be wrong.

What was the evidence we thought so convincing? There were basically two key points. One was simply the large footprint of the real estate sector, counting both direct and indirect demand (indirect impacts include everything from the lumber and steel used in housing to furniture). We initially estimated this figure to be 29 percent of GDP in 2017 but subsequently revised it down to 26 percent for 2018 and 25 percent for 2021; these figures include about 3 percent of GDP worth of imported inputs as one should do in assessing overbuilding.[9] They are still incredibly high and higher than the corresponding figures in Spain and Ireland at the peak of their pre-crisis real estate booms. In a later paper we showed that if one adds infrastructure, the total 2018 share was 33 percent and fell to 31 percent in 2021.[10] This, of course, is part of how China has compensated for its very low consumption rates. Figure 9 compares the real estate and infrastructure sectors in China with the corresponding figures for advanced economies (again including the direct and indirect impact); China's is almost double that of the United States.[11]

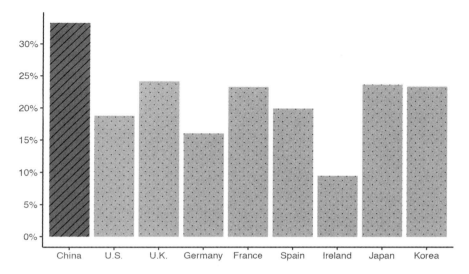

Figure 9. Real estate and infrastructure (including indirect demand) as a percentage of GDP, 2018
Data Source: Rogoff and Yang, *Economic Policy*, 2024.

Second, some regions of China were clearly becoming overbuilt. A large real estate sector is not necessarily a problem in itself for a developing economy that needs more housing, office buildings, and roads. In recent years, India has massively increased its infrastructure investment, though it still has a long way to go. This is far less the case in China, where the construction frenzy has been going on for decades, to the point where China's square meters of housing per capita has now surpassed that of much richer countries in Europe such as France, Germany, and the United Kingdom, as figure 10 illustrates. Moreover, a very large fraction of China's housing has been built since 2000 and its housing stock is overall newer than that in most advanced economies. The story with infrastructure — measured by roads, sewage pipes, railway tracks, and the like — is much the same. Like every country, China still has swaths of substandard housing without indoor plumbing, particularly in the poorer rural areas. But even if a way is found to finance the replacement of this stock, it will not nearly be enough to keep the real estate–construction engine racing at the speed it has been going up until now. Concretely, looking at the effect of housing investment

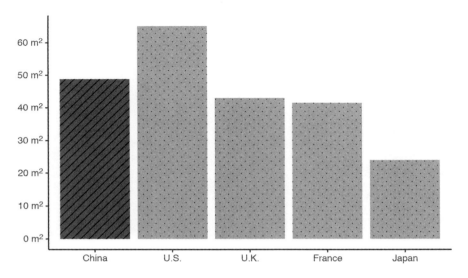

Figure 10. Per capita floor space of selected countries (sq. meters), 2021
Data Source: Rogoff and Yang, *Journal of International Economics*, 2024.

on growth, Yuanchen and I found that as much as 2 percent of the fall in China's growth rate between 2010 and today might be attributable to how the return from new housing investment has fallen as the existing stock of housing has expanded.[12] And indeed, the roughly 10 percent drop in the size of the real estate sector between 2021 and 2023 can account for virtually all of the trend decline in China's growth, and further decline appears to be ongoing.[13]

Supporting our contention of diminishing returns was broad evidence suggesting that China's rate of productivity growth has steadily slowed in recent years; indeed, controlling for investment inputs, China's total factor productivity has slowed markedly.[14] (Total factor productivity measures how much output a country is getting out of its existing labor and capital stock.) With gains in productivity quite limited, China has had to keep investment growing ever faster to maintain the same level of output growth; this is unsustainable. This is very much part of what happened to the Soviet Union and, to some extent, to Japan.

What about the fact that housing prices still appeared to be stable or rising in the premier cities on China's eastern coast? Digging deeper, and tediously going through provincial yearbooks covering over three hundred cities, we came to realize that the overbuilding problem is especially concentrated in China's poorer and "smaller" tier 3 cities. In many of these cities, prices have been falling. Tier 3 cities are the poor cousins of China's tier 1 cities — Beijing (the capital of China), Shanghai (the financial center of China), Shenzhen (the Silicon Valley of China), and Guangzhou (the trading center) — and tier 2 cities, which include the provincial capitals and a few special cities such as Tianjin, the ancient capital of China.[15] By the way, "small" means something very different in China than in Western countries. China has an astounding 21 cities with over five million people, and 145 cities with over a million people.

Although with hindsight it is easy to criticize the overbuilding in tier 3 cities, one might also say that the Chinese government was just logically attempting to spread out its 1.3 billion (now 1.4 billion) people; hence, the Hukou inter-city migration system mentioned in chapter 5. They were fighting against what economists call Zipf's law, which reflects the tendency for populations to concentrate in the largest cities. Yet the same agglomeration effects that lead to urban concentration everywhere else still hold in China. Clusters of industries learn from each other and can tap into a deep talent pool. Even social life for young people tends to be livelier. In effect, although many tier 3 cities benefited from world-class construction buildups, the top-tier jobs did not always follow, and the young people did not always stay. Now, even as China's overall population starts to shrink, there is migration from tier 3 cities to the larger tier 2 and tier 1 cities. The problems are particularly acute in the northern part of the country, where the exodus of young people is most severe: many are moving to growing cities in the south such as Hangzhou (where Alibaba was founded), Chengdu, or Xiamen. One should not conclude that China is overbuilt everywhere; the U.S. real estate crisis of 2007–2009 was concentrated in a relatively small number of states, particularly California, Nevada, Florida, and Arizona. The crisis need not include every Chinese province to have major systemic implications.

Many Westerners travel only to Chinese marquee cities. A few journalists had gone to see newly constructed cities full of empty apartment buildings, where they had been told that it was only a matter of time until the buildings were filled. One really needs to look at city-level data across all of China to put the numbers together. The problem is that China is a very large country with 1.4 billion people, and as magnificent as China's large east-coast cities may be, small and medium-size tier 3 cities account for 60 percent of China's economic output. At this writing, as much as the government may wish to hide it, the fact is that the prices in many tier 3 cities, particularly in the north, are falling. The problem has spread to many tier 2 cities as well.

Tianjin is a brisk one-hour trip by high-speed rail from Beijing. Once the ancient capital of China, it is now merely a tier 2 city, although it is sometimes host to important conferences. The buildings are magnificent in Tianjin. Still, one cannot help but feel the lack of vibrancy compared with Shanghai and Beijing. The disaster in 2015 in the port of Tianjin, where a series of explosions killed 173 people,[16] underscored that Tianjin is less developed than meets the eye. The news of the tragedy was especially jarring to me because, somewhat randomly, the port director had introduced himself to me just a year earlier at a World Economic Forum conference in Tianjin. He had handed me a bunch of glossy pamphlets, suggesting that I stop by to visit. I felt horribly about the people who had died yet also realized that the director I had just met might well end up in prison, regardless of the root cause.

A renowned architect, whose firm has engaged in major projects across China for over two decades, attended a lecture I recently gave in Spain entitled "A Tale of Tier 3 Cities."[17] Afterward, he and his spouse lamented how China's path of urbanization has all too often plowed under once-vibrant markets and meeting areas, replacing them with homogeneous structures that feel drab and lifeless. His own work, the architect explained, has always aspired to do the opposite, to bring communities together. There are no doubt many sides to the question of how to measure the quality of development. Nevertheless, my architect friend's observations corroborate what I have learned from Chinese students over the years, as well as the statistical analysis Yuanchen and I put together. In many places, the good jobs never came, young people left, and the town withered. As my high school friends from Rochester sometimes sadly joke, anyone with any get-up-and-go, got up and left.

The end of the housing boom has been extremely stressful on local government finances, especially for those many local governments that had been taking on ever-higher debt under the assumption of never-ending growth. China's system greatly encouraged such behavior. Local mayors were long explicitly judged on their city's growth rate, and there was no better way to juice the growth numbers than to spend a lot on infrastructure and real estate. If there were debt problems down the road, it didn't matter, since by then the mayor would have been promoted to run an even larger city and given the chance to build an even bigger mess. With the benefit of hindsight, I regret not asking some of the participants at my Executive Leadership Academy Pudong lecture in 2005, many of whom were city mayors, how they had been selected for advancement, and how they felt about the system, in general.

In most parts of the world, local governments are heavily reliant on property taxes. In China, property taxes were effectively banned in the 1990s because Beijing believed that they were leading to too much corruption.[18] Local governments in China have been limited to a mixture of fees and licensing taxes, which typically provide less than half what is needed. To make ends meet, local governments have relied on land sales (and resales) and so-called local government financing vehicles (LGFVs). The latter are theoretically independent public corporations set up to fund infrastructure projects and are typically repaid by user fees. LGFV debt more than quadrupled between 2012 and 2022; as of the end of 2023, it is conservatively estimated at 50 percent of GDP and is likely much higher.[19] Effectively, this is off-balance-sheet debt of local governments that is highly vulnerable to default in the event of a real estate collapse. For those not familiar with the term, think of off-balance-sheet debt as owed by a subsidiary that is effectively guaranteed by the parent entity, and so will come crashing onto local government books in the event of widespread default problems. Moreover, the local governments are not the only ones that are vulnerable. Although the big state banks have de facto central government backing, a large number of smaller local banks are highly exposed to real estate, as is the so-called shadow banking system stemming from private wealth management for wealthy individuals and corporations.

It is surprising how many China experts have long believed that the ongoing real estate slowdown has been driven almost entirely by government policy decrees aimed at slowing the housing bubble (such as requiring higher down payments on mortgages) and that if the central government were only to change its mind, the real estate bubble would be back on its merry way. It is true that the government holds many levers such as credit conditions and down-payment requirements, and these have an important influence over the market. However, such gimmicks work only up to a point. Given other spending needs such as for health care and education, there are limits to how much Chinese families are prepared to spend on rent or, for wealthier families, how many empty houses they want in their portfolio. The same applies to other types of real estate such as shopping malls and storefronts, especially now with the growing shift to online-shopping platforms, including Alibaba, JD, and Temu. Just as vast numbers of houses are underutilized, so too is the infrastructure that supports all this real estate.

The parallels to the debate in the United States over the returns on investment in infrastructure are informative. During the 1950s and 1960s, the United States made massive investments in building roads. Periodically, there have been calls to do it again—for example, by the U.S. Conference of Mayors in 1992.[20] However, in the back-and-forth of a debate that mostly took place in the 1990s, it became clear that the potential productivity gains from just building more roads and bridges were limited. The big gains from the 1950s and 1960s cannot be easily replicated. There is always work to be done on repairing existing roads and bridges; this alone will lead to a transformative rise in productivity. Of course, one can find all kinds of infrastructure projects that still have high returns in the United States—examples include improving the resiliency of the electric grid and expanding broadband access, although each has its challenges.

If China is now coming to the end of the line in the big gains it has reaped from its remarkable construction boom, what, then, to do? Workers can be reallocated and the economy reorganized, but no society has ever found this easy. If there is one commonality among post-war financial crises, it is that real estate almost always lies at the heart of them.[21] In a Western-style financial crisis, a period of fast growth supports a period of rapid real estate appreciation, which eventually morphs into a debt-fueled speculative frenzy. When it becomes apparent that high trend growth cannot be sustained, the whole process implodes; generally, the banking sector takes substantial losses, which sometimes sparks a bank run. The weakened financial sector, combined with a long period of rebuilding balance sheets, leads to a much deeper and more protracted recession than there would have been had there simply been a normal pause in growth.[22] This, of course, is exactly what happened in Japan.

Once again, this is not to say that China will have a Western-style systemic financial crisis; the central government's sweeping power to restructure and reallocate reduces that risk. Nevertheless, the slowdown poses significant financial challenges beyond simply reallocating labor and capital from real estate into more productive activities. China could re-introduce local property taxes; this would be challenging politically. Given restrictions on investing abroad (e.g., in the United States) and unreliable stock market regulation, housing constitutes the vast bulk of most citizens' wealth, which makes real estate taxes a proverbial third rail. The topic is so sensitive that for the moment, Chinese economists have been forbidden to talk about it, even in academic discussions.

Another obvious solution would be for the central government to engage in much greater revenue sharing with local governments; it has been notably reluctant to do so. As my former IMF colleague and China expert David Robinson had stressed to me, the central government has distrusted the provinces for millennia, and despite vastly better information flow today compared with the days of the emperor, that distrust remains. Still another idea would be stimulus transfers directly to individuals, especially if one diagnoses the major problem as a collapse in consumer confidence. Traditionally, China's stimulus policies have concentrated on the supply side, but the difficulties have grown to the point where supply-side answers may not be enough. However, the central government is already on the hook for local government bailouts—so much so that the IMF in 2024 was projecting China's government debt to rise to over 100 percent of GDP by 2027. China does not want to get sucked into the same debt trap as Japan, but the other options are limited.

What about increasing export growth as a remedy for slowing real estate investment? Unfortunately, many of China's Western trade partners are adopting "homeshoring" policies requiring that critical items such as chips and pharmaceuticals be produced domestically or by close allies. Even if they weren't, China's ability to grow through export expansion has inevitably become constrained by size limitations as its share of global GDP and exports has grown. On top of that, many foreign firms are diversifying production through "China plus one" strategies, which means leaving existing investments in China while redirecting new investments to other countries, from Vietnam to India to Mexico.

What about green energy and electric vehicles? Although construction workers can be retrained to build green-energy plants, or to mine for rare earths, the notion that China can retrain 20 percent or more of all workers for completely different occupations while keeping the growth engine humming is improbable. And that is not even counting the fact that both the United States and the European Union have already slapped massive tariffs on China's electric vehicles. Another idea for growth is to build satellite suburbs around select tier 2 cities to create new metropolitan areas on a scale that could allow them to mimic the success of China's tier 1 cities, which benefit from enormous agglomeration effects. Of course, the most effective approach, by far, would be to strengthen the private sector and reduce the role of the state — for example, by better protecting property rights and by providing a level playing field for private companies relative to state-owned enterprises. In recent years, things have mostly gone in the other direction.

Many seasoned China scholars were writing until fairly recently that there would be no abrupt slowdown.[23] Perhaps that will prove correct, though it may take years to find out. Statistics from China have become so politically sensitive that it is hard to know what to believe. Overall, though, between the view that China just needs to reset and will soon be on its way to having an economy twice the size of the U.S. economy, and the view that China will dramatically slow down and never even pull even, the latter appears more likely.

One more point has to be reiterated before we leave the topic of China's growth. First, for decades, China took seriously the idea that merit should be a major factor in determining bureaucratic promotions and that technical training was important — hence the training at the Chinese Executive Leadership Academy. Westerners, even those who see China as an adversary, not just a competitor, have long been stunned by the overall quality of China's bureaucrats. The system of rewarding with promotions mayors who achieve very fast growth in their cities certainly has profound flaws, but at least it creates a clear-cut metric for competition. In recent years, especially since the twentieth party congress in 2022 appointed Xi Jinping to an unprecedented third term as president, it is quite clear that political loyalty has become a bigger factor than merit.

The all-powerful seven-person Politburo Standing Committee now consists only of Xi allies, as opposed to the more balanced representation that had been the norm.[24] The broader twenty-four-person Politburo is slightly more diverse but still overwhelmingly composed of strong loyalists and, for the first time since 1992, without a single female member.[25] The head of the People's Bank of China had not traditionally been a member of the Politburo, but was at least designated an alternate. Now, even that status has been stripped, hardly an endorsement of the importance of high-quality technocratic advice on macroeconomic issues. In 2023, Xi purged the foreign minister, the defense minister, and scores of lower-level officials to tighten control.

Perhaps the unprecedented concentration of power will make it easier to navigate the difficult road ahead and to make necessary but politically unpopular decisions; left-leaning political economists who believe in having much more state control over the economy might plausibly argue that. There is a very real danger, however, that a less competent leadership will make many more and much bigger economic-policy mistakes than in the past. Well-connected thought leaders from China have told me that there is nothing to worry about; the deputies of all the main financial regulators and officials are still first-rate, even if their bosses are primarily political figureheads. And traditionally, it is the deputies who wield much of the power. One can only say, "Good luck with that."

If China's long-term growth is slowing anywhere near to the extent argued in this chapter, it deeply undermines the main argument underpinning the inevitability of the renminbi equaling and then surpassing the dollar as the world's dominant currency sometime later this century. Given that China still trails in other areas, including the rule of law, the depth and liquidity of financial markets, and the pricing of goods, it is hard to see a scenario in which China's currency is widely used in the West, at least into the foreseeable future.

CHAPTER 10

THE INEVITABILITY OF DOLLAR DECOUPLING

The fact that the Chinese economy is not likely to overtake the U.S. economy anytime soon by no means implies that the dollar will continue to effectively rule Asia. As already noted, if China were to fully decouple from the dollar and move to a more conventional inflation-targeting regime, the ramifications could be far reaching. As the world's second-most-important economy — and for many countries, the most important destination for exports and source for imports — China is already moving to price some of its trade in renminbi, and that share will likely grow as the renminbi floats more freely against the dollar. Many of China's trading partners will, at a minimum, begin to incorporate the renminbi into their exchange rate regimes, and over time the renminbi is likely to become increasingly important in the pricing of intermediate goods, particularly among countries in the Asian supply chain. The exact role the renminbi will play in global reserve portfolios depends very much on how open and liquid China makes its debt markets. But the first step is trade, and over time asset denomination can follow as global renminbi markets deepen. A shift to a much more flexible dollar exchange rate has long been manifestly in China's interests, if only because, as we have noted, China is a large country that typically faces business cycles that are very distinct from those of the United States.

Not everyone has always agreed that exchange rates between the major currencies (which nowadays would include the dollar, renminbi, euro, and yen) should freely float—two notable exceptions are the Nobel laureate Robert Mundell and the Stanford economist Ronald McKinnon.[1] These two giants in international macroeconomics independently made the case that allowing significant renminbi exchange rate flexibility would be a mistake. In fact, they both argued that a better system would have Europe and Japan, as well as China, fixing their currencies to the dollar. Mundell liked to quip that "the optimal number of currencies is an odd number less than three." I, for one, respectfully disagree. Although this might make sense in a future of global peace and harmony, the experience of the eurozone and other fixed exchange rate regimes shows how difficult fixed-rate regimes can be even within countries deeply committed to political cooperation.

Even absent geopolitical tensions, tariff wars, economic sanctions, and the cyber divide between East and West, there is ample reason for China to make the renminbi a more normal major currency—even before it competes for dominance. Just as one small example, consider the dynamics of 2023 and 2024, when China was experiencing a significant decline in growth and very low inflation even as the United States was still coming down from a boom and a couple of years of high inflation. Of course, China can create more space for interest rate independence by further closing off its capital markets, but there are limits to how successful such policies can be in a country so open to trade and where firms can exercise so many ploys for circumventing controls on both capital inflows and capital outflows.

In fact, China is already far along on a path toward decoupling the renminbi from the dollar. Technically, it set out on this path back in 2005, when China officially began pegging the renminbi to a basket of currencies, rather than just the dollar. Although the basket was weighted heavily toward the dollar and dollar-linked currencies, the subtle shift set the stage for allowing for a period of gentle appreciation that occurred between August 2005 and August 2015. Although the appreciation occurred in fits and starts, after ten years it cost 22 percent less renminbi to buy one dollar than at the beginning, a sizable movement by any measure. (Economists sometimes refer to such a path as a "crawling peg," with the exchange rate moving steadily in one direction but never too much at a time.)

THE PRESENT-DAY CHALLENGER

Given that the United States and the IMF seemed to be getting most of what they wanted, one might have expected a more enthusiastic response from Western policymakers, especially considering that China's annual current account surplus relative to GDP fell from a peak of 9.9 percent in 2007 to 2.6 percent in 2015.[2] The muted response was in part because China's trade dominance was still growing at a rapid clip, and until the 2015 stock market scare that was discussed earlier, it had continued accumulating foreign exchange reserves (roughly 70 percent in dollars) at a brisk pace.

After losing a quarter of the country's exchange rate reserves to capital outflows in 2015, Chinese authorities reformulated their basket to create greater scope for currency flexibility. The People's Bank of China at first expanded the basket to thirteen currencies, and then in 2016 to twenty-four currencies.[3] True, the currency basket is more a reference rate than a rigid target, and the authorities often take liberties to interpret the regime quite broadly. There is no question, though, that since the basket reformulation in 2015, China's exchange rate policy has begun to resemble a more flexible regime, although China does not yet have anything close to a full-blown floating rate as, say, between the dollar and the euro. Still, instead of the slowly crawling peg of 2005–2014, China's exchange rate regime now looks a bit more like what economists refer to as a "managed float," in which the exchange rate is allowed to move both up and down, but normally never too much or too fast. Still, as noted in chapter 1, China's exchange rate regime remains quite dollar-centric and a borderline case for being classified as being in the dollar bloc.

It was thought at one time that the countries of Asia needed to stabilize rates against the dollar to support efficiency within the Asian supply chain, much as European countries thought they needed the euro to promote trade within Europe. This was a key part of Mundell's and McKinnon's rationale for regional and global fixed rates. As we will discuss later in chapter 15, the Asian economies went down this road for a long time. However, the supply-chain rationale might have been overstated, at least for countries with deep financial markets and advanced economy-level regulation. Korea and Japan already allow their currencies to float against the dollar, and although both still engage in some degree of exchange market intervention, they do not fix their rates against the dollar by any interpretation. Initially after China's 2015 currency-basket reformulation, there was skepticism that China was really prepared to allow more flexibility in the dollar exchange rate. It was hard to tell for sure, in part because this coincided with a period of little movement between the euro, the dollar, and the yen, perhaps because both short- and long-term interest rates had converged across these key currencies.[4]

Indeed, the post-Covid recovery brought inflation back into the picture along with sharply elevated interest rates in the United States, Europe, and many emerging markets. The yen-dollar exchange rate — after being in a veritable coma from 2014 to 2022 — suddenly collapsed, falling from 103 yen per dollar at the end of 2020 to 157 yen per dollar in May 2024, a depreciation of 35 percent. The Korean won depreciated by 24 percent between the end of 2020 and October 2022. China, in turn, allowed the renminbi to temporarily appreciate by over 10 percent against the dollar as the pandemic unfolded in 2020, though after a couple of years the Chinese currency was back to where it started.[5]

Greater exchange rate flexibility is not a sufficient condition for expanding the use of the renminbi in international trade and finance, but it does provide motivation. As long as the renminbi-dollar exchange rate remained extremely stable, there was no particular reason for any country to consider placing a higher weight on the renminbi in its own exchange rate targeting. As the renminbi-dollar exchange rate starts to fluctuate more sharply, though, things could change dramatically, if not necessarily overnight.

When China does fully float its exchange rate, the occasional sharp fluctuations that will likely result will no doubt cause frictions in an already challenging U.S.-China relationship, and it is far from clear how these frictions will be resolved. In principle, the International Monetary Fund should be able to step in; the IMF was originally set up after World War II in no small part to navigate exchange rate disputes. But don't count on it being able to help much. An old quip about the IMF's relative, the United Nations, comes to mind, even if it is not entirely fair: "When there is a dispute between two small nations, the UN steps in and the dispute disappears. When there is a dispute between a small nation and a large nation, the UN steps in and the small nation disappears. When there is a dispute between two large nations, the UN disappears."[6]

PART III

EVERYONE ELSE'S PROBLEM

Living with the Dollar

CHAPTER 11

THE LURE OF FIXED EXCHANGE RATES

For most of the world, the question is how to live with the dollar, not how to compete with it. Typically, the starting point has been to fix the rate of exchange between the dollar and the local currency. In the post-war period, virtually every advanced economy and emerging market has tried it. Although only a few countries peg rigidly to the dollar these days, a great many tightly control short- and even medium-term movements. Understanding the problems that can arise cuts to the core of modern international economics and provides a valuable point of departure for envisioning future paths for the global financial system.[1]

There are good reasons why fixed exchange rate systems have such enduring appeal. Citizens in most developing countries and emerging markets trust the dollar far more than they trust their own central banks. A fixed rate, as long as the government reliably sticks to it, simplifies life for exporters and importers, and also helps a country's banks integrate into the global financial system. Above all, a fixed exchange rate makes monetary policy transparent and easy for the average citizen to understand. People everywhere know and trust the dollar (perhaps even more than they should, as we will see). Making the local currency convertible therefore generates trust, even more so because the dollar exchange rate is something everyone can easily see at all times.

EVERYONE ELSE'S PROBLEM

The flip side is that fixed exchange rate systems turn out to be surprisingly fragile, and when they collapse they tend to create havoc. Banks go bust, countries go into default, ministers get sacked, governments fall. The social, political, and economic fallout can lead to years of lost growth, or worse. Consider that the Russian financial crisis of 1998, sparked by an unsustainable fixed exchange rate regime, was the rocket fuel that helped propel Vladimir Putin to power. Other epoch-defining fixed exchange rate crises include the 1994 Mexican peso crisis, the 1997–1998 Asian financial crisis (which hit Thailand, Indonesia, and Korea among others), the 1999 Brazilian crisis, and the 2002 Argentine crisis. In the European debt crisis of 2010–2012, the threat of being forced to exit the eurozone and being left with a sharply depreciated domestic currency was a sword of Damocles hanging over Greece, Spain, Italy, and other distressed European economies.

The problem with having a rigidly fixed exchange rate against the dollar is that it places tight constraints on a country's monetary policy, which needs to move interest rates in synch with the Fed. Robert Mundell described the problem as a trilemma, or an "impossible trinity."[2] Countries cannot simultaneously have a fixed exchange rate, have open capital markets, and conduct independent interest rate policy. Otherwise, when interest rates are too low, capital will flee the country unless there are tight capital market restrictions.[3]

Back in the 1950s and 1960s, most economists thought the fixed exchange rate regime a solid and workable approach. The dollar-centric post-war Bretton Woods fixed-rate system supported strong growth throughout much of the world in the 1950s and 1960s (though in the 1950s Europe and Japan had intense capital controls). Widespread restrictions on international capital movements prevented speculators from bringing down the exchange rate peg at the cost of holding back financial market development, much as in modern-day China. Canada's experiment with floating from 1950 to 1962 had shown that a floating exchange rate was a viable option, although most countries preferred to live with their dollar pegs.[4]

Not everyone agreed that fixed rates were such a good idea. In a classic 1953 paper, Milton Friedman — once again the skeptic — argued that a regime of floating exchange rates, set by the market, would ultimately prove far more stable than a shaky system of fixed exchange rates set by politicians and technocrats.[5]

THE LURE OF FIXED EXCHANGE RATES

It is not that Friedman viewed fixed rates as a bad idea per se; he simply believed that policymakers would have trouble living within the straitjacket fixed rates imply, since even with all the capital controls put in place after the war, there were still periodic realignments, that is, occasions when a country (e.g., France) had to change its dollar exchange rate. On this point, Friedman would be proved correct, again and again.[6] True, Bretton Woods collapsed in no small part because the United States, at the center of the system, had trouble holding up its end of the bargain, which required it to maintain stable prices to underpin the credibility of everyone else's. The United States experienced crawling inflation that turned into a brisk walk in the late 1960s and eventually to a sprint in the 1970s. U.S. inflation wreaked havoc worldwide.

One prediction of Friedman's that proved way off the mark was his claim that floating exchange rates would move smoothly and steadily in response to inflation and interest rate differentials. Instead, floating rates proved wildly volatile. In 1976, Rudiger Dornbusch produced an ingenious explanation. His Keynesian "overshooting" model showed how volatility in monetary policy — which was certainly very unpredictable at the time — could produce amplified movements in exchange rates. Basically, since Keynesian rigidities meant it would take time for prices to adjust, the exchange rate had to absorb all the adjustment in the short run, something along the lines of Le Chatelier's principle in chemistry.[7] The exchange rate would overshoot its long-run equilibrium, only settling into it as prices fully adjusted. Although economists have since placed greater emphasis on financial market shocks, and Dornbusch's theoretical analysis has been supplanted by more-sophisticated models, the original overshooting model is still regarded as yielding fundamental insights into the connection between monetary policy and floating exchange rates.

To be fair, the rapid evolution of international capital markets also contributed to exchange rate volatility. The development of lightly regulated offshore dollar markets in London was especially problematic. From the United Kingdom's perspective, the "Eurodollar" market was a way to rebuild London as a global capital market center now that the once-dominant pound was playing second fiddle to the dollar. For American policymakers, who actually took steps to encourage offshore dollar markets in the late 1950s and 1960s, the Eurodollar market provided a way for Europeans to keep their dollars in Europe instead of tendering them for U.S. gold via official holders (mainly foreign central banks or finance ministries) and thereby draining America's limited supply.

This brings us back to Europe's transition to the euro, which was glossed over in chapter 4; now it is time to take a deeper look. As advanced-economy exchange rates began to float in the 1970s, European countries were particularly unhappy with the situation, since not only were exchange rates fluctuating between Europe and the United States, which was bad enough, they were floating between European economies themselves, each of which had its own currency. This was long before the advent of the single currency in Europe, so Germany still had the deutsche mark, France the franc, Spain the peseta, and so on. A high level of currency volatility ran counter to the main thrust of post-war European economic policy, which was to create a trading bloc that might compete as an equal with the United States.

In addition to exchange rate volatility, Europe in the 1970s was also grappling with its own out-of-control double-digit inflation — the notable exception was Germany, where inflation reached only 7 percent at its peak.[8] Once again, even in the currency chaos wrought by the collapse of the Bretton Woods system of fixed exchange rates, Germany's beloved independent Bundesbank had outperformed. The Bundesbank wasn't perfect; 7 percent inflation is anathema to the ultra-inflation-averse German public, but at least it wasn't the double-digit levels seen almost everywhere else in Europe.

Germany's neighbors, whatever their feelings about the country, coveted its deutsche mark, just as Otmar Issing had explained. Gradually the idea emerged of trying to kill two birds with one stone by having the rest of Europe stabilize their exchange rates against the German deutsche mark, much as they had done against the dollar under Bretton Woods. This would have the direct effect of stabilizing cross exchange rates across all participating European countries and, it was hoped, would indirectly help tame inflation by forcing all of Europe's central banks to follow the lead of the hard-money Bundesbank. The French sometimes referred to their peg as the "franc fort" policy. Translated to English, this means "strong franc," but the expression could also be interpreted as relating to the location of the Bundesbank in Frankfurt. Back then, the Banque de France, like all other central banks in Europe besides Germany's, was fundamentally subordinate to its all-powerful finance ministry. The idea that its interest rate policy would now be dictated in Frankfurt was shocking.

It is worth once again pointing out that at the time, neither the economics profession nor the policy world had yet figured out that if the main object was to restore low inflation, a more enduring and direct approach would have been to give national central banks much greater independence and to direct them to put a large weight on inflation stabilization.[9] One wonders whether the Eurosystem might have evolved quite differently than it did—for example, with a few of the largest countries keeping their own currencies, and other smaller currencies orbiting around them—had this approach been better understood. The undeniable advantages of having a single currency in Europe would have been lost, but so too would have been the straitjacket that produced the European debt crisis. Are we so sure that would not have been better?

In any event, the ultimate aim of European policymakers was not simply to stabilize exchange rates within Europe but to actually move to a single currency, as if there were a United States of Europe. The rationale for such a merger had been developed in the 1950s and 1960s by the economic theorists James Meade and Robert Mundell, who were thinking not so much in terms of anti-inflation credibility as in reducing transaction frictions across European states. The question, though, was how to get from A to B. A sudden merger between countries with such profoundly different interest rates and inflation rates would have produced chaos.

Europe's leaders decided to approach a currency union gradually, moving carefully until there was sufficient policy convergence, especially in inflation and interest rates, to allow a smooth landing. European policymakers were surely aware of the experience of developing countries, where pegged exchange rates often worked for a while but then blew up. They evidently believed that with better advanced-country institutions and governance, Europe would not have the same problem. They also knew, of course, that the Bretton Woods system itself had blown up, but they assumed that this was largely because the country at the center, the United States, behaved irresponsibly. Germany could be relied on to do whatever was necessary to keep its inflation low. In general, most of Europe's leading policymakers bought into this story.

U.S. economists were not so confident, particularly in light of the ongoing evolution of financial markets, which gave speculators enormous leverage and liquidity. Adopting the mathematical model that two Federal Reserve economists had developed to study why the interwar gold standard of the 1920s and 1930s collapsed, Paul Krugman famously argued that unsustainable fixed exchange rate regimes almost invariably flame out in a huge speculative attack.[10] In the Salant-Henderson-Krugman model, the government relentlessly forces the central bank to monetize its debt, which the central bank can handle until it starts running low on reserves with which to intervene. At a certain exact moment, which is known to all, speculators swoop in to scoop up the last dollars. In its simplest form the model is totally unrealistic, to say the least. For one thing, exchange rate crises are extremely difficult to predict in reality, whereas in the model the crisis comes on time like a Swiss train. However, the analysis still provided a stark example of how the bleeding could not go on forever, even if reserves could be used to postpone the day of reckoning.

Such theoretical musings did not discourage the Europeans. Populations across the continent bemoaned their nations' high inflation rates; everyone was jealous of Germany's low inflation. As Issing had explained, the rest of Europe all wished they had deutsche marks instead of their own shaky currencies. After a long period of experimentation with simply smoothing daily exchange rate movements without resisting trends, Europe moved to a system in which rates were fairly narrowly pegged against the deutsche mark. The idea was that this would create a virtuous circle in which everyone had faith in the peg, which in turn would stabilize rates even further.

For a while it all seemed to work. An early sign of trouble was when Finland's exchange rate collapsed in November 1991, falling 14 percent. Finland had festering banking problems, and its currency increasingly began to appear overvalued, especially after the collapse of the Soviet Union, Finland's neighbor and a main destination for Finnish exports. Speculators circled, and the monetary authorities eventually found that they could not fend off the attack indefinitely. Finland went through a wrenching banking crisis.[11] Having borrowed heavily abroad in dollars, and with their main income in now-devalued markkas, Finland's banks were busted.

Finnish law at the time required a parliamentary vote to change the exchange

THE LURE OF FIXED EXCHANGE RATES

rate, which is obviously nuts, since it was almost impossible to keep the news from speculators, some of whom made a killing — for example, by selling Finnish markka for deutsche marks just before the devaluation and then buying them back at a 14 percent discount just after. Not everyone got the news; the devaluation was brutal for firms engaged in the so-called carry trade, in which one borrows in the low-interest-rate currency (here, the German deutsche mark) and then holds the high-interest-rate currency (the Finnish markka). As long as the exchange rate stays fixed, it's easy money. But the markka trade blew up in the face of anyone who did not cover their bets in time. In trading, as in chess, avoiding a big loss can be as important as making a gain.

Just after the collapse, I happened to visit the trading floor of Bankers Trust, one of the world's most important foreign exchange dealers. I had never seen a major bank trading floor before, and it was hard not to look wide-eyed at the scores of busy traders at their terminals, the vaulted ceilings, and the giant TV monitors (which back then cost a fortune).

My host was a friend from my chess years, Norman Weinstein, who was the 1973 U.S. Open chess champion. Norman is extremely modest and understated; by all accounts he had become an elite foreign exchange trader. I have no way of knowing exactly how the markka devaluation might have affected Norman's book, but he was definitely in a good mood when I saw him.

Parenthetically, another friend of mine at the time, Rob Johnson — a former colleague at the International Finance Division of the Federal Reserve Board in the early 1980s — was also working on the Bankers Trust team. Evidently, Rob had been on a tour of European central banks and, fortuitously, was visiting Helsinki shortly before the crisis. George Soros, who had a great eye for trading talent, soon thereafter scooped up Rob. It was a propitious moment to be making personnel moves. Soros probably realized better than almost anyone that it was time to start building a roster for the playoffs; a lot more action was to come.

A similar attack on the Swedish krona followed in late 1992.[12] Convinced that the country's fundamentals did not merit an attack on its currency, the Swedish Riksbank told itself that as long as it hung tough, speculators would be beaten down. Policy interest rates were raised to 50 percent; one headline rate went to 500 percent. Unfortunately, the high rates were bankrupting the

Swedish banking system. When short-term rates skyrocketed, it pushed banks' borrowing costs far above their loan income. The Riksbank held tough for thirty days, but by the time it gave in, its banking system was in crisis. As John Maynard Keynes famously quipped, "The markets can stay irrational longer than you can stay solvent."

Sweden and Finland were not alone. In 1992, one country after another was felled by speculators; the casualties included Italy, Spain, and the United Kingdom. When the Bank of England threw in the towel and allowed the pound to depreciate on September 15, 1992, it reportedly lost $7 billion in an hour, including $1 billion to George Soros.

A couple of Soros's lieutenants later explained to me that the billion-dollar coup was not an overnight campaign; it took months to build positions against the pound without attracting attention. Then, when the time had come, Soros simply had to reveal his plan, and his reputation was already so great that the rest of the market followed suit.

Speculators also took down the Spanish peseta and the Italian lira, but not the French franc. The difference was that Germany decided to unleash its full firepower to back its key ally France, realizing that to do otherwise would undermine its post-war objective of peacefully integrating into Europe. When both sides of the trade — the German central bank and the French central bank — stand behind the exchange rate, it is much harder to take down, since Germany can print unlimited deutsche marks and France can print unlimited francs. That said, such a policy can work only if Germany trusts France not to abuse the privilege by printing too many francs and causing high inflation in both countries.

What was somewhat surprising about Europe's wave of exchange rate crises was that all the countries whose pegs collapsed had more than enough in reserves (including gold) to buy back the entire value of their currency supply, even without German help. So they did not seem to fit the canonical speculative-attack model in which the country just runs out of hard currency.[13] A more realistic model, proposed by Maurice Obstfeld in 1994, showed that even if the government was not spendthrift, it could still be gamed into abandoning its exchange rate by a sufficiently determined speculative attack.[14] For example, given that many mortgages in the United Kingdom had their interest rate reset every month, the Bank of England was in no position to stare down Soros and other speculators by pushing interest rates through the ceiling. There are many subtleties we need not concern ourselves with here. Suffice it to say that economists now understand that with relatively open capital markets, rigidly fixed exchange rate pegs that seem solid as a rock one day can prove quite fragile the next, particularly when a loss of confidence exposes underlying macroeconomic vulnerabilities.

CHAPTER 12

HYPERINFLATION

One might think that the exchange rate catastrophes that beset Europe in the early 1990s would have put an end to rigidly fixed exchange rate regimes. Not at all, though one has to understand the context. In the early 1990s, inflation around the world was completely out of control. Many countries were desperate, and if a fixed exchange rate could buy inflation relief for even a year or two, most did not care what might come next. Incredibly, more than forty countries had inflation rates exceeding 40 percent in 1992; this is a level of inflation that many studies have shown is almost always detrimental to growth.[1] The list of countries with very high inflation spanned much of Latin America, Africa, the Middle East, and Eastern Europe, not to mention the newly independent countries of the former Soviet Union, including both Ukraine and Russia itself.[2]

There was considerable debate among economists about how to bring an end to this inflation. Some of the most prominent and influential policy economists, including Harvard's brilliant Jeffrey Sachs (who later moved to Columbia), forcefully made the case that a fixed-rate regime was the least costly way to engineer disinflation, at least in the early years.[3] On the surface, the arguments still seem pretty compelling. After extremely high inflation hits a country, no one trusts the government to keep inflation low; even the slightest hint of a

HYPERINFLATION

rise in inflation might be enough to trigger a run from currency. An exchange rate anchor is a visible mechanism for demonstrating commitment, something the public can watch every day. The problem, though, is that assuming inflation starts coming down, how does the government engineer an exit without losing all the hard-earned credibility it gained through a painful disinflation? And what if, over time, the government's commitment weakens, particularly because of the need to keep tight control over fiscal policy?

Sachs's argument is most compelling for countries that have reached hyperinflationary levels of 40 percent or more *per month*. Table 2, which looks at the price increases between 1970 and 2000 in some major emerging markets, shows how hard inflation can be to control once it gets out of hand. The Democratic Republic of the Congo is on top with over a 10 quadrillion percent price increase (a quadrillion is a thousand trillion), thanks to three hyperinflationary episodes. Brazil had two episodes of hyperinflation and still hit 1 quadrillion percent inflation; Argentina 100 trillion percent. Obviously, inflation at these levels wipes out debt denominated in the local currency. This may be convenient for the government, but it causes major collateral damage to the rest of the economy. In a country dealing with hyperinflation, it is almost impossible for consumers or businesses to function in any kind of normal way. During the 1980s and early 1990s, hyperinflation was an epidemic of global proportions.

In the twenty-first century so far, hyperinflation and near hyperinflation have been much less frequent. Zimbabwe had inflation rates reaching 50,000 percent per year in 2008–2009, the outcome of decades of disastrous autocratic rule that destroyed a once-thriving economy in the name of socialism.[4] One of my best undergraduate students back then was from Harare, the capital of Zimbabwe. She quipped, "I don't know what data the government or the IMF are using to calculate the rate of inflation. The stores are empty; there are no prices to look at." Zimbabwe at present has abandoned an independent currency altogether and is allowing foreign currencies to be used for all payments until 2030;[5] no doubt there will be further changes. As shown at the bottom of table 2, Zimbabwe's cumulative inflation in the twenty-first century surpasses even that of the Democratic Republic of the Congo in the twentieth century, reaching 400 octillion percent. If the reader is not familiar with quadrillions (a

Table 2. Cumulative change in exchange rate vs. U.S. dollar:
January 1970–December 2001

Country	Cumulative depreciation (%) vs. dollar
Congo, Democratic Republic of the	9,924,011,976,047,800
Brazil	124,316,767,667,574
Argentina	2,855,714,286,430
Nicaragua	933,784,495,428
Peru	9,129,198,866
Bolivia	54,040,304
Turkey	7,500,585
Mexico	77,749
Indonesia	2,798
Egypt	783
Italy (vs. deutsche mark)	312
Australia	104
United Kingdom	64
Canada	39
Malaysia	23
Panama	0
Germany	−54
Japan	−59
Zimbabwe (1970–2009)	419,999,831,580,067,000,000,000,000,000
Venezuela (1970–2024)	82,409,318,181,818,100

Sources: Carmen Reinhart and Kenneth Rogoff, "The Modern History of Exchange Rate Arrangements: A Reinterpretation," *Quarterly Journal of Economics* 119, no. 1 (February 2004): 1–48; Ethan Ilzetski, Carmen Reinhart, and Kenneth Rogoff, "Exchange Rate Arrangements Entering the 21st Century: Which Anchor Will Hold?," *Quarterly Journal of Economics* 134, no. 2 (May 2019): 599–646.

thousand trillion) and octillions (a thousand quadrillion), neither was I until I started studying modern hyperinflations. Imagine if every time you check into a hotel, you need two suitcases, one with your clothes and the other with cash to pay for the room; that is what living through a hyperinflation can be like.

Another country that experienced hyperinflation in this century is the long-time progressive darling Venezuela, a nation that by some measures has larger

HYPERINFLATION

oil reserves than Saudi Arabia. Once one of the wealthiest countries in Latin America, Venezuela has suffered from decades of socialism-tinged autocratic rule. Venezuela's charismatic Hugo Chávez, who led the country down the primrose path from 1999 to 2013, was showered with praise and support—for example, by the former U.K. Labour Party leader Jeremy Corbyn and the Nobel Prize winner Joseph Stiglitz, whose writings Chávez admired.[6] Under Chávez, Venezuela's economy began a slow and steady descent despite high oil prices, in part because of a collapse in both public and private investment. Of course, it was not easy to see the full endgame to Venezuela's economic policies. Unlike banking and exchange rate crises, which tend to unfold with a bang, hyperinflation can creep up slowly, as inflation initially rises from one plateau to another.

When Chávez died in 2013, Nicolás Maduro succeeded him. Even though by then the handwriting was on the wall for the horribly mismanaged Venezuelan economy, left-leaning Western think tanks such as the Washington-based Center for Economic and Policy Research continued to periodically publish reports highly supportive of the Venezuelan government's policies.[7] In April 2013, the organization challenged the world media to give a more balanced view of Maduro's seemingly not very democratic election, producing an open letter, signed by luminaries such as the economists James K. Galbraith of the University of Texas and Robert Pollin of the University of Massachusetts, arguing that in their assessment of the polling data, Maduro was clearly the people's choice.

> It does not make sense to ignore this overwhelming statistical evidence, as the Obama administration, and almost all major U.S. media outlets, have done. As a result of this omission, many if not most Americans believe that the election was stolen or that the result is somehow in question. This is simply not believable in the face of the actual evidence.[8]

Of course, the opposition had been knee-capped. Maduro's policies accelerated the downhill slide that had been going on for years under Chávez. U.S. sanctions certainly did not help, but they were hardly the main driver.[9] Despite its astounding oil wealth, Venezuela descended into one of the worst peacetime recessions since World War II.[10] Output fell by more than 35 percent; more than seven million people, equivalent to nearly a quarter of Venezuela's population in 2022, emigrated after 2015.[11] The population suffered widespread malnutrition and lacked access to basic drugs. Inflation went through the ceiling.[12]

Unfortunately, as of this writing, Maduro continues to cling to power, having once again declared himself the winner in the election held on July 28, 2024, despite widespread concerns from world leaders and independent observers that the election was marked by fraud; independent exit polls showed Maduro getting trounced by the opposition candidate.[13]

Although the extreme monetary dysfunction that Zimbabwe and Venezuela experienced is exceptional, other, more politically stable, countries experiencing uncomfortably high inflation have long looked for a reliable cure. Indeed, sometimes leaders become so discouraged about ending high inflation that they are willing to take a leap of faith on fixed exchange rates even when told it might end very badly. Back in the 1980s, one such country was the United States' southern neighbor, Mexico. Still trying to emerge from its 1982 debt crisis, Mexico started (actually, restarted) pegging its currency to the dollar in 1988. Given the moves toward a single currency in Europe, it seemed like a reasonable idea to some. The problem was that although the U.S. Treasury at times was a cheerleader for the policy, the peg was unilateral. U.S. authorities made clear that they were not going to help support the peg; in other words, they were not going to do what Germany did in bailing out France in 1992. Our dollar, your problem.

In effect, Mexico had entered a one-sided currency peg, just as European monetary authorities had done during the first decades after World War II. Unfortunately for Mexico, international capital flows had become much larger and more volatile in the ensuing years, giving the government much less room for error.

Indeed, the adoption of the North American Free Trade Agreement (NAFTA) made things worse, as it required Mexico to open itself up more to U.S. investors. For its part, Mexico made the mistake of excessively relying on "tesobonos," which were Mexican government bonds geared to the U.S. market and payable in dollars, not pesos. Nevertheless, Mexico's exchange rate policy appeared to work for several years: inflation declined and capital inflows pushed up the dollar value of the peso. Unfortunately, Mexico's policy was just not sufficiently aligned with the United States to make the policy work indefinitely. Inflation remained well above that of the United States, and, over time, the competitiveness of the peso was declining. The peso was not literally fixed to the dollar and was allowed to depreciate gradually in a crawling peg, a concept discussed earlier in the context of China. But the peso wasn't crawling fast enough; the Mexicans feared that if they allowed the exchange rate to depreciate quickly enough to compensate for the inflation differentials, the anchor would be lost entirely. Moreover, the prospect of NAFTA encouraged higher wage demands by Mexico's politically powerful unions, which further exacerbated its competitiveness problem. By most measures, the "real" value of the peso had gotten far out of line by the early 1990s.

In the spring of 1994, Rudiger Dornbusch wrote a deeply insightful paper for a Brookings Institution conference detailing all the reasons Mexico's exchange rate was too rich, and why it would need to depreciate by 20 percent or more.[14] Dornbusch's presentation and the debate that followed proved an event of historic significance, both as a marker for how economists understand the limits of using exchange rate pegs to fight inflation, and for Mexico.

Dornbusch and his co-author, Alejandro Werner, acknowledged that one could make the case that Mexico's apparently overvalued exchange rate might have just reflected all the great economic reforms the country had been making in the run-up to the free-trade agreement, which was set to be implemented on January 1, 1994. And Mexico seemed to have tamed the unsustainable budget deficits that had led to its 1982 debt crisis. In principle, membership in NAFTA itself was going to provide a huge boost for productivity in Mexico, effectively integrating it into the U.S. market.

Dornbusch and Werner argued, however, that another, less benign, explanation better described the situation, particularly given that Mexico's current account deficit had swollen to 7 percent of GDP, a very high level by normal standards.[15] Dornbusch and Werner argued that the huge trade and current account gaps could be closed only through an exchange rate devaluation. The only question was whether the devaluation should occur before or after a new president took office in December 1994. Their perspective was not universally shared, although there were some at the International Monetary Fund who were also worried. However, as the IMF historian James Boughton later wrote, the optimists at the IMF outnumbered the worriers.[16]

EVERYONE ELSE'S PROBLEM

The Brookings conference session at which Dornbusch and Werner presented their paper included two supremely qualified discussants: Guillermo Calvo, an influential Argentine-born macroeconomist, and Stanley Fischer, a former World Bank chief economist who would soon become the second-in-command at the IMF.

The discussion was extraordinarily sharp and insightful. Still, one is struck by how much of the focus was on finding a way for Mexico to keep an exchange rate peg of some form as an anchor to fight inflation. Dornbusch and Werner did emphasize that, as a rule, the extreme step of using a fixed exchange rate as part of a plan to stabilize inflation has to be temporary and after a period has to give way to a more flexible arrangement. That, however, once again leaves open the question of how to make a smooth transition without being taken down by speculators.

Calvo hit the nail on the head when he argued that if Mexico was already in as deep a hole as Dornbusch and Werner claimed — he was not sure himself whether that was true — then the best plan was for the U.S. Treasury to simply backstop Mexico, serving as a lender of last resort. This was all well and good, but if the United States did that, it would create the same kind of problem the Germans faced in Europe; namely, deciding how much help they could promise without creating a moral-hazard problem. That is, if a big "one-time" bailout convinces Mexican politicians that the United States can always be gamed into doing it again, what is to discourage the Mexican government from re-digging the fiscal hole the United States has just filled in? Let's just say that the U.S. authorities probably did not trust Mexican fiscal policy any more than Germany trusted Italian or Greek fiscal policy. Dornbusch and Werner's paper quickly became very well known among economists; it took longer to seep into Wall Street's consciousness.

On December 20, 1994, the new government of Ernesto Zedillo — whom James Boughton describes as overseeing the cleanest (least corrupt) administration Mexico had known to that point — allowed the peso to fall by 15 percent.[17] It is a standard move for a new administration to absorb inevitable adjustment pain early on when it can blame the previous administration. (There is the old joke about the Soviet dictator Stalin giving his eventual successor Khrushchev two letters and telling him to open the first when he gets into big trouble and open the other when he gets into big trouble a second time. The first letter says, "Blame everything on me." The second says, "Write two letters."[18])

The markets went berserk. Eventually the peso dropped not by 15 percent, not by 20 percent, but by over 50 percent before rising somewhat over time. To prevent Mexico from having to default, the United States and the IMF bailed out Mexico. President Clinton, together with the Treasury secretary, Robert Rubin, and his international economics deputy, Larry Summers, managed to find a source of money that Congress could not (back then) block—the exchange stabilization fund, which was intended to be used for dealing with currency volatility.

The peso depreciation, coupled with the sharp rise in Mexican interest rates needed to prevent the peso from depreciating even further, decimated the banking system for much the same reasons as occurred in Europe. Mexico, having just suffered a lost decade of growth after its 1982 debt crisis, again experienced a prolonged slowdown.

A year later, in 1995, Maury Obstfeld and I took a more radical view of events, essentially arguing that for most cases, the only question is when, not if, a rigidly fixed exchange rate regime will collapse.[19] We surveyed the history of exchange rate pegs and showed that in almost every situation in which a country had moderately open international capital markets (that is, open to speculation), its fixed exchange rate regime collapsed within five years; there were only a few exceptions. We argued that fixed exchange rates are sustainable only in rare circumstances and that most countries should instead adopt a flexible exchange rate regime with inflation targeting. We emphasized that this would be much more effective if coupled with central bank independence.

Thus, the Brookings panel discussion around Dornbusch and Werner's paper was wrong in one essential element. Mexico didn't just need a one-time devaluation, or even a one-time devaluation followed by faster depreciation. It needed to scrap the whole idea of focusing monetary policy excessively on the exchange rate to stabilize inflation. Our paper highlighted some Asian currencies that might run into trouble—we noted that the Thai baht, whose peg to the dollar had hit the five-year mark, was a case to be looked at closely. As is usually the case for financial crises, it was hard to predict the timing exactly. It turned out we were a couple of years early.

CHAPTER 13

WHEN EXCHANGE RATE PEGS OUTLIVE THEIR SHELF LIFE

In the summer of 1997, I was invited to the IMF to give a one-week course on recent topics in international economics, built around my treatise with Maurice Obstfeld *The Foundations of International Macroeconomics*; one of my lectures was on the fragility of fixed exchange rates.[1] Stanley Fischer, who had served on my MIT Ph.D. thesis committee, by then was the second-in-command at the IMF. He called me to his office to discuss whether it would be a good idea for Jordan to adopt a fixed exchange rate regime, an idea the IMF had been discussing with Jordanian authorities. Needless to say, my response was that it was an option to be considered only in dire circumstances. Otherwise, a fixed rate was a dubious idea that might at best work for a few years and probably no longer; after that, there would be a debilitating crisis. Jordan did not adopt a fixed exchange rate in the end; had the Jordanian authorities been serious about it, the news from Asia a few days later would have derailed their plans.

When the Thai baht plummeted by more than 15 percent on July 2, 1997, it came as a complete shock to most of the world, which somehow thought Asia was immune to the problems Europe had experienced with fixed rates. By December 1997, the baht was down almost 50 percent.[2] Although polemicists were quick to blame the IMF, the reality was a good deal more nuanced. For one thing,

Thailand — like Mexico before its crash — was running a gaping current account deficit totaling 7 percent of GDP. Moreover, unbeknownst to the IMF, Thai authorities had quietly been running down their dollar reserves using forward contracts on the baht-dollar exchange rate. Essentially, the forward contracts committed the authorities to sell dollars for baht a few months hence, which has very similar effects to buying baht for dollars today but is much less visible than making the purchases outright. Pinning down the expected future exchange rate helped keep the current rate in line. The IMF had not been properly informed.[3]

The underlying problems gnawing away at the baht peg were very typical of a brewing exchange rate crisis, although there were some important nuances. Importantly, the Thai government itself had not been running large deficits, even though the country as a whole was borrowing from the rest of the world. In contrast, domestic financial firms, including both banks and trusts, had been borrowing in dollars, and a lot of the money was being used to fund domestic real estate purchases. This debt paid high interest rates compared with U.S. debt, despite the fact that the baht was pegged to the dollar, and attracted foreign buyers. These buyers might have been lulled into a false sense of security by the country's high growth rate (which averaged roughly 9 percent the decade prior), believing that the housing and land being purchased would surely go up in price over time and thereby secure their loans.

When the exchange rate plummeted, the flaws in this logic were laid bare. The dollar value of Thai real estate portfolios dropped sharply, so much so that the loans on many properties, especially foreign dollar loans, exceeded the properties' value; many debtors went into default. The plunge in value was exacerbated as financial firms trying to meet customer withdrawals were forced to sell repossessed properties at fire-sale prices. This, in turn, led to a downward price spiral that pulled even more property loans underwater; that is, zombie loans took down healthy ones. The coup de grâce for Thailand's economy was a sudden stop in foreign lending that made it extremely expensive for even strong Thai borrowers to roll over any debt coming due. The once high-flying Asian miracle economy entered a deep recession. In principle, the IMF could have come in big immediately and filled the gap to prevent the rot from spreading far and wide. It took time, however, to accurately assess the situation, especially after it became clear that the Thai central bank had previously been less than forthcoming about its intervention book.

Over the course of the next few months, contagion spread to Indonesia (August) and Korea (November) as foreign speculators hunted for other inflexible exchange rate regimes to take down and as locals in Asia also lost confidence. What followed was devastation, the quantitative dimensions of which are so severe that it is almost numbing to recite them.

The Indonesian rupiah crisis started unfolding in July and August of 1997 but intensified going into 1998; the rupiah ultimately fell from a stable pre-crisis value of around 2,600 rupiah per dollar to as low as 11,000 rupiah per dollar in January 1998, and then 14,000 rupiah per dollar in July of 1998. In Indonesia, a lot of foreign-currency borrowing had been done by companies instead of financial firms. But in the end the catastrophic effect on the economy was the same; per capita output fell by over 14 percent from peak to trough.[4] The fact that the Indonesian government had defaulted on its debt only three decades earlier did not help.[5]

The crisis also engulfed South Korea, where banks were the main borrowers from abroad and again a lot of the funds ended up in real estate. The Korean won fell from 800 per dollar in 1996 to almost 1,400 in 1998 (at times even lower). Despite a $58 billion loan from the IMF, the Korean economy still suffered a massive recession; GDP growth per capita fell to negative 6 percent from over 5 percent each year in the decade prior.[6]

Malaysia is an interesting case that is much studied. Some credit Prime Minister Mahathir Mohamad for daring, in the face of standard IMF advice, to institute controls to prevent foreign speculators from abruptly pulling their money out of the country.[7] That IMF advice was that it was fine to tax money on its way into the country, which often included funds from expats living abroad, so as to discourage overly rapid inflows. However, it was counterproductive to stop foreign investors from exiting in a crisis, since it might then take a long time to persuade them to come back. Despite the prime minister's bold steps, Malaysia did not escape a severe recession, and its currency still fell by almost 50 percent against the dollar.[8] Some people had told me that most of the big foreign investors managed to get out despite the controls. Evidently that was wrong.

In 1999, I engaged in a debate/discussion with George Soros on the lessons from the Asian financial crisis, hosted by the London School of Economics; the audience consisted of faculty and students, as well as a couple of other prominent financiers and researchers from the Bank of England and the U.K. Treasury. To his credit, Soros was already thinking about big issues related to re-imagining international financial institutions, even if there were reasons to be quite skeptical about some of the details, as I argued at the session and will come back to in chapter 17. After a lively discussion, I turned to Soros and whispered so that no one could hear it, "You pulled most of your money out of Malaysia in time, right?" Knowing how successful his fund had been in navigating (and sometimes catalyzing) exchange rate crises again and again — Soros and his team were the best of the best at this game — I assumed he would say "yes" or "mostly." Instead, Soros grimaced and shook his head from side to side.

There is much more to be said about the Asian financial crisis (or as the Asian countries call it, "the IMF crisis"), but for our purposes it is enough to know that exchange rates were at the heart of the problem. Virtually all the banking and financial crises across Asia were intimately linked to failed fixed exchange rate regimes. Regulators had allowed banks, financial firms, and companies in Asia to go deep into dollar-denominated debt. Herein lies one of the political economy challenges of fixed rates, one that comes up again and again. To maintain the fixed (stable) exchange rate, authorities need to convince investors that the regime is going to last indefinitely. This makes it difficult for the regulatory arm of the government to discourage firms from taking on dollar debt. The government cannot on the one hand say, "Our government will never ever devalue," and then insist that firms not borrow abroad in dollars because "there is just too big a risk that we might change our minds."

In the summer of 1998, the central bank of South Korea held a conference on the implications of globalization for world financial markets. The impact of the won's massive devaluation could be felt everywhere, from the price of taxis to the ultra-low cost of McDonald's hamburgers. (It was only to look; I am definitely not above eating at McDonald's, but I love Korean foods such as bibimbap.)

EVERYONE ELSE'S PROBLEM

My presentation was based on an update of my 1995 paper with Obstfeld, which had argued that, for the vast majority of countries, having a rigidly pegged exchange rate is a dangerous policy choice unless there are severe constraints on capital markets, which in turn have their own issues. A few participants, including one noted central banker, pressed me on whether Argentina or Hong Kong might be exceptions; my answers were suitably cautious given the unpredictability of exchange rate crises, though my skepticism probably showed through. We will deal with the collapse of the Argentine currency board in 2002 in the next chapter.

Hong Kong's peg is different from almost any other: Hong Kong keeps massive reserves—enough to buy back its money supply several times over—which makes its currency much tougher to take down. A prominent currency trader once explained to me, "Yes, the Hong Kong dollar can be taken down by a sufficiently intense attack. But the first few waves of speculators will get slaughtered." During the Asian financial crisis, the Hong Kong dollar did in fact come under attack, which forced the Hong Kong Monetary Authority, Hong Kong's central bank, to raise interest rates sharply to discourage speculation. Unlike the European countries, which ultimately folded under the pressure of high interest rates, Hong Kong did not. When the Hong Kong stock market started falling sharply as foreign investors started trying to pull their money out, the Hong Kong Monetary Authority took the extraordinary step of spending $15 billion to buy up shares. Make no mistake, it was a huge gamble. However, given that Hong Kong's status as a global financial center was the island state's best bargaining chip to maintain its de facto independence from China, the gamble made sense. In game theory, having the other side believe that you are absolutely obsessed with sticking to your position can be an advantage. So it was for Hong Kong pitted against the world's speculators.

Upon returning to Princeton, where I was a professor at the time, I received a personal letter signed by the chief executive of the Hong Kong Monetary Authority, Joseph Yam. Yam wanted me to understand that there wasn't the slightest chance of Hong Kong ever abandoning its dollar peg, because the central bank was totally committed to it. Yam proved correct; the Hong Kong currency peg is still in place today, though how much longer it will last now that Hong Kong's short-lived era of independence appears to have ended is unclear.[9]

One can imagine that someday China will convert Hong Kong's economy to the renminbi as part of its project to internationalize its currency, particularly as the renminbi begins to float more against the dollar. For now, Beijing evidently believes that Hong Kong is still far more useful to China if it keeps the dollar peg.

After the Asian financial crisis of 1997–1998, fixed exchange rate regimes, notably including Russia's and Brazil's, continued to collapse. Russia's economy in the 1990s was in deep crisis after the fall of communism and the breakup of the Soviet Union. Between 1992 and 1996, the consumer price level rose by over 11,000 percent; not quite hyperinflation, but for the average Russian retiree on a fixed ruble income that distinction was irrelevant. In 1997, however, things started looking more stable; inflation had come down to a "mere" 17 percent.[10] To build on its gains, the Russian Federation agreed to an IMF program aimed at bringing inflation down even further to 8 percent; a central component of the program was a fixed dollar-ruble exchange rate beginning in January 1998. If this sounds suicidal, remember from our earlier discussion about Jordan that the IMF still considered fixed rates a viable anti-inflation strategy and that the idea was still being endorsed by some leading economists as a best practice.

Unfortunately, Russia's program required an unrealistic degree of discipline by fiscal authorities and implausible forbearance from speculators. The Russian peg came under pressure after a month. However, having seen the catastrophic results in Asian countries that had submitted to speculators, the Central Bank of Russia persisted in trying to maintain the peg, and inflation continued to fall. By July 1998, Russia had concluded a large financing program with the IMF aimed at stabilizing fiscal policy and shoring up confidence in the ruble. The IMF put in $15 billion, the World Bank $6 billion, and the Government of Japan another $1.5 billion. It was not enough. In August 1998, the central bank finally threw in the towel. Russia changed to a floating rate, defaulted on its domestic debt, and instituted a moratorium on its payments to foreign creditors, which is also a form of default.[11]

The ruble exchange rate collapse and the Russian default nearly led to a global economic crisis. A large hedge fund, Long-Term Capital Management (LTCM), held a significant position in Russian government debt at the time of the default, as did several other Western hedge funds. What made LTCM different was that its main business model involved a quite simple arbitrage between newly issued long-term U.S. Treasury bonds and "off-the-run" bonds (say, a bond issued a week earlier) that were obviously near perfect substitutes but are sold in the secondary market at a small discount. At the time of the Russian default, LTCM held a position in an astounding 5 percent of the global fixed-income market, which led to a liquidity panic that briefly froze the U.S. Treasury bill market, the world's largest and most liquid financial market. Traders stared in stunned silence as their screens literally froze; a Yale professor who was on the trading floor at the time reported to me that he had never seen anything like it in his life. Imagine the most liquid market in the world freezing up. Eventually, the Federal Reserve Bank of New York stepped in and organized a bailout.

Brazil, a country that had suffered from serial hyperinflation, was the next major fixed exchange rate regime to fall. Like the others, Brazil had sought to find a way to stabilize inflation and decided to use the exchange rate. Starting in July 1994 it had fixed its exchange rate to the dollar, creating a new currency — the real — in the process. Under the "Real Plan," Brazil's exchange rate was allowed to depreciate but not nearly as fast as prices were rising, which quickly led to massive overvaluation.[12] The world had seen that movie before in many places, not least in Mexico, the second-largest country in Latin America after Brazil.

With extremely high inflation and glacial exchange rate depreciation, Brazil had become a rather expensive destination and was becoming more expensive by the day, as Natasha and I learned when we spent our delayed honeymoon in Brazil in December 1995. I had been to Brazil a couple of times for conferences and loved the country, and I thought Natasha would too. She had traveled widely as an international television producer for the Sesame Street Workshop, and before that as a documentary filmmaker and journalist; it was hard to find a place she had not been. We persisted with the plan even though, as we started tallying up the cost, it looked to be significantly more expensive than we had budgeted and we were forced to continually scale back our aspirations. Our previous attempt at a honeymoon in June had been cut short because Natasha had to rush back to Moscow after a group of armed men, dressed in Russian military uniforms, seized her team's Sesame Street production office in Moscow, taking the crew's life-size Elmo doll with them. Later, we jokingly referred to that as our "minimoon." The overpriced Brazil trip became our "moneymoon."

Stopping in Rio on the way to our final beach destination in the north, we met up with a couple of my former Ph.D. students, one from Berkeley and one from Princeton, who had returned to Brazil after their studies. Afonso and Cristina were great hosts, and it was fascinating to hear their perspective on life in Rio. At some point, the nerdy economist in me could not control myself from asking: Aren't you aware of how expensive Rio has become compared with New York? Doesn't that bother you? How can the government expect to maintain a nearly fixed exchange rate with the dollar when inflation in Brazil is so much higher than in the United States? Isn't it likely that Brazil's fixed rate will inevitably blow up, as Mexico's did? They said that things were not so obvious, citing many local and foreign experts, including the IMF, who were all broadly supportive of what the government was doing.

The various arguments sounded a lot like the ones authorities in Mexico had been making in the run-up to their exchange rate crisis in December 1994: basically yes, an exchange rate attack might happen, but it was far from a certainty. Importantly, Brazil's capital markets were far from fully open, as we learned from having to pay in advance through vouchers for almost everything on the trip, one way the government made sure that tourists couldn't take advantage of the much more favorable black-market exchange rate.

Both of my former students are exceptional economists and had already published in very top academic journals. Each went on to become quite influential later. The fact that they believed that Brazil's seemingly unsustainable exchange rate policy had a reasonable chance of working—to bring down inflation without causing a crisis—certainly made an impression and gave me some pause. Then again, having lived through the chaos of Brazil's two near hyperinflations, perhaps the fact that the fixed exchange rate regime might blow up some day wasn't the deal-breaker for them that it was to me. If the country could get a few good years out of it, maybe the economy would be in a stronger position when problems came, something along the lines of what Jeffrey Sachs had implicitly been arguing.

Brazil's fixed rate (crawling peg) did last a couple more years, reaching roughly the five-year marker Obstfeld and I had identified as the shelf life for the majority of fixed-rate regimes. When the Brazilian real peg came crashing down in early 1999, it crashed hard.[13] Ironically, much as in the Russian case, the crash happened just as the peg had finally succeeded in squeezing most inflation out of the system. Unfortunately, this success came too late; cumulative price hikes had left the real far overvalued, the current account deficit was 5 percent of GDP, and the economy was sliding into recession. The bulk of the government's domestic debt was short term and needed to be rolled over within the year. It was an accident waiting to happen. After the Russian default in 1998, capital flows from abroad dried up. Within a short period, the Brazilian currency fell from 1.20 reais per dollar at the beginning of 1999 to 2.15 reais per dollar in February; that is, one Brazilian real bought only 56 percent as many dollars as before.[14] Given Brazil's history with hyperinflation, there was an understandable degree of panic.

In a remarkable turn of events, the president of Brazil, Fernando Henrique Cardoso, took the bold step of appointing the forty-one-year-old Arminio Fraga to head Brazil's central bank. Until that point, Fraga had been working as a trader for George Soros, whose fund presumably was making money off Brazil's currency woes. Critics in Brazil thought the Fraga appointment was like having the fox guard the henhouse. What Fraga did was even more shocking; instead of opting for a devaluation of the currency or a crawl with a much faster rate of depreciation, he produced a plan that involved floating the currency. To consider how radical this was at the time, recall the postmortems on the Mexican crisis, many of which advocated some version of sticking to a peg.

If there is no peg, how to anchor inflation? Following the example of several advanced economies, most notably including New Zealand, Canada, and the United Kingdom, Fraga instituted inflation targeting, whereby, very crudely put, the central bank sets forth targets for the path of inflation and adjusts its short-term policy interest rates as needed to keep inflation on track. This had not previously been done in emerging markets; Mexico's central bank, under Guillermo Ortiz, instituted its own version of inflation targeting a couple of years later, in 2001. What made Fraga's move so astounding was that central bank independence is normally a key institutional requirement for inflation targeting to succeed. Without independence, the central bank will constantly be forced to succumb to political influence – for example, inflationary finance, where the central bank prints money to soak up government debt, without worrying about the effect on inflation. Fraga managed to use inflation targeting as a mechanism to assert de facto central bank independence, even though there was no legislation to that effect. President Cardoso's strong public support was critical. It must be added that even with Fraga's extremely thoughtful implementation of central bank independence, it still might not have worked without a major loan from the IMF to bridge the transition to stability, especially in 2002, when Brazil was coming under fire from international speculators in anticipation of the election of the left-wing president Lula da Silva (who served for eight years, and then returned as president again in 2023).

While at the IMF, I traveled to Brasilia, the capital in the north of Brazil where the central bank was located, just to understand better for myself whether the central bank's operating independence was to be believed. I also needed to decide how to advise the IMF's managing director, Horst Köhler, on plans to offer Brazil a $40 billion bailout loan. I was impressed by what Brazil was doing, and my assessment probably helped a little in pushing through the loan, as Köhler knew me to be skeptical of undertaking large bailouts without forcing foreign lenders to write down their debts first. Years later, the idea of forcing creditor write-downs in unsustainable debt situations became a core tenet of IMF policy (at least in theory); back then it was heretical.

I got to meet the former president Cardoso a few years later when I gave a lecture in São Paulo, after which he gave comments. It is always something of an out-of-body experience to meet a leader whom you have followed for years and whose policies and decisions have been so consequential. Personally, I view Fernando Henrique Cardoso as one of the great Latin American leaders of the twentieth century. Given my early research on the topic, perhaps I am a little biased by his courageous decision to give the central bank so much de facto independence and to stick by it when the going got tough. Formal central bank independence took much longer. It was finally granted in 2021 (technically only "autonomy" was granted), and although the topic remains fraught politically, there is little question that Brazil's central bank is one of the country's most trusted institutions.[15]

Now, with three decades of hindsight after our "moneymoon" in Brazil, I perhaps better understand my Brazilian students' perspectives on the 1990s exchange rate peg, which seemed reasonable to them but patently unsustainable to me. In reality, after a prolonged era of ultra-high inflation and hyperinflation, and with a still-nascent democracy after years of military dictatorship, there was no way to wave a magic wand and have a stable monetary regime overnight. There had to be some transition, and the 1994 Real Plan, for all its limitations, has to be credited as a critical first step out of an extremely difficult situation. Without the intermediate exchange rate stabilization phase, it would have been well-nigh impossible for Fraga's inflation-targeting regime to have taken root. In this sense, Columbia's Jeffery Sachs (whose recommendation of fixed rates was mentioned in chapter 12), and my students Cristina and Afonso, who were happy if Brazil could get just a couple of decent years, had a point. After a period of extreme monetary distress, sometimes a pegged exchange rate system can be the "least bad choice," even if it makes another deep crisis a few years down the road inevitable.

Nevertheless, Brazil's transition to stability is not yet complete. Despite its impressive revolution in monetary policy, Brazil still has some of the highest real interest rates in the world, particularly for consumer lending, and is typically in competition with Turkey for having the highest real interest rates of any emerging-market economy. It is a complex problem, and there are many causes, but certainly the legacy of recurrent very high inflation is one that Brazilians have not yet entirely forgotten. Many macroeconomists have the idea that if a country introduces inflation targeting, the problem is permanently solved. As I shall argue in the last part of this book, this view is quite naive, even for a country like the United States.

CHAPTER 14

LEBANON AND ARGENTINA

Unique or Prototypical?

Perhaps the most remarkable case of a dollar peg is Lebanon's from 1997 to 2019. The fact that Lebanon managed to hold on to its rigidly fixed rate despite extremely high debt and persistently large deficits was long one of the great anomalies in international finance, given that Lebanon is situated in a difficult neighborhood, with borders to both Israel and Syria. Before being torn apart by a brutal civil war that began in 1975, and even for some time after the civil war began, Lebanon was the region's most reliable financial center, effectively the Switzerland of the Middle East.

Given how exchange rate pegs were falling one after another in the late 1990s and early 2000s, few economists imagined the peg would last nearly as long as it did when Lebanese prime minister Rafic Hariri, accompanied by his finance minister, economy minister, and central bank governor, came to the IMF in November 2002. Meeting Hariri was one of the most intellectually and emotionally impactful experiences of my time at the IMF. Hariri had come to the IMF in advance of a donor conference for Lebanon to be held in Paris. The Lebanese government was not seeking IMF resources. However, Lebanon's donors—mainly Arab countries such as Saudi Arabia—wanted the IMF's help to stabilize the country's economy. Presumably, with a strong macroeconomic framework in place, aid funds could be employed effectively. Hence Prime Minister Hariri paid a visit to Horst Köhler, the IMF's managing director, who in turn asked me to come to the meeting at his office.

The managing director had me sit next to him. Facing us were Hariri and his three ministers. The prime minister somberly explained his country's challenges with reconstruction, how important it was to receive the planned aid, and how he hoped the IMF might be helpful. Rafic Hariri exuded gravitas and experience; he commanded confidence.

Köhler was sympathetic, but he knew he had to be realistic; there was one thorny issue that particularly concerned him about the sustainability of Lebanon's plan. He asked me to explain why, after so many exchange rate crises, the IMF had become skeptical about the sustainability of overly rigid fixed exchange rates.[1]

Addressing the Lebanese prime minister, I discussed how the experience of Europe, Asia, Mexico, Brazil, and most recently Argentina had led many economists, including myself, to believe that rigidly fixed exchange rates can be very problematic. Given Lebanon's high debt, high government deficits, and seemingly unsustainable current account deficits, its fixed exchange rate regime had to be considered quite vulnerable. Had Lebanon considered moving to a more flexible regime before going to donors? Hariri listened patiently and then said something to the effect of, "Well, we view our dollar exchange rate peg as an important source of stability, and we are not considering changing it at this time." He then turned to his ministers to elaborate. One of them explained that standard Western economics is based on the idea that wages and prices are very inflexible in the short run; canonical Keynesian monetary policy and exchange rate prescriptions flow from this. Lebanon is a completely different kind of society where people are used to bargaining over everything and the notion of rigid wages and prices just does not hold. Thanks to this, its economy does not need the exchange rate to cushion shocks in the same way as most advanced economies.

The next morning, I learned that the finance minister wanted to meet privately. My staff quickly found a small interior meeting room with a window to the hallway. We sat at opposite sides of a long, narrow wooden table, each accompanied by one aide. The minister wanted to revisit the discussion of Lebanon's exchange rate regime. He assured me that both his ministry and the central bank fully understood the inherent risks. However, there was something further that the IMF should know before even lightly suggesting that Lebanon abandon an exchange rate system that had so far remained intact. Although I do not have the exact quote, it was something to the effect of, "You do realize that there are some very 'heavy people' who have their money in Lebanon? If the finance ministry were to announce tomorrow that Lebanon is going to change its fixed dollar exchange rate, I would be found floating face down in the Beirut River the next day." Point taken.

In the end, Lebanon kept its exchange rate peg, despite its high debt and persistent deficits. The finance minister stayed alive. Observing this normally impossible achievement — maintaining a fixed rate while perpetually bleeding reserves — was like watching a magician levitate his assistant on stage.

At the donor conference in Paris later in November 2002, the international community pledged some $4.4 billion, although only $2.5 billion was ultimately delivered. In exchange, Lebanon agreed to privatize key industries, pay down debt, cut recurrent expenditures, and increase tax revenues.[2] Although it always appeared likely that Lebanon was receiving money through the back door to prop up the regime, the exact contours of that aid are still not fully clear.

I was back teaching at Harvard when news of Hariri's assassination broke in 2005. With the memory of our meeting still fresh in my mind, it was pretty jarring. For Lebanon, it was tragic to lose such a great leader, and it was a defining moment in Middle East politics, marking Lebanon's long descent into Iranian-backed Hezbollah dominance. The experience of Lebanon also shows that there are extreme cases in which politics can trump both economics and financial markets for an exceptionally long time. In 2019, Lebanon effectively ended its fixed exchange rate regime and has since defaulted on its debt.

Lebanon is a very important country geopolitically, but its GDP is a twentieth of Argentina's, which has been a vastly bigger borrower from the IMF. When I arrived in Washington as chief economist at the IMF in the summer of 2001, Argentina was already in deep trouble. It had gone through recurrent programs with the IMF, which kept giving Argentina funds to temporarily plug the holes in the country's fiscal plumbing and to bolster confidence. By August 2001, the country was clearly in a tight spot; it already had a lot of debt that needed to be refinanced, and it was still running deficits. Like Brazil and Mexico in the 1990s, Argentina had what seemed to be a greatly overvalued exchange rate. This time, it wanted another $10 billion.[3]

Argentina, like Lebanon, had managed to keep its fixed exchange rate longer than Obstfeld and I would have guessed possible. In part, this might have been because it had adopted a stronger kind of exchange rate peg, a currency board, which for younger readers one might say is more akin to a dollar "stablecoin," a topic we will turn to in a later chapter.

In principle, the Argentine government was holding one dollar of hard currency reserves for every peso the central bank issued, so pesos were fully backed at the official one-to-one dollar exchange rate. Advocates of currency boards will tell you that this is all there is to it. In reality, there was the tough question of what to do in case of a bank run, since the Argentine central bank had barely enough dollars to cover the peso currency supply, much less serve as a full-blown lender of last resort to the country's dollar-based financial system. Recall that when the Hong Kong dollar was attacked in 1998, the Hong Kong Monetary Authority not only had enough dollars on hand to buy back all the paper currency and bank reserves it had outstanding; it also had enough to cover checking (or "current") accounts as well. Since the government is only directly guaranteeing paper currency (and bank reserves), not every liability in the financial system, it may seem excessive to hold dollars to bail out banks and not just the government. The problem is that a run on the banking system can quickly swell the currency supply.

Be that as it may, by mid-2001 Argentina no longer had enough dollar resources even to back its currency supply. On top of that, the government had issued a large quantity of bonds abroad (over $100 billion) and was running a large government deficit.

It would not be giving away any great secrets to say that the IMF's management and senior staff were in constant meetings about whether another loan just might work this time, whether the exchange rate system was sustainable, and in general, how to help. More than any other time, it struck me how messy the real world is compared with the models we economists have developed. Still, having a firm and active grasp of core economic models proved quite useful as a frame of reference across endless days of policy debate, as we kept circling back to the same set of problems, including Argentina's perennial difficulties in balancing its budget and its rigidly fixed exchange rate regime. Not only do standard open-economy macroeconomic models help crystallize some important truths, but knowing them makes it much easier to remember what you said the previous day! Being clear and consistent in policy advice is important, though one must also remember that even the best economic models have their limitations.

The Argentine government definitely wanted the money, ostensibly to help its people, though surely also so that it could cling to power. From the perspective of Argentine citizens, however, there were big downsides. What was the use of getting another IMF loan if the money was going to be used to pay off creditors, especially if Argentina was going to end up defaulting anyway?

As painful as defaulting on private creditors might be, these creditors can typically be browbeaten into negotiating a partial default so that the country can resume normal activities. Admittedly, the negotiations can take years. Nevertheless, defaulting on the IMF, which is regarded as the uber-senior creditor in international-finance circles, is much harder to do, even for Argentina. Why not let Argentina first come to a deal with its foreign lenders to write down its debt and only then come in? Alas, as already emphasized, such thoughts were still considered too radical.

By taking even more IMF money, it was as if the Argentine government were placing a bet with a bookie with little chance of success, and when that bet failed, Argentine citizens would have to pay it back. Economists refer to such loans as "gambling for redemption." The overwhelming sentiment of the IMF's professional staff was that the odds of success were slim. That was certainly the private-sector view: Argentine government debt that summer was selling at a steep discount.

At one point, grasping at straws, the U.S. Treasury thought that it had found a clever financial-engineering solution to the problem. The Treasury wanted the Argentines to use IMF funds to buy back a portion of their own debt, which was, after all, selling at a deep discount. If Argentina's debt was selling for twenty-five cents on the dollar, then one dollar of IMF aid could be used to retire four dollars of loans, or so the Treasury thinking went. Buybacks of various sorts were all the rage in the 1980s, and the idea was showered with praise by nongovernmental organizations, political leaders, and the media. Unfortunately, on deeper inspection by economists, the whole idea of buybacks turned out to be extremely dubious.[4] The problem is that when a poor, developing economy owes far more than it is ever likely to repay, even a very large percentage reduction in the face value of its debt might still not be enough to make the country solvent; all that happens is that the market price of the remaining debt gets bid up. In reality, buybacks end up being a boondoggle for creditors. They get cash up front from the sale without giving up any meaningful leverage in extracting maximal future repayments. By 2001, this insight had become common wisdom — except evidently to the upper echelons of the U.S. Treasury Department. Fortunately, there were some staff at the Treasury who got the point, and after some back-and-forth with the IMF research department, the buyback idea was killed.

Ultimately, the Argentine government got its $10 billion loan. The IMF and the U.S. Treasury Department probably understood the situation to be hopeless but did not like the optics of appearing to abandon Argentina, especially after all the complaints about the IMF's handling of the Asia crisis in the 1990s. Also, there were a couple of important players who insisted that "it just might work" and argued that this was a "Diamond-Dybvig" multiple-equilibrium problem and that the loan might help coordinate speculators on the "good" equilibrium.[5] Douglas Diamond and Philip Dybvig were awarded the Nobel Prize in 2022 for articulating circumstances in which having a lender of last resort with deep pockets and powerful taxation tools could prevent bank runs and make everyone better off. It's a beautiful piece of work that I regularly teach.

Unfortunately, its rationale for large-scale bailouts is often abused by policymakers looking for a rationale to bail out financial-sector firms or, in the case of the IMF, countries. Part of the Diamond-Dybvig model's undeniable elegance comes from making the simplifying assumption that the borrower is completely trustworthy and is not going to try to game the system. In practice, a borrower (or financial firm) that is not so trustworthy will have every incentive to take big risks knowing that it will keep the rewards if things go well and get bailed out if things go badly.

Given Argentina's recurrent defaults and its difficulties meeting the targets set out in earlier IMF programs, appeals to the Diamond-Dybvig analogy seemed a painful stretch, trying to produce a technical rationale for what was fundamentally a political decision to bail out a country that had thoroughly lost the confidence of the private sector. In the end, the bailout failed spectacularly. Argentina's endemic fiscal and current account deficits continued, speculators kept up the pressure, and Argentina kept bleeding its scarce remaining dollar reserves to satisfy the market.

As chief economist at the IMF, I was careful not to give any public commentary on Argentina. However, in December 2001, in preparing an update to the *World Economic Outlook*, we pretty much had to include an extended discussion of Argentina's economic challenges. The *World Economic Outlook* predicted that the Argentine economy would likely face a third consecutive year of recession (however optimistic the IMF's August 2001 program might have once been) and further stated, "Argentina has continued to battle with a recession since then [August], reigniting doubts regarding the sustainability of the fiscal position and the exchange rate regime."[6]

Until then, the IMF had studiously refrained from drawing any connection between Argentina's persistent yawning deficits and its exchange rate regime, despite this issue being at the heart of the best-known models of speculative attack on fixed exchange rate regimes. The wording on fixed rates and deficits in the *World Economic Outlook*'s discussion of Argentina was approved by the IMF's executive board without controversy — which was a surprise — probably because the optimists were growing very few in number.

Out in the world, though, there was a belief that the IMF might stand by Argentina with yet another loan if needed to prop up its fixed-rate regime for a couple more months. So, when it came time for me to present the *World Economic Outlook* findings at the usual press conference, the new wording, buried as it was in chapter 3, commanded attention. When pressed to speak about the issue, I matter-of-factly stated, "The mix of fiscal policy, debt, and the exchange rate regime is not sustainable. The authorities recognize that, and it is also discussed in the *World Economic Outlook*."[7]

Within a few days, Argentina went off its fixed exchange rate; shortly thereafter it defaulted on its debt and began a long cycle of renegotiation. At the time, it was the largest sovereign default in history (later to be surpassed by Greece). Famously, even as the Argentine government was telling creditors in 2002 that it needed a massive haircut on its $100 billion debt, data on international capital flows from the Bank for International Settlements showed that private Argentine citizens had squirreled away at least that much in Miami—money that the Argentine government's creditors could not reach.

As of this writing, Argentina is once again the IMF's most problematic debtor, this time because in 2019 the IMF once again made a large loan without first forcing private creditors to write down their debt and thereby effectively assumed a large chunk of that private debt. It is a dance that never seems to end.

Policymakers' attraction to fixed exchange rates began to wane after the 1990s and particularly after Argentina. Over time, the advice from places like the IMF became that, with rare exceptions, no country should consider having too rigid an exchange rate. In fact, at one point, the IMF's Stanley Fischer suggested that the world would likely gravitate toward two polar extremes: either countries would have a fairly flexible exchange rate, or if a group of countries wanted to sustain fixed rates among themselves, they would need to adopt a common currency. It may be possible to temporarily fix an exchange rate in anticipation of a country's eventual entry into a currency union as, for example, Belgium and Austria did—they pegged to the deutsche mark in the early 1980s and then moved smoothly into the euro. Estonia later did the same.

There are exceptions to the rule. Among larger economies, we have already mentioned Hong Kong; another is Saudi Arabia. Saudi Arabia's foreign revenues are overwhelmingly in oil, which is priced in dollars. Moreover, its oil reserves are still plentiful, with the marginal cost of extraction low by international standards. At present, Saudi Arabia is a large net creditor to the rest of the world. Going forward, however, maintaining the peg could prove more difficult, particularly as the country engages in massive investment—notably in its Saudi Vision 2030 projects—to transition away from oil dependence. As currently planned, the projects involve investment at a level that could require hundreds of billions of dollars in foreign borrowing, which would obviously increase the vulnerability of a rigidly fixed exchange rate. As just one example, "The Line" project envisions a narrow linear city of over 100 miles stretching from dessert valleys to the Red Sea, and housing nine million residents, with no roads and no cars.[8] It is a commendably visionary project, but it's hard to see how Saudi Arabia's current fixed exchange rate regime can survive such a radical transformation of the country's business model, especially since it implies going from being a major creditor to being a major debtor.

LEBANON AND ARGENTINA

The general principle is that it is better to exit from a position of relative strength than to wait to be forced to exit when overwhelmed by speculators. As we have seen earlier in discussing China, this is easier said than done, though not impossible.

CHAPTER 15

THE TOKYO CONSENSUS

In economics, the questions never change, just the answers.
—JON EATON

So fixed exchange rates are out, right? After their 1997–1998 debt crisis, countries across Asia reported to the IMF that they had decided to adopt flexible exchange rate systems. Yet even a casual glance at their dollar exchange rates showed that in most cases, they were not floating all that much or all that fast. What was going on?

With Asia's two main trading partners, China and the United States (or "Chimerica," as the financial historian Niall Ferguson termed it[1]), on a dollar standard, there was still a very strong incentive for most Asian countries to at least maintain relatively stable dollar exchange rates. For one thing, the so-called Asian supply chain had continued to develop. Intermediate goods would be sourced throughout Asia, sometimes sequentially: cotton produced in the Philippines might be spun into cloth in Thailand, dyed in Vietnam, then assembled in China, all for export to the United States. This trade in turn was linked to a web of financial transactions, which quite naturally were also indexed to dollars. All of this happened organically, essentially driven by network effects that policymakers had to find a way to accommodate.

In principle, Asia could have created a currency union aimed at supporting intra-Asian trade just as the euro was to support intra-European trade. In the early 2000s, this would have been politically infeasible given that Japan's economy was still considerably larger than China's; and although fading, there was still some lingering distrust from events surrounding World War II. China had nowhere near reached the level of institutional development at which the renminbi could be contemplated as an alternative to the dollar. Foreign investors could not even acquire renminbi bonds. To put things in perspective: When, in 2016, the IMF's treasurer needed to acquire renminbi bonds to integrate the renminbi into the IMF's index of core currencies (its special drawing rights, to be discussed later in chapter 17), the IMF still had to place and confirm orders by fax.

A currency union without either of the region's two most important economies would be pointless. India — with its high tariffs and relatively isolationist development strategy — was not in the game, despite its rapidly expanding outsourcing sector.

A number of influential left-leaning economists pushed for restoring strong capital controls,[2] advice that some highly interventionist socialist governments outside Asia welcomed with open arms. In 2003, Argentine president Néstor Kirchner and Brazilian president Lula da Silva signed the "Buenos Aires Consensus" on macroeconomic policy and capital controls, which was intended to run counter to the "Washington consensus" that called for relatively open markets and stable macroeconomic policies.[3] In practice, Venezuela was of the same mind. None of these countries fared particularly well in the ensuing two decades, despite high prices for their commodity exports through much of the period. The Buenos Aires Consensus was a dud.

Fortunately, Asia's policymakers were reluctant to follow this path. Given that their economies were far more open to trade than Latin America's, capital-control leakage would have been extremely difficult to control. We have already mentioned Europe after World War II, for example, where capital controls were extensive on paper. However, rampant use of under- and over-invoicing of exports and imports dramatically muted their effect. Leakage of this kind amounted to as much as 30 percent of trade for some European countries.[4]

Thus, to stabilize their exchange rates against the dollar, the Asian economies would have to go it alone. The United States certainly wasn't going to help.

Instead of looking to the United States and Europe, which had by and large abandoned exchange market intervention by the 1990s, Asian countries looked to Japan, which for years had successfully intervened in the foreign exchange market to stabilize its currency against the dollar. Whatever Asian politicians' lingering post-war bitterness, they enormously respected Japan's economic success and turned to it as a model to emulate. Perhaps it was politically impossible to call it the "Tokyo consensus." Nevertheless, to a large extent, that is what it was: modified, perhaps even improved, but following the Japanese example more than any other.

One key element was to hold large quantities of (mostly) dollar reserves, even though exchange rates were no longer fixed. By the end of 2002, Japan had amassed a war chest of nearly half a trillion dollars in reserves (today it is roughly $1.2 trillion).[5] Across East Asia, and later South Asia, and eventually even Latin America, everyone else started to do the same. It is sobering to think that, as of the end of 2023, India had foreign exchange reserves of over $600 billion, Brazil about $300 billion, and South Africa much less but still $50 billion.[6]

Piling up dollar reserves is quite an expensive proposition, as interest rates on U.S. Treasuries tend to be much lower than the rates on the domestic debt issued to buy it; after all, the dollar is the global safe asset. A number of Western commentators lamented that Asian countries were not instead relying on the IMF.[7] They evidently did not understand that a big part of the rationale for the reserve buildup was that Asian economies never, ever, wanted to submit again to an IMF program, which they viewed as part and parcel of their painful 1990s recessions. This might not be fair to the IMF given that part of its role in any country is to let its political leaders blame the IMF for the austerity their impecuniousness or poor financial regulation would have led to, regardless. Be that as it may, fear of a second "IMF crisis" was a compelling political argument for countries to build up war chests so that they could bail out their own financial systems if needed. Conveniently, it also gave ample ammunition to help stabilize exchange rates.

Normally, the United States and Europe would have complained about such behavior and pointed to the IMF's Articles of Agreement, as the United States did with China. However, after the disastrous 1997–1998 crisis, and especially after all the criticism that followed, neither the United States nor the IMF was inclined to challenge the Asian reserve buildups.

Besides, the IMF had let Japan accumulate reserves for decades, long after the Bretton Woods fixed exchange rate regime had collapsed. Why shouldn't the rest of Asia be allowed to do the same? As discussed in detail in chapter 3, the United States did crack the whip in 1985, when it forced Japan to allow its exchange rate to appreciate under the Plaza Accord. However, although Japan yielded on allowing the yen to rise sharply, the Bank of Japan soon returned to accumulating dollars. The United States pressured Japan to stop from time to time, as I witnessed at a meeting in 2003 on the perimeter of the IMF annual meetings in Dubai. The U.S. officials insisted that Japan needed to start setting an example for China. At the meeting, the Japanese finance minister seemed to agree and acquiesce. I left the room thinking that the whole issue had been settled, and continued to believe that until I looked at the data quite some time after. In fact, what I had witnessed was a master class in diplomacy. Japan continued to accelerate its intervention in the dollar-yen market, and its reserves climbed 30 percent to over $800 billion by the end of the year. Japan was setting an example for China, just not the one the United States intended.

The fact that Asian central banks were accumulating dollars is not quite enough to explain why they were so successful in dampening short-term exchange rate volatility compared with most open economies. As we have already seen in our postmortem of the early 1990s European exchange rate crises, even if a country has enough reserves to buy back its entire currency supply, speculators can still stare the central bank down if its underlying policies are inconsistent.

Thus, accumulating reserves was a piece of the puzzle, but not the complete solution (unless those reserves were as massive as Hong Kong's). Three further factors helped. First, Asian countries restored some of their international capital controls, particularly on inflows of funds. Second, and much more importantly, they improved domestic regulation, strengthening capital requirements on banks, for example. Although not technically a restriction on international capital flows, domestic capital requirements force banks to worry more about their collateral positions (the liquid assets they have to deal with loan losses or bank runs). Forcing banks to pay more attention to their capital structure generally makes foreign exchange market intervention more effective because it constrains banks' ability to fully take advantage of any arbitrage opportunities that might arise and that could potentially work against the central banks' intent.

This point is so fundamental, and so little understood, that it is worth a brief digression to expand on it. Suppose, for example, that the Japanese central bank were to buy yen bonds and sell U.S. dollar bonds with the intent of strengthening the yen-dollar exchange rate, a routine operation. The basic idea is that with fewer yen bonds and more dollar bonds out there, investors will bid more for Japanese assets. If banks were to try to take advantage of the new situation by borrowing in yen at a low interest rate (essentially creating new yen debt quite similar to what the central bank just tried to soak up), and then investing in U.S. dollars at a higher interest rate (also a routine operation), their actions would counter the central bank's, undoing some or all of the exchange rate effects. Collateral requirements limit banks' ability to engage in such arbitrage. Thus when one talks about international capital market restrictions, as policymakers and economists so often do, it is very important take into account domestic capital market regulations at the same time.

The third critical adjustment that many Asian countries made was to give their central banks greater agency, if not outright independence. The Bank of Japan itself gradually asserted greater independence from the all-powerful Ministry of Finance, both legally — for example, through an amendment to the Bank of Japan Act in 1997 — and operationally, through the formal adoption of inflation targeting in 2013.[8] The Bank of Korea followed a similar path, and other Asian central banks were also gradually given more resources over time, which allowed them to strengthen their research departments and gain stature.

Maintaining low inflation is a critical element of perhaps the most important development in Asian finance, which has been to deepen domestic markets. For starters, this broadens the market for government debt, allowing governments to place public debt without having to tap dollar markets. Also, deeper domestic capital markets make it easier for producers of non-traded goods, whose revenues are in local currency, to borrow in local currency instead of dollars, which thereby reduces the country's overall foreign exchange risk.

One leading international policymaker who emphasized this point quite clearly was Zeti Akhtar Aziz, the governor of Bank Negara Malaysia, the central

THE TOKYO CONSENSUS

bank of Malaysia, from 2000 to 2016 and the first woman in that position. Dr. Zeti was at one point the longest-serving central bank governor in the world. She is widely respected and the recipient of many awards and had even been considered by some as a possible candidate for managing director of the IMF (though at least through the writing of this book that post has always been held by a European). Dr. Zeti emphasized that although deepening domestic markets is hard work, requiring multifaceted improvements in regulation and governance, many emerging-market central banks were determined to do it. Fast forwarding to the present, there is no question that the improvements have been notable, as Dr. Zeti had predicted, and not just in Asia. That said, there is still ample room for improvement. Even today, Asian stocks tend to trade at lower price-earnings ratios than U.S. or European stocks, in no small part because capital market regulation (including transparency, antitrust, and corporate governance) is less developed throughout most of Asia.[9]

Last but not least, central banks were careful to soften their pegs, allowing for modest adjustment in day-to-day fluctuations and potentially large adjustment in the event of a crisis. For example, instead of the kind of rigid dollar peg that China had instituted from 1995 to 2005, Singapore and Malaysia adopted softer exchange rate pegs that allowed movement within narrow bands. Why should having a small amount of wiggle room make such a big difference? Wouldn't investors just blow right through it? Although one cannot say with confidence — the academic literature has not yet really addressed this question — my conjecture (already hinted at in chapter 13) is that by weakening the commitment to the peg, the government sends a strong signal to the private sector that it needs to allow for the possibility that the fixed exchange rate might one day move a lot. By injecting some risk into the game, the central bank can blur the bullseye painted on its back when a rigid peg starts to look unsustainable.

While all of this was going on, research on understanding the workings of Asia's evolving new exchange rate regimes lagged, in part because of the wide gap between how countries were actually managing their exchange rates and what they were reporting publicly. Despite extensively intervening to stabilize their exchange rates, most Asian economies told the IMF that they had adopted flexible exchange rates, and the IMF duly recorded their regimes as flexible in its official exchange rate classification document.[10]

It was only after the appearance of a couple of academic articles showing how absurd this was that the IMF began to include more nuance in its characterization of exchange rate regimes to better fit reality. In an article published in 2004, Carmen Reinhart and I showed that virtually half the countries that reported to have a flexible exchange rate arrangement in their official pronouncements to the IMF had a de facto inflexible regime, and vice versa.[11]

One must give Asian policymakers their due. By putting a bit more "sand in the wheels" of their financial systems, without necessarily using heavy-handed controls, and by having ample reserves on hand, Asia's central banks could stabilize exchange rates more effectively than economists had previously imagined.[12]

In sum, many emerging markets, particularly in Asia, did not so much reject the Washington consensus as choose to adopt key elements and insert their own improvements. Asian policymakers understood that although capital controls and financial market regulation have their uses, they cannot compensate for deep inconsistencies in macroeconomic policies. Asian policymakers thus built up reserves, strengthened regulation, and introduced some controls (particularly on inflows); the end result looked a lot more like a Tokyo consensus than a Buenos Aires consensus.

CHAPTER 16

FIXED EXCHANGE RATES REDUX

> An economist is someone who sees something
> in practice and asks if it is possible in theory.

Many economists in the early 2000s, including me, regarded Asia's steady buildup of dollar reserves as exacerbating problematic imbalances in the global economy—a euphemism for the U.S. current account deficit, which at that time was absorbing most of the world's surpluses, much of which was emanating from Asia and the Middle East. While in the end access to massive global capital inflows almost surely exacerbated the excesses that led to the United States' real estate crisis that started in 2007 and the global financial crisis in 2008, research over the ensuing decade highlighted many subtleties that had not before been recognized. Maybe Asian policymakers had gotten their exchange rate policies (mostly) right.

In a series of highly original papers, three economists at Deutsche Bank—Michael Dooley, David Folkerts-Landau, and Peter Garber, all former academics—argued that Asia was just following the same development strategy as Europe had used after the war, employing a mix of intervention and capital controls to maintain an undervalued exchange rate in order to promote growth.[1] They described the international monetary system as having evolved into a Bretton Woods II system analogous to the post-war Bretton Woods system, which mainly encompassed the United States, Europe, and Japan. In their view, this was not a dangerous and unfair system about to blow up into crises. They argued that the Asian economies—and a few others elsewhere that emulated them—were following a very reasonable development strategy. Instead of complaining, U.S. borrowers, both public and private, should be happy with how the system allowed Americans to access enormous sums of money from abroad at far lower interest rates than might otherwise be the case. The core contributions in the "Deutsche Bank trio" papers were famously memorialized in Ben Bernanke's celebrated "global savings glut speech" in 2005, which drew heavily on their ideas.[2]

The Deutsche Bank trio's message was that if Asia was to be accorded the same latitude the United States had given post-war Europe, then its big current account surpluses should be tolerated or even welcomed. It was a clever argument, implicitly chastising the United States and Europe for having a double standard in not accepting from Asia economic policies they had condoned for themselves. The analogy was very far from perfect. Post-war Europe, for example, had not run consistently large trade surpluses against the United States; many countries had run deficits. Instead, Europe mainly accumulated dollars by selling assets such as land and factories, as we shall explore further in chapter 21. And it is far from clear that Europe's exchange rates were undervalued. In fact, with only a couple of exceptions (mainly Germany), post-war Europe needed capital controls to protect their overvalued exchange rates, and to conserve precious dollars. By contrast, as explained in the previous chapter, most Asian economies were really following Japan, the modern success in their own neighborhood, not Europe from another era. In particular, they were, if anything, holding down their exchange rates against the dollar, not propping them up. Thus the Tokyo consensus is a more accurate description of the East Asian development model.

Still, the Bretton Woods II analysis was provocative and deeply insightful. Perhaps the technical piece of the trio's original analysis that was the most strained—even though most leading policy economists apparently agreed with it—was the idea that China was relying mainly on intervention to indefinitely maintain an artificially undervalued exchange rate, and thereby gain a competitive advantage. We have already addressed this issue, but it bears repeating in this context. A country's competitiveness depends not only on the exchange rate but also on its domestic prices and wages. If China makes imports more expensive relative to its exports by temporarily holding down its exchange rate — either through intervention or by using conventional monetary policy — then local and global demand will shift toward Chinese goods and bid up their prices. In the long run, the resulting inflation will undo any competitive advantage gained by keeping its exchange rate from appreciating. Thus, if market forces are making the real exchange rate appreciate (the exchange rate adjusted for national price differences), monetary policy can at best slow them down, and certainly not for years on end.[3]

In fact, as again we have discussed earlier, the exchange rate undervaluation story misses perhaps the most important device the Chinese authorities were using to keep their economy so hypercompetitive: the steady migration of millions of people each year from agrarian rural China to its cities and manufacturing centers. The real problem that Western economies were facing was a never-ending stream of impoverished rural Chinese being lifted out of desperate poverty each year through the chance to work in the productive city centers. Exchange market intervention might have contributed to the supposed undervaluation of China's currency, but it was likely secondary. Nevertheless, many aspects of the trio's analysis were spot on, in particular the notion that Asia's high savings rate was helping push down global interest rates, thereby easing borrowing conditions in the United States.

A second qualification to the trio's thesis was that the inflow of cheap funding from Asia was of unalloyed benefit to the United States. It was not. It might have been if U.S. banking regulators had been more attuned to the so-called capital inflows problem instead of thinking that financial crises happen only to emerging markets. When foreign capital pours into a country with fragilities in its financial regulation, it can painfully expose the gaps. Thus, whereas record U.S. borrowing from abroad did not by itself cause the global financial crisis, it surely added fuel to the fire.

It is not as if regulators saw nothing strange going on. During the mid-2000s, Alan Greenspan, the Federal Reserve chair, gave numerous speeches in which he noted that the gaping U.S. current account deficit had come alongside a rush by Americans to take out second mortgages on their homes and a stunning drop in the personal savings rate from 6 percent in 1993 to 1 percent in 2005.[4] A chunk of these loans, effectively coming from Asia but intermediated by the U.S. financial system, contributed to the subprime mortgage crisis. Unfortunately, although Greenspan and his staff thought enough of the correlation to make it a recurrent theme in his speeches, that insight did not translate into tighter financial regulation. If the IMF were advising an emerging market that was experiencing a large capital inflow, one of its core pieces of advice would be to tighten financial regulation as a first line of defense. The United States did not do so.[5]

Disagreeing with the Fed chair's view in that era was futile. I once had the experience of speaking immediately after Chairman Greenspan at a conference. It was at the CATO Institute in November 2003.[6] Greenspan was absolutely at the height of his fame—he had earned the moniker "The Maestro"—and the huge audience soaked up his every word with rapt attention; his speech was covered live by several business news channels worldwide.[7]

Speaking directly after the chair of the Federal Reserve is not an easy assignment. You have to fight through the noise of all the camera crews loudly packing up and clearing the room, and then try to seem unfazed while half the audience is exiting—some of them to file their stories, others to call their trading desks, and others just to take a coffee break, having arrived quite early to get a seat. And some of those still in the room are whispering and exchanging thoughts excitedly on what they just heard.

Greenspan had focused his remarks on the massive U.S. current account deficit, giving all the ways the borrowing gap might get closed and explaining why—thanks to the depth and diversity of the U.S. economy—basically nothing was likely to go wrong. My remarks took a darker view of the global imbalances. I noted that when a country is borrowing at this scale—the United States was soaking up more than half of all the trade surpluses the rest of the world was generating—there can be unknowns lurking, and I raised the possibility of a destabilizing exchange rate depreciation. Back in late 2003, at the time of the conference, it had not yet occurred to me that the biggest problems for the United States were rooted in regulatory failures, failures that all the borrowing from abroad would inevitably amplify; that epiphany came later while I was working on my book with Carmen Reinhart ahead of the 2008–2009 global financial crisis. Still, it seemed Panglossian to just assert that the U.S. current account was not telling us anything about risks posed to the United States and the world.

FIXED EXCHANGE RATES REDUX

A journalist came up to me afterward, perhaps the only one of the dozens in attendance that had stayed for our panel. "So, when do you think the U.S. current account might lead to problems?" he asked. I mentioned the Dornbusch quote on how crises take longer to happen than you think (cited at the beginning of chapter 8); that did not seem of any interest to him. The journalist responded, "So you mean nothing is likely to happen in the next few weeks?" "Quite unlikely," I responded. The journalist grimaced and clearly decided there was nothing to write about.

The U.S. current account deficit has since fallen sharply, from a peak of 6 percent of GDP in 2006 to an average of only 2.5 percent over the past decade, although that decrease is more the result of the United States suddenly becoming self-sufficient in oil than of a renaissance in manufacturing.[8] China's current account surplus has fallen from 10 percent of GDP in 2007 to less than 2 percent in 2024,[9] in part as a result of the Trump-Biden tariffs. The friction between the two countries has grown dramatically.

To be fair, emerging markets have continued to find ways to mitigate the challenges they face in having to live with the dollar. In the first years after the start of the Covid pandemic, none of the large emerging markets (including Mexico, Brazil, Indonesia, Vietnam, South Africa, and even Turkey) experienced obvious debt distress—not according to the International Monetary Fund, and not according to market interest rate spreads. They instead typically let off steam by allowing their exchange rates to depreciate in response to the global emergency circumstances.

The resilience of large emerging markets in the immediate wake of the pandemic has been something of a surprise for economists given the explosion of interest rates and the sharp appreciation of the U.S. dollar that occurred post-pandemic, and given the slowdown in China that has been the main export destination for more than half of emerging markets. Sure, there were some cases such as Turkey where inflation soared to nearly 100 percent, and where a crisis appeared to be just around the corner. It has not come yet, though, perhaps in part because of all the profits Turkey reaps from helping funnel gray-market goods from Europe into Russia.

The main credit has to go to how emerging-market policymakers have adapted to the dollar-centric world, building up reserves, allowing some ex-

165

change rate flexibility, issuing most government debt in local currency, and frankly, for the most part, adopting relatively conservative monetary and fiscal policies. Emerging central banks have become more independent, and notably they did not make the mistake that advanced economies made after the pandemic by waiting too long to raise interest rates. Instead, given their long experience with major shocks, they knew to raise interest rates proactively, mitigating if not stopping the later rise in inflation. On fiscal policy, emerging markets in the twenty-first century have never bought into the "debt is a free lunch" philosophy that has infected both political parties in the United States, an issue we will return to later. In fact, whereas the U.S. Treasury and Federal Reserve were busy shortening the duration of U.S. debt to benefit from ultra-low short-term interest rates, many emerging markets were willing to pay a premium to lock in low long-term rates. This was a major failure by the United States and could well cost taxpayers potentially hundreds of billions of dollars per year in the coming decade.

At the same time, it is important not to be overly generous to emerging-market policymakers; it is too soon to know whether any large, systemically important emerging markets will have a crisis in the near term. At the IMF we had a saying, "Beware of star pupils."

The Deutsche Bank trio had exposited some of the benefits to the Asian economies' approach of seeking stability in their dollar exchange rates. What about the costs, for example, of losing exchange rate flexibility as a tool for managing stabilization policy? How would their economies adjust in the face of, say, a sudden drop in domestic demand? In principle, allowing the exchange rate to depreciate can help cushion the blow by encouraging citizens to buy more domestic goods and fewer imported ones. Outside of extreme shocks such as the pandemic, most Asian economies did not appear to be doing this.

In one of the most influential international economics papers of the past couple of decades, the French-born, British-based economist Hélène Rey advanced a remarkable proposition: she essentially argued that in the twenty-first century, global financial shocks had become the main source of volatility for most emerging markets and that in this case having a flexible exchange rate is not as helpful for routine short-term stabilization as most economists believed.[10] Before we explore her arguments, it is helpful to step back and briefly review the history of emerging-market capital market integration, as well as conventional thought regarding what kind of exchange rate regime might work best in managing it.

Before World War II, many of today's emerging markets, particularly across Africa and Asia, were still colonies. Integration into global capital markets, such as it was, came mainly through their colonizers, and mainly for the colonizers' benefit. After the war, as one country after another gained independence, most former colonies remained relatively closed to international capital flows. The situation began to change in the 1980s, as countries attempted not only to tap international lending but also to find ways to both diversify risk and access foreign technology. Despite sensitivity to being "recolonized," many countries relaxed restrictions on foreign direct investment, allowing foreign firms to build new factories as well as to acquire existing ones. Local firms that remained independent benefited from stock market liberalizations that enabled foreigners to invest in emerging-market equities. Stock market development was supercharged by the privatization of nationalized companies ranging from utilities to railroads to mining companies, especially as many governments shifted from heavy-handed socialism to more market-oriented economies.

Advanced-economy mutual funds, hedge funds, and pension funds took note of these changes, and advanced-economy regulators started to give these institutions more latitude to diversify into emerging markets. At a deeper level, demographic forces also played a role. Advanced-economy populations were starting to age and save for retirement, whereas emerging markets were still relatively young. The flow was in both directions, as emerging-market wealth holders sought diversification and safety in advanced economies. Many policymakers and academics hailed the changes, albeit with notes of caution from some, particularly on the choice of exchange rate regime.

At least that is how it was framed until just over a decade ago, when Rey argued that exchange rate flexibility is of little use in hiding from the vicissitudes of the global financial cycle. Loosely speaking, the global financial cycle reflects the "risk-on, risk-off" herd behavior of global investors that leads to a remarkable degree of international asset price correlation. The co-movements also have to do with how markets process information about common fundamentals — say, a spike in oil prices or an uptick in Chinese exports that could be indicative of higher global demand in general. Regardless, one robust feature of the global financial cycle is that money tends to flow in and out of emerging markets with a surprisingly high level of synchronicity most of the time, regardless of whether a country is on a fixed or flexible exchange rate regime. This applies to all kinds of liquid capital flows, including bonds, equities, and bank loans. Foreign direct investment — for example, when foreign firms build local factories — is by nature much stickier.

The core problem is that despite enormous growth in recent decades, the typical emerging-economy capital market is still a minnow in the ocean of global capital flows. Particularly when there is a panic or significant rises in risk, foreign investors are notoriously indiscriminate or ignorant, or both. A country's exchange rate regime, or more generally the quality of its policies and institutions, certainly matters, but in the short run these are overwhelmed in a stampede.

Why are capital flows so indiscriminate? It would be hard to overstate how uninformed we Americans are about geography. I confess that as a teenager, when I decided to go by train from France to Yugoslavia to compete in a chess tournament, I had no real idea of what countries I would pass through traveling from Rennes to Zagreb. In the film *Dog Day Afternoon*, from 1975, the actor Al Pacino plays a thief named Sonny, who is holed up inside a bank with hostages. As he and his partner Sal negotiate with the police for a safe escape, Sonny turns to Sal and asks, "Is there any special country you wanna go to?" "Wyoming," Sal suggests. Sonny immediately shoots back, "Sal, Wyoming is not a country." Sal could just as well have been a representative American investor.

Rey further argues that the global financial cycle has become such a major driver of booms and recessions in emerging markets that countries need to find proactive policies to resist it; simply having a flexible exchange rate is not enough. Unfortunately, there are no simple solutions. Part of the answer, she suggests, lies in persuading advanced economies to regulate their own financial systems more vigilantly, especially because large global banks are major channels through which the global financial cycle transmits. Given how inward looking most countries are in their financial-regulation policy, brokering change is going to be a heavy lift, especially in the United States, which is going to look out for its own interests or, in this case, the interests of U.S. banks and financial firms. In the meantime, emerging markets need to try to better regulate their own financial institutions, particularly to dampen lending booms that amplify housing bubbles and other speculative excess.

Regardless, Rey argues that if emerging markets want to have more independent monetary policy, the exchange rate is not a sufficient release valve. It is necessary to have some capital market restrictions; exchange rate flexibility does not matter as much as commonly thought. She disagrees in particular with how Robert Mundell framed exchange rate policy. As discussed in chapter 11, Mundell posited that countries face a "trilemma" in that it is impossible to have fully open capital markets, a fixed exchange rate, and an independent monetary policy. Rey argues that, in fact, the core problem is a dilemma. Countries that want independent monetary policy need to have capital controls. A floating exchange rate is not enough.

Rey's work has helped motivate efforts to understand whether there are intermediate solutions involving some modest use of capital controls and intermediate exchange rate flexibility; we have already mentioned the Asian model as well as Gita Gopinath's research. Although there have been some exciting first steps, achieving clear answers still seems far away.[11]

We do know that countries facing frequent demand or cost shocks can still benefit enormously from having a flexible exchange rate. This is why countries that depend heavily on commodity exports—for example, Canada, New Zealand, Australia, and Chile—often allow shocks to their commodity export basket to be passed through in large part to their exchange rate.[12] That is, if the prices of milk and lamb's wool go up sharply, New Zealand is more likely to allow its exchange rate to appreciate to reflect the higher value of these major exports than to allow the change to pass through quickly to its overall consumer price index. Importantly, during both the global financial crisis and the pandemic, most emerging markets allowed sharp depreciations of their exchange rates to offset the shock, often on the order of 10 to 20 percent. So dilemma or trilemma, it is clear that exchange rate flexibility matters a lot for dealing with very large shocks.

To punctuate the importance of dollar dominance in all of this, Rey argues that although there are many drivers of the global financial cycle, perhaps the most important—or at least the one that can be most concretely identified—is Federal Reserve interest rate policy, which she shows to be very correlated with global financial conditions.[13] Given the outsize weight of the United States in the global equity and bond markets, and the fact that so much global debt is dollar linked, it is easy to believe that Federal Reserve policy plays a central role. Whether this is in fact causal, or just a correlation with the Federal Reserve reacting to global financial conditions, continues to be debated. Nevertheless, the broad point that emerging markets are acutely vulnerable to global financial flows, regardless of their exchange rate regime, is something emerging-market finance ministers and central bankers have become acutely aware of.

PART IV

ALTERNATIVE CURRENCIES

CHAPTER 17

GLOBAL CURRENCIES

The idea of a world currency holds perennial appeal among leading economists. The great John Maynard Keynes envisioned a new, more cooperative global economic system after World War II, and looked to create a global currency to inhabit it. He called for a global central bank or "Clearing Union" to issue the "bancor," derived from the French *bancaire*, meaning "bank gold."[1] Keynes's global governing body would have apportioned the bancor among national central banks according to each nation's share of world trade. Keynes's vision included a scheme for dealing with persistent surplus and deficit countries, particularly to eliminate what he believed to be the "beggar thy neighbor" exchange rate policies of the 1930s. Private international capital markets would be constrained by strict controls, an interesting twist given that Keynes had made quite a bit of money speculating on currencies, and indeed had helped others in the Bloomsbury group do the same. I leave the details to Keynes's biographers to sort out; suffice it to say that the proposal was politically unrealistic at every level, now more so than ever. Economists today don't even completely buy the beggar-thy-neighbor characterization of the 1930s; as one country after another left the gold standard so that it could stimulate its economy through inflation, global demand increased, as economic historian Barry Eichengreen famously demonstrated.[2]

173

ALTERNATIVE CURRENCIES

Toward the end of World War II, with the United Kingdom in economic shambles and the United States holding all the cards, Keynes was clearly hoping that the United Kingdom could preserve at least a modicum of post-war leverage in a global financial system that it had ruled for more than a century. The U.S. negotiator at the Bretton Woods meetings, Harry Dexter White, would have none of it. With all the money and financial power, the United States' preferred post-war monetary system prevailed. Whether Harry Dexter White later became a Soviet spy is yet another sub-plot and has been a matter of passionate dispute among White's biographers.[3]

For now, the closest that Keynes's bancor has come to realization is in the United Federation of Planets' "credits" in Gene Rodenberry's television series *Star Trek*. The series paints a post-capitalist, utopian socialist future; for the series' intensely committed fan base, the world of *Star Trek* is almost reality.[4] And before one of them writes to me, yes, I know, *Star Trek* came out in the late 1960s, so if the International Monetary Fund ever did become a world central bank, it actually would be life imitating art.

Keynes's idea of a world currency has re-emerged in recent years, particularly now that central bank digital currencies are starting to come into play. When the former Bank of England head Mark Carney proposed introducing a synthetic global digital currency to reduce dollar dependence, the idea was greeted with understandable enthusiasm in many circles, especially by many central bankers who regard the centrality of the dollar as destabilizing in their countries. They see Federal Reserve interest rate policy as helping propel a global financial cycle: foreign capital rushes in when investors see low interest rates and relative economic calm in the United States, but then races out even faster when interest rates and risk perceptions turn.[5] And even worse, they see U.S. authorities as having too much control over the global payments system and the flow of information embedded in it. The rest of the world is keen to see the development of an alternative global currency in which other countries, besides just the United States (or another hegemon such as China), have a say.

With all due respect to the remarkable achievements of the euro, it should be pretty obvious now why a global currency won't work. Without political and fiscal union to complement monetary union, a global currency is a recipe for discord and financial crisis. So far, the eurozone has managed to continually evolve, although it has careened from one crisis to another; perhaps one day Europe will reach a level of political unity that will cement the single currency in perpetuity. However, a global currency would have to deal with even larger income gaps, cultural differences, and political chasms than Europe has ever had to face. If a politically cohesive group of European countries has had to navigate so many challenges—the euro is still a work in progress—how is a global currency ever going to work?

Nevertheless, there already exists a nascent global currency with a well-defined governance structure—or at least that is how some would portray it. Back in 1969, the International Monetary Fund introduced the SDR (short for "special drawing right"), which many believed would be a first step toward a global currency. The SDR itself was the outgrowth of many proposals for creating a multilateral currency to substitute for dollar reserves, including plans offered by Yale's Robert Triffin, MIT's Franco Modigliani, and the IMF's research director Edward Bernstein, among others.[6] When I was a graduate student at MIT, Modigliani—a Nobel Prize winner—was legendary for falling asleep in seminars and then suddenly waking up and asking a brilliant and perfectly timed question. (Evidently, the trick was to keep his eyes closed for a few minutes after waking up.) So it does not surprise me that his 1971 plan for reforming the international monetary system is as thorough and comprehensive as anyone's. Modigliani's plan, however, is as totally unrealistic as Keynes's bancor proposal had been. Among other things it requires the United States to redenominate its Treasury bills into SDRs for any foreign central bank that asks, and to make a legally binding international agreement (presumably to be adjudicated by the IMF) to reduce the U.S. deficit whenever it is deemed "excessive" or to increase it whenever it is deemed "insufficient."[7]

The most important thing to know about the SDR is that it is not a currency in any conventional sense. Rather, the SDR is fundamentally an accounting unit that is indexed to a basket of currencies consisting of the U.S. dollar (43 percent of the basket), the euro (29 percent), the Chinese renminbi (12 percent), the Japanese yen (8 percent), and the U.K. pound sterling (7 percent).[8] As of mid-August 2024, one SDR was worth $1.34.[9]

There is no paper SDR currency, and private individuals or firms are not able to directly hold it. There do exist SDR-denominated bonds that private entities can hold; the World Bank periodically issues them to fund its loans to developing countries. The payouts, though, are not in SDR but in one of its constituent currencies, typically dollars.

Instead, the SDR is a "reserve currency" that can only be held by governments in the form of accounts at the IMF. Even in this sense, it is still an accounting unit; should a government cash in its SDRs (as low-income countries typically do soon after they are issued), it receives payments in the form of dollars or other constituent currencies. In normal times, the SDR has simply been an accounting device that the IMF uses to index loans and capital contributions. Hence, when you read a newspaper headline that Argentina is getting a $44 billion loan from the IMF, the amount is technically set in SDRs, and the interest rate is indexed to the rate on the corresponding mix of the underlying national treasury bonds plus a small premium to cover the IMF's lending costs. By the way, the IMF's lending rate is obviously a very good deal for any developing country or emerging market such as Argentina, which would otherwise be paying a much higher rate for hard currency borrowing (e.g., borrowing in dollars or euro). It is polemic nonsense to describe the IMF's lending rate as usurious, as critics sometimes claim.

If this were all that was involved, there would be nothing to it; just a political charade by a U.N. family organization that for ideological reasons doesn't want to admit that the dollar is king. Sure, one can argue that SDR reserves are hedged, except that a simpler way to do that would be to hold a basket of currencies as national central banks do, although more typically the basket is 60 percent dollars rather than 43 percent, as in the SDR.

By denominating all its assets and liabilities in SDRs, the International Monetary Fund does take pressure off its treasurer in managing exchange rate risk. More importantly, it doesn't have to haggle with countries over how their IMF reserves are being held, or with borrowers about how its loans are indexed. There is, however, a much more fundamental property of SDRs that makes them more exceptional. Specifically, with the agreement of its membership, the IMF can essentially spin them out of thin air. Given that SDR payouts are in hard currencies such as the dollar and the euro that are easily spent in world markets, and that these can be issued only by national central banks, where does the money come from? Is it magic?

GLOBAL CURRENCIES

One would think so given the standard claim that SDR allocations cost advanced countries very little, as Treasury Secretary Janet Yellen testified to Congress in 2021.[10] Following similar logic, a number of important thought leaders, including George Soros and Joseph Stiglitz, have argued in favor of issuing SDRs at scale on a perennial basis as a tool for development aid, and not just in global emergencies.[11] (Soros would make use of rich countries' existing holdings.) "Basically it is printing money," Stiglitz told the *Guardian* in 2023, in calling for up to $300 billion per year in new SDR issuance.[12] The logic is that since developing-economy debtors essentially cover the interest payments on any SDRs they borrow, there is really no cost. Countless nongovernmental organizations — for example, Oxfam — often call for the issuance of SDRs as a way of redistributing income from rich to poor. This is a worthy cause, but is the SDR really such a powerful all-purpose instrument?

I have watched my magician friend David Blaine perform some of his incredible card tricks a dozen times now, and I still cannot figure them out. (Our mutual connection was the former world chess champion Bobby Fischer.) I can, however, help elucidate how the SDR works. This is not to say that new issuance is always and everywhere a bad idea; there are emergencies in which it is the only option to get money quickly to poor countries, however inefficient it may be. Still, this is a case in which readers should see through the financial-engineering magic.

To explain the SDR requires a deeper dive into the workings of the International Monetary Fund, which has already been referred to many times in this book. Without understanding the IMF's governance, capacities, and limitations, there is no way to understand its pseudo-currency. We will focus on the essentials.

The International Monetary Fund is a multilateral (that is, multicountry) government agency that was formed, along with its sister agency, the World Bank, at the end of World War II. The two are sometimes referred to as the "Bretton Woods sisters," since they grew out of the same meeting in 1944 that produced the post-war exchange rate system.[13] Today, the IMF has 190 member countries and is broadly charged with maintaining global financial stability. It is somewhat akin to a United Nations for global economic issues, but with a few major caveats.

ALTERNATIVE CURRENCIES

The IMF's executive board, which must approve all major decisions, consists of only twenty-four directors. Each director typically represents multiple constituencies; only a few countries — including the United States, the United Kingdom, Germany, France, Japan, China, and yes, Russia — have their own seats.[14] Second, and even more importantly, the votes of the twenty-four members are not equal. Rather, votes are apportioned according to how much paid-in capital each country has contributed. This capital is the core of the IMF's financing capacity and is lent on a rotating basis, a fundamental accounting issue that sometimes seems to escape debt jubilee enthusiasts: the IMF is limited on the new loans it can make until old loans are repaid. As things stand, Europe's voting share far exceeds its present-day weight in the global economy, particularly as Asia has emerged. Germany alone has almost as large a vote as China even though its economy is a quarter the size. At this writing, the IMF is pushing for an adjustment to increase China's share so that it is more in line with reality. So far, no agreement has been reached. This, in no small part, is because under the current IMF rules, the United States' 16.5 percent voting share is enough to give it veto power over major financing decisions, a privilege no other director enjoys.

Full disclosure: During my tenure as chief economist and director of research at the IMF from 2001 to 2003, I was asked to produce analyses of the SDR. This included a major report to the IMF's executive board, submitted jointly with the IMF's Treasury Department, reporting on the status of the SDR, including suggestions for the future.[15] Presumably the reader will infer from the discussion in this chapter that whereas the report certainly categorized potential uses of SDRs, including in global emergencies, it did not evangelize transforming the SDR into a global currency, nor did it promote routine issuances of SDR as a good way to provide development aid. But I am getting ahead of myself.

The IMF has "printed money," that is, made so-called special allocations of SDRs a few times, starting in the early 1970s. By far the most significant allocations were the $250 billion issued in August 2009 as the global financial crisis unfolded and the $650 billion issued in August 2021 during the pandemic.[16] These headline numbers grossly overstate the actual amounts at stake because the SDRs are allocated according to voting shares in the IMF (e.g., the United States has 16.5 percent of shares and so gets 16.5 percent of the SDRs).[17]

Aid is a good thing, but this is a bit like giving a million dollars to every billionaire so that you can give $1,000 to needy families. Middle-income emerging markets are worthy, but should they get far more SDRs per capita than low-income countries? When low- and middle-income countries spend their SDRs, the funds effectively come from contributions that the other members (essentially the advanced economies) make, which are generally paid for by issuing government debt. In return, those members are given interest-bearing SDRs. (I am omitting many details that do not matter here.) The rich countries, by convention, are expected not to spend their holdings. Effectively, the rich countries allow the developing economies to benefit from the rich countries' low borrowing rates for whatever purpose the developing-country governments deem appropriate; unlike normal IMF loans, special SDR allocations carry no conditionality. This is part of the "magic," though not the whole story.

A second part of the magic is the implicit assumption that most developing economies and emerging markets can be relied on to repay the IMF because it is a senior lender. This is certainly an overstatement even for large emerging markets (witness Argentina) and is poppycock for very-low-income countries.[18] In fact, the IMF wrote off debt from low-income countries in 1996, and it will almost certainly have to do it again for a great many of the pandemic-era loans it made to low- and low-middle-income countries, if not all of them. This is not intended as a criticism, just a prediction.

Unfortunately, the 1990s debt-forgiveness approach is much more complicated to implement today because China has become a very large creditor and there is a lot more private-creditor debt than in the 1990s. Any write-down of IMF or World Bank debt thus must be organized so that the funds are not simply redirected to repay other creditors, who may not want to be as generous. There are other subtleties having to do with the seniority structure that we need not get into here.

Advocates of SDR allocations might well respond that the preceding analysis is missing a critical component. If the IMF floods the world with SDRs, they will become more common, more liquid, and more money-like, so it makes sense for these loans to bear a very low rate since they provide a "convenience yield." This attempt to elevate the SDR to a global currency is, unfortunately, wishful thinking. The would-be moneyness of the SDR will inevitably run into the brick wall of dollar dominance, not to mention other superior vehicles such as the euro. It is going to be very hard for a new currency managed by a loosely governed global institution to compete, the basic point we started out with. Saying that making new SDR allocations is akin to printing money is not far from saying that issuing food stamps, as the United States does, is like issuing a currency. Food stamps have long been a great program; this does not mean they are a free lunch for taxpayers, so to speak. SDR allocations may very well be a good thing in some circumstances; if so, it is not because making SDR allocations is like printing money.

One further argument that has been made in favor of printing SDRs is that they provide a non-transparent way of giving aid in a world in which many countries, particularly the United States, might not tolerate it otherwise. That is, the non-transparency—the hocus pocus—is a feature, not a bug. This line of argument admits the reality that the SDR is far from a free lunch but claims that the SDR is an easier sell to legislatures than grants because no one really understands SDRs. It is a plausible argument, but only up to a point. If the SDR is routinely used as a backdoor channel for large-scale aid packages, as many well-meaning grandees have proposed, and if such loans are repeatedly written off, the U.S. public will eventually see behind the curtain. SDR issuance will become impossible, even in emergency situations when it is most needed.

To be clear, I favor vastly increased aid to be channeled from advanced countries to low-income countries. Indeed, for several decades, across both journal papers and op-eds, I have argued that a much larger proportion of advanced-economy aid to poor developing economies should come in the form of outright grants, not loans.[19] That is, no interest, no repayments. Recently, I published a proposal for a global carbon bank that would require funding of at least $100 billion per year, and perhaps several times that.[20] However, trying to fund that aid through financial-engineering tricks to fool the public is short-sighted and would be a mistake. SDRs are not a magical global currency that cuts through all our myriad differences, and they are not costless if one knows that much of the debt will eventually have to be written off.

From a moral and economic perspective, there is great appeal to having a well-thought-out internationally managed currency replace the U.S. dollar; such a system is potentially more efficient and fairer, and scholars should keep working on it. However, as long as we live in a Westphalian nation-state system, instead of the United Federation of Planets in *Star Trek*, such plans do not yet appear realistic.

Indeed, the great concern in the international community today is not about whether the IMF will gain the power to issue a world currency; it is whether the IMF will stay intact as geopolitical tensions rise and continue to represent virtually every country in the world. Hence the appeal of supposedly stateless world currencies, as we turn to next.

CHAPTER 18

CRYPTOCURRENCIES AND THE FUTURE OF MONEY

Cryptocurrencies such as bitcoin have significant uses in the global underground economy that undeniably give them long-term value. And, as we shall see, the global underground economy is massive—easily 20 percent of global GDP, on par with the economic size of Europe. However, there is absolutely no chance that any cryptocurrency will supplant the dollar as the dominant currency in legal, tax-compliant transactions, except perhaps in a post-nuclear apocalyptic *Mad Max* dystopian future. It is important to understand why those who are convinced otherwise are dead wrong; the reasons cut to the heart of money and dollar dominance.

Yuval Noah Harari's brilliant book *Sapiens* contains an exceptionally eloquent passage on money, often quoted in Silicon Valley circles, that has mesmerized the crypto community.[1] It is beautifully written but deeply misleading. Harari argues that at its core, money is simply a social convention. If everyone comes to accept something as money, whether giant stones as on the Micronesian island of Yap or rice as in medieval Japan, then it indeed becomes money. Long before Harari's 2011 book, economists had constructed supremely elegant government-free theoretical models to capture this same idea, using carefully constructed mathematical frameworks every bit as eloquent in their own way as the writing in *Sapiens*.[2]

Unfortunately, such theories go much too far in empowering private choice and understate the powerful tools the government has to coordinate and coerce. As Marco Polo observed, Kublai Khan's subjects accepted the emperor's tree-bark currency on pain of death for refusal. When a modern-day government issues a national currency, it has an essential advantage over any substitute or private currency: It can pay all its employees and suppliers in its currency, and it can insist that government currency be used to pay taxes. It can issue debt denominated in its currency; the U.S. dollar's status as "legal tender" means that U.S. dollars must be accepted if used to pay any debt. Last but not least, the government can require its currency to be the legal unit of account in a broad range of activities—for example, bookkeeping for tax records and legal documents. All these channels combine to create network effects that give the government currency an insurmountable advantage. If that's not enough, the government can add more restrictions, such as requiring that bank deposits be denominated in government currency.

If a government overplays its very strong hand and issues far more currency than the public has use for, the currency's value will plummet and prices will soar. This happened, for example, in Weimar Germany in the 1920s, in many emerging markets in the 1980s and 1990s, and in Venezuela and Zimbabwe in the twenty-first century, all cases discussed previously. If the government currency is viewed as nearly worthless, people will go to great lengths and take considerable risks to avoid using it, whatever the rules and regulations. These extreme examples, though, only underscore the limits of what can be achieved by a government through coordination and coercion. In general, the government's advantages are formidable; countries such as Turkey and Argentina have routinely had episodes of high double-digit inflation without the public abandoning the government currency. Harari and the earlier theoretical literature he alludes to are eloquent, but it is specious to suggest that the choice of currency depends mainly on social convention and history and that there are multiple possible equilibria where different currencies can prevail. Crudely put, if China were to absorb some other country, that country's currency would eventually disappear and be replaced by the renminbi, no matter how much fondness its people attach to using their legacy currency as a medium of exchange.

If a competitor to the government's fiat currency should prove resilient, despite the aforementioned advantages the government currency enjoys, the government can further tip the scales by adopting laws and restrictions that make the competitor less liquid.

Except for the intense lobbying efforts against regulation, it should not be all that difficult to at least ringfence the use of cryptocurrencies, especially as the vast majority of people engage with cryptocurrencies using "exchanges" that are far easier to regulate than blockchain transactions themselves. That is because most people find trading cryptocurrencies "on chain" (on the blockchain) to be too difficult and to require too much technical savvy; who wants to irreversibly lose all their money by accidentally typing in a wrong address? Exchanges, despite all their efforts to cloak themselves in blockchain language, are really just banks. Loosely speaking, think of holding bitcoins on the blockchain as akin to having hundred-dollar bills, whereas holding bitcoins at an exchange is like holding money at a bank. Some of the same features that make the bank accounts convenient to use also make them much easier, in principle, for the tax authorities, law enforcement, or a court to trace. And the same would be true for cryptocurrency exchanges if they were subject to regulations fully parallel to those banks are subject to. Without getting into the weeds, let's just say that at present, this is far from always the case.

Using exchanges, individual investors don't really need any cryptocurrency savvy. They can acquire cryptocurrency, say bitcoin or ether, by paying in fiat currency such as the dollar, making use of the exchange's user-friendly interface; the exchange will deal as needed with the blockchain. The fiat value of your crypto, should you wish to have it exchanged back into dollars, fluctuates with the market. Meanwhile, since not everyone asks for their cryptocurrency back at the same time, the exchange can make handsome profits by lending its holdings at rather high interest rates. All of this indeed makes an exchange more or less like a bank, but with one massive difference: there is no government lender of last resort standing behind the exchange, and there probably won't be until the sector becomes regulated more in parallel with legacy banks, which unfortunately may not happen until cryptocurrencies become part of some much larger financial crisis. Again, the government ultimately holds the key levers, even if that realization has not fully sunk in.

Of course, even if there were no exchanges (that is, no crypto banks), cryptocurrencies could still exist on the blockchain, but they would be far less useful in transactions, and there would still be many steps governments could take to rein in blockchain transactions. We will come back to this. Without the liquidity exchanges provide, however, the challenge cryptocurrencies pose to fiat currencies would be far smaller. The dollar would be nothing without the banking and financial systems that stand behind it. Right now, there is a huge political battle, particularly in the United States, over regulation of exchanges and crypto. In the near term, cash donations from the crypto industry will no doubt trump anything an economist might say (no pun intended), but one should have little doubt where things need to go in the long run.

History has repeatedly shown that no private-sector currency can expect to win at a game in which governments make the rules, at least not indefinitely. Although most major innovations in currency have emanated from the private sector, in each case the government has eventually regulated or simply appropriated the new technology. Private coinage existed long before the king of Lydia (in present-day eastern Turkey) introduced the first stamped coins in the seventh century B.C. Over time, neighboring states similarly took over minting. Standardized coinage allowed Alexander the Great, a student of Aristotle, to stretch out his empire; he used this then cutting-edge technology to pay and provision even his most far-flung troops.

The private sector also invented paper money. Chinese merchants introduced the idea of proxy notes that could be redeemed for coins to avoid the dangers of transporting large amounts of coins long distances — in ancient China such notes were called "flying money." (The image of money falling out of a suitcase and being scattered to the wind is now cliché but must have seemed otherworldly twelve centuries ago.) In due time, provincial governments and then the emperor usurped the right to issue the notes. Few things shocked Marco Polo more than paper money back in 1275, when he visited the court of Kublai Khan. His eloquent rendition describes how Khan's mint, as if through alchemy, turned worthless tree bark into a store of value that citizens throughout the land accepted as payment without question. Europe, where the printing press had not yet been discovered, was dazzled. Thus, the long history of money shows that each time a new private-sector innovation or refinement comes along, the government will eventually either steal it or regulate it into submission.

ALTERNATIVE CURRENCIES

Dyed-in-the-wool crypto believers may think it is impossible to regulate cryptocurrency; one hears "the code is the law" or "crypto is censorship resistant." The problem with this logic — as I have already emphasized — is that even if governments cannot ban cryptocurrencies entirely, they can certainly create laws that make them difficult and expensive to use, and thereby quash the network effects needed for any cryptocurrency to compete with government currency.[3] (My skepticism about a private cryptocurrency replacing the dollar is not to deny the distinct possibility that blockchain technology will have a revolutionary impact on finance in other ways, but I leave that topic for another day.[4])

If I had to predict when meaningful crypto regulation will unfold, my guess is that it will happen within the next ten to fifteen years. But then I once thought that about Big Tech, which so far has proved far too optimistic.

Indeed, when Apple became the first trillion-dollar company in mid-2018, one of Silicon Valley's all-time most successful investors called me out of the blue. He got straight to the point: "Now that there has been the first one-trillion-dollar tech company, how long will it be before there is a two-trillion-dollar tech company?" he asked. He explained to me his thesis of why this might happen sooner than you think; the force of his logic was impressive. A central element was that the top tech firms are making so much money that they can afford to bid away top talent from the rest of the economy, which makes Wall Street like them even better. A second reason was that tech firms are best positioned to exploit a world of very low interest rates, which make very-long-term projects viable even if they don't pay off for decades — for example, space exploration, self-driving vehicles, or artificial intelligence. Wall Street trusts tech firms to find ways to keep succeeding, in part because their talent pool gives them a capacity to pivot that no other sector can match.

The investor's analysis was incredibly clear and incisive. Unfortunately, because I write on macroeconomic and financial policy, and sometimes speak to leading policymakers, it is my practice not to actively manage my boring portfolio. Otherwise, maybe I would have thought about taking advantage of this great stock tip. Nevertheless, I tried pushing back. Won't the trillion-dollar headline bring forward the day that policymakers finally try to limit Big Tech's monopoly power, especially the ability of big firms to force small competitors to sell under threat that their intellectual property will be cloned? Isn't social media undermining our political system, promulgating slander, and at least partly responsible for the mental-health crisis, especially among young people? Regulation of Big Tech is one area where I broadly agree with the sometimes-radical ideas of my Cambridge, Massachusetts, neighbor Senator Elizabeth Warren.[5]

The investor was unperturbed, arguing that regulation is conceptually difficult and politically fraught. The pathbreaking article rethinking antitrust law for the Big Tech era, written by Warren's protégé Lina Khan in 2017, clearly did not faze anyone in Silicon Valley, and as of this writing, her determined efforts as President Biden's chair of the Federal Trade Commission to take on Big Tech have stumbled in the courts. This, however, is almost certainly not the last word.[6] For example, it was a rare big win for the government when in August 2024 a U.S. district court ruled that Google had violated antitrust laws in trying to preserve its search monopoly, though it is much too soon to say what this ruling will ultimately signify.[7]

In the case of digital-currency regulation, which is still in the early innings, one hopes officials will wake up before it is once again too late. Government monopoly over currency is essential for dealing with financial crises and for avoiding public debt crises. A bitcoin standard would have many of the same problems as the gold standard. It could perhaps provide intermittent stability, but at the cost of generating much larger crises when they do come. Moreover, without the ability to engage in countercyclical Keynesian monetary policy, business cycles could be far more severe. These kinds of concerns are not very popular in certain quarters of the crypto community, as I know well from dozens of indignant emails — and even some death threats — after the publication in 2016 of my book on the past, present, and future of currency.[8]

It was fortunate indeed that the first major crypto-linked crisis did not cause a worldwide recession. When FTX (short for Futures Exchange) went bankrupt in 2022, most of the world, including many people working in cryptocurrency, did not seem to fully grasp the bank-like nature of cryptocurrency exchanges. When it was discovered that FTX had lost a large sum on speculation, a run ensued, and FTX collapsed just as a bank would have in the days before deposit insurance and government bailouts became the norm. The only difference is that FTX was housing deposits linked to cryptocurrency rather than fiat currency. Almost overnight, FTX's founder, Samuel Bankman-Fried (SBF), went from being feted everywhere as the tech world's newest Steve Jobs to being accused of massive fraud and becoming its newest Elizabeth Holmes. The latter is the Stanford graduate who founded the biotech firm Theranos, whose value peaked at $10 billion before the firm went bankrupt.[9] (I never owned shares in Theranos, but I do own a black turtleneck sweater—Holmes's signature look, borrowed from Steve Jobs. After the firm's ignominious collapse, my children told me I had to stop wearing it.)

Despite having written forcefully on cryptocurrency regulation in my 2016 book and then later contributing to a Group of Thirty report on the topic in 2019, I had not previously paid much attention to SBF when, in April 2022, I was invited to appear on a new weekly cryptocurrency show that Bloomberg had launched. The show was mainly aimed at crypto enthusiasts. The producer asked whether I would be willing to appear on the show with Samuel Bankman-Fried. I said yes, actually having no idea who he was. A quick Google search showed that at age twenty-nine, SBF was worth more than $20 billion ($26 billion at one point before FTX went under).[10] In the end, SBF ducked the appearance at the last minute, leaving me to be interviewed alone, which is a shame. I still wonder what he would have said when asked whether more oversight was needed to prevent crypto banking panics; my guess is that his answer would have been quite insightful even if not 100 percent believable.

Anyway, having ignored SBF until then, I started to occasionally tune in to his commentary after that. One had to be impressed by SBF's realization that serious regulation was inevitable, and he even claimed to want it. Many others in the industry would rant about the Securities and Exchange Commission and its head Gary Gensler. Why can't the SEC be more supportive or at least leave cryptocurrencies alone so that great financial innovation can continue apace? they would ask. On the other hand, it was worrisome to read that SBF and his colleagues at FTX were making tens of millions of dollars in political donations. Officially, SBF was only interested in being "helpful" to the conversation in Washington. When have we heard that before? In the run-up to the 2008–2009 financial crisis, financial-sector firms trumpeting fantastic new innovations topped political donor lists to both parties.

Recognizing that positive publicity adds leverage to lobbying, FTX produced a clever ad for the 2022 Super Bowl featuring the comedian Larry David constantly dismissing the great inventions of history leading up cryptocurrency exchanges. It was a lot cheerier than Crypto.com's exceedingly dark Super Bowl ad in which the actor Matt Damon tells the audience to buy crypto because "fortune favors the brave." Bankman-Fried lined up other celebrity endorsements, including the sports legends Tom Brady (football), Stephen Curry (basketball), David Ortiz (baseball), and Naomi Osaka (tennis). SBF knew how the game was played.

I finally met Samuel Bankman-Fried in person at a conference shortly before FTX's ignominious collapse. No one at the conference was aware of what was about to unfold, and SBF was still being lionized. In retrospect, one wonders whether SBF himself knew just how bad things would get; he was certainly still projecting great confidence about his firm's future. In for a penny, in for a pound, one supposes. Other cryptocurrency leaders have rightly said that one cannot paint the whole space with SBF's brush; there have always been con artists in finance, yet banking and finance have survived and thrived. Cryptocurrency's vulnerability to runs, though, is a much deeper problem that is not so easily dismissed.

At the opposite end of the spectrum from crypto evangelists are those, such as the noted economist Nouriel Roubini and the legendary investor Warren Buffet, who have claimed that bitcoin is fundamentally worthless, a pure speculative bubble. At the World Economic Forum in Davos, Switzerland, in January 2024, the financial titan Jamie Dimon described bitcoin as "hyped-up fraud."[11] These views, shared by a number of top economists, are as naive as Bankman-Fried's evangelism. Sure, it is easy to see the bubble element, especially in our celebrity-crazed culture. When Elon Musk appeared as a guest star on NBC's *Saturday Night Live* comedy show, the price for dogecoin dropped sharply after Musk's character facetiously described the cryptocurrency as "a hustle," and one can find endless other examples.[12] Bubble behavior, however, is not the whole story. Just as Yuval Noah Harari's explanation of money offers far too much hope to bitcoin evangelists, the idea that cryptocurrency is good for nothing except speculation ignores cryptocurrencies' killer app: the sprawling underground economy.

Perhaps this is because very few economists think about the underground economy, since they don't know how to quantify it. Nor does the government, as mentioned in chapter 7 as one reason it is difficult to pin down the true value of national output. Thanks to big data, however, that situation is changing. The issue is so fundamental to understanding whether bitcoin and other cryptocurrencies might have genuine uses in making payments, and not just as speculative assets, that one cannot ignore it.

The World Bank, in an extensive 2021 study surveying a range of methods, estimated that the average size of the underground economy in advanced economies is on the order of 17 percent of gross national income. The estimates for developing economies are even higher: 32 percent. Of course, the underground economy is by design difficult to trace, so any quantification is a "guesstimate." Nevertheless, as we shall see, newer techniques suggest that these orders of magnitude are not far off.

If so, given that the ultimate source of rents accruing to any currency comes from underlying transactions demand, the stakes for becoming the payment mechanism of choice for the underground economy are quite substantial. Historically, cash has been the medium of choice for stealth transactions. It is no coincidence that the overwhelming share of the world's paper currency supply is in large-denomination notes, and the lion's share of these appear to be used underground.[13] And there is a lot of it sloshing around. Governments know how much they print; they just have little idea where it is. For example, as of the end of 2022, 82 percent of the value of U.S. currency was in hundred-dollar bills, which amounts to roughly fifty-five hundred-dollar bills in circulation for every person living in the United States, or $22,000 in hundreds for each family of four. The exact whereabouts are mostly unknown. Although most estimates (including my own) suggest that roughly 50 to 60 percent of the total are held abroad, that still leaves a staggering amount sloshing around in the United States.[14]

Similar currency statistics apply in every advanced economy and in most emerging markets. With perhaps over a trillion dollars' worth of paper currency overseas, supplying paper currency to the global underground economy has been a huge business for the United States, even if — as I've argued for decades — governments that focus on the benefits and fail to look at the costs are being penny-wise and pound-foolish.[15] If private cryptocurrencies can compete in this market, not to mention expand it because they can be used online, the potential rents are huge.

By the way, if I seem obsessed by this topic, it might trace back to my days as a wandering professional chess player, when I was surprised more than once by the wads of large-denomination bills that a tournament sponsor or simultaneous-exhibition sponsor seemed to have stashed in their closet. As a teenager, although I did indeed wonder what was going on, I was just happy they were supporting chess, which, one supposes, is similar to how most beneficiaries of tax evasion feel.

Early estimates of the size of the underground economy were essentially derived by looking at cash demand itself, a somewhat circular reasoning but back then the best that could be done. In the mid-1980s, Edgar Feige, a colleague of mine at the University of Wisconsin–Madison, was one of the pioneers in this area, and his work is probably what first piqued my professional interest.[16] Over time, more-sophisticated methods came into use; these methods tried to infer unregistered economic activity from observable variables such as electricity demand (or much more recently nighttime light emission visible to satellites). Another variable might be the use of credit and debit cards relative to cash outstanding. There are also approaches that involve building full-scale macroeconomic models to infer unmeasured activity from inconsistencies in the data. All these methods are very indirect.

Quite recently, however, Francesco Pappada, of the Paris School of Economics, and I have developed a new approach, one that is arguably far more straightforward and transparent than earlier methods, although it does require manipulation of large databases.[17] It involves looking at reported tax receipts relative to what they should have been according to the national survey data on consumption that is used to compile national accounts. This new approach is particularly applicable to Europe, where the value-added tax constitutes an especially important component of government revenues. Typically the VAT system provides a big incentive to hide transactions from the government—the tax is on the order of 20 percent, sometimes higher—and people have found many clever ways to avoid paying it. An estimate of the size of the underground economy can then be imputed from the shortfalls in tax revenue country by country and

Table 3. Size of the informal or underground economy relative to GDP in Europe (selected countries), 1999–2020 average

Country	Size of underground economy (as % of GDP)
Greece	36
Italy	31
Spain	24
Portugal	24
France	14
Germany	13
Finland	10
Denmark	9
Sweden	6

Source: Francesco Pappada and Kenneth Rogoff, "Rethinking the Informal Economy and the Hugo Effect," *Journal of the European Economic Association* (forthcoming). In general, the underground economy derives mainly from tax and regulatory evasion, but also includes illegal activity. The construction of table 3 employs the authors' "EVADE" algorithm, which compares broad measures of consumption from survey data in each country with reported value-added tax receipts, taking into account differing rates by countries and by goods categories, including exemptions. The algorithm also takes into account that the authorities are much better at enforcing the valued-added tax on imports than on domestic sales, and that exports to countries outside the European Union are exempt from the VAT.

year by year across Europe. Our estimates for the size of the underground economy are given in table 3.

These figures may seem staggering, with Italy's underground economy at 31 percent of GDP and Greece's even higher at 36 percent. However, the estimates are not so different from those derived using earlier, much less direct methods such as those surveyed in the World Bank study. Our results also match up well statistically with a number of reasonable benchmarks; countries with high tax rates tend to have a larger underground economy, for example.[18] Given the estimates for Italy, Spain, and Greece under the newer, more transparent method, the World Bank's estimates of a 32 percent average across developing economies appear quite plausible.

What does all of this have to do with the value of cryptocurrency? Bitcoin (and other cryptocurrencies) may have little legitimate use in legal, tax-compliant transactions, but if it is indeed widely used in facilitating trade in the underground economy, then one cannot say it is a purely speculative asset. One can complain that regulators are inept and that law and tax enforcement are weak, but not that the fundamental value of bitcoin should be zero — unless the frame of reference is a society in which no one ever breaks the rules. In fact, there are a great many studies suggesting that bitcoin is used in a broad range of illegal activities, and bitcoin is the overwhelming currency of choice in ransomware attacks and in dark-web markets. However, its use appears to be much broader than that. What evidence might lead one to think that?

Unlike cash, for which most of the evidence on underground use comes from tax seizures, drug- and human-trafficking arrests, and the like, evidence of the underground use of bitcoin can be gleaned from the electronic vapor trail it leaves. One approach takes advantage of the fact that some blockchain addresses are known, and then uses that information to identify transactions connected to known illicit activities. Law enforcement authorities have already shown the ability to track down bitcoin successfully on a number of occasions.[19] Even sophisticated evasive measures such as "tumbling" that mix and repackage bitcoins to make them untraceable have not proved 100 percent regulation-resistant; founders of illegal tumbler sites have learned that they cannot easily evade the long arm of the law.[20]

The preceding discussion refers to "on-chain transactions" in which bitcoins are directly traded from one wallet to another.[21] We have already noted that the overwhelming majority of bitcoin trades go through exchanges, which, again, are basically to cryptocurrencies what banks are to paper currency. Taking advantage of the fact that some exchanges with worldwide footprints have posted all their trades, including the exact time stamp, the quantity of bitcoins traded, and the fiat currency used to make the trade, Clemens Graf von Luckner, Carmen Reinhart, and I investigated whether this trade information could be used to determine whether bitcoins are being used for transactions in general and international transactions in particular, including capital flight.[22] Our approach exploited the fact that bitcoins trade in small fractions out to the satoshi (defined as one hundred millionths of a bitcoin). In many cases, the data reveal rapid-fire identical-size trades (measured in bitcoins) within a very short time window — for example, a purchase of bitcoins with Argentinian pesos and then a sale to convert the bitcoins into U.S. dollars.

ALTERNATIVE CURRENCIES

Given that the odds of seeing two trades that are identical in size down to the satoshi is something like the odds of seeing two identical-size snowflakes, chances are that the trades are performed by the same entity, using bitcoin as a "vehicle currency" to convert one fiat currency to another (in our example, pesos to dollars). It is not possible to get into all the details here, except to mention that with a high volume of trades, one has to control for the possibility that some share of the matches are purely coincidental. This is essentially a generalization of "the birthday problem": in a room of thirty random individuals, there is a 70 percent chance that two will have the same birthday. Controlling for this factor still suggests that bitcoin is being used for transactions, not just as a store of value.

Not surprisingly, the cross-border outflows are particularly large from countries with intense capital controls, including Nigeria, Venezuela, Ghana, Argentina, and Russia. There are many exciting new approaches to studying these issues; the example I have provided is just one.

In researching our paper, my intrepid young co-author Clemens found himself in Lebanon in 2020, a year after its remarkably long-standing fixed dollar exchange rate — which was discussed extensively in chapter 14 — had collapsed, with the country now in default and foreign exchange transactions essentially shut down. Clemens needed a way to get paper dollars; fortunately, he had bitcoins. In his search for a place to exchange bitcoins for cash, he found a hole-in-the-wall shop in a seedy part of Beirut.

Befriending the shop owner after a couple of visits thanks to his impressive knowledge of blockchain, and also checking transactions in and out of the shop's public bitcoin wallet, Clemens realized that his own bitcoin sales were minuscule compared with the many hundred-thousand-dollar trades this crypto boutique was routinely handling. Why doesn't this place get robbed all the time, even given the armed guard on the street? he wondered. Then Clemens awkwardly realized that he was in the middle of a Hezbollah-controlled part of the city. Because Hezbollah has been designated by the United States as a terrorist organization and is on the financial sanctions list, it is cut off from the global banking system. This means that it must find other means to send and receive money from abroad. Apparently, this unpretentious shop was a Hezbollah bank.

Some uses of bitcoin are quite sympathetic — for example, finding yourself cut off from normal banking services, as Clemens experienced. Ukrainian refugees have reported using bitcoin to carry funds across borders, since it is safe and far easier to cash in across Europe than Ukraine's currency, the hryvnia.

To be clear, nothing is completely safe. Bitcoin keys may be virtually unbreakable, but their owners' bodies are not, and a thief can potentially force you to enter the codes needed to transfer your currency to the thieves' blockchain wallets. Some bitcoin multimillionaires who moved to tax havens in warmer climates, such as Puerto Rico, have learned this lesson the hard way, or so I was told recently by an early crypto pioneer who had moved back to the mainland.

It will be interesting to see the extent to which bitcoin (or other cryptocurrency) comes to serve as a substitute for hundred-dollar bills as a store of value for those who might be in need of a fast escape. Portability in a crisis is one of the prime reasons the U.S. hundred-dollar bill is so popular abroad. Indeed, over the years, the U.S. Treasury has sometimes looked at phasing hundreds out of circulation in light of the well-documented role they play in facilitating all kinds of crime and tax evasion worldwide. Whenever the idea is raised, the biggest pushback invariably comes from foreign countries.

One such instance was during the late 1970s, according to my Group of Thirty (G30) colleague the late John Heimann, who was comptroller of the currency at the time. Evidently, the idea was scrapped because of protestations from the French, many of whom still held on to hundred-dollar bills and greatly prized what they termed their "running money."[23] After all, if your country has already been invaded twice in a century, you never know when it will happen again, as Heimann observed. French president Macron's warnings to Europe about the rising risks of war no doubt have some once again considering what they would do if forced to move across borders. Of course, with inflation, any hundreds they carry will only buy what a fifty did thirty years ago.

The clear and demonstrated use of bitcoin in the global underground economy, and possibly also its value as "running money," means that even if not routinely used in the legal economy, bitcoin can still have fundamental value. It can hardly be considered completely worthless. If bitcoin were used in transactions representing even, say, 10 percent of the value of the global underground economy ($2 trillion per year), and if its value in facilitating underground transactions were 3 percent (a very-low-end estimate for illegal or tax-evading transactions; most credit card companies in the United States charge 2 percent on transactions, and American Express gets 3 percent) that would still be a $60 billion per year market, with bitcoin yielding that return in perpetuity. Viewed from this perspective, bitcoin exchange-traded funds, which have been allowed by U.S. regulators since January 2024, enable ordinary U.S. investors to buy an asset that services the global underground economy. Given that bitcoin likely helps facilitate all the same illicit activities as the hundred-dollar bill, one might well ask whether U.S. regulators should be so tolerant. Would U.S. regulators allow one of the big financial firms to develop a product that is linked to the global black-market value of blood diamonds and that can be used for terrorist financing? They seem to have no problem with indexing to cryptocurrencies.

Indeed, though it is difficult to prove definitively, one strongly suspects that a part of goods trade between Russia and China has made use of cryptocurrencies to evade U.S. financial sanctions. Even if bitcoin per se is not being used directly in this trading, bitcoin could serve as collateral for certain types of stable coins (discussed below) that are more convenient for transactions, much as short-term U.S. Treasury securities are used to collateralize financial trades. In some sense, the use of bitcoin as collateral might be considered another fundamental application that gives it value.

Wait, you ask, don't blockchain trades leave a permanent record so that the authorities can always trace them? If so, how can bitcoin be used for underground-economy transactions? The short answer is that they can almost always be traced, but it can be costly for authorities and, in the case of international transactions via an offshore exchange, requires a high level of international cooperation. If cryptocurrency is used to commit a terrorist attack, such cooperation will be relatively easy to achieve. For small tax-evasion cases, say a Nigerian citizen evading a few thousand dollars in taxes by conducting transactions in a Finnish-based exchange, the cost of enforcement is prohibitive. My conjecture is that if the day ever comes when authorities can effortlessly and costlessly trace bitcoin, its value will collapse. At present, that day is far off.

We now turn to stablecoins, which are a very different animal than bitcoin, though some of the appeal is the same. There are a few distinct kinds of stablecoins, but the two most widely used coins, tether and USD coin (USDC), are by far the most important. Both have their value fixed at one dollar, although on occasion they trade for less. Stablecoins have become popular over time precisely because cryptocurrency prices are so volatile. Indeed, tether is more traded than bitcoin, although as of mid-August 2024, bitcoin has a far larger market cap ($1.1 trillion compared with $116 billion for tether and $34 billion for USDC).[24]

Central bankers tend to be far more open minded about integrating stablecoins into the financial system than integrating cryptocurrencies with their wildly gyrating prices. Dollar-linked stablecoins provide a potential alternative to bank debit accounts and credit cards as a payment mechanism. If sufficiently regulated — and this means that regulators must be able to easily identify the underlying holder at all times, which is not always the case now — stablecoins also might provide an alternative to a central bank digital currency (discussed in chapter 19) that could prove attractive to the Fed. For example, in contrast to having just a single government provider of digital currency, there can be multiple private dollar-linked stablecoins that create an ecosystem where competition and innovation can thrive. The most sophisticated stablecoins are already far more developed than any central bank digital currency.

There are, however, three key issues. First, if a stablecoin provider does not have a lender of last resort behind it, it will be subject to runs unless the stablecoins are sufficiently backed by safe dollar securities such as Treasury bills; there is a very close analogy with runs on fixed exchange rates.[25] Second, it is the stablecoin provider, not the government-owned central bank, that collects the interest payments on the securities it holds. Third, if stablecoins became sufficiently pervasive and convenient, they could disintermediate banks in the sense of bidding away the ordinary depositors who provide a critical component of the capital that banks rely on to make loans; the same issue comes up in the next chapter with central bank digital currencies. All three issues can be addressed in principle, although there are many obstacles and complications. For example, at present, even though interest rates have risen sharply, the major stablecoins are reluctant to pay interest because doing so would radically change their regulatory status, and they would be required to register as securities with the U.S. Securities and Exchange Commission. That problem could be fixed, of course, but only by the government.

Legacy financial firms (banks) are plenty nervous about losing business to dollar-linked stablecoins, and for the moment are heavily lobbying regulators to restrict stablecoins — and will likely keep doing so until they have their own stablecoin product. As for having access to the Fed's balance sheet in the event of a run on a stablecoin, the issues are pretty much the same as with any bank or financial institution. Explicit insurance creates a moral-hazard problem. Capping the amounts insured for any individual is a partial solution, but in practice it is very hard for the government to avoid protecting all depositors no matter how large. In the end, although stablecoins offer new technological possibilities in transactions, the regulation issues are really very similar to old-fashioned banking and must be taken up if stablecoins continue to grow in importance.

In sum, cryptocurrencies can definitely compete for business with the dollar in the global underground economy, and this is a source of fundamental value. However, naive crypto evangelists who believe that their superior technology will allow non-state or private currencies to outcompete government currencies in the legal economy should look at the long history of money. The private sector may drive innovation, but over the long run, the government holds the cards. The crypto industry can pour money into Washington, as it did during the 2024 U.S. Presidential campaign, following the path Samuel Bankman-Fried had pioneered. This may work for a while, but eventually, perhaps soon, a crisis of one sort or another will make it clear that the government needs to establish a much more comprehensive regulatory regime in which innovation can thrive but where crypto is no longer the Wild West.

CHAPTER 19

CENTRAL BANK DIGITAL CURRENCIES

Many of the world's major central banks, including the European Central Bank, the Bank of England, and the Bank of Canada, are far along in developing their own central bank digital currency, or "CBDC." At first, CBDCs may be mainly for wholesale use by banks and financial firms, but in due time, many central banks will likely issue retail CBDCs that can be used by individuals. In its simplest form, a retail CBDC could be like having your own Venmo account at the central bank. Or it could be a central bank token, or even a government-sanctioned cryptocurrency, depending on its privacy properties. Indeed, as we shall see, there are dozens of alternative approaches to implementation, some so different that it is hard to think of them as belonging to the same species.

Central banks were initially a bit slow to respond to the explosion of digital currencies in part because, as one major central bank head explained to me a decade ago in commenting on my 2016 book's call for introducing coherent regulation, "Right now, cryptocurrencies don't seem to be doing any serious harm, and we don't want to get in the way of all the innovation."

Nowadays, central banks are no longer holding back, and there is something of a frenzy in CBDC development. Over 90 percent of BIS-member central banks have been exploring the issue;[1] the People's Bank of China's "e-CNY" was already entering beta testing as the pandemic broke out. The burst of official interest would have eventually happened anyway, but the proximate trigger came in 2019, when Facebook, with its two billion users, proposed its "Libra" cryptocurrency, throwing the central banking community into a frenzy. Facebook's token (which was not actually a full-blown cryptocurrency) was effectively blocked first by Swiss and then by U.S. regulators, and the project was abandoned—for now. I was sad for the sake of a couple of former Ph.D. students of mine who had joined Facebook's elite Libra development team, but nevertheless thought regulators had, for once, made the right decision.

There are two distinct rationales for CBDC development. Most countries present their CBDCs as a way of enhancing payment efficiency and financial inclusion, essentially improving the legacy financial system rather than replacing it. A side benefit is that the process helps them better understand cryptocurrencies, including how to potentially regulate them.

For some countries, another rationale is equally important: deflating if not necessarily dethroning the dollar—at a minimum, preventing it from penetrating more deeply into their own trade and finance and, more ambitiously, taking a slice of the dollar's international business. These central banks are hoping that blockchain technology might help overcome the size and network effects that have made the dollar so pervasive. After all, if stateless bitcoin can carve out a substantial market, why not a digital currency backed by a well-funded state actor?

The race to have the leading CBDC is one the United States could almost surely win, were it so inclined, given the dollar's strong initial position and the United States' broad lead in technology. Officially, the Federal Reserve began exploring the potential "benefits and risks" of (retail) CBDCs in early 2022.[2] It is understandable that the United States has been slow to act; why rock the boat when, under the current system, the dollar is king?[3] What if developments in digital currencies undermine the dollar's position in some unforeseen way—say, by creating highly liquid markets for other currencies that diminish the dollar's network advantages, or by introducing alternative "rails" for international payments that lie outside the authority of U.S. regulators?

I cannot help but think back to the Eastman Kodak Company. Back in the 1960s and 1970s, Kodak was making a fortune selling and developing film; the main profits were never in the cameras themselves. My father, an avid photographer, thought it well worth the trouble and cost of mailing in his pictures to be developed by Kodak rather than having them developed at the local pharmacy; so did a great many other people. Then, in 1975 Kodak's Rochester research center produced the first digital camera, eliminating the need for film and setting the stage for the company's demise. Probably nothing like this will happen to the dollar, yet if you are winning at the currency game as it is now played, why would you want to lead the charge for change?

Moreover, given that the United States has by far the world's deepest and most liquid financial markets, no country has more to lose if a CBDC cybermeltdown — or state-sponsored cyberterrorism — were to occur. It is very difficult to get the kinks out of any large-scale new payments system without being able to run it for a while and make adjustments over time through trial and error.

The existing payments system, for all its limitations and flaws, has been developed and stress-tested for decades. The North Koreans, the Chinese, the Russians, and the Iranians have long been working around the clock to hack it to steal money from large banks and cripple the U.S. financial system. It is certainly true that more goes on in the shadows than the public is ever told. I am fully willing to accept that the July 2024 CrowdStrike outage, which crippled airlines, businesses, and both of my computers, was not a cyberattack. But I am not 100 percent sure we would ever be told the full truth if it was. Over the past decade, I have participated in several high-level cybersecurity conferences with leading scientists from top universities and heads of intelligence agencies from several major U.S. allies. After a day of listening to all the vulnerabilities, and some of the little-reported intrusions that have already occurred, I usually want to hide under a bed. One piece of good news is that so far, attacks on the financial sector have not been disastrous, yet things are clearly getting more precarious; major banks are increasingly reporting very sophisticated attacks by what are clearly state-sponsored actors.

Cyber risk is probably not even the leading concern for most central banks, not yet anyway. As the existing financial system is constructed, banks play a key role in providing loans to small and medium-size businesses, and this role is not easily replaced. In fact, in most parts of the world, including Europe, banks play a major role in funding even large corporations, given the underdevelopment of bond markets.

ALTERNATIVE CURRENCIES

Much as everyone likes to dump on banks, so far technology has had difficulty duplicating their ability to develop long-term relationships with local businesses. These relationships enable banks to make loans that are too small for the bond market. Given that small and medium-size businesses are a major source of innovation and jobs creation in the U.S. economy, the government cannot simply allow banks to disappear overnight.

In principle, banks do not need to rely on bank deposits for their funding, and in fact most also issue bonds. Bond funding, however, is considerably less dependable than deposits, which are famously "sticky." That is, there is a large retail base of depositors who do not pay close attention to nuances such as risk; why should they when the government explicitly guarantees an individual's deposits in any one bank for up to $250,000? If that is not enough, you can spread your money around to multiple banks; there are services that will do this for you at very low cost. Moreover, even if you have billions of dollars in a single bank and it fails, the government has shown time and again that it will bail you out to avoid "contagion." When Silicon Valley Bank went bust in March 2023, some of its depositors had accounts with several billion dollars; they were all bailed out.[4] And it will happen again, no matter what regulators and politicians tell us.

For some progressive economists, having a CBDC that undermines the power of the legacy banking structure is one of its most attractive features; they do not mind giving the central bank more direct control over all lending in the economy. Indeed, the fact that CBDCs can pay interest—a clear advantage over paper currency—can be used to help vacuum funds quickly out of private banks. In one approach, the central bank would use the CBDC to soak up all retail deposits, then turn around and lend the funds back to the banks, perhaps through an auction. (There are also less extreme versions.)[5] Banks would remain lending institutions but would no longer be deposit-taking institutions. This intriguing idea is completely viable; the problem is that it creates an enormous temptation for the government to favor some kinds of lending over others, as is the case in, say, China or India. Conservatives, of course, loathe the idea of giving so much power to the government, but many centrists, too, are concerned that a CBDC would become a political football.

True, there are evolving technological alternatives to many services that banks provide. So far, however, they have not developed nearly enough to replace bank lending. In China, Alibaba pioneered making low-interest-rate loans to regular commercial customers, using data that it had on these same customers as buyers. There are various internet lending platforms that make use of rating systems. China has hundreds of these; the United States has a few. So far, they have only been able to play a niche role. Still, Big Tech has huge advantages over legacy banks in collecting and using data, and top bank executives remain very nervous about it. Banks also have staff and branches tailored to the old era, expenses that Big Tech competitors would not start out with. For the moment, regulatory guardrails have prevented Big Tech from pushing aside banks. Needless to say, this is a very active area of engagement.

All the above concerns—cyber risk, system failure, disintermediation, and excessive government power—underscore why any new financial technology must be implemented gradually, and why, ideally, experimentation should take place first in much smaller countries than the United States. The Fed will want to see the glitches worked out somewhere else. The United States has been slow to adopt new innovations in virtually every new transaction technology for the past few decades. It was slow to put chips in credit cards; there was a period when it was sometimes difficult to use U.S. credit cards in Europe, which had adopted chip technology much earlier. The United States was slow to introduce real-time clearing (that is, almost immediate clearing) for small-scale retail transactions. The FedNow instant payment system only started gradually rolling out in July 2023; the Nordic countries already had such a system up and running for years. Real-time clearing sharply reduces credit risk and ought to eventually lead to lower credit card fees, which, given the United States' highly developed financial system, are absurdly high.[6]

Assuming that the Fed does wait a long time before plunging in, there is the outside risk that a CBDC from another central bank could gain a foothold that proves difficult to break. The European Central Bank appears well on its way to issuing a digital euro, at least for use on the wholesale level. The euro already controls significant market share; if the digital euro develops during a period when Europe is becoming more cohesive and the United States less so, the possibility that a digital euro could extend the currency's reach could suddenly become quite real. For China, a digital renminbi might provide a helpful advantage in persuading Asian neighbors and possibly some commodity producers to step up use of China's currency, which would pave the way for more decisively breaking away from the dollar bloc, something that is likely to happen anyway.

Concern over competition from other central bank CBDCs—including from the United Kingdom on account of its world-class financial system—was a major impetus for the White House and the Federal Reserve to announce that they are looking into the issue. Perhaps the mere threat that the United States might someday introduce a digital dollar will be enough to discourage some other central banks from introducing their own CBDCs. A common saying in chess is, "The threat is stronger than the execution." Maybe, but surely other central banks will call the United States' bluff or, as in the case of China, will want to make plans for setting up a parallel currency anyway.

Given its geopolitical aspirations, most immediately in the Taiwan Strait and the South China Sea, China is surely planning for contingencies in case the United States imposes stringent financial sanctions, as it has with Russia. Regardless, if China wants the renminbi to be used more internationally, developing a clearing system that runs independently of the existing international payments system is an extremely appealing prospect. Whether such a system requires a state-run CBDC as opposed to, say, privately run Alipay, is far from clear. Consumer enthusiasm for China's CBDC has been limited, in part because it lacks the broad functionality of Alipay and other private e-currencies. Of course, it is much easier in China than it would be in the United States for the government to simply insist that everyone use its payments mechanism.

The threat that any foreign CBDC poses to U.S. markets is small, if only because the U.S. government can impose severe restrictions that prevent widespread use. One does not want to minimize the difficulties of this step, but restrictions would almost certainly be imposed. The Securities and Exchange Commission has been quite creative in putting restrictions on cryptocurrencies (too creative according to its critics), and the same methods could be applied, which presumably even a crypto-crazed president would allow.

In the near term, though, the dollar might be most vulnerable in the global underground economy, discussed in the preceding chapter. Is it dirty pool for foreign central banks to court businesses in the global underground economy?

American officials will have trouble complaining, given that the U.S. Treasury has been profiting for decades with its hundred-dollar bills.

Perhaps a useful way to give a flavor of the debate, and the incredible range of options in play, is to discuss a competition hosted by the Monetary Authority of Singapore (the country's central bank) in the fall of 2021.[7] The competition attracted virtually every major player in the game, from leading banks and financial firms to tech companies to late-stage startups.[8]

Singapore is exactly the kind of place one could see issuing an early CBDC that set standards for other countries, in part because of its advanced and sophisticated financial sector and in part because Singaporeans are used to rapid change in a way most Americans could not begin to fathom. Modern Singapore, as portrayed in the 2018 movie *Crazy Rich Asians*, with its gleaming skyscrapers, expensive cars, and world-class theme parks, is a far cry from the backward, developing country in Bing Crosby and Bob Hope's classic 1940 film *The Road to Singapore*, with its grass huts and pedal-driven carriages. Singapore is in constant competition with Hong Kong to be the most important financial center in Asia. At this moment, Singapore has perhaps moved ahead, as China's crackdown on Hong Kong's independence undermines the credibility of the rule of law, which is very strong in Singapore despite the fact that corruption is still rife in the region. (If you ever get a chance to read Bradley Hope and Tom Wright's book about the incredible 1MDB scandal, *Billion Dollar Whale: The Man Who Fooled Wall Street, Hollywood, and the World*, you will understand why it was a sensation in Singapore. Somewhat poetically, the scandal involves the financing of Martin Scorsese's film *The Wolf of Wall Street*, starring Leonardo DiCaprio and Margot Robbie.)

I was asked to serve as one of the judges for the three-hour final event of the competition, which was broadcast live on Singaporean television. For me, it turned out to be a way to get a glimpse into the diverse questions that arise as one digs deeper and deeper into digital technologies. The call for proposals gave a twelve-point laundry list of criteria the CBDCs were to fulfill, from efficiency to security to inclusiveness to interoperability. The latter covers everything from the ability to interact with legacy bank systems to interacting with CBDCs from other countries.

ALTERNATIVE CURRENCIES

The contestants included a dizzying array of computing giants, major banks, and credit card companies, but also blockchain and stablecoin operators, crypto banks, identification specialists, operators of cross-border payment systems, and many others. The ultra-brilliant group was remarkably diverse, representing every continent in the world and different educational and socioeconomic backgrounds.

There was at least one element that every presentation had in common: the rapture consumers could be expected to experience whenever making a payment with a CBDC. Evidently, there can be no greater joy in life than paying for one's morning coffee with central bank digital currency. Otherwise, not surprisingly, the contestants from the major banks and credit card companies mostly offered systems that would keep the current system as intact as possible, enhancing it rather than replacing it. Conversely, most of the tech outsiders wanted to phase out legacy systems as fast as possible. One can expect big battles with banks initially having the upper hand, but not necessarily forever.

One problem that some presentations addressed, and others did not, is how to handle international transactions, given that each country has its own rules and regulations. One would think that international interoperability should be easy to set up, but to make a long story short, it is not, which is probably why many participants decided to leave the topic, important as it is, to another day.

Every presentation did address how to balance the government's need to be able to audit transactions (to enforce taxes and security regulations) with people's desire to have some transactions remain completely private. Most of the proposals basically boiled down to having different systems and security depending on transaction size. Typically, for small transactions, the payer would only have to demonstrate that they have the funds and would not be asked to give extensive identifying information. To transact larger amounts, they would need to reveal more. The problem with this kind of multiple-tier system is that ultimately funds have to be able to flow across the different tiers; otherwise each tier would just be a separate currency. And it is precisely when information flows across tiers that privacy data is vulnerable. Simply put, as things stand, trying to move money from a high-privacy small account to a low-privacy big account, or vice versa, compromises the high-privacy account. So far, no CBDC platform has completely solved this problem, despite some claims to the contrary.[9]

All in all, for me, Singapore's CBDC hackathon was a wake-up call both to the speed at which the technology is advancing and to the huge stakes that are attracting a significant slice of the world's top technology talent. Some of these super-smart people really think that a state-sponsored digital currency can compete with the dollar in a way that has not been feasible with legacy financial systems, that is, banks. Near term, one should be quite skeptical, but it would be foolish to ignore the possibility longer term.

PART V

THE PERKS AND BURDENS OF BEING THE DOMINANT CURRENCY

CHAPTER 20

PERKS OF CURRENCY DOMINANCE

Aside from the sheer exhilaration of power—which is not to be discounted as a component of national welfare—just how much is dollar dominance worth to the United States? One very concrete benefit is that foreigners are willing to hold surprisingly large quantities of U.S. debt, which helps drive down the interest rates the U.S. government has to pay. Foreign central banks held $6.7 trillion of U.S. Treasury bills as of mid-2024; if other foreign investors (mainly institutional investors such as sovereign wealth funds) are included, the figure rises to $8.2 trillion.[1]

Surely one of the reasons dollar debt sells at a premium—that is, pays a lower interest rate—is that the United States has the deepest and most dynamic financial markets. This makes U.S. Treasury debt very easy to sell quickly and without excessive transaction costs; that is, U.S. debt is very liquid. It is also very safe, at least in the literal sense of getting repaid dollar for dollar as promised (that is, ignoring surprise inflation). The U.S. legal system generally supports strong creditor rights; by and large foreign investors can expect to get paid. The fact that the United States is a military superpower is not to be discounted either. Japan could someday be threatened by China, and Europe is already threatened by Russia.

A less obvious, but extremely important factor underlying demand for U.S.

government debt, especially short-term Treasury debt, is its widespread use as collateral in worldwide financial transactions. This collateral use gives an almost money-like feature to Treasury bills that contributes to what economists have termed their "convenience yield," which compensates for a lower interest rate. It has long been understood that people are willing to hold zero-interest paper currency because it helps facilitate transactions and provides privacy in ways that interest-bearing assets cannot yet fully duplicate. The exponential growth in global financial markets over the past five decades has similarly created a special demand for U.S. Treasury bills.

Here, being the dominant currency really does matter. In principle, a trader can use German bunds or Japanese JGBs as collateral, and they are often used as such. However, because so much of the world's financial markets is dollar based, U.S. Treasury debt is particularly useful. In a seminal paper a decade ago, Annette Vissing-Jorgensen and Arvind Krishnamurthy estimated the convenience yield to be about half a percent, an order of magnitude we will see more than once in this chapter.[2]

Another more subtle reason why dollar interest rates might be lower than otherwise stems from the fact that empirically the dollar tends to appreciate (go up in value against other currencies) during crises and to fall back down in more normal times. Markets typically offer a premium on assets that retain or increase their value during downturns, as this makes them a hedge.

Just to clarify: When we say the dollar pays a "lower" interest rate, we mean lower given the total amount of debt the U.S. government has issued; most evidence suggests that the United States faces a normal downward-sloping demand curve for its debt, even if the slope is very slight. That is, to elicit higher demand, even the U.S. government must pay a higher interest rate.[3] To put it more crudely, the fact that the world loves dollar bonds doesn't mean its appetite is bottomless.

The convenience yield is a tight and well-defined concept, albeit one that applies only to government debt. A far broader and more encompassing concept— "exorbitant privilege"—takes account of the myriad advantages the United States, including both the government and the private sector, enjoys from financial globalization. Ever since the French finance minister Valéry Giscard d'Estaing introduced the poetic term in the mid-1960s, exorbitant privilege has become a focal point in discussions and debates about the role of the dollar.[4] At the time, the president of France, Charles de Gaulle, famously wanted to restore France's stature as a global leader on the world stage, for example, by making the country a nuclear power. Although he apparently never actually used the term "exorbitant privilege" in any public speeches, de Gaulle clearly believed that the post-war exchange rate system gave France the short end of the stick, and in the end French insistence on redeeming dollars for gold helped bring down the post-war exchange rate system. The denouement for Bretton Woods came shortly after his death in 1970.

Although it was a speech by Giscard d'Estaing in 1965 that popularized the concept of U.S. dollar privilege, economists had already been debating for some time the benefits to the United States of being the reserve currency. Two splendid papers published in 1964, one by Chicago's Robert Aliber and one by Walter Salant of the Brookings Institution, weighed the costs and benefits of being the world's "reserve currency."[5] (As discussed in chapter 1, the global monetary setup was a bit different back then; the U.S. dollar, and the U.S. dollar alone, was still theoretically convertible to gold by governments, although most did not do so for fear of destabilizing a system that seemed to be working for everyone, even if de Gaulle did not see it that way.) Aliber and Salant both emphasized that the dollar's reserve-currency status — governments could hold the dollar in lieu of gold knowing that it could be converted — gave the United States broad scope to borrow from abroad at a relatively low interest rate and a large degree of flexibility in choosing when to exercise this privilege. Salant further argued that it was the flexibility to borrow in periods of great need, not the somewhat lower interest rate in normal times, that constituted the crux of the benefit to the United States of issuing the reserve currency.

A modern-day economist would emphasize the distinction between dealing with an idiosyncratic supply shock, such as the need to quickly increase military spending, and a global demand shock, such as the 2008–2009 financial crisis or the 2020 pandemic. Either way, it is still a great advantage to have broad access to global capital markets in times of duress. As a very young Michael Jordan (the basketball and marketing legend) cleverly retorted when unexpectedly pressed to choose between Diet and Classic Coke at his first press conference (he was hawking both): "Coke is Coke. They both taste great."[6]

PERKS AND BURDENS

Salant's back-of-the-envelope calculation suggested that the lower borrowing cost was worth at least 0.8 percent of GDP and ventured that the ability of the U.S. government to borrow heavily in times of extreme need was likely worth far more. It is quite remarkable how well Salant's estimates have stood up to much more sophisticated modern techniques, which require a full-blown macroeconomic model to reach a conclusion. There are a range of estimates, but a study by the Georgetown economist Matthew Canzoneri and co-authors is indicative of the order of magnitudes scholars find.[7] Their calculation, which necessarily requires a lot of assumptions and modeling choices, suggests that the direct borrowing benefit the United States enjoys amounts to about half a percent per year's worth of consumption; that is a bit lower than Salant's estimate, also given that U.S. consumption is roughly 70 percent of GDP. Nevertheless, in today's economy that would be over $120 billion per year. Canzoneri and his co-authors further calculated the benefits of being able to borrow more when the need was greatest to be worth another quarter of a percent.

The astute reader will notice that the estimates by Canzoneri and his co-authors do not quite agree with Salant's conjecture that the single greatest advantage to being a currency hegemon is being able to borrow big when need is greatest, instead finding it half as important as lower borrowing costs. One should not conclude that Salant was necessarily wrong; macroeconomists have generally struggled with quantifying how risk is reflected in aggregate behavior. For example, why, on average over long periods, do stocks pay such a high return compared with bonds?[8] It certainly seems that the times when the rest of the world is most in awe of U.S. borrowing capacity are precisely during very difficult circumstances when the United States seems to be able to binge on stimulus like a drunken sailor while most other countries are experiencing severe fiscal duress.

The idea of having governments borrow promiscuously in peacetime is relatively new—perhaps the most transformative legacy of the Keynesian revolution, even if Keynes himself had a more measured view than some of his later disciples.[9] In earlier times, the country bestowed with the dominant currency would use its privileged borrowing status mainly to finance wars. Douglass North and Barry Weingast famously argued that the Glorious Revolution of 1688 produced fundamental changes in British institutions that made the

United Kingdom a more credible borrower and helped it match up to the far more populous France.[10]

The birth of the Bank of England in 1694 came with a slew of fundamental reforms that helped secure property rights, protect wealth, and in general, put an end to crude confiscatory government. Great Britain's enhanced borrowing capacity helped pay for ships and mercenaries in its wars against France, a country whose population of around twenty million was almost four times England's at the turn of the eighteenth century. During Great Britain's (and subsequently the United Kingdom's) long reign as issuer of the dominant currency, it was constantly fighting wars, from small battles to maintain or defend its colonies to the Napoleonic Wars. Then there were World Wars I and II. In wartime, the United Kingdom ran substantial deficits; in peacetime it typically ran surpluses. Of course, Britain's wars helped produce and protect its vast colonial empire; Britain's overseas wealth spun off great profits that substantially offset its debt-servicing costs.

The United States has run a very different kind of empire, forging itself into the world's largest international debtor. Starting from its privileged position as the center country in the post-war Bretton Woods system, the United States has since expanded its use of debt considerably, albeit in fits and starts. The United States ran massive deficits to finance World War II as the dollar emerged the undisputed global currency, but then raised taxes significantly to help finance the Korean War of the early 1950s. The United States then went back to using deficit financing to pay for the Vietnam War of the 1960s and early 1970s, in addition to a raft of new social programs. There is widespread agreement that this decision helped catalyze the Great Inflation of the 1970s thanks to a very accommodating Federal Reserve, albeit one confronted with a difficult set of circumstances.

The 1970s experience did not dissuade President Ronald Reagan from slashing taxes in the 1980s; when the public woke up at the end of his "Morning in America" policies, they had a whopping debt hangover. Since then, U.S. debt has mostly drifted up with a brief slowdown during Bill Clinton's presidency in the 1990s, when (by the way) the economy did quite well anyway.

It was during the twenty-first century that the United States' fiscal profligacy really kicked up a head of steam. President George W. Bush (the younger Bush) borrowed heavily to finance the U.S. invasion of Iraq; rather than raise taxes, he followed Reagan and cut them. Barack Obama later had little choice but to borrow heavily in dealing with the financial crisis he inherited from Bush (although the financial deregulation overshoot that led to the crisis had started earlier under Clinton). He might have been able to borrow even more had he been willing to offer the Republican-controlled Congress tax cuts. That move was left to Donald Trump, who borrowed big to finance tax cuts after taking over from Obama. He then later had to borrow a great deal more to counter the pandemic. Joe Biden continued to borrow to fight the pandemic, probably well past the point it was warranted. On top of that, the Biden administration also borrowed to finance ambitious progressive social and industrial policies. It has become standard fare in American politics to watch each party rail against deficits when they are out of power but hungrily embrace deficits when in control and able to advance their own agenda. Going forward, almost all official projections of future U.S. debt levels assume that massive further borrowing, rather than higher taxes, will be used to deal with the coming bulge in retirements and old-age dependency as the baby boomer generation ages. As shown in figure 11, the Congressional Budget Office projects the debt-to-GDP ratio to reach 166 percent by 2054; that is probably an understatement.[11] Much of the sharp rise over time comes from the bulge of old-age support payments, mainly Social Security and Medicare, coming up as the baby boomer generation hits peak retirement years.

Some very recent estimates suggest that the premium on U.S. debt might be far higher than Salant's 0.8 percent. For example, Zhengyang Jiang, Arvind Krishnamurthy, and Hanno Lustig estimate that foreigners earn an extra convenience yield of 2 percent on U.S. Treasury holdings.[12] At today's debt levels, this implies a direct savings to the U.S. government of up to $140 billion a year on foreign holdings alone (rising to $600 billion, or about two-thirds of the annual U.S. military budget, if the extra yield is also as large for American holdings). An important caveat is that some of the very high estimates of the U.S. government borrowing premium are drawn from the period of ultra-low real interest rates that prevailed until recently, which might tend to exaggerate the premium for reasons that will become apparent later in chapters 25 and 26

PERKS OF CURRENCY DOMINANCE

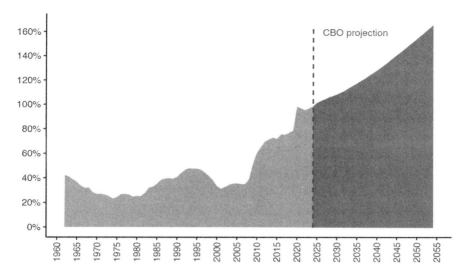

Figure 11. Privately held U.S. government debt as a percentage of GDP, 1962–2054
Data Source: Congressional Budget Office.

on fiscal sustainability. Of course the premium might also fall if China's affinity for the dollar declines.[13]

So far, we have been discussing concrete quantifiable benefits to dollar dominance. There are certainly other major benefits that may not easily translate into dollars, but definitely do translate into raw power, which is in many ways what the rest of the world most resents. The Federal Reserve's capacity to print unlimited dollars in an economic or financial crisis effectively gives the American government enormous leverage over the evolution of the global payments system. This not only allows it to tilt the playing field toward U.S. banks, but potentially gives it privileged access to information on people and purchases all over the world.

In some ways, the dollar has also become a de facto branch of the U.S. armed services. For over three decades now, the United States has increasingly weaponized financial sanctions as an alternative to military intervention. To say that China has been watching U.S. actions to punish Russia would be an understatement. As I have repeatedly emphasized, fear of sanctions is a major impetus underlying China's drive to internationalize the renminbi, to develop its own central bank digital currency (as discussed in chapter 19), and to create parallel rails for clearing international financial transactions away from the prying eyes of U.S. authorities. China's payment system has already been accepted by some other countries. U.S. allies, who sometimes see shades of gray where Americans see black and white, are also concerned about U.S. financial sanctions overreach. Dismissing the allies as spineless, as the U.S. commentariat so often does, misses genuine disagreements that could later come back to bite the United States if it ignores them.

The ability to monitor global transactions and impose financial sanctions is great for the U.S. government but creates strong incentives for the rest of the world to circumvent not only the dollar but all parts of the plumbing of the international financial system over which the United States exerts control (major credit cards, dollar bank transfers, and the like). In the next chapter, we expand the discussion to include benefits of currency dominance not only to the public sector but to the private sector as well.

CHAPTER 21

EXORBITANT PRIVILEGE OR TAXATION WITHOUT REPRESENTATION?

The French concept of exorbitant privilege that Giscard d'Estaing had in mind was far more sweeping than just the direct borrowing benefits accruing to the dollar's reserve-currency status. After World War II, American private businesses and individuals had swept into Europe buying up businesses and building factories. While European governments had to hold low-yield U.S. Treasury debt in order to defend their dollar pegs, private American citizens were plowing funds into high-return European investments. My great-aunt Henrietta, a U.S. citizen, had a factory in Bologna, Italy, as a manufacturing base for the high-fashion shoes she designed for the U.S. market, a dream that she would never have been able to afford in New York. Such businesses paid off handsomely as post-war Europe rebuilt and started pulling somewhat closer to U.S. productivity and income levels. Giscard d'Estaing's thesis that Europe needed its own currency to rebalance global economic power was a key driving force in the creation of the single currency in Europe.

Giscard d'Estaing become president of France in 1974 and went on to become one of the key architects of the euro. Back in 1997, I was among the faculty who had the honor of meeting the former president when he came to give a speech at Princeton University entitled "The European Monetary Union: The Making of a Global Currency." I confess to being one of those in the audience who was skeptical that the euro could ever challenge the dollar, especially given the eurozone's lack of a coherent fiscal framework, not to mention the lack of a Europe-wide lender of last resort. When the chance came, I asked a question along those lines, drawing on the insights of my colleague Peter Kenen, who was also sitting in the audience, and Maurice Obstfeld, my longtime co-author. Giscard d'Estaing firmly insisted that we Americans need to understand that the single European currency is ultimately a political project, a path to lasting peace and prosperity in a continent that had suffered two world wars in one century, and that the European political project overrides any economic concerns. The former president was enormously eloquent, and quite emotional, in his response. As we have discussed, the euro has certainly had its troubles but at present is still thriving, even if the continent is struggling to grow. Overall, though, one would have to concede that, so far, Giscard d'Estaing was more right than wrong.

In any event, his concerns about the United States' exorbitant privilege continue to be borne out by events. The United States has been able to run immense current account deficits—at times reaching 6 percent of GDP—year after year. Yet, until recently, the United States' net international investment position—the market value of all assets held by Americans abroad (including debt, equity, and direct foreign investment) less the market value of all such assets held by foreigners in the United States—has deteriorated remarkably slowly. Just to be clear, a country's current account deficit is the sum of net public plus net private borrowing from abroad; it is not just government borrowing. In recent years, the current account deficit has fallen to around 2 to 3 percent of GDP, again mainly because of the fracking revolution, which sharply reduced U.S. dependence on imported fossil fuels. Still, 3 percent of GDP in 2023 amounted to over $800 billion.

It was not always so. For the first few decades after World War II, the U.S. current account typically showed a modest surplus. Foreign governments might have been soaking up U.S. Treasury bills, but U.S. investors were sending at least as much money back into the rest of the world. After being in steady surplus throughout the 1960s, the U.S. current account dipped ever so slightly into deficit in 1972, as shown in figure 12.[1] President Nixon was reportedly panicked. The Nixon-era current account deficit was a mere baby step compared

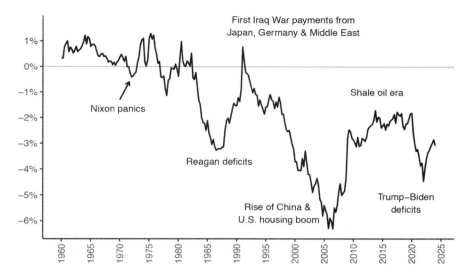

Figure 12. U.S. current account balance as a percentage of GDP, 1960–2024
Data Source: Federal Reserve Bank of St. Louis.

with what happened in the 1980s, when Ronald Reagan slashed taxes and ran large government budget deficits. Since then, the U.S. current account has consistently been in the red, except for a slight positive blip in 1991. That surplus happened only because of cash payments to the U.S. government from Saudi Arabia, Kuwait, Japan, and Germany in lieu of direct military support for President George H. W. Bush's war on Iraq (Desert Storm). U.S. borrowing peaked in 2005 and 2006 in the run-up to the financial crisis.[2]

Given the long string of deficits, it is hardly surprisingly that the United States eventually went from being a net creditor to a net debtor nation. The change appears to have occurred in the late 1980s, though identifying an exact date is nearly impossible mainly because some assets and liabilities are very hard to mark to market in the same way as traded stocks and bonds. This is especially the case for plants and equipment and, to a lesser extent, real estate.

For years, one of the big puzzles was why, given the prodigious rate at which Americans were borrowing from abroad, the United States was not falling deeper into debt than the official statistics appeared to show. One especially curious period was 1998–2010, when U.S. net foreign liabilities went up at a snail's pace compared with how much the United States was borrowing. For example, by 2010, cumulative U.S. current account deficits amounted to 45 percent of U.S. income, but net liabilities to foreigners increased only 17 percent.[3] What was going on?

Just looking at the current account is misleading because it does not include capital gains and losses on existing assets. For example, if all your wealth is in a house that you bought for $200,000 and then over the course of the year it becomes worth $300,000, your wealth can go up even if your expenditures exceed your salary by $20,000.

As it happens, foreign investments in the United States have long been tilted heavily toward bonds, particularly short-term bonds (a roughly 60–40 ratio of debt to risky assets). U.S. investments abroad have been exactly the opposite — roughly 60 percent in stocks or direct foreign investment. This fact alone means that on average, Americans typically earn higher returns; over long periods, stocks outperform bonds. Direct foreign investment, where U.S. companies or individuals build plants or buy privately owned firms abroad, is another form of investment that, if anything, pays an even higher return. (The same would apply to direct foreign investment in the United States.)

My aforementioned great-aunt Henreitta, starting from almost nothing with her shoe factory in Italy, eventually did well enough to return to the United States and become an artist. She had a good eye for artistic talent—she was a very early customer of Andy Warhol, who drew pictures of her shoes for an advertisement in *McCall's* magazine. Had Henrietta bought U.S. bonds, she would have deeply regretted it after the high-inflation 1970s. Had she bought an early Warhol, she could have retired much sooner.

The United States' higher-risk and higher-return portfolio means that even if Americans' wealth is sapped thanks to high spending relative to income, the loss might be muted by the higher return it gets on its assets. The economists Pierre-Olivier Gourinchas and Hélène Rey were perhaps the first to point out just how impactful this phenomenon is, especially in a world in which gross investment flows are quite large.[4] (At present, Gourinchas is chief economist at the IMF.) Even if its current account were in balance, the United States could be accumulating large claims on the rest of the world at the same time that the rest of the world was accumulating large claims on the United States. In a simple

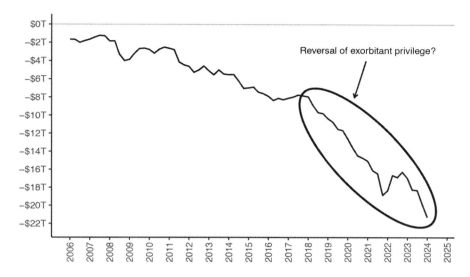

Figure 13. U.S. net foreign asset position, 2006–2024
Data Source: Federal Reserve Bank of St. Louis.

case, a German investor buys Ford Motor Company bonds (which are relatively low risk), and Ford invests the money in a German auto plant (which might have quite a high return but is much riskier). Initially, the trade is a wash and does not affect the net savings captured in the current account. But over time the German auto plant is likely to produce more income flowing back to the United States in the form of profits than Ford will have to pay out in interest to the German investor.

Gourinchas and Rey actually showed something stronger than this; they showed that across all classes of investments the United States receives a higher return than it pays to foreigners. There was initially some controversy over this result because it is difficult to construct the data properly, but over time the result has seemed to hold up. There are many reasons, but the most fundamental is simply that U.S. investments tend to be less risky.

Recently, the scenario has flipped, as figure 13 illustrates.[5] As of the first quarter of 2024, U.S. net foreign liabilities had jumped to 72 percent of GDP, up from 17 percent in 2010, and exceeded the United States' accumulated current account deficits back to 1990.[6] Did the United States' exorbitant privilege suddenly disappear? Not necessarily. It is still the case that the United States invests disproportionately more in stocks abroad compared with foreigners who invest disproportionately more in bonds. What has changed over the past decade, however, is that U.S. stocks have vastly outperformed foreign stocks, so foreigners who invested in the United States have done far better than Americans who have diversified abroad. (Recall the stunning outperformance of the U.S. stock market relative to the European stock market shown in figure 5 in chapter 4.) As of this writing in mid-2024, there have been few investments better than Apple, Meta (Facebook), Alphabet (Google), Microsoft, Amazon, Nvidia, or Tesla.[7] Whether this past decade will prove anomalous and foreign risky assets (such as stocks) will outperform U.S. risky assets over extended periods in the future is anyone's guess. For what it is worth, my guess is that the next decade will see a significant rebalancing of U.S. and foreign equity returns, even if Europe fails to close the income gap.

The net foreign investment position of the United States is also quite sensitive to the dollar exchange rate, and the dollar, too, has had a good run, at least well into 2024. When the dollar outperforms against, say, the euro, the return on investing in the United States versus abroad increases. This is also not something that can be relied on to continue. In fact, to remind the reader, even though exchange rates themselves are notoriously difficult to predict or explain, the *inflation-adjusted* exchange rate has more predictability. A good rule of thumb is that when the dollar exchange rate rises significantly over a relatively short period, even after adjusting for inflation differences between the United States and its trading partners, there is a high chance that it will at least partly reverse over a few years, either through higher inflation in U.S. trading partners or through a depreciation of the exchange rate.

The United States' exorbitant privilege is an active area of research, and there are many rabbit holes one could go down. It suffices to briefly mention a couple here. The economists Ricardo Hausmann and Federico Sturzenegger have argued that statisticians at the U.S. Bureau of Economic Analysis badly underestimate the historical size of U.S. assets held abroad and thus wildly understate the capital gains those assets have accrued. Therefore, they conclude, the value of U.S. assets abroad is far greater than the official numbers indicate. In particular, they reasoned that legacy U.S. plant and equipment abroad likely spin out much higher returns than locally held companies, thanks to access to U.S. technology and capital. One piece of evidence supporting their view is the fact that U.S. companies have long typically reported much larger returns on their direct foreign investments than have foreign companies operating in the United States.

Hausmann and Sturzenegger ingeniously attributed the differential to "dark matter," meaning the unseen (or understated) value of U.S. assets abroad.[8] A higher valuation for the assets would bring the returns (basically the profits divided by the estimated value of the investments) down to earth. In a later paper with the economist Ellen McGrattan, the Nobel Prize–winning economist Edward Prescott made a similar argument.[9] Part of the answer might lie in the way that multinationals report profits, using accounting tricks like transfer pricing to exaggerate what the foreign subsidiary was earning in the low-tax foreign country and understate profit in the high-tax United States. Dark matter is still a bit of a mystery, and I will leave it at that.

A second rabbit hole comes from new big-data techniques that, combined with the gradual opening up to researchers of proprietary data sets, have allowed much closer examination of the comparative returns of firms at home and abroad. The economists Carol Bertaut, Stephanie Curcuru, Ester Faia, and Pierre-Olivier Gourinchas have found that financing flows seem to follow the same winner-takes-all (or most) pattern that so much else in the modern economy does, and this has particularly benefited U.S. firms of late, allowing them to earn larger returns compared with foreign-owned firms that have more difficulties with financing.[10] However, these economists still found that the root of the U.S. advantage is that Americans have a greater appetite for risk in their foreign investments than do foreigners in U.S. investments.

The great MIT economist Charles Kindleberger had an explanation back in the mid-1960s, just as complaints about exorbitant privilege were reaching an early crescendo.[11] Kindleberger pointed out that the United States had a more developed financial system than any other country, which allowed it to be "Banker to the World." The United States would take in investments from foreigners seeking a safe place to park their money, and then lend out to risky projects abroad. This is very much what we see today. Which brings us to the question of what, exactly, is exorbitant about this aspect of the U.S. privilege, and how intimately is it connected with dollar dominance?

PERKS AND BURDENS

One perspective is that the United States benefited from not being a battleground in World War II, thereby gaining a giant first-mover advantage in the global economy. On top of that, the post-war Bretton Woods exchange rate system helped enshrine the United States at the center of the currency system. As generous as the post-war Marshall reconstruction plan was, it also shaped Western Europe into free-market economies that the United States could do business with, strengthening U.S. hegemony. The French would have preferred a more balanced system, such as the tripartite arrangement at the end of the 1930s, which required the United States to take some of the responsibility for fixing the exchange rate; the precise details are not critical here but can be found in *Monetary War and Peace* by Max Harris.[12] The main point is that such responsibility would have forced the United States to hold significantly more foreign-currency reserves (including French francs). France could have held correspondingly fewer dollars. Whether such a system would have been workable in a global economy that had become so asymmetric is an open question.

There is, however, another way of looking at things, one that suggests that it was not just a turn of world history that made the United States banker to the world but a set of legal institutions far better suited to being a banker country than France could ever be. In particular, there is Andrei Shleifer and Robert Vishny's thesis that the Anglo-American legal system provides a more predictable environment for creditors and thus for the flourishing of modern finance. Before their work, there was a common view among legal scholars that all the various major legal systems—including the French, German, Spanish, and Scandinavian systems (all generally based on civil law consisting of codified statutes and ordinances), and the Anglo-American systems (based on common law, which combines the passing of laws with case precedent), were just different approaches to solving the same problems. Each was thought to have its advantages and disadvantages, with none to be strictly preferred with respect to the financial sector. Shleifer and Vishnay argued that, in fact, this was not the case, compiling massive cross-country comparisons to make their point.[13] As just one example, in many countries (e.g., France and Brazil) bankruptcy judges are famously biased in favor of debtors.

Notably, as the U.K. economy recovered from World War II, London remained the financial capital of Europe. It remained so even after the birth of the euro in 1999, and remains so even after the Brexit vote in 2016. The European Central Bank is located in Frankfurt, and the German economy has long surpassed the British economy in size. Yet Frankfurt is far behind London as a financial center. Paris is a minor player by comparison, despite the hopes France had pinned on the euro.

The preceding discussion focused narrowly on the legal system; certainly, there are other important institutional differences that might underpin the United States' (and the United Kingdom's) ability to be a global financial intermediary. For example, there has historically been a high level of trust that the United States will not arbitrarily seize foreign assets, and will respect foreigners' tax residency, given that taxation is another way to partially seize assets. Concern over maintaining this reputation, aside from legal issues, has been an obstacle in the seizure of the Russian central bank's hard currency reserves. The fact that U.S. states are allowed to compete with each other to induce foreign investments is another advantage to the United States.

As investors in foreign assets, Americans have another advantage that is almost unique: historically, the United States has been a nation of immigrants. Immigrants to the United States, especially those who are first- or second-generation, typically still have strong connections to their native land and have good knowledge of local institutions. This gives them a large comparative advantage in channeling U.S. investment funds back home, in essence helping to fill in the weak financial markets that constrain entrepreneurs in much of the world.

This effect shows up strongly when one looks at, say, how much foreign direct investment in Germany comes from U.S. counties or states with large German immigrant populations, or how much investment in Italy comes from regions of the United States that historically have had large concentrations of Italian immigrants (e.g., my hometown, Rochester, New York). As it happens, during the period of mass German immigration to the United States at the end of the nineteenth century, the Midwest was relatively attractive for immigrants, and many settled there. A big wave of Italian migrants arrived at the beginning of the twentieth century, when the West was particularly attractive, and many Italians settled there. Conversely, the effective ban on Chinese immigration between 1882 and 1965, which also affected much of Asia, left the existing Asian

227

American populations concentrated as well; even today 30 percent live in California. Again, to dig into the weeds, it is necessary to make sure the correlations are not caused by spurious factors. However, recent research by the economists Konrad Burchardi, Thomas Chaney, and Tarek Hassan have offered clever ways to deal with this issue.[14]

In recent years, as the rest of the world has amassed greater concentrations of wealth, and as foreign families have anchored their connection to the United States by sending children to U.S. colleges, the foreign direct investment channel may have become more of a two-way street. This has arguably already led to some offset to the investing advantage the United States gets from its large and diverse immigrant populations (notably, foreign investors earning high returns in U.S. tech startups).

There is also the possibility that Americans have a different attitude toward taking risks. For better or for worse, the entire structure of America's system rewards risk-takers — perhaps because of more generous bankruptcy laws — and this is reflected in investment choices. Or a much simpler explanation would be that Americans are much richer than citizens of other large countries, and rich people can afford to take bigger risks. Of course, one of the reasons there are competing notions of exorbitant privilege is precisely because the United States today enjoys so many interlocking advantages that mutually reinforce each other.

One final point. Although the original exorbitant-privilege debate contrasted the United States and Europe, in today's era of financial globalization much of the action is between advanced economies vis-à-vis emerging markets and developing economies. We have already discussed how emerging economies especially have built up central bank reserves to help stabilize their exchange rates and financial systems; 60 percent might be dollars but most of the rest is in yen, euro, and the currencies of other advanced economies. The fact that low-interest-rate Japan has long enjoyed exorbitant privilege is well known.[15] More broadly, the same holds true for most advanced economies, albeit not necessarily to the same degree as for the United States.[16] So being rich is good; being rich and the United States is even better.

CHAPTER 22

SMALL WAYS THE UNITED STATES HELPS COUNTRIES DEAL WITH DOLLAR DOMINANCE

It has to be said that in recent years, the U.S. Federal Reserve has been quite clever in finding ways to bend its rules slightly — or one might say interpret them generously — so as to share just a bit of its privileged position with the 96 percent of humankind that lives elsewhere. A number of observers have gotten very excited about the idea that the Fed could and should share even more.

The Federal Reserve's mandate, however, requires that it focus only on the welfare of the United States. It can consider the impact of its policies on the rest of the world only to the extent there is blowback on the United States. When the Fed chair Paul Volcker sharply raised interest rates in the 1980s to fight runaway U.S. inflation, the fact that his policies triggered a debt crisis in Latin America was a concern, but mainly because these countries had huge debts to the U.S. banking system. That may seem brutal, yet Fed independence just does not extend to its own foreign policy.

Policymakers from emerging markets nevertheless have vigorously critiqued the Fed for being so inward looking. For example, India's central bank head Raghuram Rajan argued in 2014 that the Federal Reserve was paying insufficient attention to the ripple effects of its policies on emerging markets as it exited from ultra-loose monetary policy.[1] His arguments were compelling and cogent, but to little avail.

PERKS AND BURDENS

Before turning to the central bank dollar swap lines, which is perhaps the most interesting and important, let's dispense with two others. First, there is the Fed's participation in the Bank for International Settlements' bimonthly Global Economy Meetings, which the Fed chair regularly attends along with the heads of twenty-nine other central banks; another twenty-two central bank leaders are allowed as observers.[2] Skeptics may view these meetings as superficial; I know I did before having any policy experience. That view is wrong. A lot of information gets exchanged—information a savvy market participant could make tens of billions of dollars off, information that allows central bankers to make much better forecasts and hence better policy. One highlight of these meetings is the Fed chair's assessment of where the U.S. economy is going. Of course, the chair is not going to outright say what the next interest rate move is; however, by sharing forecasts and candidly answering questions, the Fed chair likely reveals a lot. (That is no small part of why financial conferences have long been willing to pay exorbitant speaking fees to former Fed chairs and governors, especially right after they step down from office, although the restrictions on this have tightened somewhat in recent years.) No wonder central bank governors from Asia, Africa, and Latin America will endure painfully long flights over long distances to attend the BIS meetings. Although there are no private participants in the main meetings, it should be noted that there are representatives from several countries with extremely large sovereign wealth funds, including Norway, Singapore, Saudi Arabia, and China, to name just a few. One of my former colleagues, the late professor Richard Cooper, a pioneer on the topic of international policy coordination, was absolutely incensed about this, which he regarded as tantamount to allowing insider trading. Cooper's claim is worth further consideration, though I will leave it to scholars of international financial organizations to debate the point.

There are other ways the United States helps out more directly. The most important is as the largest shareholder of the International Monetary Fund (discussed in chapter 17). At the Marrakesh meetings in October 2023, the United States agreed to a 50 percent increase in IMF core quota lending resources, which would bring the IMF's total quotas close to a trillion dollars.[3] (Core quota resources are the rotating funds used for standard IMF bailout loans — for example, to Greece and Argentina.) The deal was years in the making and had to overcome countless obstacles; little doubt the prospect that after 2024 the IMF might be dealing with a much more skeptical U.S. administration helped concentrate their minds. Christine Lagarde, the president of the European Central Bank and a former head of the IMF, reportedly termed the shockingly successful boost as the "Marrakesh Miracle." It was a milestone. Still, considering that the IMF already has programs in nearly a hundred countries (as of January 2024), and that its resources are simply dwarfed by the size of world capital markets, a trillion dollars is not as big a "bazooka" as it sounds. The total amount of global debt (public plus private) was $235 trillion at the end of 2023.[4] True, this comparison is exaggerated since advanced-economy government debt alone accounts for more than a quarter of the total. However, given the $12 trillion central banks hold in foreign exchange reserves, or the trillions of dollars sloshing about in world capital markets each day, one does not want to overstate how much the United States helps through the IMF.[5]

This brings us to the most important sharing tool the Federal Reserve has at its disposal and, in the near term, the one likely to be the center of continuing discussion. Central bank "swap lines" are a way the Federal Reserve can help countries suffering dollar liquidity crises, provided the Fed judges the collateral they put up to be essentially riskless. For example, as the pandemic unfolded in February and March of 2020, the flight to dollar safety put pressure on dollar markets worldwide, both in advanced economies and in emerging markets that were experiencing large outflows of capital. The Fed eventually stepped in by activating swap lines that offer foreign central banks short-term dollar lines of credit with foreign central bank liabilities as the collateral.[6] At their peak, the swap lines reached almost $450 billion in 2020, as figure 14 shows.[7] As one can see from the figure, foreign central banks drew on these swap lines even more strongly during the 2008–2009 global financial crisis, when they peaked at $582 billion. The much smaller spike from late 2011 to early 2012 coincides with the European debt crisis.

These loans are referred to as "swap lines" because there is a firm commitment to unwind the trade and repay the loans in full, with no exchange rate risk to the Fed. The idea actually dates back to the 1960s, when U.S. officials sup-

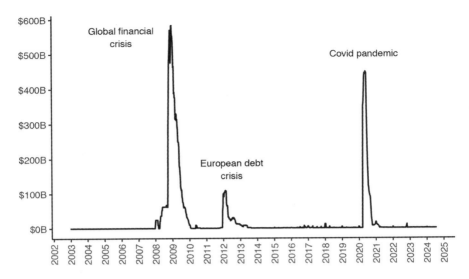

Figure 14. Foreign central bank use of Fed dollar swap lines, 2003–2024
Data Source: Federal Reserve Bank of St. Louis.

ported the development of Eurodollar markets in London by offering swap lines to the Bank of England so that it would not be compelled to cash in its own U.S. Treasury bills for gold every time it needed to stabilize the market.

In theory, by making trades with foreign central banks, the Fed is taking on the highest-quality debt a country has to offer. What's in it for the Fed? Aside from stemming crises that could affect the United States, the potential availability of swap lines in crises encourages foreign regulators to take a more relaxed attitude toward dollarization of their financial markets, thereby expanding networks and dollar hegemony. In doses, it is good business.

Access to dollar funding is extremely valuable in a major crisis, even for countries that have large dollar reserves. For example, during the global financial crisis, Korean markets came under enormous dollar funding strains even though the Bank of Korea had $240 billion of reserves.[8] Remarkably, as soon as the Fed swap line was announced, the pressures dissipated. During that period, the Fed also issued swap lines to a raft of other central banks, including those of England, Japan, Brazil, New Zealand, and Mexico.[9] Importantly, the Fed charges a fee for its swap lines (it charged 0.5 percent during the global financial crisis and then only 0.25 percent during the pandemic), and does not allow large balances to persist after a crisis subsides.[10]

The most obvious downside to swap lines is that the collateral the Fed holds in return for its loan is non-dollar-denominated foreign government debt, even if the immediate counterparty is the foreign country's central bank. It may be the safest form of debt a country has to offer, but that does not make it completely safe. Although the risk of default is small, it is not completely trivial, especially given that swap lines peak in situations of maximum global stress, when resilience to a further shock is at a low point. The Fed recognizes the very small risk of default. It also knows that unless it is willing to help foreign central banks in a global panic, dollar dominance will suffer.

Officially, the Fed has to say that swap lines are effectively riskless; it is proscribed from taking on credit risk without explicit Treasury backing. Of course, it is folly to assume that advanced-country default is impossible, and it is probably only a matter of time until some extraordinary circumstance pushes an advanced country to the brink. Advanced countries have defaulted in the past, even if it has been eight decades or more for most. The United Kingdom and France defaulted on their World War I debts to the U.S. government in 1931; Japan and Germany defaulted on their debts to private creditors during World War II. Brazil and Mexico defaulted in the 1980s, and many times before that.[11] During the pandemic, they all got swap lines. It worked out well and most likely would again; this does not mean repayment is a sure thing. Not so long ago, many experts were saying that inflation had been dormant for so many decades that we could safely assume it would never happen again. Before the 2008–2009 financial crisis, many a top economist, most famously Robert Lucas, confidently declared that advanced economies would never again experience a large financial crisis anything like the Great Depression of the 1930s.[12] By the same token, advanced-country sovereign default can happen; swap lines are a calculated risk, not riskless. Risk would become a much bigger consideration if, in the future, swap lines were dramatically scaled up or extended to countries that have a relatively recent history of default.

Even if one sets aside the issue of default risk and assumes swaps with major advanced economies' central banks to be 100 percent safe, there is another interesting question: How would expanded use of swap lines affect the discounts that the U.S. government and private sector currently receive on dollar borrowing? If dollar swap lines were dramatically beefed up so that they could be accessed on a regular basis, and at scale, it would certainly encourage other countries to issue vastly more dollar debt, both public and private. And this surge in supply of dollar debt could eat into the U.S. government's borrowing "privilege."[13]

Countries that are not beneficiaries of swap lines complain that swap lines go only to "friends of the Fed." Some have argued that the IMF should fill in the gap, even if it means extending swaps to countries that are significant credit risks. Unfortunately, such plans have the potential to run afoul of the same limitations we saw in the case of trying to make IMF special drawing rights into a world currency; the IMF has a different mandate than the Federal Reserve and can be expected to be much softer on its borrowers and far more amenable to aiding developing countries. As we saw with the discussions over whether to lend more money to Argentina (discussed in chapter 14), it is very hard in real time to recognize the line between a liquidity crisis and a solvency crisis, and there is always great pressure on policymakers to view everything as a liquidity crisis so that they can claim that a bailout is risk free and will cost nothing.

That said, even though the Federal Reserve has been somewhat discriminating in selecting which countries get swap lines, in practice, the entire world dollar funding market — even small countries that are not "friends of the Fed" — has benefited. Global dollar markets are deeply intertwined. By flooding the largest economies with dollars, the Fed is effectively taking some of the pressure off dollar liquidity everywhere.

It should be noted that in anticipation of perhaps someday establishing the renminbi more firmly as a global currency, the People's Bank of China has also been experimenting with renminbi swap lines, albeit still on a very small scale compared with the Fed or even the European Central Bank.[14]

Precise estimates of the quantitative effects of swap lines are difficult to pin down, in part because there have really only been two major swap-line episodes in the modern floating era (the global financial crisis and the Covid pandemic), and in part because the swap lines have come along with myriad other policy measures. For example, at around the same time that swap-line use burgeoned in March 2022, the Fed unveiled a plethora of other facilities that backed everything from municipal bonds to junk bonds.[15] Nevertheless, it is possible to somewhat disentangle these effects by using very-high-frequency data—that is, by looking at market rates right after swap lines are announced, and by taking advantage of the fact that not all countries received swap lines simultaneously and that many countries did not receive swap lines at all. One recent study found that countries that received swap lines saw liquidity premiums in their markets fall (relative to countries that did not receive swap lines), their exchange rates appreciate, and so-called covered interest parity deviations fall; the latter is a measure of the strength of bank balance sheets.[16] These results do not tell us anything about how the swap lines might eat into exorbitant privilege, and with only two major episodes of swap-line issuance in recent decades, there just isn't enough data.

The issue of expanded Fed and IMF swap lines surely deserves further deliberation, and this is an area where there might be ways to improve the current global exchange rate system, at least marginally, without major institutional changes. Of course, as the experience of the European debt crisis illustrates, it is difficult to extend open-ended sovereign credit without improved global governance.

One can get a glimmer of the Fed's thinking about the limits to swap lines from transcripts of its meetings during the global financial crisis. (The pandemic-era transcripts have not yet been released by the Fed, since there is generally a five-year delay before publication.) For example, in discussing a proposal to establish swap lines with Singapore, Korea, Brazil, and Mexico in October 2008, Board members noted that these countries had ample reserves as collateral, had adopted prudent policies (in the staff's judgment), and most importantly, cared about staying on good terms with the United States.[17] In a conference call in May 2010, the Fed discussed the possibility of reactivating its swap lines with the ECB and, in particular, an assessment of eurozone governance risks.[18]

In sum, there are ways the United States helps other countries manage the costs of having to deal with the dollar, and Americans can point to these. Mostly though, the U.S. dollar policy is to let everyone else manage for themselves.

CHAPTER 23

COSTS OF BEING A DOMINANT CURRENCY

As we have seen, the United States gains clear quantitative benefits from issuing the dominant global currency, in addition to amorphous benefits such as privileged access to information and an enhanced ability to impose financial sanctions. Are there significant costs to maintaining dominant-currency status? The main drawback that Robert Aliber and Walter Salant worried about six decades ago — the fear that persistent inflation would induce foreign central banks to trade dollars for gold en masse — is gone. The dollar is no longer convertible into gold; U.S. Treasury debt no longer has gold clauses.

To be clear, there can still be a run on U.S. Treasury bills. For example, people sometimes ask what would happen if China "weaponized" its dollar reserves ($2 trillion as of 2024), by dumping them all at once.[1] There is little question that there would be a spike in yields even if the Federal Reserve itself temporarily soaked up all the debt China was selling. It would be traumatic. However, even if the Chinese sale led to higher interest rates and temporarily higher inflation, it would not take down the system.

That said, in today's world where political brinkmanship has become routine, anything is possible. If a U.S. president capriciously announced that the United States might tax or withhold debt payments to certain countries, the resulting flight from Treasuries could be worldwide. Total foreign holdings of

COSTS OF BEING A DOMINANT CURRENCY

U.S. debt today are four times China's holdings alone. One would hope that the U.S. Treasury and Federal Reserve have war-gamed such "black swan" scenarios. Nevertheless, all in all, it is probably fair to say the vulnerability to a run today is vastly less than it was under Bretton Woods, when the dollar was backed with gold.

Are there any big drawbacks to dominant-currency status now that there is no commitment to back the dollar with gold? We will look at a couple in this chapter. One is quite clear-cut and purely economic, having to do with disproportionate losses the United States incurs on its global portfolio in downturns. The United States incurs these disproportionate losses in part because it is banker to the world and holds a relatively risky portfolio, and in part because the dollar tends to appreciate in global downturns. We will start with the other cost, which is less obvious but potentially much larger.

One can debate the extent to which military power is an essential ingredient to currency dominance, but not too much. Spain, the Netherlands, and the United Kingdom were all formidable military powers during their currencies' peak years of influence. Since World War II, the United States has been a global superpower. At the very least, military power and currency dominance are complements: dollar dominance makes it easier to finance the military and, in particular, to fund sudden buildups.[2] A more subtle point, too, is that the United States' military power may also give it additional leverage in establishing the rules and setting the policies for international financial markets and international financial institutions. It's not that U.S. negotiators are so crude and say "It's our bomb and we're going home" if they don't get their way (except perhaps at times Donald Trump). Yet military power gives important negotiating leverage over a broad swath of issues; at least there is a strong game-theoretic argument for believing so. The basic idea of recognizing interlinkages between finance, trade, and security issues has become a hot topic in international political economy research.[3]

The United States today spends vastly more on its military than does any other country: 3.7 percent of GDP in 2024. France spent barely 2 percent; Germany and Italy about 1.5 percent of their much smaller GDPs; and Canada even less. And this does not even take into account that European spending is fragmented and inefficient, with everyone wanting to be in charge and chronic

Figure 15. U.S. military expenditures as a percentage of GDP, 1947–2024
Data Source: Federal Reserve Bank of St. Louis.

difficulty in coordinating weapons development and production. Russia's invasion of Ukraine in 2022 has led to a modest rebalancing, although it is not clear whose defense spending will go up more in the long run, the United States' or Europe's. It is the United States whose spending decreased the most after the fall of the Berlin Wall, and if its share increases to anything like it was three decades ago, the implications for the U.S. budget will be staggering.

Figure 15 is particularly striking. U.S. military spending as a share of GDP was 6.8 percent at the end of the 1980s and reached 11 percent during the Vietnam War era.[4] To reach 6.8 percent today, the United States would need to spend close to $900 billion a year more on defense than it currently does; to reach 11 percent, it would need to spend over $2 trillion more.[5] By contrast, the expenditures of the United States' main allies never rose much above 3 percent of GDP over this entire period according to statistics from the Stockholm International Peace Research Institute.[6] If the ongoing second Cold War persists, or worse yet deepens, unwinding the peace dividend could be a staggeringly expensive proposition.

Admittedly, it is hard to know how much spending will have to go up and, in particular how recent developments in drone warfare, artificial intelligence, and space warfare will affect costs. Clearly the United States will need to be at the cutting edge in these areas given advantages China has in others—for example, its vastly greater shipbuilding capacity and the fact that it can get away with compensating its military personnel far less than the United States does. (In my college years, a Navy midshipman once explained to me that part of the Soviet Union's cost advantage over the United States in shipbuilding was all the money it saved on amenities and safety features. One suspects this is also true of China today.)

Europe's reluctance to share the burden of mutual defense has famously become a sticking point in transatlantic relations. While other U.S. presidents have not been as crude and bombastic as Donald Trump, who threatened to withdraw from NATO, his frustrations are generally shared. Indeed, when liberals succeed in cutting defense budgets, the message sent to Europe is clear enough, that there is an expectation that other rich countries will step up to fill in the gap.

Given the historical disparity, there is a lot of ground to make up. Even if Europe were to vastly increase its military expenditures overnight, this would only be a first step toward making up lost ground from years of forgone investment—for example, in ships, missiles, and equipment, not to mention technology. Part of the way Europe and Japan pay for their superior social nets is by spending less on their military. Imagine if the United States could expand its social programs by $500 to $600 billion per year by scaling back military spending to the same share of GDP as its largest allies.

Perhaps it is unfair to pick on France, but let us do it anyway. Only a week before Russia's invasion of Ukraine in February 2022, the National Defense and Armed Forces Committee of the French National Assembly issued a scathing report on French preparedness. It stated that the country no longer had enough ammunition to sustain a high-intensity war and would run out in just a few weeks in the event of a "bitter" conflict.[7] In fact, had France been put in a position in which it had to expend ammunition at the same rate as the Ukrainian army, its armed forces might have run out of bullets in a few days. Understandably, some American military leaders view Europe's weak contribution to its own defense as weaponized incompetence, as one intimated to me in a conversation during the European debt crisis. We were together with two of his lieutenants on a small antique military vessel after I had spoken at a security conference. He asked whether Europe, given its debt morass, could still be relied on to pay its share of joint weapons development projects. Although I answered, "Yes, I would definitely assume so if the commitments were clearly specified," my companions remained skeptical.

Does the United States carry so much of the burden of defending its allies because Americans like it that way, or because it gets gamed into doing so? Back in 1968 the economists Mancur Olson and Richard Zeckhauser developed an economic theory of alliances, arguing that the United States is at a strategic disadvantage in trying to get smaller European countries to contribute to NATO.[8] Their idea was that if smaller European countries are setting their defense budgets individually, they have a huge incentive to free ride and not pay their fair share of the costs. If, for example, the Netherlands decides to spend a little less on defense, it is not going to make a decisive difference to the collective deterrence NATO provides. By contrast, when the much larger U.S. economy devotes an extra 1 percent of its GDP on defense, it really moves the needle. Political scientists have since pointed out that the Olson-Zeckhauser thesis does not necessarily explain other collective-action problems between the United States and Europe; for example, Europe has done more on the environment. Nevertheless, six decades after its publication, and despite the coordinating device of the European Union, the Olson-Zeckhauser thesis still rings true for the NATO alliance. No, we should not be too impressed if Europe achieves its modest 2 percent spending target in the wake of Russian aggression.

If the European Union ever progresses to the point of meaningful political and fiscal integration, the situation both for NATO and for the dollar's dominant-currency status might be different. For now, that day seems far off, although France's president, Emmanuel Macron, has raised the possibility of at least partially addressing the coordination problem by issuing EU-wide defense bonds; of course this would have to done at scale.[9] Nevertheless, without deep integration of Europe's defense industries, the cost of scaling up defense capabilities might still be prohibitive. There are many obstacles to integration, ranging from disagreement over who would control a more united European military-industrial complex to fears of German rearmament (within and outside Germany).

COSTS OF BEING A DOMINANT CURRENCY

A European economist suggested to me recently that there might be an unspoken French concern that if Germany began rearmament in earnest, German firms would soon dominate defense and nuclear sectors that are, for the moment, dominated in Europe by France. That would be especially painful, as there are precious few manufacturing areas in which France is competitive.[10] Nevertheless, Macron has warned that Europe "can die" without a stronger military, and the president of the European Commission, Ursula von der Leyen, has proposed subsidizing the defense industry, though others worry that having Europe become a superpower would destabilize transatlantic relations.[11] Perhaps just as Europe came together to deal with its debt crisis, the European project will move forward on this occasion as well. If Europe ever did become a military superpower, the euro would almost surely gain on the dollar, even outside its home base.

There are those who believe that the United States should drastically cut its military spending regardless, opining that a large fraction of military spending is invariably wasted. This is no doubt the case, and there is a lot of political pork in military spending. That said, the value of some defense expenditures becomes apparent only when a nation fails to make them and suffers the consequences. One is reminded of the Constitutional Convention in 1787, where a delegate is said to have proposed limiting the size of the U.S. army to 5,000 troops. In response, George Washington, having just led an understaffed, underfed, and underequipped Continental Army, quipped that he was fine with that, as long the constitution also stated that no invading foreign army could have more than 3,000 troops. James Madison, who later became the country's fourth president, said much the same in the *Federalist Papers*.[12]

Overall, it is hard to sustain the role of a dominant currency without being one of world's geopolitical superpowers. Europe can hide behind the shield of the United States, but it lacks both leverage and competence over many critical issues. The global financial system depends on rules, and as we suggested earlier in this chapter, the country that is both an economic and a military superpower has enormous power to shape the rules. Thinking otherwise is dangerously naive.

As noted at the outset of this chapter, economists have also focused on a second, and very different, cost of dollar dominance—that of providing insurance to the world in case of severe global downturns and, to a lesser extent, in recessions. There are two main components. One has to do with the fact that the dollar tends to appreciate in a crisis, as funds generally pour into the United States, partly because the United States is considered a low-risk debtor, and partly because U.S. markets are especially deep and less likely to freeze up. The rise in the dollar has the effect of increasing the foreign-currency market value of U.S. assets in foreign portfolios and decreasing the dollar market value of foreign assets in U.S. portfolios. It may sound odd to call this "insurance," but it does make investments in dollar-denominated bonds a better hedge against crises. We have previously noted that this is one of the reasons U.S. Treasury debt might pay a lower interest rate than it would otherwise.

In a "risk-off" market panic, where investors stampede to reduce the riskiness of their portfolios, the dollar can go up a lot. During the global financial crisis, a broad trade-weighted index of the dollar against its trading partners shot up over 10 percent between September 2008 and March 2009 before things first began to turn around. The same thing happened again during the pandemic, when the trade-weighted dollar increased by over 5 percent.[13] Just as the United States is not the only advanced country to earn some measure of exorbitant privilege, the dollar is not the only "safe" currency in this regard. In a crisis, investors often also flee to the Japanese yen and the Swiss franc.

A second dimension of U.S. insurance derives precisely from its "banker to the world" function. Remember that compared with foreign holdings of U.S. assets, U.S. holdings of foreign assets tend to be more in equities and generally in riskier assets. Normally, these yield a high return, but in a downturn, stock prices tend to collapse. Foreigners also lose money in U.S. stocks, but since a big share of their U.S. investments are in things like Treasury bills, they tend to lose much less. Being banker to the world means having to take it on the chin sometimes when it is especially painful. Sometimes instead of exorbitant privilege, the U.S. pays an "exorbitant duty."[14]

Does the cost of providing insurance to the rest of the world fully offset the benefits of exorbitant privilege? As discussed in chapter 20, it would take a full-blown empirical model with myriad assumptions to examine this question. One's strong intuition is that the insurance costs are not so large compared with all the benefits the United States gets, in part because deep U.S. markets allow risks to be spread extremely efficiently, a point the former Fed chair Alan Greenspan often emphasized. In most standard economic models, to get a really large number for the insurance cost that comes with exorbitant privilege, one would need to assume that Americans who are investing abroad are extremely risk averse, which somewhat contradicts the fact that they are making such risky investments.

A qualification to the "insurance" result is that it presumes that U.S. macroeconomic policy dysfunction is not the *source* of the crisis. Suppose that to fund a politically motivated tax cut or spending increase the U.S. government runs a very large deficit, and out of concern for employment, the Fed does not allow interest rates to rise enough to contain inflation. In this situation, it is quite possible that the dollar exchange rate would depreciate rather than appreciate. One can come up with other examples, though of course just because a crisis is caused by U.S. macroeconomic policy malfeasance doesn't mean the dollar loses, as exemplified by the Great Depression of the 1930s and the 2008–2009 global financial crisis.

To conclude, although global currency dominance is indeed a great franchise, it comes with some significant costs, especially the costs of being a military superpower, and is not quite the unalloyed benefit that it is sometimes portrayed as.

PART VI

PEAK DOLLAR DOMINANCE

CHAPTER 24

CENTRAL BANK INDEPENDENCE

The Bulwark of Currency Dominance

"Climate is systemic risk, climate is systemic risk," a dozen protestors chanted as they pushed their way onto the stage where I was participating in a panel discussion with Jay Powell, the Fed chair; Gita Gopinath, the IMF's second-in-command; Amir Yaron, governor of the Bank of Israel; and Pierre-Olivier Gourinchas, the chief economist at the IMF and moderator of the panel. At first, we did not know what was happening and it was pretty unsettling. It was November 9, 2023, only a month after Hamas terrorists had brutally massacred 1,200 Israeli men, women, and children, provoking an outsize Israeli retaliation. There were already intense protests and counterprotests across the United States, not least at my own university, Harvard. The IMF organizers had invited Governor Yaron six months earlier, before any of this had happened. With everything going on in the Middle East, probably no one expected Yaron to come, but he did, despite knowing that IMF security might not be able to protect him. After the initial shock, we quickly realized that the protestors were not after Governor Yaron.

"Jerome Powell, by refusing to take climate risk as a systemic crisis, you are putting us at risk of an economic disaster. Climate change will heighten the risk of a banking crisis. Because of your negligence, the American people will have to take a 15 percent loss of GDP," one of the leaders, a twenty-something young woman, started reciting.

As the protestors quickly lined up onstage a foot or two behind him, Powell appeared remarkably calm despite briefly cursing into the hot mic. I would have been terrified. Meanwhile, Pierre-Olivier alertly pulled the rest of us off the stage, especially as we had no idea what was next. With a slight delay, live streaming of the event was cut off. Natasha, however, sitting near the front with my adult children, Gabriel and Juliana, captured every bit of it.

After the IMF pulled together enough large and beefy-looking security staff to escort (or more accurately shove) the protestors out of the room, the audience went quiet and waited for what was next. Remarkably, Powell returned after perhaps fifteen minutes and gave the rest of his speech, quite composed — just a day in the life of the Fed chair.

We will come back to the environment, an area we can all agree is supremely important to the world, though the IMF climate protestors vastly overrate the Fed's place in the hierarchy of institutions dealing with the green transition. This is not to mention the limits of the Fed's instruments and the tight boundaries within which it is free to act independently of democratically accountable elected leaders. As Chairman Powell stated as he resumed his remarks, the primary focus of the Fed needs to be on fulfilling its congressional mandate of maintaining stable inflation and maximum employment.

Although external challenges to dollar dominance and stability are serious enough, the greatest vulnerabilities come from within. In a world of pure fiat money, where there is no commodity backing to currency, trust in the Federal Reserve's commitment to keeping inflation (reasonably) stable is the single most important bulwark that stands between global economic stability and a return to the macroeconomic stone ages — that is to say, the 1970s. Anyone who thinks that Federal Reserve independence is etched in stone is naive. The Fed cannot hold out forever if political pressures to inflate are too powerful, especially if fiscal policy is patently unsustainable. The president controls appointments to the Fed Board; Congress controls the Fed's budget and can in principle re-absorb the Fed into the Treasury in the blink of an eye. The Fed has to bend sometimes, as it did in the pandemic.[1] If, however, the central bank caves too often and too easily, gradually inflation expectations will rise, and instability will ensue.

CENTRAL BANK INDEPENDENCE

It is surprising how many academic and policy economists have come to believe that controlling inflation is a purely technocratic problem that has been thoroughly solved. The assumption of low inflation is hardwired into the modern New Keynesian models that fill the pages of the top academic journals and that are now extensively used by central banks. To be precise, these models take as given that on average, the central bank will always achieve its inflation target over the long run. They take this as a matter of faith. There is no allowance for the possibility that external pressures to inflate might undermine central bank credibility, at least from time to time. Perhaps this is because in the years after the global financial crisis, when interest rates and inflation rates collapsed globally, high inflation was the last thing anyone was concerned about. In the post-pandemic world, with higher real interest rates, deglobalization, and geopolitical frictions, political pressures on central banks to hold down interest rates, thereby allowing higher inflation, will inevitably increase.[2]

Why? Well, first, no government wants to pay high interest rates on its debt, and now more so than ever. When Paul Volcker came to the Federal Reserve at the end of 1979, U.S. government debt was 30 percent of GDP, partly thanks to the unexpected double-digit inflation in the 1970s that gutted the value of long-term government bonds. Not so today. As of mid-2024, the U.S. debt-to-GDP ratio stood at 121 percent; it would have been even higher but for the unexpected burst of pandemic inflation.[3] Each 1 percentage point increase on the average interest rate paid on all federal debt held by the public adds almost $300 billion to the federal deficit. It took a lot of courage to sharply raise interest rates as Paul Volcker did in the 1980s, when he took interest rates well into double digits; today it takes even more courage to raise rates half as much.

The stock market does not like high real interest rates either. There are various ways to look at it; if one holds the growth of dividends constant, then a higher real interest rate (adjusting for inflation) cuts into the discounted present value of earnings. More simply put, when the real interest rate is high, the case for choosing stocks over bonds becomes less obvious.[4] During periods of high stock market growth, the financial sector and financial media invariably heap praise on the chair of the Fed; not so much when the Fed has to raise interest rates to control inflation.

There are also pressures from the rest of the economy. Most people love low interest rates. When financing costs are low, it is cheaper to buy a house or a car, or anything purchased on credit. And precisely because low interest rates tend to push up the price of stocks and housing, people feel wealthier, borrow more, and spend more. For a long time, Americans facing low interest rates have behaved as if savings was for suckers. Private-equity funds that took out massive loans to buy companies made spectacular profits, as did ordinary Americans who took out second mortgages on their homes or stretched to borrow for their first ones.

Last but not least, politicians love to cut taxes and raise government spending to flatter voters' perceptions of their competency, especially in the run-up to elections.[5] The political budget cycle is a well-documented phenomenon all over the world.[6] Again, the short-term political pressures on central banks are almost all toward lowering interest rates. Even though voters certainly care about price increases, the effects of interest rate cuts on inflation tend to come with a lag relative to the more immediate impact on growth. Fundamentally, at any point in time, the short-term benefits of lower interest rates typically outweigh the short-term costs in terms of higher inflation, which tends to pick up with a lag and can last for an extended period. The Fed understands perfectly well the consequences of short-term thinking; that does not mean its political overseers (Congress and the president) will always have the same agenda, especially in the run-up to an election.

A political economy story fits the facts of the 1970s, the last period of high inflation before the 2020s, a lot better than any technocratic explanation. Inflation actually started edging up in the mid to late 1960s, as President Lyndon Johnson embarked on his Great Society social-spending programs while at the same time ramping up U.S. involvement in the Vietnam War. There are certainly parallels to today: the United States has dramatically increased domestic spending while funding major proxy wars on two continents (and counting).

It was only after inflation got completely out of control during the mid to late 1970s that President Jimmy Carter turned to the former Treasury official Paul Volcker to vanquish it. Although the tough steps that Volcker took were supported by many economists, they were not an easy sell politically and met with enormous resistance. As a junior economist at the Fed in the early 1980s,

I watched builders, farmers, car dealers, and others march one after the other on the Fed. They were angry. Auto dealers flooded the Fed's mailroom with keys from cars they couldn't sell; idle builders and carpenters mailed the Fed two-by-fours (wooden planks) for which they had no use.

Back in August 1979, when Volcker arrived as chairman of the Fed, few countries endowed their central banks with any significant independence from their treasury departments. Only the Bundesbank and the Fed could be regarded as truly independent central banks; the Bank of England wasn't granted independence to set interest rates until 1997. Watching the Volcker Fed up close led me to formulate a theory that offered a new rationale for having an independent central bank, and for choosing central bankers who are more "conservative" than society as a whole, in the sense that they are known to place a high weight on controlling inflation compared with short-term output stabilization. Equivalently, as my 1985 paper showed, the independent central bank can simply place significant weight on hitting an inflation target.[7]

Earlier work, especially the Nobel Prize–winning work of Finn Kydland and Edward Prescott in a paper entitled "Rules Rather than Discretion," had identified the importance of credibility in formulating monetary policy.[8] However, their conclusion that the problem could be solved by simply having a firm policy rule had two big drawbacks. It did not come to grips with how to keep politicians from constantly undermining the Fed; rules are made to be broken. Even more critically, it did not account for the constantly morphing nature of the financial system, which would defy any attempt to enshrine a mechanical rule. Having an independent central bank with a strong commitment to stabilizing inflation solves these problems.

At the time, the idea of instituting an independent central bank with an anti-inflation character or mandate was rather radical, and it was a long multiyear struggle to get my paper published as it suffered one rejection after another. At the time the profession was searching for new mathematical monetary policy formulas, and the idea of proposing an institutional solution to the inflation problem was apparently too radical. Indeed, if the Fed media office had looked more closely before the paper went out to journals, I might never have been allowed to circulate it — especially the "conservative central banker" (with respect to inflation) part—in the first place. Fortunately, the analysis involved just enough mathematics to discourage careful reading by anyone outside of academia, especially journalists, and the paper slipped through.

The idea for making the central bank both independent and exceptionally inflation focused had come partly from watching Volcker's predecessor, the hapless G. William Miller, who was appointed by President Carter as Fed chair in 1978. My own Federal Reserve career overlapped with Miller's for only six weeks. But it was enough to see that he was doing the opposite of what was needed. Instead of forming a long-term strategy for defeating double-digit inflation, Miller veered from one short-run problem to another, overly concerned about what the next day's newspapers would say.

It did not help that most of the financial journalists at the time did not understand monetary policy any better than G. William Miller did. The basic point Miller failed to grasp is that by persistently aiming for lower short-term interest rates (the Fed only directly controls the overnight rate), he was driving *up* long-term interest rates because no one believed that he was serious about stopping inflation. And long-term interest rates—for example, home mortgage rates—are the most important ones for the economy. This may sound preposterously simple, yet the point still eludes most of the news reporting surrounding Fed meetings, which focuses disproportionately on how very-short-term rates will evolve in the near term. That is akin to looking only one or two moves ahead in chess.

Decades later, I learned from former Carter White House staffers the story of how Miller landed the second-most-powerful job in Washington. It turned out to be mostly by chance. Miller, then the CEO of the industrial conglomerate Textron, apparently made a good impression in a visit to Washington just when the Carter White House was desperately looking for a new Fed chair. Belatedly recognizing the mistake, and to clear the way for the appointment of someone with a serious plan for defeating inflation, Carter had to offer Miller the position of secretary of the Treasury.

The Fed's experience, along with the independent German Bundesbank's success in maintaining relatively stable inflation, inspired many other countries to take steps to insulate monetary policy from political pressures. In the 1990s, the designs of the European Central Bank, the Bank of England, and many other central banks were patterned off either the Bundesbank or the Fed model, with the refinement of making inflation targets more specific (per a main example in my paper). Central bank independence has generally been one of the major successes of modern macroeconomics and has paved the way for a huge turnaround in central bank performance.

If you don't believe that central bank independence matters for inflation stability, consider that during the first hundred years of the Federal Reserve's existence, from 1913 to 2013, the U.S. consumer price level increased by a factor of twenty-four(!), with spikes during the First World War and the Great Inflation of the 1970s, among other periods.[9] The scourge of inflation has been tamed only in the last few decades. Looking at the abysmal track record of the earlier period, one can understand why after the pandemic spike in inflation in 2022, the Fed was so intent on showing its determination to bring inflation back to target. It showed that it was willing to sharply raise its short-term policy interest rate in order to keep long-term inflation expectations anchored.

High and variable U.S. inflation may not be the end of the world, but it is certainly not a good thing either. Inflation leads to myriad distortions in the real economy and wreaks havoc with the financial system, especially as there is no such thing as high and stable inflation. The period of very low inflation that prevailed for almost three decades before the pandemic played a central role in establishing the dollar as a reasonably stable store of value. By encouraging more people, firms, and nations to trust the dollar, the era of low inflation helped build up the base of dollar users and applications, reinforcing and strengthening dollar network effects. The network effects will not unwind overnight if the Fed once again loses the plot on inflation, but they will gradually erode. There will be substitution into other currencies—for example, the euro, the Swiss franc, and perhaps the Japanese yen. Chinese efforts to internationalize the renminbi will certainly benefit. The U.S. financial sector, which has flourished under a stable dollar standard, will shrink. Even if the U.S. dollar remains on top, its competitors might gain a foothold in some regions, a broader theme we have mentioned before and will return to in the last chapter.

So, if the case for central bank independence has now become so clear, why should there be any concern going forward? One problem is that in the low-inflation era, too many people started to take stable inflation for granted. They began to ask what other challenges central banks might be repurposed to tackle, for example, global warming.

Up until recently, most young people, even serious academic researchers, believed that inflation would never come back. Before 2022, my Harvard students, though they patiently listened to my lectures on inflation, clearly believed that it was of little relevance to their own lives. I might as well have been telling them they should listen to Frank Sinatra, the music of another generation. Even today, after the sustained post-pandemic inflation outbreak, the majority of professional macroeconomists appear lulled into believing that the risks of high inflation are trivial into the foreseeable future, now that the lesson has been learned — again, classic "this time is different" thinking.

There is a lot of inertia in academic economic research as well. For well over a decade after the global financial crisis in 2008–2009, researchers had convinced themselves that the problem in the future for central banks was disinflation, not inflation. For a while, most advanced-economy central banks struggled to get inflation up to their target of 2 percent.[10] A talented young Swedish graduate student approached me at one point, after months of feverishly working on why central banks kept undershooting their inflation targets. Exasperated, he declared, "If you told me that inflation will only happen again when the Federal Reserve Board does a special rain dance, I would believe you."

A remarkable outpouring of creative if questionable ideas on how to solve "lowflation" filled the pages of top economics journals. One idea was that the Fed should employ "helicopter money," an old Milton Friedman paradigm made famous in a speech in 2002 by Ben Bernanke, who was then a Federal Reserve governor and later became chair. Friedman's image of helicopters flying all over the country dropping bundles of cash is a metaphor for having the government make cash transfers to everyone (as happened multiple times during the pandemic), and then paying for it by having the central bank directly print money. For a time, this earned Bernanke the moniker "Helicopter Ben."[11] When interest rates were zero and nothing seemed to increase inflation, helicopter money was lauded by numerous policy luminaries as a brilliant solution.[12] After all, what could be the downside? Even if it did not work to create inflation, at least people would have some extra spending money.

CENTRAL BANK INDEPENDENCE

Having the government make transfers to people is not at all a bad idea in a recession. Having the unelected Fed Board decide who gets the money is absurd. The right to impose taxes and make transfers lies with Congress. If helicopter money is really such a great idea, Congress can always choose to issue debt and make payments to anyone it wants, and the Fed can buy up the debt. (We will come to "modern monetary theory," an extreme variant of this approach, in the next chapter.) If the Fed were to try helicopter money on its own, central bank independence would quickly become a distant memory; perhaps the Fed would even lose its headquarters and have to move back to the U.S. Treasury building where it was housed from 1913 to 1937. I hesitate to name all the major academic and policy economists, not to mention prominent journalists, who have advocated this dubious idea.

As already noted, with ordinary interest rate policy paralyzed during the long zero-bound era—when central banks brought their short-term interest rates down to zero or even slightly below it—many serious people became convinced that inflation would never again be a great concern, and pressures grew on central banks to do something else with their independence and power to print money. There were strong cries from progressives for the Fed to direct more of its energies toward reducing inequality, dealing with social justice, and yes, healing the environment. These are all worthy goals. The question is whether central banks have the expertise, policy instruments, or democratic accountability to be taking a lead role in achieving any of them.

The Fed is particularly ill-suited to play anything more than a secondary supporting role in environmental policy; the central bank doesn't have the ability to impose carbon taxes or regulate emissions; nor does it have the requisite staff expertise. The Fed is not the Environmental Protection Agency. The main rationale for Federal Reserve independence is to keep a lid on inflation. Even if progressives succeed in temporarily turning the Fed into a financial EPA, its efforts will backfire without support from the elected branches of government. The endgame will be a complete loss of Federal Reserve independence, with potentially dire consequences for inflation stabilization and growth over the long run.

Some central banks, the European Central Bank in particular, have sought to find a back door to justify using their regulatory powers to redirect lending and investment away from legacy fossil fuels and toward green energy. The ECB uses the thin pretext that several decades from now environmental problems will become a predominant source of financial risk, and it worries them that banks are not adequately accounting for this risk. This is a wild stretch for many reasons, one being the very long time horizons involved and another being the implication that the ECB understands the business risks that global warming poses better than the banks themselves do. At least in the case of the ECB, it is following a very clear directive from its constituent governments that Europe aims to be a leader in the green transition.[13] This is simply not the case in the United States, at least for now.[14]

Academic economists continue to take up with relish the idea that Federal Reserve policy can and should do much more to reduce wealth and income inequality. From a purely intellectual perspective, the research is fascinating, especially on the technical side, and it is certainly valuable to better understand how interest rate cycles affect wealth and income distribution.[15] From a practical policy perspective, however, it makes little sense to have the Fed concentrate on inequality as opposed to price stability. Its core instrument, the interest rate, is ill-suited for performing surgical redistribution of income and wealth. The Fed's dual mandate to maintain stable prices and maximum employment already stretches its capacity; it is not possible to precisely hit two targets when it has only one truly effective instrument, the short-term policy interest rate. Congress and the president have ample tools and power to take extensive action on redistributing income, and they do it all the time. Pushing the unelected Fed to consistently bypass or reverse the actions of elected officials is again a fast track to loss of independence and high inflation.

The issues regarding the use of interest rate policy to address social justice are similar. The Federal Reserve has regulatory power to ensure that the banking sector does not engage in discriminatory behavior, and it should coordinate with other financial regulators and Congress on appropriate guidelines. But addressing demands for social justice should not be a further target for interest rate policy; that is for Congress and the judicial system. Pressures on central banks to implement broad-ranging political agendas are very real. Textual analysis of their speeches suggests that central bankers are being pushed hard to engage in such issues.[16]

So far, we have discussed attacks on central bank independence from the left, where a lot of the action and ideas have been in recent years. However, the Fed has also come under assault from the right, some of whom believe that having an independent Federal Reserve invests too much power in unelected officials. During the 2024 presidential campaign, a group of Donald Trump's advisers floated the idea of requiring the Fed chair to consult with the president on interest rate changes, and after a while, Trump himself embraced it.[17] Suffice it to say that even if a president were able to do this (most likely, legislation would be required), markets would quickly pour a cold bucket of water on it. Inflation expectations would rise, the dollar would tank, markets would be destabilized. The Trump team's proposal, however, follows in a long line of ideas that have been floated from the right.

In 2009, the Republican senator Ron Paul's best-selling book *End the Fed* argued for a return to the gold standard. In the 1980s, President Ronald Reagan flirted with the idea. Even today, goldbugs will tell you that the pre-war gold standard was oh-so-much better than the current regime. Yet in reality, the gold standard had many problems, not least periodic deflation, recurrent financial crises, and worst of all, acute vulnerability to speculative attacks. The idea still comes up periodically in the press. In a sense, the invention of bitcoin in 2009 was aimed at addressing similar disquiet with government fiat currency.

In 2011, the famed conservative economist and Federal Reserve historian Allan Meltzer started writing about how the Federal Reserve's "quantitative easing" policies would end up fueling inflation. Under its quantitative easing policies, the Federal Reserve issues bank reserves (traditionally thought of as a form of "money") to buy up assets, mostly long-dated U.S. Treasury bills and mortgage-backed securities.[18] Reserves are funds that banks keep at the Federal Reserve, and they are often pooled with paper currency as a form of money since they can be converted to cash at any time. Meltzer worried that eventually, all this "money printing" would lead to high inflation.[19] He asked quite pointedly whether it really made sense to flood the market with so much money. A number of other prominent, mostly right-leaning, economists signed on to this view.

Meltzer, a brilliant monetary economist and author of the definitive history of the Federal Reserve, was wrong on this one, or at least so I argued in a debate with him at a conference in March 2012.[20] What had changed since his seminal earlier work on monetary policy was that the Fed started paying interest on bank reserves in October 2009. This made bank reserves — debt the Fed owes banks — a lot more like interest-bearing short-term Treasury bills than paper currency, which pays zero interest. So bank reserves do not necessarily burn a hole in private-sector pockets — that is, create more pressure for inflation — any more than ordinary U.S. debt.

The 2024 Republican presidential candidate Vivek Ramaswamy called for narrowing the Federal Reserve's existing mandate to include only stabilizing inflation. To guard against mission creep, Ramaswamy further proposed cutting the Federal Reserve staff by up to 90 percent so that it simply would not have the capacity to take on so many issues.[21] This would be throwing out the baby with the bathwater; the Fed's staff is essential not only for its analysis of the effects of monetary policy but also for the myriad areas in which the Fed is involved in regulation. The U.S. financial system is constantly evolving and, unless properly regulated, poses large systemic risks to economic stability.

Then again, Ramaswamy was not entirely off base either. A friend of mine recently wrote to me after retiring as the head of research for a regional Federal Reserve Bank. My friend claimed to have been the last person doing research on monetary policy at his shop; everyone else was studying the environment and inequality. A glance at the bank's website confirmed this; let's just say this particular bank was not on the East Coast. This kind of mission creep in central banking has become a global phenomenon.

Although there is no space here to go into detail, the rise of central bank independence has proved phenomenally successful in emerging markets, far more so than I would have ever guessed back in the early 1980s. (The Brazilian central bank was highlighted in chapter 13.) This independence, nascent as it may be, has played a key role in allowing many emerging markets to shift a large fraction of their government borrowing — even borrowing from foreign creditors — into local currency. More stable prices have at the same time helped promote the deepening of domestic financial markets. As noted in chapter 15 on fixed exchange rates and the Tokyo consensus, the adoption of more conservative macroeconomic policies has played a big role in helping emerging markets better weather a range of severe shocks over the past two decades, including the global financial crisis, the pandemic, the slowdown in China, and the post-pandemic inflation in the United States.[22] (Once again, this is not to rule out the possibility of things going sharply downhill again for emerging markets this decade.) As also emphasized earlier, many central banks — including in countries that follow the Tokyo consensus — officially say they are inflation targeters but in fact give a very large weight to exchange rate stabilization, far above and beyond what inflation targeting would call for.

Finally, a word about artificial intelligence and how it might affect pressures on central banks in general and the Federal Reserve in particular. Although I am certainly no AI expert, I have enjoyed a window into developments through chess, which has been on the frontier of AI research for over six decades, and I have been able to interact with a number of the leading researchers. As a graduate student at MIT in 1976, I got to play several games against Richard Greenblatt's famous program. Greenblatt holds a great place of distinction among coders, who consider him to be one of the founders of the hacking community (in the good sense). Greenblatt's 1970s program was only a notch below master level, not yet good enough to be able to win or draw against a top player (unless over a very large number of games), but far above the average club player. The experience was a little bit unnerving (what if I become the first grand master to lose to a computer?). Although I managed to win all the games, the window into the future it provided played a role in my decision to give up competitive chess completely just a few years later (and except for a single one-on-one exhibition blitz game against the world champion Magnus Carlsen in 2012, I have not played a single game since).[23]

It was no surprise to anyone that computers eventually became better than humans. In 1997, the then world champion Garry Kasparov lost to IBM's "Deep Blue" machine in a celebrated match that is often marked as one of the major advancements of the twentieth century.

The programs kept improving steadily, and even more importantly, the computers they ran on kept getting faster and faster. At first, chess players learned to beware of playing "gambits" (in which one gives up material for space and initiative) against computers. Gambits can often work against a human, who is more likely to make mistakes when thrown on defense. A computer, however, would simply gobble up the proffered material, calmly walk a tightrope on defense for as long as it takes to consolidate, and then eventually take advantage of its extra material to win. Human play absorbed these insights to some extent.

And then suddenly, it all changed. Just when the existing programs seemed to be reaching almost godlike strength, along came DeepMind's neural-network program AlphaZero in 2016. It not only destroyed older-generation programs but also led to a complete rethinking of the game. AlphaZero was far less materialistic than its predecessors, often throwing caution to the wind to attack, much like players from the so-called Romantic era of the nineteenth century. The influence on human play was profound. The world champion Magnus Carlsen absorbed the new ideas especially quickly and reinvented himself; once a player who aimed to slowly wear down his opponents, he became a swashbuckling attacker. His new hyperaggressive approach yielded enormous competitive success and placed him very far above his contemporaries, with a solid claim to be "The GOAT," along with Bobby Fischer and Garry Kasparov. Fans were delighted. The constant flow of fresh ideas coming from computer chess has only continued, with today's best programs able to beat the 2016 version of AlphaZero as badly as it beat its predecessor.

And here is the biggest surprise. Through all of this, human chess has flourished; games have become richer and more exciting, and there has not been the surfeit of draws one might expect as top players keep refining their strategies. Yes, there have been some rule changes to speed up play and to make cheating more difficult—for example, subjecting players to metal detectors, restricting live audiences, and delaying broadcast of the move. There will likely be further adjustments to force human players to have to think on their feet rather than rely excessively on computer-aided preparation. But so far, the necessary changes have not been terribly radical.[24]

Indeed, chess incomes have likely gone up, although there are many causes, not least the rise of streaming and the large number of parents who would prefer that their children learn chess rather than watch TikTok videos. The huge success of the Netflix series *The Queen's Gambit* also helped, in part by bringing more girls and young women (and others) into chess. The takeaway is that, on the one hand, AI does not necessarily mean the end for humans. On the other hand, the progress in chess programs—which if anything has been accelerating, even almost thirty years after Kasparov lost to IBM's Deep Blue — is sobering. Those who are thinking only about what the next generation of ChatGPT-type programs will do are not thinking far enough ahead.

Back to economics and central banking. Obviously, AI can go in many different directions, depending very much on how it is regulated. A lot of thorny questions need to be resolved. One point of view is that AI will be globalization redux: that it will relentlessly drive down costs, benefiting firms at the expense of workers, but nevertheless make it easier overall for the Fed and other central banks to keep inflation low while maintaining full employment. If so, then AI-driven deflationary pressures might partly offset inflationary pressures coming from deglobalization, rising global tensions, and populism. In any event, it is unlikely that the deflationary forces from AI will dominate in the near term. Indeed, the near-term development of AI could be inflationary given that it will likely require very large investments in energy and computing. It is also possible that AI will lead to sharply greater internal conflict within societies given how it could upend jobs and reshape the distribution of income. That, too, could lead to inflationary pressures.

Perhaps the biggest challenge of all to central banks, however, will be long-term pressures from unsustainable government-debt trajectories, a topic we turn to next.

CHAPTER 25

DEBTOR'S EMPIRE

The United States' Achilles' Heel

Whether U.S. government debt is a runaway express train or a minor inconvenience is somewhat in the eyes of the beholder. Both views are extreme. The first overstates the speed and urgency with which adjustments must be implemented; the second is far too complacent about risks and too sanguine about real interest rates returning permanently to their ultra-low post-financial-crisis levels.

If the United States does run into problems making the fiscal adjustments needed to fund its debt, it will create a major and recurrent problem for the world that could unfold in higher interest rates, greater inflation, financial instability, or more intense financial repression – or more likely than not, all four. It would not be good for the dollar's brand.

Financial repression looms large in what follows; it is a hidden tax few people understand. It typically occurs when the government forces financial institutions to hold more of its debt as part of a program of holding down interest rates. Economists have long understood the widespread use of financial repression in developing economies and emerging markets; it is discussed extensively in *This Time Is Different*. In recent years, particularly after the global financial crisis, it became much more prominent in advanced economies as well.[1] Perhaps one attraction to governments of the financial-repression tax is that even though it inevitably ends up being almost entirely passed on to middle-income depositors, few realize it is going on. Moreover, by forcing financial institutions to hold more government debt than they might otherwise choose, financial repression reduces private-sector investment.

Indeed, some of what finance economists refer to as the "convenience yield" of government debt (first mentioned in chapter 17) might be interpreted as at least partially due to financial regulation; the government creates rules and regulations that make it "convenient" to hold large quantities of government debt to meet liquidity and collateral requirements. Later on in this chapter, I will return to the issue of financial repression in the context of the distinction between foreign and domestic holders of U.S. debt.

As the world watches the United States flounder in dealing with its debt policy, one concern is that it will reinforce trends to diversify (especially coming from China), which could push up U.S. interest rates further and cause the United States to flounder even more in response. Obviously, the unstable dynamic could be curtailed by clear and forceful leadership, but the current divisive political environment in the United States might make that difficult.

Before diving any deeper into the topic of debt, let's get one thing straight: It is simply not true that all U.S. government debt is "safe" — certainly not in real terms, that is, adjusting for inflation. U.S. bondholders suffered a significant loss from unexpected inflation after the pandemic in the early 2020s and a truly massive loss during the high-inflation 1970s. Why is it important to emphasize this point? Unfortunately, over the past decade especially, as young economists came to fervently believe that inflation could never happen in their lifetimes (many told me so), policy studies and journal papers almost ubiquitously came to refer to U.S. government obligations as "safe" debt. This lazy language drives some of us crazy, but it has become embedded in both academic and policy discussion. Very-short-term U.S. debt (e.g., one-month Treasury bills) can be considered safe, perhaps, since inflation tends to evolve slowly. For longer-term debt, this is more than just an abuse of language; it is a fundamental misconception. There has to be a safety valve; back in the days of the gold standard, when all debt was effectively indexed and inflating down debt was not possible, the primary safety valve was often "safe" short-term debt.

At present, outright default by the United States is highly unlikely given the easier route of inflation, since under 10 percent of U.S. debt is indexed to inflation. Yet the United States has defaulted in the past—in particular, during the 1930s, when President Franklin Roosevelt abandoned the gold clause in U.S. debt, much the way a country abandons its fixed exchange rates. History is written by the victors, and Americans tend to conveniently forget that the U.S. Supreme Court ruled that the 1930s abrogation of the gold standard was, in fact, a default.[2] A Harvard Law School colleague of mine once tried to persuade me that this was not really a default, since the U.S. Supreme Court simultaneously ruled that no significant harm was done to creditors and awarded them collectively only one dollar.

No harm? How did foreign central bankers, who thought their dollars were as good as gold, feel? By this logic, when Argentina abandoned its dollar peg in 2002, it was not really a default to foreign creditors either, given that the Argentine Supreme Court was fine with it. If inflation-linked debt ever became a much larger share of total U.S. debt, how sure are we that no future president would seek a way to effectively abrogate the inflation link out of frustration that U.S. debt had become almost immune to partial default through inflation? Isn't that pretty much what happened in the 1930s when President Roosevelt abrogated the clauses that indexed U.S. debt to gold?

We have already seen that the United States' "safe" debt stood at over 120 percent of GDP by mid-2024, nearly quadruple its 1980 level and double that in 2007.[3] Recall from figure 11 in chapter 20 that the Congressional Budget Office expects U.S. debt to rise much further over the next three decades, and that is based on optimistic assumptions.[4]

The notion that government debt is a proverbial free lunch has so thoroughly pervaded the Washington establishment that there is little appetite for reducing deficits. The belief that interest rates will remain ultra-low forever has become deeply embedded in politics on both sides of the aisle, whether it is Republicans who believe that taxes can be sharply cut without reducing spending, or Democrats who believe that spending can be massively raised even if they cannot push through higher taxes.

Even though many liberals absolutely hate George W. Bush's vice president, Dick Cheney, the vast majority now implicitly agree with the archconservative's famous view that "Reagan proved deficits don't matter."[5] Leading progressive economic commentators periodically recycle their columns arguing that ordinary Americans are foolish to care so much about the national debt, which (they argue) can reliably be serviced cheaply and easily. In his 2019 presidential address to the American Economic Association, Olivier Blanchard, a giant in academic macroeconomics research, went further to suggest that, thanks to ultra-low interest rates, higher debt can be financed through growth alone without necessarily ever having to raise taxes, not just in the United States but across advanced economies worldwide, at least up to a point.[6] Many right-leaning policy economists and politicians seem to agree, regularly claiming that debt concerns should never get in the way of growth-enhancing tax cuts; the *Wall Street Journal*, among other conservative outlets, regularly embraces this perspective.

Financial regulators also seem to share this Alfred E. Neuman "What, me worry?" view of dealing with debt in the future, as the U.S. government casts an ever wider and more generous safety net over the bond market and financial firms. In 1873, when Walter Bagehot wrote *Lombard Street*, he recommended that in a financial crisis, a lender of last resort should lend freely against good collateral, but at a penalty interest rate.[7] For decades, Bagehot's principle was the mantra of central bankers. In the twenty-first century, increasingly confident of the bottomless demand for government debt, the philosophy is something closer to "When in doubt, bail it out."

Figure 16 illustrates just how much U.S. government debt has swollen. Remarkably, the amount of marketable U.S. government debt is now roughly on par with that of all other advanced countries combined; a similar comparison would hold for corporate debt.[8] It is also important to note that in addition to explicit marketable debt, there are also very substantial "hidden debts" — for example, the debt implicit in the government's periodic generous bailouts of financial firms. In March 2023, after several small and medium-size banks had become actuarially bankrupt as a result of sharply rising interest rates, the Federal Reserve created a generous new facility that backstopped capital losses estimated by several researchers to be over $2 trillion.[9] Despite all protestations to the contrary, the U.S. government has continually increased the size and scope of its implicit bailout guarantees, creating what might be termed "the financial welfare state."

For a long time, neither explicit nor implicit borrowing seemed to matter.

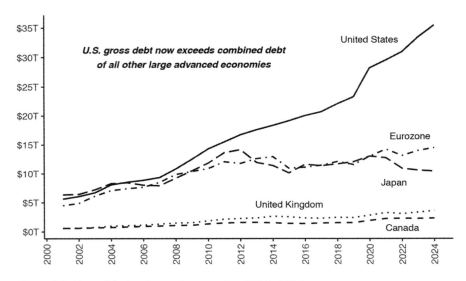

Figure 16. Gross debt in advanced economies, 2001–2024
Data Source: International Monetary Fund.

Even as U.S. debt ballooned, the cost of servicing the debt, in terms of total annual interest payments, remained steady. At times, interest payments declined, even as the stock of debt rose. This was mainly thanks to the fact that real interest rates fell off a cliff after the global financial crisis: the return on inflation-indexed ten-year U.S. Treasuries averaged near zero from 2012 through 2021. Real interest rates on short-term debt were sharply negative. When real interest rates on Treasury bills are negative, it means that bondholders are effectively paying the U.S. government for the privilege of holding its "safe" debt; they may be receiving interest payments, but each year inflation devalues the purchasing power of the remaining principal and interest payments so much that the bondholders are losing on net.[10]

This has been a very convenient situation for policymakers and politicians; over time the idea has been embraced by many in the economics profession. In his widely celebrated "secular stagnation" speech at an IMF panel session in Washington in 2013, Larry Summers argued that the very low real interest rates reflected a new era of insufficient aggregate demand and a general belief that the age of strong growth was over for a long time to come. The idea of secular stagnation dates back to another Harvard professor, Alvin Hansen, who crafted the idea during the Great Depression of the 1930s.[11] Until Summers, though, no one had thought to draw a parallel. Hansen, of course, was eventually proved wrong; after World War II, the United States enjoyed decades of strong growth, as did Europe and Japan, and interest rates rebounded from their near-zero level during the Great Depression.

Fed chair Ben Bernanke shared the stage with Summers when he gave his speech (as did I, though no one will remember) and tried to push back, arguing that economic forces would eventually push the real interest rate to be positive, so secular stagnation could not hold indefinitely. For what it is worth, I noted in my remarks that a major part of the drop in real interest rates had to be a legacy of the 2008–2009 financial crisis that spooked investors, consumers, and regulators, and it should not be expected to last indefinitely. Secular stagnation did not last forever after the Great Depression, why should it now?

An influential book by Robert J. Gordon strongly seconded the "lower forever" view. Gordon's fascinating book basically asserted that humankind had a great ride for 250 years following the Industrial Revolution, but now that many of the most economically consequential inventions had already been invented, one could no longer expect a similar pace of technological progress. His list of highly economically important inventions included the railroad, the internal-combustion engine, running water, and the television.[12] If Gordon's thesis was correct, this time secular stagnation was here to stay.

I would sometimes try out Gordon's ideas on my older colleagues in the sciences, both at Harvard and at MIT. One distinguished physicist couldn't believe that so many economists on Wall Street, in academics, and at the Fed really believed that economically impactful inventions had radically slowed down for good. "Don't economists understand that breakthrough inventions such as Shockley's 1947 transistor sometimes take many years to fully implement?" (The second generation of computers were built with transistors instead of vacuum tubes.) Young assistant professors in the sciences were even more shocked, and many argued that the pace of technological change today is more rapid than ever.

A similar idea to Gordon's had been advanced independently by the Silicon Valley entrepreneur Peter Thiel and the former world chess champion Garry

Kasparov. In 2012, I participated in a public debate with them on the topic "innovation versus stagnation" at the legendary Oxford Union.[13] I argued that the "long-term stagnation" view was underestimating the coming economic impact of the world of AI; my concern was that technology would evolve too quickly for humans to adapt, not that it would be too slow. After the debate, the audience voted by choosing one of two grand doors to walk out of—which was quite theatric. The outcome looked to be close, though I never found out who actually won.

My view that secular stagnation was a post-crisis phase, not a permanent fixture, was indeed pretty far outside the consensus. That became acutely apparent when, after stepping down as Fed chair in 2014, Bernanke reportedly began telling private audiences that he did not expect to see 4 percent short-term interest rates again in his lifetime.[14] Given that Bernanke was only sixty years old at the time, this was quite a statement.[15] Only eight years later, the Fed's short-term policy rate reached 5.5 percent.

Despite my views being so far outside the professional consensus, I kept making the point that secular stagnation is not forever in my talks and writings. No one wanted to hear it; too many people were deeply intellectually invested in the view that interest rates would stay low forever, and anyone saying otherwise must be in favor of "austerity." For example, at a conference in London in November 2016, I remarked, "In nine years, nobody will be talking about secular stagnation."

Why not ten years? I explained to the audience that I had already been making the point for a year, including in a debate before the G7 finance ministers and central bankers in Dresden in which Summers also took part. After a year of saying "ten," it did not feel right to keep moving the goalposts; hence, "nine." The quip might have been lost to posterity except that one of my co-panelists, Brad DeLong, quoted me on his blog.[16] The conference had been closed to media and was, at least I thought, being held under "Chatham House rules," under which ideas can later be shared but not attributed to any specific individual. Admittedly, no one else was really arguing with secular stagnation at the time, and of course now I am extremely grateful that someone put my prediction in the record.

For years, faith in low interest rates consumed Washington. Not only did the United States borrow heavily to take advantage of near-historic low interest rates; the U.S. Treasury and the Fed doubled down by issuing relatively short-term debt, in essence betting taxpayers' money that interest rates would not go up.[17] Homeowners perfectly well understand that if they get a variable rate mortgage to finance their home, they might enjoy a lower interest rate now, but they take a risk it will go up in the future. The Treasury and the Fed decided instead that the risks of rates going up were sufficiently low that it was better to just pay the lower short-term rates than pay a premium to lock in the low rates.

In a 2016 *Project Syndicate* column, I urged that the U.S. government consider locking in the low rates by issuing more thirty-year debt, which was then paying 2.25 percent interest, even though this was at a premium to short-term debt, which was then paying zero. Progressives went into convulsions.[18]

Robert Skidelsky, a British economist famous for his biography of Keynes, wrote a response as if my call for caution on low rates was advocating "austerity." Presumably, this was because my suggestion would require "diverting" to debt service funds that could be used to pay for new spending programs, devil may care about rising rates in the future. Skidelsky argued that the risk of high debt ever leading to problems was inconsequential and noted that Japan had debt of 230 percent of GDP (never mind two lost decades of growth).[19] My article had stated:

> But the government should not operate like a bank or a hedge fund, loading up on short-term debt to fund long-term projects. It is too risky. With net U.S. government debt already running at 82 percent of national income, the potential fiscal costs of a fast upward shift in interest rates could be massive.[20]

One would think that those routinely arguing for greater use of debt to pay for social programs would favor having a longer maturity structure to protect against a later crisis that might force sharp short-term cutbacks. Fifty-year floods may not happen often, but a country that doesn't prepare for them will eventually run into trouble.

That same year, 2016, I presented a research seminar in a large, almost full, auditorium at the U.S. Treasury and was invited to meet afterward with the team of experts in charge of managing the U.S. debt. Treasury Secretary Jack Lew, although not present at my talk, did stop by at lunch. Everyone listened patiently as I explained my arguments that the Treasury might be taking too much interest rate risk and listed reasons why one should expect long-term rates to rise eventually. It was to no avail. Who can blame them when so many prominent academic voices were insisting that the risks were minimal and that having to spend more money on debt service inevitably meant less spending on something else — in other words, "austerity."

Such thinking is always a very-short-term perspective; future economic historians can later decide whether the Treasury was right. At the moment, it appears that the Treasury missed a golden opportunity to lock in low rates on behalf of the American taxpayer. In October 2023, as yields on 10-year U.S. Treasury bonds neared 5 percent, more than triple their 2016 lows, the legendary investor Stanley Druckenmiller slammed Treasury Secretary Janet Yellen for not locking in long-term rates, calling it "the biggest blunder in Treasury history." He also noted that Steven Mnuchin, who served as Treasury secretary under Trump, missed the same chance.[21]

"Almost everyone expected interest rates to be low forever," the *Economist* observed in November 2023.[22] In a 2019 article entitled "On Secular Stagnation in the Industrialized World," Łukasz Rachel and Lawrence Summers showed that real interest rates had been in steady decline for more than three decades. They argued that, but for recurrent massive budget deficits across industrialized economies, on top of changes in old-age pension systems starting in the early 1970s, neutral (full employment) real interest rates would have been 3 percent lower — that is, deeply negative.[23] Academic economists were falling all over themselves to explain why real interest rates were in such steep decline; all the most prominent papers suggested that rates were likely to fall further still. Leading causes were postulated to be demographics (an aging population needing to save more for retirement), a long-term trend decline in productivity, and growing inequality. The top academic journals were replete with papers with explanations of decline, largely reinforcing confidence in "lower forever."[24]

Popular books followed suit. Stony Brook University economist Stephanie Kelton's best-selling 2020 book *The Deficit Myth* argued that as long as a country can issue debt in its own currency, it can and should use this capacity to expand social programs, leaving it to the Federal Reserve to issue bank reserves to soak up the debt.[25] Kelton's arguments calling for central bank–financed deficits were particularly influential with progressives, most notably Representative Alexandria Ocasio-Cortez, who argued that deficit spending could be used to substantially help pay for her Green New Deal. Kelton later described AOC's endorsement as having an "Oprah effect" on modern monetary theory.[26] To be fair, Kelton did note that inflation could eventually ensue, even if the media blitz had smothered this qualification. The empirical question is just how quickly inflation pressures become a problem, a question intimately connected with just how far the United States can stretch its exorbitant privilege.

The idea that U.S. debt is a cow to be milked became common wisdom throughout much of the economics profession, which led to a sea change in views among academic economists on the role of fiscal policy. A poll of American Economic Association members posed the proposition "Management of the business cycle should be left to the Federal Reserve; activist fiscal policies should be avoided." In 2000, 72 percent either agreed or agreed with proviso and 28 percent disagreed. By 2021, the results had flipped: 67 percent disagreed and 33 percent agreed or agreed with proviso.[27]

Until this volte-face, fiscal policy was generally considered too political to be employed in routine macroeconomic stabilization policy. The revisionist professional-economist consensus apparently takes a stunningly positive spin on what a real-world U.S. Congress is capable of, at odds with many decades of experience. Milton Friedman emphasized that because of inevitable political haggling, fiscal policy tends to come online late in the cycle, providing stimulus only after a recovery is underway and lasting for too long thereafter. (Exactly what happened again after the pandemic recession.) On top of that, when rushed, a large portion of the expenditures tend to be misdirected and wasteful.

The belief that the United States' politically charged Congress can perform surgical short-term demand management as well as the relatively technocratic Fed is hard to fathom, although of course in extreme cases such as the financial crisis and the pandemic, fiscal policy needs to share center stage with the Fed. That was not the question American Economic Association members were being asked, though.

Lastly, if the progressive vision of how to use debt is to increase government spending, then surely the Republican version has been to use debt finance to pay for tax cuts. Conservatives might reasonably argue that cutting taxes is somewhat less costly since tax cuts stimulate growth. However, as already noted, in practice U.S. tax cuts have almost always raised the deficit significantly, both in the short run and the long run, so both sides are effectively relying on the same free-lunch argument.

CHAPTER 26

THE SIREN CALL OF "LOWER FOREVER" INTEREST RATES

It is probably fair to say that the belief in "lower forever" correlates with much greater concern among academic economists about finding ways to reduce within-country "communitarian" inequality.[1] If one sees great benefit to expanding the footprint of government, it is only human nature to want to believe that there might be a supercheap way to do it, as modern monetary theorists and Representative Ocasio-Cortez posited. As someone who is generally in favor of greatly expanding the social safety net in the United States, especially for low-income citizens, I am puzzled why progressives shoot themselves in the foot by arguing for the heavy use of deficit spending rather than increased taxes to pay for it.

Counting on lower-forever real interest rates is a very risky proposition. Why should the country that aims to stay on top for several more centuries, if possible, choose to make bets that will almost surely blow up someday? My long-standing guess is that the average real interest rate on ten-year inflation-indexed U.S. Treasury bonds will be much higher in the 2020s and 2030s than the near-zero average level in 2012–2021. Of course long rates will fall sharply in a recession, although not as much as short rates, but they will rise again during normal times.

As discussed in the previous chapter, there have been many serious research papers that reach a different conclusion, typically arguing that some mix of fading demographics, weak trend growth, and rising inequality will keep pushing real interest rates ever lower throughout the twenty-first century. That may be right. However, some of the explanations come across as ex post rationales rather than convincing theories. What is particularly striking is how many of these proposed explanations break down when one looks at longer time horizons. In the case of demographics and productivity trends, for example, most of the literature looks at data only for the past few decades. Yet, over longer horizons, the correlations disappear or even reverse, as my work with Barbara Rossi and Paul Schmelzing on seven hundred years of real interest rate history has shown.[2]

Although there are very plausible reasons why interest rates might fall in the future, there are also strong forces pushing in the other direction. These include the massive rise in global debt (public and private), the first spurt coming during and immediately after the global financial crisis and the second during and for some time after the pandemic. There has also been a generalized rise in borrowing even in calmer times. Nature abhors a vacuum, and with real rates extremely low it is natural for investors and (dis)savers to push the envelope. If former vice president Al Gore is right that the next few decades will see one billion climate refugees crossing borders,[3] the pressures on debt and spending will be staggering for all advanced economies, regardless of whether they welcome people in or try to lock them out. And Gore is certainly right about the need to sharply raise investment to mitigate global warming.

Sooner than that, if the worldwide rise in populism leads to greater income redistribution, that too will increase aggregate demand, since low-income individuals spend a higher share of their earnings. In addition, some of the trends purportedly promising lower-forever interest rates may reverse. As noted already, the peace dividend seems to have evaporated. An aging population saves for retirement, but an elderly retired population needs to dissave to support itself. The rise of tech has led to a period in which less physical capital is required in production. That trend, too, could turn with the significant investment needed to support AI's voracious appetite for energy and computing power. Then again, the one thing that's for sure is that the real interest rate is quite volatile, so some of these arguments may later prove ex post rationales as well.

"LOWER FOREVER" INTEREST RATES

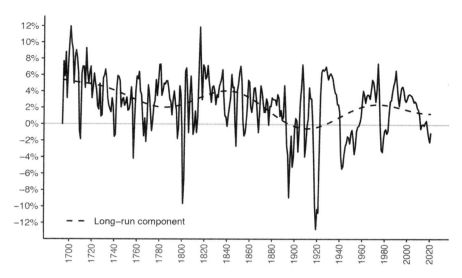

Figure 17. U.K. real interest rate with long-run component, 1694–2022
Data Source: Rogoff, Rossi, and Schmelzing, *American Economic Review*, 2024.

Figure 17 takes a very-long-run view of long-term real interest rates; it goes back four centuries for the United Kingdom. Figure 18 for the United States is a century shorter but delivers the same message.[4] In both figures, the dashed curve is an estimate of the underlying long-term trend movement, which does not necessarily evolve linearly. There are two important takeaways. First, although there was an overall downward trend in real rates for centuries (likely driven by rising liquidity and declining default risk), this downward underlying trend may have softened or even reversed over the past hundred years. Second, the figures make clear that real interest rates are extremely volatile, and on balance, when big shocks happen, such as the "secular stagnation" plunge after the global financial crisis, they tend to die out over time. In particular, the post-1980 fall in real rates that Rachel and Summers emphasized (marked in figure 18) looks considerably less convincing when viewed from a centuries-long perspective. This should hardly be surprising; after the inflation of the 1970s, Fed chair Paul Volcker was forced to push short-term real interest rates to unprecedented levels to tame inflation. It took a long time for the high interest rates to unwind, in part because the public remained scared that inflation would

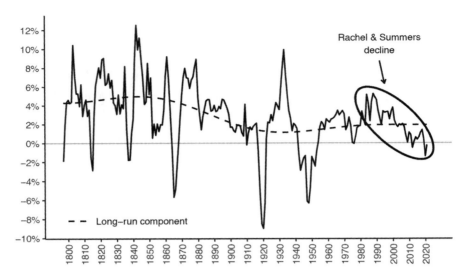

Figure 18. U.S. real interest rate with long-run component, 1797–2022
Data Source: Rogoff, Rossi, and Schmelzing, *American Economic Review*, 2024.

come back. This fear was built into long-term interest rates. Thus, looking at the trend in real interest rates starting only in 1980 tends to greatly exaggerate any downward trend, even if there still is one. And the trend one sees in figures 17 and 18 can hardly explain the steep drop after the 2008 global financial crisis and again during the pandemic, which are clearly best interpreted as transitory shocks that will mostly dissipate over time. There have been ultra-low-rate eras (relative to the trend), as well as ultra-high-rate eras; so far, they have all ended.

The interest rate is a key source of action determining the sustainability of debt, mainly because it is typically quite volatile. The other main determinant, aside from the path of deficits, is the economy's underlying growth rate. If the average growth rate of the economy is higher than the average interest rate the government is paying on its debt, then there exists the possibility that the country's debt burden, relative to income, might fall even if the government just kept rolling over all principal and interest payments. Then again, there are countless instances when countries with strong growth rates and low interest rates suddenly ran into debt problems; real interest rates and growth rates are highly

"LOWER FOREVER" INTEREST RATES

volatile. One also needs to ask whether hidden financial-repression taxes are artificially lowering interest rates through what amounts to a hidden tax.

For example, many freshman economics textbooks will tell you that the United States paid down its World War II debt mainly through high growth. However, those who make that claim have clearly never looked at the role that financial repression played in the early post-war period or that very high inflation played in the seventies. The economists Julien Acalin and Lawrence Ball found that the U.S. debt-to-GDP ratio would have been 74 percent in 1974 rather than the actual 23 percent without the help of these factors. Others have shown that even in the extreme case when debt is fully financed by growth, the resulting distortions and displacement of private investment can still outweigh any benefits.[5]

Indeed, one can argue that the long-run trend in the difference between the interest rate and the growth rate has, if anything, been positive for over a century, even with financial repression.[6] That should not be terribly surprising. The past hundred years marks the rise of the welfare state and major increases in the cost of waging war, both of which created distortions that undermined economic growth or, at the very least, sharply undermined gains from productivity. This further calls into question the idea that the government can ignore debt.

Regardless of the relationship between the interest rate and the growth rate, the United States is running deficits at such a prolific rate that it is likely headed for trouble in almost any scenario.[7] Within the next three decades, the entire United States as a whole is projected to look like today's Florida, with over 22 percent of the population 65 or older.[8] This will drive up the costs of Social Security and especially Medicare, and at the same time reduce the size of the tax-paying labor force.

A relatively new phenomenon in modern times is the rapidly growing population of the very old, say 85 and older, many of whom require a high degree of care and supervision, as the British economist Charles Goodhart has emphasized.[9] Old-age entitlements and rising debt-service costs will increasingly dominate spending, reducing space for other expenditures such as the green transition, defense, infrastructure, and education and training. Politicians are always saying that they plan to cut discretionary spending, yet there is not much room left to cut. Pruning military spending in the face of rising world tensions is wishful thinking. It certainly is possible to cut old-age entitlements and to make payments means-tested, but politically this has been a third rail. That may change. Indeed, one might argue that in practice, pension-fund obligations may be thought of as junior to general debt obligations.[10] If over the long run, the United States ends up, say, making Social Security means-tested in order to balance the budget, this would be an example of de facto default on this junior debt. And if the budget stress is severe enough, there could be other similar pullbacks on entitlement promises as well.

As health-care spending grows and constitutes an ever-larger share of total consumption expenditures, particularly for the elderly, there are going to be continuing philosophical battles over how to pay and how to distribute, battles involving moral questions that are not easily resolved.[11] In the past, the United States has benefited from immigration; that too has become increasingly complicated given the lack of a coherent policy. All in all, the odds that the system can reset without having a serious crisis seem low. A debt crisis can take many forms, but most would involve higher, more unstable inflation and much higher nominal interest rates, as well as potentially a long-lasting hit to central bank credibility.

Is there any cost to just allowing the debt to rise? Some point to Japan, whose debt was over 250 percent of GDP in 2024, as having proved that high debt is not an issue. Not an issue for what? Japan suffered two decades of lost growth. As noted earlier, it is difficult to disentangle all the reasons for Japan's low growth, including demographic decline and rising competition with China. But this does not make it an example to emulate. True, Japan has not had a government-debt default crisis, and it need not given that virtually all its government debt is denominated in yen. Nevertheless, as highlighted in chapter 3, Japan's high debt unquestionably poses risks of a financial, debt, or inflation crisis if interest rates rise from their extremely low levels of late 2024, in which case the government risks having very little fiscal space to respond.[12]

The U.S. government has many cards to play and, as issuer of the dominant currency, more capacity to borrow than other countries. Still, the basic tools are the same: default (not likely, but in the present political environment cannot be ruled out), inflation (which would have to be at a very high level to have a significant impact because so much U.S. debt is short term and 10 percent is indexed to inflation), and financial repression (basically forcing Americans to hold debt, directly or indirectly). None of these would be pretty or painless. The U.S. dollar is not going to sink to the depths portrayed in the dark futuristic film *Civil War*, where in one scene the protagonists have to buy gasoline using Canadian dollars because the U.S. dollar has become nearly worthless, presumably through very high inflation. The fact that this is not going to happen does not mean, however, that Americans will never see unexpected bursts of 10 percent inflation, as they did after the pandemic. As I argued in the previous chapter, the more difficult political and economic environment that central banks face today implies that another inflation burst is more likely than not over the next decade. And even if very high debt does not contribute to inflation pressures, it can create other problems.

In 2010, when Carmen Reinhart and I first conjectured that very high debt might affect growth, it caused a firestorm of criticism. The controversy continues to this day, mainly in TikTok and Twitter feeds that are deeply misinformed. Still, *Nature* magazine (not particularly known for economics) recently reported on a new cash prize for catching "errors" in papers, although it might just as well have been touting a prize in polemic misrepresentation.[13] Unfortunately, most of the public is deeply confused about the difference between deficits (the excess of current spending over taxes) and debt (how much the government owes thanks to cumulative deficits).[14]

To be clear, deficit spending and tax cuts are generally good for growth in the short run. The entire point of preserving fiscal space is precisely to be able to engage in aggressive countercyclical policy in the event of deep recessions and financial crises, or to be able to ramp up spending quickly in the event of a natural disaster or war. Having very high debt, by contrast, makes it more difficult, and certainly riskier, to engage in large-scale borrowing as needed in a crisis. High debt can also crowd out private investment that is necessary to sustain high productivity growth, even in normal times.

If one is a firm believer in lower-forever interest rates, there is no tradeoff. Borrow a lot today, and then, if necessary, borrow even more tomorrow. As should be clear by now, this is a very risky strategy that rests precariously on very optimistic assumptions — faith-based assumptions really — about the future path of long-term interest rates and growth in the face of rising debt burdens.

What constitutes high debt? Without quantitative benchmarks, however crude, it is a meaningless concept. In our short 2010 thought piece, we divided countries into high- and low-debt "buckets" as a rough first pass at the problem. We observed that, on average across twenty advanced economies, the median growth rate of those with debt in the highest bucket (90 percent of GDP) was about 1 percent less than that of countries in the lower buckets.[15] Given that this was a conference paper limited to six pages (a normal paper might be twenty to forty journal pages not counting online appendixes), we posited a correlation but did not engage in formal statistical tests, although we widely shared our novel debt data and published our sources, allowing the IMF to later clone and extend it. Polemicists interpreted our result as saying that growth collapses when debt crosses over the 90 percent of GDP threshold by even a hair, but that is a nonsensical interpretation. As we clearly stated in our writings, arguing that growth suddenly falls when debt goes from 89 percent to 90 percent of GDP is a bit like saying that a car crash becomes much more likely at one mile per hour over the speed limit, or that a person is much more likely to suffer a heart attack when their cholesterol level goes from 199 to 200. A decade of subsequent research has supported our broad conjecture that high debt is associated with lower medium-term growth. (Again, being able to borrow can be very good for growth in the short run; owing a large debt is a drag.)

Paul Krugman, a Nobel Prize–winning economist, is a leading proponent of the view that very high debt should be of relatively little concern for any advanced economy. With his *New York Times* columnist hat, the renowned progressive economist must have published some twenty-odd articles, books, and blogs, polemically arguing that large debt-financed stimulus spending should be used indefinitely to fight financial crises and pandemics, and expressing far less interest in other ideas such as private-sector debt write-downs (during the global financial crisis) or facilitating a more rapid escape from crippling lockdowns (after the pandemic). It is not as if the United States failed to allow debt to rise after the global financial crisis: the debt-to-GDP ratio went from 63 percent at the end of 2007 to 101 percent at the end of 2012, and that was on top of a major (albeit much needed) new health-care program, Obamacare. And then during the pandemic, when policymakers embraced the bigger-for-longer deficits theory, debt rose from 107 percent of GDP at the start of 2020 to 121 percent of GDP at the start of 2022.[16] The likely excessive stimulus supported growth but painfully turbocharged inflation. Indeed, had the Biden administration been successful in passing the trillions of dollars in additional deficit-financed stimulus it proposed, instead of being a vote short in the Senate, post-pandemic inflation and interest rates would likely have gone far higher.

Of course, major crises often prove an opportunity to permanently expand the size of government, and many progressives lean into fiscal stimulus precisely in hopes of achieving this. Fair enough. Krugman periodically holds out France, which happens to have by far the largest tax burden of the major advanced economies, as an ideal. France is certainly great to visit, even if its per capita GDP is far below that of the United States, and the European Union cannot pull its weight geopolitically.

Although debt-financed stimulus spending is certainly warranted in a deep recession, was it really the only idea for digging out of the global financial crisis, which had its roots in defaults by low-income subprime debt holders? Shouldn't other instruments have carried some of the burden? There is a strong case that a policy of targeted debt write-downs for low-income homeowners would have been an efficient way to help revive the economy, hitting at the heart of the problem rather than just treating the symptoms. One approach, which I spoke widely about, was to institute a federal program to subsidize or write down distressed subprime mortgages, perhaps in return for, say, 25 percent of the appreciation if the homes ended up rising in value. Of course, this would have increased federal debt in the short run, but by much less in the long run, which is what matters. My suggestion drew the attention of former president Bill Clinton, who cited it in his 2011 book,[17] and I also had the opportunity to discuss it with then president Barack Obama and then vice president Joe Biden in a meeting in the Oval Office of the White House in December 2010. The University of Chicago professors Atif Mian and Amir Sufi, in their deeply researched and influential 2014 book, similarly argued that much more attention should have been given to debt write-downs instead of just open-ended stimulus.[18]

And what about the possibility of having the Federal Reserve temporarily relax its inflation targets to stimulate the economy, as mentioned earlier, which might well have succeeded had it been tried early on and definitely would have if the Federal Reserve had been willing to consider temporary negative short-term interest rates?[19]

Going forward, it is clearly right that if real interest rates return to their historic post–financial crisis lows, benchmarks from the past will need to be re-evaluated. A country can have vastly more debt if the financing cost is negligible. On the other hand, what happens if real interest rates over the next decade stay elevated and growth slows or if there are large unexpected fiscal needs? Should countries bet the farm on lower-forever interest rates?

Our 2010 analysis applied to all advanced countries as a group, so certainly as the issuer of the dominant currency, the United States faces much softer constraints, but that is mainly because a significant fraction of U.S. debt is held internationally.[20] In general, this is very good for the dollar, but at the same time it creates a higher level of vulnerability than if all debt were held domestically. Some economists have argued that there is a modern-day "Triffin dilemma" because of the risk of what would happen in the event that foreign holders of U.S. debt were seized by a sudden loss of confidence.[21] This issue is closely related to the question of whether China could weaponize its reserves that was discussed at the outset of chapter 23, but there are many more layers.

As mentioned earlier, Robert Triffin was a professor at Yale University. Testifying before Congress in 1960, he famously predicted that the post-war Bretton Woods fixed exchange rate system had inherent inconsistencies that made it unsustainable.[22] As the reader knows by now, the Bretton Woods system had the U.S. dollar at the center, and in principle foreign governments could cash in their dollar reserves for gold anytime they so chose. Triffin pointed out that fast-growing Europe and Japan were building up dollar reserves far faster than the United States was expanding its gold supply and that, as a result, if enough countries were to cash out their Treasury bills at the same time, the United States would not be able to handle the demand. Moreover, he observed, because of inflation, the $35-an-ounce price for gold was looking increasingly too low, which made it all the more tempting for foreign central banks to exchange their dollars for gold. Although Triffin's forecast did not come true for another decade, he was undeniably quite prescient.

"LOWER FOREVER" INTEREST RATES

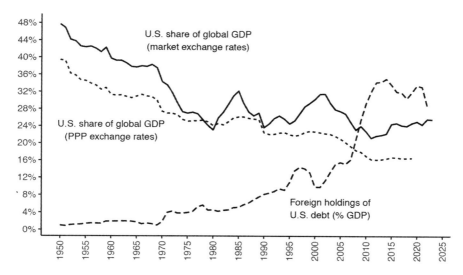

Figure 19. Falling U.S. income share, rising foreign holdings of U.S. debt: the modern-day Triffin dilemma

Data Source: Total Economy Database (market exchange rates); Penn World Tables (PPP exchange rates); Treasury International Capital System (foreign holdings of U.S. Treasury debt).

The claim that there is an analogy to the present situation—that we are confronting a modern-day Triffin problem—is correct up to a point. Figure 19 captures the problem in stark terms; the United States' share of global GDP is falling, but its debt to foreign bondholders is rising.[23] However, it is also true that the U.S. government no longer promises to exchange gold, silver, or anything else for dollars. The U.S. Federal Reserve does promise to keep "stable prices," which it interprets to mean about 2 percent inflation. If the world had as much faith in that promise as it once did in the promise to exchange dollars for gold (which admittedly was far from perfect by the 1960s), then the effect would be much the same, and figure 19 would suggest that a blowup is coming. The parallels break down because the possibility of letting off steam through bursts of inflation is well understood and will eventually get built into interest rates. If the United States repeatedly has bursts of inflation as it did after the pandemic, even if only once every ten to fifteen years, the inflation risk premium on dollar bonds will increase, the United States will enjoy a lower level of exorbitant privilege, and of course there will be more financial instability. Things will be even worse if the United States is seriously challenged in a major conflagration or if an extremely populist administration is swept into power, controlling the presidency and both houses of Congress. The 1970s Vietnam war era was also a setback for the dollar, and the sharply divided electorate incentivizes both parties to put pedal to the metal on deficits whenever they control the Presidency and both houses of Congress. During the 2024 election, the Harris and Trump campaigns seemed to be competing on who could promise to run the largest deficits, albeit on this point, Trump probably won.

Where the Triffin dilemma parallel holds most directly is that there is far less the U.S. government can do to lock in foreigners than it can do to lock in domestic residents. In particular, with domestic residents, the United States can engage in financial repression by, say, expanding regulations to make banks a captive audience for debt, as discussed earlier. These costs get passed on to depositors in the form of lower interest rates on deposits, higher fees on services, and higher rates on loans. In essence, financial repression is a form of taxation that can only be directed at domestic residents. It typically hits low- and middle-income households much harder than wealthy households, which have ample means for diversifying into other assets. Financial repression won't work with foreign holders, who can pull their money out.

Regardless of the exact parallel to Triffin, there is little question that the entire world is vulnerable to the vagaries of U.S. policy. When the United States takes outsize risks — say it issues too much debt or keeps interest rates too low for too long (or both) — it puts the entire global economy at risk. The fact that the United States does not internalize the costs that its actions impose on the rest of the world means that it is likely to take bigger risks than it would otherwise.

Before I close this chapter and turn to future risks, it is useful to touch on one further topic. If not secular stagnation, what explains the cycle of crises the world has found itself in over the past three decades? An alternative view is that the world has been in the grip of a "debt supercycle" with financial crises in Japan and emerging Asia in the 1990s, in the United States and Europe in the late 2000s, and now China in the 2020s. I am hardly suggesting that the debt supercycle explains every ebb and flow of the global economy. It does, however, have a deep and sustained impact on growth in the region(s) where it is centered at a given time, and on financial markets everywhere.

The cycle is transmitted across regions to varying degrees through financial market effects and through savings flows. As already discussed in chapter 15, very low Asian interest rates were a major factor driving capital flows into the United States, pouring fuel on the deregulation-induced fire that produced the U.S. subprime mortgage crisis that eventually morphed into the global financial crisis.[24] Unfortunately, U.S. policymakers, and many academics, insisted that massive U.S. borrowing from abroad was just a healthy expression of financial globalization, without considering the possibility that it might expose vulnerabilities.

As noted in chapter 4, the link with the European debt crisis, a near extinction event for the euro, is much easier to draw. Yes, there were vulnerabilities: Spain and Ireland had housing-price bubbles even greater than in the United States; Greece's government was on an unsustainable borrowing binge; Iceland and Cyprus had financial-governance problems that large pools of money from Russia made much worse. Yet it is also possible that but for the 2008–2009 crisis, which was centered in the United States and reflected deeply inadequate regulation, the euro might have had longer to mature as a currency system and been better able to handle its own crises — for example, the debt crisis in Greece or the housing crisis in Spain — when they eventually came.

How is China's current economic malaise connected? The world lavished praise on China's stimulus policies in 2010–2011 without fully recognizing the extent to which they concentrated on supporting real estate and infrastructure and planted the seeds of today's imbalances. Having revved up the real estate engine, the government felt obliged to keep providing further rounds of stimulus, some coming from the central government and others catalyzed by regulatory changes that launched the "local government financing vehicles" that have disastrously boomeranged today.

Wait, you ask. If China is now gripped by its own form of a financial-crisis slowdown, won't the real interest rate effects ripple through the world, with low demand in China pulling down real interest rates everywhere? Yes, except that there are several reasons that the effect will be sharply muted. First, although

China is the world's second-largest economy, it is far less integrated into global financial markets than Japan, Europe, and especially the United States. Second, and equally important, the world is in a new era with respect to trade with China, with far less tolerance for massive Chinese trade surpluses that have the effect of pouring capital into the West. So, in fact, a disproportionate share of the impact on real interest rates will be felt in China itself.

Some of the policies a government should want to follow to counter the debt supercycle are not so different from those for combating secular stagnation — for example, implementing stimulus policies such as large-scale transfers to individuals or spending on infrastructure, partly financed by debt and partly financed by progressive taxes. Still, if the growth slowdown is recognized as ultimately transitory rather than permanent, the right fiscal policies are those that are temporary and targeted instead of open-ended and bottomless.

Where will the debt supercycle go next? At this moment, the answer is less obvious than it was a decade ago, when one could clearly point to China, or at least, so I argued. There are several candidates. With higher interest rates likely to continue to put pressure on housing prices in much of the world, there are many countries where house prices have risen sharply and are now quite vulnerable. Indeed, prices have started to fall in some countries. Japan is vulnerable, as noted in chapter 3, thanks to its exceptionally high government debt and the continuing challenge of lifting interest rates from ultra-low levels. And although the large middle-income emerging markets have had two relatively calm decades, despite having experienced one crisis after another from 1982 to 2002, the situation is far more dire in smaller lower-middle-income countries and developing economies in general, with well over half already either in a state of technical default or the practical equivalent. If all these problems are exacerbated by higher interest rates, inflation, and policy volatility coming from the United States, the next ten years could be quite difficult.

Is this prognosis too dark? My analysis is intended to be balanced; it is just that the challenges ahead for the global financial system are formidable.

There has been only one time in my professional life when I allowed myself to be deliberately hyperbolic — at the time it seemed like the only sensible position. It was August 19, 2008, just a few weeks before the collapse of Lehman

"LOWER FOREVER" INTEREST RATES

Brothers, which marked the beginning of the most intense period of the global financial crisis. I was giving a speech to a conference held in Singapore but organized by the Rating Agency of Malaysia; it was not a particularly large audience, perhaps sixty to seventy people including a couple of young journalists. My presentation focused on a research paper Carmen Reinhart and I had written back in January 2008, which (as mentioned in chapter 4) pointed to flashing red lights suggesting that the United States might be at risk of a financial crisis. (That material also became chapter 13 of our book *This Time Is Different* the following year.) In addition to that, however, I also made some other rather bold predictions:

> The U.S. is not out of the woods. I think the financial crisis is at the halfway point, perhaps. I would even go further to say, "the worst is to come." . . . We're not just going to see mid-sized banks go under in the next few months, we're going to see a whopper, we're going to see a big one, one of the big investment banks or big banks. . . . Probably Fannie Mae and Freddie Mac — despite what U.S. Treasury Secretary Hank Paulson said — these giant mortgage guarantee agencies are not going to exist in their present form in a few years.[25]

Having given many major press conferences as the IMF's chief economist, I knew how to make news, but that was certainly not my intention. In this instance, my comments were intended only to give the audience a candid assessment of where things stood. They were not so different from comments I had made several times earlier in the summer — for example, at a major conference in July on the island of Gotland in Sweden, with many policymakers, journalists, and leading political figures present. I had also given the same speech to an executive-education program in Madrid, where the feedback from the mid-level bankers in attendance was that my analysis of the global financial system was too depressing compared with the uplifting remarks of the previous speaker, a famous Spanish soccer coach.

Timing is everything, and by mid-August, the mood had changed. My read of the Federal Reserve and Treasury officials I knew well was that they thought that the market would be "ready" for them to let a large bank go given that they had made clear how distasteful they found it to bail out Bear Stearns debt holders back in March. (The troubles of the important investment house Bear Stearns were mentioned earlier in chapter 4.)

My remarks made front-page headlines across Asia and Europe. Commenting on an article about my remarks, Floyd Norris of the *New York Times* wrote, "Of the economists I know, Ken Rogoff is among the least inclined to sound excited or hysterical. In my experience he speaks calmly, and with well-considered sentences. This makes this article all the more scary."[26]

As it turned out, the predictions came true: the U.S. economy went into a deep recession, one of the world's largest investment banks failed, and the U.S. government was forced to assume the massive debts of the collapsing mortgage giants. The point of this prequel to the conclusion is not to scare the daylights out of anyone but only to provide a frame of reference for what follows.

CHAPTER 27

THE END OF THE PAX DOLLAR ERA?

The legendary Danish chess grandmaster, Bent Larsen, when asked whether he preferred to be lucky or good, replied "both." Lucky and good certainly describes the post-war economic trajectory of the United States dollar. Too often, though, Americans forget the "lucky" part of the equation. Had Russia liberalized its economy in the mid-1960s, had Japan not allowed itself to be browbeaten into a destabilizing currency appreciation in the mid-1980s, had France not insisted on including Greece in the euro in 2001, or had China moved to a full-fledged floating exchange rate regime in 2010's, the dollar would likely still be on top, but perhaps not nearly to the extent it is today. In any of these alternative realities, U.S. interest rates would probably be higher; the dollar's exorbitant privilege less.

The dollar franchise has also had the benefit of several outstanding post-war Presidents and Fed chairs, and it has been strong enough to survive eras of mediocrity in one or both. Despite the paralyzing divisiveness that has been tearing apart the country in recent years, the dollar will continue to survive. However, that does necessarily mean it will indefinitely continue to be as dominant or as stable as it has over the past eight decades. Indeed, there are many other reasons to believe the Pax Dollar era has peaked.

For one thing, there is a huge appetite for alternative transactions vehicles among friends and foes alike, outside the prying eyes and the global reach of U.S. authorities. Certainly, the U.S.'s promiscuous use of financial sanctions is a major factor pushing China to loosen its still-close ties to the dollar. As the renminbi-dollar rate becomes more volatile, the rest of Asia will also be forced to strike a new balance, given China's importance in global trade. The rise of cryptocurrencies and central bank digital currencies that aim to create new non-dollar pipelines for global finance are expressions of this demand. Nothing major has happened yet, but the dollar-dominated financial system is hardly immune to disruption. Even the euro, although down, is not out as a competitor, especially if the Russian invasion of Ukraine ultimately forces the greater fiscal and political unity that should have been a prerequisite for sharing a common currency in the first place.

The greatest dangers to the dollar supremacy, however, come from within, and it does not matter which party is in power, especially if one or the other has too much of it. The past few decades of rising dollar dominance have created a false sense in U.S. political circles (and among many economists) that ultra-low interest rates are almost certainly the future norm. Their complacency is classic "This Time Is Different" thinking. History suggests that the ultra-low real interest rates that prevailed in the years after the global financial crisis should always have been viewed as a temporary deviation from much longer-term trends. Ex-post rationales for "lower forever," such as secular stagnation (permanently lower growth) and adverse demographics, have important elements of truth, but were vastly overblown, especially by those wanting to believe that outsized deficits can be sustained forever, and that any thoughts of reining them in, either via higher taxes or lower spending, must be summarily dismissed as unacceptable "austerity."

If rapidly rising debt is left unchecked, and there seems to be little political appetite to rein in massive deficits, the United States and the entire world is in for a sustained period of global financial volatility marked by higher average real interest rates and inflation and more frequent bouts of debt and financial crises. Former U.S. vice-president Dick Cheney's "deficits don't matter" hypothesis seemed to be a good call when interest rates kept dropping and dropping. Now, with interest rates normalizing (outside recessions), the jig is up.

There is also unwarranted complacency concerning inflation. Economists have convinced themselves that high inflation is a solved problem. As a technocratic matter that is true, but the political economy roots of inflation remain, which is why another bout of high inflation over the next five to ten years is not only possible but likely, especially if there is another major shock such as a cyber war or a pandemic. Nor can one presume that politicians will always find central bank independence convenient. Donald Trump's proposal that the President have a direct input into Fed policy is particularly blunt, but even a more conventional administration in the future may follow suit, particularly in times of extreme economic or fiscal distress.

Is all of this too alarmist? If one learns nothing else from examining the evolution of the global currency system over the past seven decades, it should be that surprising changes can and do happen. If runaway U.S. debt policy continues to crash up against higher real interest rates and geopolitical instability, and if political pressures constrain the Federal Reserve's ability to consistently tame inflation, it will be everyone's problem.

A postscript: Virtually all of what I have had to say here is intended to be objective analysis that does not depend on which party controls power in the near term. Just as this book goes to press, however, it has become apparent that Donald J. Trump has won a resounding victory in the U.S. Presidential election. One can only say that, for better or for worse, the title of this book, while inspired by Nixon-era Treasury Secretary John Connolly's beatdown of his foreign colleagues five decades ago, captures only too well the America-first philosophy of the new administration. President Trump may be exceptionally direct in his exercise of raw U.S. economic power. However, as we have seen, there is a long history of the United States allowing competitors to do well but not too well, especially if their success threatens to diminish the dominance of the U.S. economy and the dollar. This is nothing new. American arrogance and exceptionalism have sometimes served U.S. interests, but they also helped trigger the Great Inflation of the 1970s and the 2008–2009 Global Financial Crisis. One can hope for a long period of strong growth and low inflation, but it would be folly to ignore the many "this time is different" Pax Dollar assumptions built into today's markets that may well be upended over the next decade, if not much sooner.

NOTES

CHAPTER 1. INTRODUCTION

1. For readers interested in more detail, table 1 gives a sweeping history of the global safe asset and the corresponding exchange rate system.

2. Kristi Oloffson, "Top Ten Things You Didn't Know About Henry VIII," *Time*, June 24, 2009.

3. Kenneth Rogoff, *The Curse of Cash* (Princeton, N.J.: Princeton University Press, 2016).

4. Carmen Reinhart and Kenneth Rogoff, *This Time Is Different: Eight Centuries of Financial Folly* (Princeton, N.J.: Princeton University Press, 2009).

5. Kenneth Rogoff, Barbara Rossi, and Paul Schmelzing, "Long-Run Trends in Long-Maturity Real Rates, 1311–2022," *American Economic Review* 114, no. 8 (August 2024): 2271–2307.

6. With income weighted at market exchange rates; see figure 2 in text.

7. Although the full-blown transition to a dollar standard took place only after World War II, the late 1930s witnessed England, the United States, and France attempting to partially restore the role of gold through the Tripartite Agreement of 1936. The financial historian (and my former Ph.D. thesis student) Max Harris argues that the pact in many ways already elevated the dollar above other currencies and was a precursor to the post-war system. Max Harris, *Monetary War and Peace: London, Washington, Paris, and the Tripartite Agreement of 1936* (Cambridge: Cambridge University Press, 2021).

8. Hector Perez-Saiz, Longmei Zhang, and Roshan Iyer, "Currency Usage for Cross Border Payments," Working Paper No. 2023/72 (International Monetary Fund, March 2023).

9. See Patrick McGuire, Goetz von Peter, and Sonya Zhu, "International Finance Through the Lens of BIS Statistics: The Global Reach of Currencies," *BIS Quarterly Review*, June 2024, 9.

10. See McGuire, von Peter, and Zhu, "International Finance Through the Lens of BIS Statistics," table 6C.

11. Ethan Ilzetzki, Carmen M. Reinhart, and Kenneth S. Rogoff, "Rethinking Exchange Rate Regimes," in *Handbook of International Economics*, vol. 6, ed. Gita Gopinath, Elhanan Helpman, and Kenneth S. Rogoff (Amsterdam: Elsevier, 2022), 91–145. See also Carol Bertaut, Bastian von Beschwitz, and Stephanie Curcuru, "The International Role of the U.S. Dollar," *FEDs Notes*, October 6, 2021.

12. Anna Hirtenstein, "The Dominant Dollar Faces a Backlash in the Oil Market," *Wall Street Journal*, December 28, 2023.

13. Emine Boz et al., "Patterns of Invoicing Currency in Global Trade: New Evidence," *Journal of International Economics* 136 (May 2022): 677–719.

14. Figure 1 is updated from Ethan Ilzetzki, Carmen Reinhart, and Kenneth Rogoff, "Exchange Arrangements Entering the Twenty-First Century: Which Anchor Will Hold?," *Quarterly Journal of Economics* 134, no. 2 (May 2019): 599–646. It is constructed using an algorithm that considers how a country's exchange rate actually behaves; official pronouncements are considered only if they are consistent with what the central bank actually does. There are other ways to assess the dollar's importance in any given country; they mostly all give the same overall impression.

15. Operationally, if it wants to dampen dollar currency fluctuations, a central bank typically either moves its interest rate in close correspondence with that of the U.S. Federal Reserve (to relieve pressures on the currency from capital racing in and out of the country) or uses its dollar reserves to intervene directly in the foreign exchange market.

16. Data source for figure 2: For market rates, Total Economy Database (The ConferenceBoard), www.conference-board.org/data/economydatabase/total-economy-database-productivity ("© 2024, The Conference Board, Inc. All rights reserved); and for PPP rates, Penn World Tables (Groningen Growth and Development Centre) http://www.rug.nl/ggdc/productivity/pwt/"www.rug.nl/ggdc/productivity/pwt/. For further details, see Feenstra, Robert C., Robert Inklaar and Marcel P. Timmer (2015), "The Next Generation of the Penn World Tables" *American Economic Review,* 105(10), 3150-3182, available for download at http://www.ggdc.net/pwt"www.ggdc.net/pwt. The market exchange rate measure is clearly sensitive at any point in time to the value of the dollar. Other countries' incomes are converted to dollars at market exchange rates and at purchasing power parity exchange rates. The reader should note the same databases, the Total Economy Database and the Penn World Tables, are referred to later in this book in abbreviated form.

17. China's 2023 GDP was $17.8 trillion and the United States' was $27.3 trillion. International Monetary Fund, *World Economic Outlook* (October 2024).

18. United Nations, Department of Economic and Social Affairs, Population Division, *International Migrant Stock* (New York, United Nations, 2019).

19. Rong Qian, Carmen M. Reinhart, and Kenneth Rogoff, "On Graduation from Default, Inflation and Banking Crises: Elusive or Illusion?," in *NBER Macroeconomics Annual 2010*, ed. Daron Acemoglu and Michael Woodford (Chicago: University of Chicago Press, 2011), 1–36.

CHAPTER 2. THE SOVIET CHALLENGE

1. Paul A. Samuelson, *Economics: An Introductory Analysis* (New York: McGraw-Hill, 1961), 830.

2. "Professor Predicts Soviet Growth Will Overtake the United States," *Harvard Crimson*, October 17, 1960.

3. Daniel Patrick Moynihan, "The Soviet Economy: Boy, Were We Wrong!," *Washington Post*, July 11, 1990.

4. Walt Rostow, *The Stages of Economic Growth: A Non-Communist Manifesto* (Cambridge: Cambridge University Press, 1960).

5. J. Michael Montias, "On the Consistency and Efficiency of Central Plans," *Review of Economic Studies* 29, no. 4 (October 1962): 280–290.

6. Martin Weitzman, "Soviet Post-War Economic Growth," *American Economic Review* 60, no. 4. (September 1970): 676–692.

7. J. Michael Montias, *Artists and Artisans in Delft: A Socio-Economic Study of the Seventeenth Century* (Princeton, N.J.: Princeton University Press, 1982).

8. Angus Maddison, *Economic Growth in Japan and the USSR* (New York: Norton, 1969), 111.

9. Gus Weiss, "Duping the Soviets: The Farewell Dossier," *Studies in Intelligence* (Center for the Study of Intelligence), 1996, www.cia.gov/resources/csi/studies-in-intelligence/1996-2/the-farewell-dossier/. See also Sergei Kostin, Eric Raynaud, and Richard V. Allen, *Farewell: The Greatest Spy Story of the Twentieth Century*, trans. Catherine Cauvin-Higgins (Las Vegas, Nev.: Amazon Crossing, 2011).

10. The Soviet Union's industrial and military espionage foreshadows China's much larger program in the twenty-first century. William C. Hannas, James Mulvenon, and Anna B. Puglisi, *Chinese Industrial Espionage: Technology Acquisition and Military Modernisation* (New York: Routledge, 2013).

11. Yakov Feygin, *Building a Ruin: The Cold War Politics of Soviet Economic Reform* (Cambridge, Mass.: Harvard University Press, 2024).

12. Bernard Gwertzman, "Fischer Now a Chess Hero in the Soviet," *New York Times*, July 23, 1971.

13. Natasha Lance Rogoff, *Muppets in Moscow: The Unexpected Crazy True Story of Making Sesame Street in Russia* (New York: Rowman & Littlefield, 2022).

14. Anna Ivanovna, Michael Keen, and Alexander Klemm, "The Russian Flat Tax Reform," Working Paper No. 2005/16 (International Monetary Fund, January 2005).

15. Arkady Dvorkovich later went on to become deputy prime minister of Russia from

2012 to 2018, and after that president of the World Chess Federation (FIDE). He remains president of FIDE as of this writing even though Russian chess players are only allowed to play in most international tournaments under the FIDE flag or that of another country.

16. "Top Russian Economist Mau Charged in Large-Scale Fraud Case," *Reuters*, June 30, 2022.

CHAPTER 3. JAPAN AND THE YEN

1. Maybe they meant that the second line served box lunches; I never tried it.

2. Michael E. Porter, *The Competitive Advantage of Nations* (New York: Free Press, republished with new introd., 1998).

3. C. K. Prahalad and Gary Hamel, "The Core Competence of the Corporation," *Harvard Business Review* (May/June 1990): 79–90.

4. Ezra Vogel, *Japan as Number One: Lessons for America* (Cambridge, Mass.: Harvard University Press, 1979).

5. "Boz Confession: Bolt Out of Blue," *Los Angeles Times*, October 16, 1986.

6. The classic postmortem on the episode is the methodologically pathbreaking paper by Steven Berry, James Levinson, and Ariel Pakes, "Voluntary Export Restraints on Automobiles: Evaluating a Trade Policy," *American Economic Review* 89, no. 3 (June 1989): 400–430.

7. "Joint Venture with GM," Toyota, *75 Years of Toyota*, part 3, chap. 1, sect. 3, www.toyota-global.com/company/history_of_toyota/75years/text/leaping_forward_as_a_global_corporation/chapter1/section3/item2.html.

8. Ulrike Schaede, *The Business Reinvention of Japan: How to Make Sense of the New Japan and Why It Matters* (Palo Alto, Calif.: Stanford University Press, 2020).

9. Kevin Roose, "Kodak's Dubious Cryptocurrency Gamble," *New York Times*, January 30, 2018.

10. Over the same period, greater Rochester, including its sprawling suburbs, has grown slightly.

11. Justin Murphy, "Superintendent Who Led East High's Revival to Leave for UR post," *Democrat and Chronicle*, March 24, 2023.

12. In 1955, Japanese per capita GDP was 22 percent of U.S. per capita GDP on a PPP basis and 13 percent using market exchange rates; by 1991, the PPP figure was 81 percent and the market exchange rate figure was 126 percent. Penn World Tables (for PPP) and Total Economy Database (The Conference Board) (for market exchange rates).

13. Japan spent less than 1 percent of GDP on military expenditures during the period 1961–2019. SIPRI Military Expenditure Database. See figure 15 (chapter 23) for U.S. figures.

14. Among international economists, James Baker is especially famous as the architect

of the "Baker Plan," which provided debt relief to a score of middle-income emerging-market countries, thereby helping to end Latin America's "lost decade."

15. G10 finance-minister meetings are off the record. In their superb biography of James Baker, Peter Baker and Susan Glasser note that Baker liked to brag that he had been both the youngest and oldest member of the Eagle Lake Rod and Gun Club in Texas. Peter Baker and Susan Glasser, *The Man Who Ran Washington: The Life and Times of James A. Baker III* (New York: Doubleday, 2020).

16. Carmen Reinhart and Kenneth Rogoff, *This Time Is Different: Eight Centuries of Financial Folly* (Princeton, N.J.: Princeton University Press, 2009).

17. Kenneth Rogoff, "Time-Series Studies of the Relationship Between Exchange Rates and Intervention: A Review of the Techniques and Literature," Federal Reserve Staff Studies No. 132 (Board of Governors of the Federal Reserve System, 1983). See also Kenneth Rogoff, "On the Effects of Sterilized Intervention: An Analysis of Weekly Data," *Journal of Monetary Economics* 14 (1984): 133–150.

18. On September 11, 1985, the yen-dollar exchange rate was 244, on September 11, 1986, it was 156, and by December 31, 1987, it was 121. "Japanese Yen to U.S. Dollar Spot Exchange Rate" (series: DEXJPUS), FRED (Federal Reserve Bank of St. Louis).

19. An excellent source for understanding how deep Japan's financial problems already were by 1992 is Christopher Wood, *The Bubble Economy: Japan's Extraordinary Speculative Boom of the '80s and the Dramatic Bust of the '90s* (New York: Atlantic Monthly Press, 1992).

20. Kunio Okina, Masaaki Shirakawa, and Shigenori Shiratsuka, "The Asset Price Bubble and Monetary Policy: Japan's Experience in the Late 1980s and the Lessons," *Monetary and Economic Studies* (Bank of Japan) 19, no. S-1 (February 2001): 395–450; "Nikkei Stock Average, Nikkei 225" (series: NIKKEI225), FRED (Federal Reserve Bank of St. Louis); and author's calculations.

21. Bryan Burrough and John Helyar, *Barbarians at the Gate* (New York: Harper Row, 1989).

22. See Wood, *The Bubble Economy*.

23. To be fair, not all the investments were duds, and Japanese investors today have nevertheless managed to achieve a large, if quiet, footprint.

24. Data source for figure 3: "Households; owner-occupied real estate including vacant land and mobile homes at market value" (code: LM155035015.Q), from table B.101 ("Balance Sheet of Households and Nonprofit Organizations"), Financial Accounts of the United States (Z.1), Board of Governors of the Federal Reserve System; "Japan—Spot Exchange Rate, yen/US$" (code: RXI_N.B.JA), Foreign Exchange Rates (H.10), Board of Governors of the Federal Reserve System; "Estimated Values of Houses and Residential Land," table 4-1, 2019 National Survey of Family Income, Consumption and Wealth, Statistics Bureau of Japan.

Data source for figure 4: "Total equity market: Market capitalization," Statistics Portal,

World Federation of Exchanges, https://statistics.world-exchanges.org. All series are for domestic market capitalization. U.S. exchanges are the American Stock Exchange, NASDAQ, and the NYSE. The Japanese exchange is Japan Exchange Group (Tokyo and Osaka).

25. Richard Meese and Kenneth Rogoff, "Empirical Exchange Rate Models of the Seventies: Do They Fit Out of Sample?," *Journal of International Economics* 14, nos. 1–2 (February 1983): 3–24.

26. The Bank of Japan and several other Japanese ministries were well ahead of the curve in providing many publications in English. My thesis adviser, Rudi Dornbusch, had explained to me that usually the only countries that reliably translated government financial statistics into English were those who borrowed a lot of money from abroad. In the early 1990s, Japan, already a large net creditor to the world, was an exception.

27. Natalia V. Bhattacharjee et al., "Global Fertility in 204 Countries and Territories, 1950–2021, with Forecasts to 2100: A Comprehensive Demographic Analysis for the Global Burden of Disease Study 2021," *Lancet* 403, no. 10440 (May 18, 2024): 2057–2099.

28. "Labour Force Survey," 2023, Portal Site of the Official Statistics of Japan website, https://www.e-stat.go.jp.

29. Robert M. Solow, "A Contribution to the Theory of Economic Growth," *Quarterly Journal of Economics* 70, no. 1 (1956): 65–94.

30. Korea has a population of 51.5 million; Taiwan, 23.3 million; Hong Kong, 7.6 million; and Singapore, 5.9 million—a collective population of 88.3 million. Japan has a population of 124.0 million. International Monetary Fund, *World Economic Outlook* (April 2024).

31. Okina, Shirakawa, and Shiratsuka, "The Asset Price Bubble and Monetary Policy."

32. Total Economy Database (The Conference Board).

33. For an excellent discussion, see Takeo Hoshi and Anil Kashyap, "Japan's Financial Crisis and Economic Stagnation," *Journal of Economic Perspectives* 18, no. 1 (Winter 2004): 3–26.

34. Christina Romer and David Romer, "New Evidence on the Aftermath of Financial Crises in Advanced Economies," *American Economic Review* 107, no. 10 (October 2017): 3072–3118.

35. World Bank database, GDP, PPP (current international $).

36. "Real Residential Property Prices," BIS Data Portal, https://data.bis.org/topics/RPP.

37. Tim Hornyak, "Japan Has Millions of Empty Houses. Want to Buy One for $25,000?," *New York Times*, April 17, 2023.

38. The U.S.'s and Japan's debt-to-GDP ratios are based on gross debt, taken from the International Monetary Fund, *Fiscal Monitor* (October 2024). As discussed earlier, an unexpected burst of high inflation is akin to a partial default on long-term nominal bonds because it means that creditors are being repaid with dollars that buy fewer goods than they had

originally anticipated; had they known that high inflation was coming, they would have charged a higher interest rate to compensate.

39. Ulrike Schaede, *The Business Reinvention of Japan: How to Make Sense of the New Japan and Why It Matters* (Stanford, Calif.: Stanford University Press, 2020).

40. Japan's 2023 GDP was $4.2 trillion, whereas China's was $17.8 trillion. International Monetary Fund, *World Economic Outlook* (October 2024).

CHAPTER 4. THE SINGLE CURRENCY IN EUROPE

1. Kenneth S. Rogoff, "The Optimal Degree of Commitment to an Intermediate Monetary Target," *Quarterly Journal of Economics* 100, no. 4 (November 1985): 1169–1189.

2. Martin Feldstein, "The EMU and International Conflict," *Foreign Affairs*, November/December 1997.

3. See, for example, Peter Kenen, "The Theory of Optimum Currency Areas: An Eclectic View," in *Monetary Problems of the International Economy*, ed. Robert Mundell and Alexander Swoboda (Chicago: University of Chicago Press, 1969), 41–60; Maurice Obstfeld, "EMU: Ready or Not?," *Essays in International Finance* (Princeton IES), no. 209 (July 1998).

4. Commission of the European Communities, Directorate-General for Economics, *One Market, One Money: An Evaluation of the Potential Benefits and Costs of Forming an Economic and Monetary Union* (Brussels: Office for Official Publications of the European Communities, October 1990).

5. Data source for figure 5: "Total equity market: Market capitalization," Statistics Portal, World Federation of Exchanges, https://statistics.world-exchanges.org. All values are for domestic market capitalization. U.S. exchanges are the American Stock Exchange, NASDAQ, and the NYSE. European exchanges are the Athens Stock Exchange, the Belarusian Currency and Stock Exchange, the BME Spanish Exchange (all cities), the Borsa Italiana, the Bratislava Stock Exchange, the Bucharest Stock Exchange, the Budapest Stock Exchange, the Bulgarian Stock Exchange, the Cyprus Stock Exchange, Deutsche Börse AG, Euronext (all cities), the Ljubljana Stock Exchange, the London Stock Exchange (now LSEG), the Luxembourg Stock Exchange, the Malta Stock Exchange, MICEX, the Moscow Exchange, NASDAQ OMX and Nordic (all cities), the Prague Stock Exchange, the SIX Swiss Exchange, the Ukrainian Exchange, the Vienna Stock Exchange, the Warsaw Stock Exchange, and the Zagreb Stock Exchange.

6. The currencies phased out at the founding of the euro in 1999 were the German deutsche mark, the French franc, the Italian lira, the Dutch guilder, the Austrian schilling, the Belgian franc, the Irish pound, the Finish markka, the Portuguese escudo, the Spanish peseta, and the Luxembourg franc. Greece (the drachma) joined in 2001.

7. Ling Hu Tan, "IMF Engagement with the Euro Area Versus Other Currency Unions," in *Background Papers for the IMF and the Crises in Greece, Ireland, and Portugal*, ed. Moises Schwartz and Shinji Takagi (Washington, D.C.: IMF Independent Evaluation Office, 2017), 63–95.

8. The two African currency unions were pegged to the French franc and then to the euro; the Caribbean currency union was pegged to the U.S. dollar. These currency unions involved vastly poorer and smaller economies than the eurozone, and the two African currency unions were post-colonial arrangements effectively subsidized by France, though one might argue exploited as well.

9. "Currency Composition of Official Foreign Exchange Reserves" (COFER), IMF Data (International Monetary Fund).

10. Like figure 1, figure 6 is based on the algorithm and data set (updated) from Ethan Ilzetzki, Carmen Reinhart, and Kenneth Rogoff, "Exchange Arrangements Entering the Twenty-First Century: Which Anchor Will Hold?," *Quarterly Journal of Economics* 134, no. 2 (May 2019): 599–646.

11. International Monetary Fund, *World Economic Outlook* (April 2024).

12. Ethan Ilzetzki, Carmen M. Reinhart, and Kenneth S. Rogoff, "Why Is the Euro Punching Below Its Weight?," *Economic Policy* 35, no. 103 (July 2020): 405–460.

13. Data source for figure 7: Penn World Tables (Groningen Growth and Development Centre) (to 2019), www.rug.nl/ggdc/productivity/pwt/; Total Economy Database (The Conference Board) (from 2020), www.conference-board.org/data/economydatabase/total-economy-database-productivity.

14. Total Economy Database (The Conference Board).

15. "Demography Could Be Yet Another Force for Divergence Within the EU," *Economist*, January 11, 2020.

16. Hassan Afrouzi, Marina Halac, Kenneth Rogoff, and Pierre Yared, "Changing Central Bank Pressures and Inflation," *Brookings Papers on Economic Activity* 2024, no. 1, 205–241.

17. European Council, "Economic Governance Review: Council and Parliament Strike Deal on Reform of Fiscal Rules," press release, February 21, 2024.

18. International Monetary Fund, World Economic Outlook Press Conference (Dubai International Convention Center, Dubai, September 18, 2003).

19. The most quantitatively significant issue seemed to be the costs that European businesses had to absorb to keep accounts in multiple currencies; the European Commission's 1990 monograph *One Market, One Money* suggested that these costs might reduce euro area GDP by as much as 1 percent. (When I sat next to a high-powered accountant on a plane a decade later, she explained that modern software had essentially eliminated currency-conversion accounting costs.)

20. Kenneth Rogoff, "NAChos and ECUs: Issues in the Transition to European Monetary Union" (paper presented to the Board of Governors of the Federal Reserve System Academic Consultants Meeting, Washington, D.C., November 19, 1991).

21. Martin Feldstein and Charles Horioka, "Domestic Savings and International Capital Flows," *Economic Journal* 90, no. 358 (June 1980): 314–329; Olivier Blanchard and Fran-

cesco Giavazzi, "Current Account Deficits in the Euro Area: The End of the Feldstein-Horioka Puzzle?," *Brookings Papers on Economic Activity* 2002, no. 2, 147–209.

22. Stephen Mihm, "Dr. Doom," *New York Times*, August 15, 2008.

23. Carmen Reinhart and Kenneth Rogoff, "Is the 2007 U.S. Sub-Prime Financial Crisis So Different? An International Historical Comparison," *American Economic Review* 98, no. 2 (May 2008): 339–344.

24. "Same as It Ever Was: What Do Earlier Banking Crises Reveal about America's Travails Today?," *Economist*, January 10, 2010.

25. Patrizia Baudino, Jean-Philippe Svoronos, and Diarmuid Murphy, "The Banking Crisis in Ireland," FSI Crisis Management Series No. 2 (Bank for International Settlements, October 2020). See also Patrizia Baudino, Mariano Herrera, and Fernando Restoy, "The 2008–14 Banking Crisis in Spain," FSI Crisis Management Series No. 4 (Bank for International Settlements, July 2023).

26. In February 2009, I was asked to come to Reykjavík to meet for two days with the prime ministers of Sweden, Denmark, Finland, Norway, and Iceland to discuss the implications of the global financial crisis in general, and how to help Iceland in particular. It was a difficult time. The normally packed plane from Boston to Reykjavík (which I have taken many times en route to Europe to save money) had only four passengers. After we deplaned, one of them caught up to me and asked, "Are you Ken Rogoff?" Startled, I asked who he might be. "I am the IMF representative to Iceland." Iceland was in some ways fortunate both that its crisis came early and that it is relatively small (its population is under 400,000), which allowed its banks to default in ways that were not later open to Ireland.

27. For example, Kenneth Rogoff, "The Euro's Pig-Headed Masters," *Project Syndicate*, June 3, 2011.

28. Carmen Reinhart and Kenneth Rogoff, "Growth in a Time of Debt," *American Economic Review* 100, no. 2 (May 2010): 573–578 (and 2013 online errata).

29. Kenneth Rogoff, "Inflation Is Now the Lesser Evil," *Project Syndicate*, December 2, 2008.

30. Mario Draghi, speech at the Global Investment Conference (London, July 26, 2012).

31. Chris Miller, *Chip War: The Fight for the World's Most Critical Technology* (New York: Scribner, 2022).

32. Carmen Reinhart and Kenneth Rogoff, "Financial and Sovereign Debt Crises: Some Lessons Learned and Those Forgotten," in *Financial Crises: Causes, Consequences, and Policy Responses*, ed. Stijn Claessens et al. (Washington, D.C.: International Monetary Fund, 2014), 141–156.

CHAPTER 5. THIS TIME IS DIFFERENT

1. Kenneth Rogoff and Yuanchen Yang, "Peak China Housing," Working Paper No. 27697 (National Bureau of Economic Research, August 2020).

2. "Measuring the Universe's Most Important Sector," *Economist*, November 2021.

3. The pathbreaking paper on how fast-growing Asian countries have inevitably run into diminishing returns, such that high investment cannot indefinitely produce very high growth, is Allwyn Young, "A Tale of Two Cities: Factor Accumulation in Hong Kong and Singapore," in *NBER Macroeconomics Annual* 1992, ed. Olivier Blanchard and Stanley Fischer (Cambridge, Mass.: MIT Press, 1992), 13–53. However, the idea came into the popular conversation after the brilliantly clear exposition in Paul Krugman, "The Myth of the Asian Miracle," *Foreign Affairs*, November/December 1994.

4. Adam Posen, "The End of China's Economic Miracle," *Foreign Affairs*, September/October 2023.

5. See Stella Yifan Xie, "China's Economy Won't Overtake the U.S., Some Now Predict," *Wall Street Journal*, September 2, 2022, and Rick Newman, "China's Economy May Never Eclipse America's," *Yahoo Finance*, August 21, 2023.

6. Data source for figure 8: Penn World Tables (Groningen Growth and Development Centre).

7. Here, I am defining the dollar bloc as in figure 1, using the algorithm from Ethan Ilzetzki, Carmen Reinhart, and Kenneth Rogoff, "Exchange Arrangements Entering the Twenty-First Century: Which Anchor Will Hold?," *Quarterly Journal of Economics* 134, no. 2 (May 2019): 599–646.

8. Gish Jen, *Thank You, Mr. Nixon* (New York: Knopf, 2022).

9. "Monthly Foreign Exchange Reserves, 2002," State Administration of Foreign Exchange, published September 20, 2011, www.safe.gov.cn/en/2011/0920/578.html.

10. Just to be clear, as an accounting matter, a country's current account is equal to the difference between its national savings and investment rates. When the two are exactly equal, the country is saving just enough to pay for all its own investments in things like factories, new equipment, and structures. If savings is less than investment, the country will have to borrow from abroad, running a current account deficit, and vice versa if savings is higher than investment.

11. Juann H. Hung and Rong Qian, "Why Is China's Saving Rate So High? A Comparative Study of Cross-Country Panel Data," Working Paper No. 2010-07 (Congressional Budget Office, November 2010).

12. The so-called Balassa-Samuelson-Harrod effect is one of the more empirically durable relationships in international macroeconomics. There are certainly exceptions, and it most typically shows up strongly only in exceptionally fast-growing economies; 1950s–1980s Japan is the canonical example. See Kenneth Rogoff, "The Purchasing Power Parity Puzzle," *Journal of Economic Literature* 34, no. 2 (June 1996): 647–668.

13. Kevin Honglin Zhang and Shunfeng Song, "Rural–Urban Migration and Urbanization in China: Evidence from Time-Series and Cross-Section Analyses," *China Economic Review* 14, no. 4 (January 1, 2003): 386–400. See also Joe Myers, "You Knew China's Cities Were Growing: But the Real Numbers Are Stunning," World Economic Forum, June 20, 2016.

14. Jiangze Bian et al., "Leverage-Induced Fire Sales and Stock Market Crashes," Working Paper No. 25040 (National Bureau of Economic Research, September 2018).

CHAPTER 6. ZHU RONGJI'S UNCANNY FORECASTS

1. Evidently the inspiration for Melua's song had come on a trip to Beijing, where a tour guide made the claim.

2. In a back-to-the-future move, my proudly liberal hometown of Cambridge, Massachusetts — aka "The People's Republic of Cambridge" — has replaced a significant fraction of its streets with bike lanes, although so far the number of bike riders is very small compared with the number of people who rely on cars and buses.

3. The film is the third in Hiroshi Inagaki's *Samurai* trilogy, *The Duel at Ganryu Island* (1956).

4. Joseph Stiglitz, *Globalization and Its Discontents* (New York: Norton, 2002).

5. Jeremy Bulow and Kenneth Rogoff, "Cleaning Up Third-World Debt Without Getting Taken to the Cleaners," *Journal of Economic Perspectives* 4, no. 1 (Winter 1990): 31–42.

6. My remarks at the Stiglitz debate were later published on the IMF website as an open letter, dated July 2, 2002. Where I really took issue was with Stiglitz's characterization of the IMF's junior economists as third-rate, which seemed like punching down, and his personal attacks on Stanley Fischer, when he impugned Fischer's ethics for taking a job in the financial sector after retiring from the IMF. Fischer, to me, was one of the greatest leaders the IMF has ever had. A decade later, in 2014, President Obama appointed Fischer as vice chair of the Federal Reserve, a position he served with great distinction.

7. Guillermo Calvo and Carmen Reinhart, "Fear of Floating," *Quarterly Journal of Economics* 117, no. 2 (May 2002): 379–408.

CHAPTER 7. THE PEOPLE'S BANK OF CHINA

1. Menzie Chinn and Hiro Ito, "What Matters for Financial Development? Capital Controls, Institutions, and Interactions," *Journal of Development Economics* 81, no. 1 (October 2006): 163–192.

2. Ayhan Kose et al., "The Effects of Financial Globalization on Developing Countries: Some Empirical Evidence," Occasional Paper No. 220 (International Monetary Fund, September 2003).

3. Little did I know that a few years later, in 2008, I would be offered membership in the Group of Thirty (G30), an influential consultative group that counts among its members many leading current and former policymakers, and that Governor Zhou would be my colleague in those informal meetings for years to come.

4. A decade later, in 2014, when China first decided to self-report its portfolio on a one-off basis, China had indeed diversified somewhat, with dollar holdings down to 70 percent of its portfolio; that share dropped to 57 percent when reported again in 2022. Matthew

Ferranti, "Estimating the Currency Composition of Foreign Exchange Reserves" (Ph.D. dissertation, Harvard University, May 2023). (Matthew is a former Ph.D. thesis student of mine.)

5. Agence d'Architecture A. Bechu & Associés, *China Executive Leadership of Pudong* (2005), https://bechuetassocies.com/uploads/projets/pdf/celap-university_5b2d1.pdf.

6. John Foley, "Jiang Zemin Made China Richer and More Unequal," *Reuters*, November 20, 2022.

7. Charmain Maria Jacob, "Mumbai Overtakes Beijing to Become Asia's Billionaire Capital," *CNBC*, March 27, 2024.

CHAPTER 8. PRELUDE TO CRISIS

1. Katherine Rushton, "Ken Rogoff Warns That China Is the Next Bubble to Burst," *Telegraph* (London), May 17, 2014.

2. Robert N. McCauley and Chang Shu, "Dollar and Renminbi Flowed Out of China," *Bank for International Settlements Quarterly Review*, March 2016, 26–27.

3. Andrew Ross Sorkin, "A Warning on China Seems Prescient," *New York Times*, August 24, 2015.

4. Yu Yongding, "China's Misguided Exchange Rate Machinations," *Project Syndicate*, August 24, 2017.

5. "China Registers 415 Million Motor Vehicles, 500 Million Drivers," *Xinhua News Agency*, December 12, 2022.

6. Alyssa Abkowitz, "Facebook's Mark Zuckerberg Goes Running in 'Hazardous' Beijing Smog," *Wall Street Journal*, March 18, 2016.

7. Emily Shrider and John Creamer, "Poverty in the United States: 2022," Report No. P60-280 (U.S. Census Bureau, September 2023).

8. Richard Jackson, "The End of the One-Child Policy," Commentary, Center for Strategic and International Studies, October 29, 2015. Today, many other factors, including the high cost of housing and education, have continued to hold down birth rates even with the restriction relaxed.

CHAPTER 9. THE END OF HIGH GROWTH

1. "National Database," National Bureau of Statistics of China, 2023, www.stats.gov.cn.

2. Penn World Tables (Groningen Growth and Development Centre), www.rug.nl/ggdc/productivity/pwt/.

3. Financial crises are not the only way populism interrupts growth; the stunning riots across Chile in October 2019 come to mind. See Amanda Taub, "'Chile Woke Up': Dictatorship's Legacy of Inequality Triggers Mass Protests," *New York Times*, November 3, 2019. I, for one, did not see this coming despite having visited Chile only a few months earlier to give a presentation at the central bank's annual research conference.

4. Although China enjoys a world-class reputation for building infrastructure, there are still quality problems at times; for example, in May 2024 rain caused a 59-foot section of highway to collapse, reportedly killing at least 48 people. Alisha Rahaman Sarkar, "Highway Collapse in China Kills at Least 48 People," *Independent* (London), May 2, 2024.

5. Kenneth Rogoff, "Debt Supercycle, Not Secular Stagnation," in *Progress and Confusion: The State of Macroeconomic Policy*, ed. Olivier Blanchard et al. (Cambridge, Mass.: MIT Press, 2016): 19–28.

6. Edward Glaeser et al., "A Real Estate Boom with Chinese Characteristics," *Journal of Economic Perspectives* 31, no.1 (Winter 2017): 93–116.

7. Hamming Fang et al., "Demystifying the Chinese Housing Boom," *NBER Macroeconomics Annual* 30 (2015): 105–166.

8. For example, "Bernanke: Subprime Mortgage Woes Won't Seriously Harm the U.S. Economy," *CNBC*, May 17, 2007.

9. Kenneth Rogoff and Yuanchen Yang, "Peak China Housing," Working Paper No. 27697 (National Bureau of Economic Research, August 2020), and online addendum "The Size of China's Real Estate Sector."

10. Kenneth Rogoff and Yuanchen Yang, "Rethinking China's Growth," *Economic Policy* 39, no. 119 (July 2024): 517–548.

11. Data source for figure 9: Rogoff and Yang, "Rethinking China's Growth."

12. Data source for figure 10: Kenneth Rogoff and Yuanchen Yang, "A Tale of Tier 3 Cities," *Journal of International Economics* 152 (November 2024): 1–27.

13. Kenneth Rogoff and Yuanchen Yang, "China's Real Estate Challenge," *Finance and Development* (forthcoming).

14. See "People's Republic of China: Selected Issues," Country Report No. 2023/081 (International Monetary Fund, February 2023).

15. There is actually no official city tier classification, though there is an informal one. Yuanchen and I categorize Beijing, Shanghai, Guangzhou, and Shenzhen as tier 1 cities. Tier 2 cities include two municipalities directly under the central government (Tianjin and Chongqing), four cities under separate state planning (Dalian, Qingdao, Ningbo, and Fujian), and twenty-five provincial capitals (Shijiazhuang, Taiyuan, Hohhot, Shenyang, Changchun, Harbin, Nanjing, Hangzhou, Hefei, Fuzhou, Nanchang, Jinan, Zhengzhou, Wuhan, Changsha, Nanning, Haikou, Chengdu, Guiyang, Kunming, Xi'an, Lanzhou, Xining, Yinchuan, and Urumqi). This classification is also broadly in line with other methods of grouping cities on the basis of GDP, income level, or population size and is widely used in the literature. See Rogoff and Yang, "A Tale of Tier 3 Cities."

16. Caroline Mortimer, "Tianjin Explosion: Gigantic Crater Left by Chinese Factory Accident Revealed," *Independent* (London), August 19, 2016.

17. Rogoff and Yang, "A Tale of Tier 3 Cities."

18. Keyu Jin, *The New China Playbook: Beyond Socialism and Capitalism* (New York:

Penguin, 2023). I was Keyu's adviser, both for her undergraduate and graduate Ph.D. theses at Harvard.

19. Rogoff and Yang, "Rethinking China's Growth." The IMF estimates LGFV debt and includes it as part of general government debt under its augmented definition. For details, see "People's Republic of China: 2022 Article IV Consultation Staff Report," Country Report No. 2023/067 (International Monetary Fund, February 2023).

20. Camille Gardner and Peter Henry, "The Global Infrastructure Gap: Potential, Perils, and a Framework for Distinction," *Journal of Economic Literature* 61, no. 4 (December 2023): 1318–1358.

21. Carmen Reinhart and Kenneth Rogoff, *This Time Is Different: Eight Centuries of Financial Folly* (Princeton, N.J.: Princeton University Press, 2009).

22. The importance to the U.S. economy of having banks with strong balance sheets was first emphasized in 1983 in a classic paper by Ben Bernanke, for which he was awarded the 2022 Nobel Prize in economics. The original paper was basically a thought piece. Later in the 1980s, Bernanke, together with Mark Gertler, fleshed out the analytics. Ben Bernanke and Mark Gertler, "Inside the Black Box: The Credit Channel of Monetary Policy Transmission," *Journal of Economic Perspectives* 9, no. 4 (Fall 1995): 27–48. Richard Koo later coined the term "balance sheet recessions" in the context of Japan. Richard Koo, *Balance Sheet Recession: Japan's Struggle with Uncharted Economics and Its Global Implications* (New York: Wiley, 2003). Carmen Reinhart and I provided a large multicountry database that allows one to not only examine all the qualitative features of financial crises but also compare quantitative characteristics, which turned out to be remarkably similar across countries and historical episodes, especially in how crises unfold after they have begun. We looked not only at output but importantly also real estate prices, current accounts, stock prices, unemployment, and debt, among other metrics. By looking at a broad array of markers, it is possible to draw much deeper and more meaningful comparisons than by looking at output alone. Reinhart and Rogoff, *This Time Is Different*.

23. See Eswar Prasad, "Has China's Growth Gone from Miracle to Malady?," *Brookings Papers on Economic Activity* 2023, no. 1, 243–270, and accompanying discussion by Kenneth Rogoff. See also Nicholas Lardy, "How Serious Is China's Economic Slowdown?," *Realtime Economics* (blog), Peterson Institute for International Economics, August 17, 2023.

24. Neil Thomas, "Xi Jinping's Power Grab Is Paying Off," *Foreign Policy*, February 5, 2023.

25. Caroline Kapp, "Female Representation Regresses in China," *Council on Foreign Relations*, October 28, 2022.

CHAPTER 10. THE INEVITABILITY OF DOLLAR DECOUPLING

1. Robert Mundell, "EMU and the International Monetary System: A Transatlantic Perspective," Working Paper No. 13 (Austrian National Bank, 1993); Ronald McKinnon, *The Unloved Dollar Standard* (Oxford: Oxford University Press, 2012).

2. "Balance of Payments: Total Net Current Account for China, P.R., Mainland" (series: CHNBCAGDPBP6PT), FRED (Federal Reserve Bank of St. Louis).

3. Keith Bradsher, "China to Track Renminbi Based on a Basket of Currencies," *New York Times*, December 11, 2015; John Clark, "China's Evolving Managed Float: An Exploration of the Roles of the Fix and Broad Dollar Movements in Explaining Daily Exchange Rate Changes," Staff Report No. 828 (Federal Reserve Bank of New York, November 2017).

4. Ethan Ilzetzki, Carmen Reinhart, and I conjectured in 2020 that the low volatility of major currency exchange rates was just a manifestation of the fact that so many central banks found themselves stuck at the zero lower interest rate bound. We argued that once policy interest rates came off the zero lower bound and started to vary significantly across countries, exchange rate volatility would rise sharply (and so it has—in the case of the yen and even the renminbi, far more than we might have guessed). Ethan Ilzetzki, Carmen Reinhart, and Kenneth Rogoff, "Will the Secular Decline in Exchange Rate and Inflation Volatility Survive COVID-19?," *Brookings Papers on Economic Activity* 2020, no. 1, 279–332.

5. Spot exchange rates (series: DEXCHUS, DEXKOUS, and DEXJPUS), FRED (Federal Reserve Bank of St. Louis).

6. Kenneth Rogoff, "Can the IMF Avert a Global Meltdown?," *Project Syndicate*, September 6, 2006.

CHAPTER 11. THE LURE OF FIXED EXCHANGE RATES

1. My former Ph.D. student Oleg Itskhoki was awarded the Clark Medal in 2022 as the top economist under 40 at any American university, in no small part for his fresh explanations of a range of empirical puzzles in the exchange rate literature. One such puzzle was the finding that standard monetary models of exchange rate behavior cannot beat a random-walk model of exchange rates, even after the fact. See Richard Meese and Kenneth Rogoff, "Empirical Exchange Rate Models of the Seventies: Do They Fit Out of Sample?," *Journal of International Economics* 14, nos. 1–2 (February 1983): 3–24. Another was the purchasing power parity puzzle. Empirically, after a shock to the real exchange rate (the nominal exchange rate adjusted for price differentials), it takes on average three years for half the shock to dissipate, whether through nominal exchange rate or relative price adjustment. See Kenneth Rogoff, "The Purchasing Power Parity Puzzle," *Journal of Economic Literature* 34, no. 2 (June 1996): 647–668. Oleg's work with Dimitri Mukhin suggested that a significant share of the volatility that drives flexible exchange rates is due to financial shocks. If so, then fluctuations in the real exchange rate can be sharply curtailed simply by fixing the nominal exchange rate (e.g., the yen price of a dollar)—a novel argument for exchange rate stability, although this is just the cutting edge in an active area of research.

2. This was an earlier incarnation of Mundell, who relished pushing against the status quo. As Rudi Dornbusch once joked, when the world was on fixed exchange rates, Mundell argued for floating; but then when it went on floating, he argued for fixed. Later it was gold. Mundell was Dornbusch's Ph.D. thesis supervisor at the University of Chicago.

3. To say the least, it is a bit more complicated than that; for example, the government can put off adjusting interest rates temporarily by intervening in the foreign exchange market. Central bank hard currency reserves, however, are not a bottomless pit. Eventually, the government has to take action to bring macroeconomic policy into line or make capital controls much stricter. It can defy the trilemma for a time, but not forever.

4. Lawrence Schembri, "Canada's Experience with a Flexible Exchange Rate in the 1950s: Valuable Lessons Learned," *Bank of Canada Review*, Spring 2008, 3–15.

5. Milton Friedman, "The Case for Flexible Exchange Rates," in *Essays in Positive Economics* (Chicago: University of Chicago Press, 1953), 157–203.

6. Hugo M. Kaufman, "A Debate over Germany's Revaluation 1961: A Chapter in Political Economy," *Weltwirtschaftliches Archiv* 103 (1969): 181–212.

7. Rudiger Dornbusch, "Expectations and Exchange Rate Dynamics," *Journal of Political Economy* 84, no. 6 (December 1976): 1161–1176.

8. "Inflation, Consumer Prices for Germany" (series: FPCPITOTLZGDEU), FRED (Federal Reserve Bank of St. Louis).

9. The idea of employing central bank independence as an alternative mechanism for achieving inflation stability was first formally developed in Kenneth S. Rogoff, "The Optimal Degree of Commitment to an Intermediate Monetary Target," *Quarterly Journal of Economics* 100, no. 4 (1985): 1169–1189.

10. Paul Krugman, "A Model of Balance of Payments Crises," *Journal of Money, Credit and Banking* 11 (August 1979): 311–325; Stephen Salant and Dale Henderson, "Market Anticipations of Government Policies and the Price of Gold," *Journal of Political Economy* 86, no. 4 (August 1978): 627–648.

11. Lars Jonung, Jaakko Kiander, and Pentti Vartia, "The Great Financial Crisis in Finland and Sweden," Economic Papers No. 350 (European Commission, December 2008).

12. Claes Berg and Richard Grottheim, "Monetary Policy in Sweden Since 1992," BIS Policy Papers No. 2 (Bank for International Settlements, 1997).

13. Maurice Obstfeld and Kenneth Rogoff, "The Mirage of Fixed Exchange Rates," *Journal of Economic Perspectives* 9, no. 4 (Fall 1995): 73–96.

14. Maurice Obstfeld, "The Logic of Currency Crises," *Cahiers économiques et monétaires* 43 (1994): 189–213.

CHAPTER 12. HYPERINFLATION

1. See Carmen Reinhart and Kenneth Rogoff, *This Time Is Different: Eight Centuries of Financial Folly* (Princeton, N.J.: Princeton University Press, 2009), chap. 12.

2. A partial list of the very high-inflation countries in 1992 includes countries in Latin America (Brazil, Uruguay, Nicaragua, and Peru), sub-Saharan Africa (Angola, Nigeria, Sudan, and Zimbabwe), and the Middle East and North Africa (Turkey, Iraq, Lebanon, and Yemen), as well as the former Soviet bloc countries (Poland, Bulgaria, Ukraine, Croatia,

Estonia, Mongolia, Kazakhstan, Turkmenistan, Uzbekistan, and Russia). For a complete list, see Kenneth Rogoff, "Globalization and Global Disinflation," in *Monetary Policy and Uncertainty: Adapting to a Changing Economy* (2003 Economic Policy Symposium proceedings) (Kansas City, Mo.: Federal Reserve Bank of Kansas City, 2004), 77–112.

3. Jeffrey Sachs, "The Transition at Mid-Decade," *American Economic Review* 86, no. 2 (May 1996): 128–133.

4. "Zimbabwe Inflation Spirals Again," *BBC News*, February 14, 2008.

5. "Zimbabwe Extends Multi-Currency System to 2030," *Reuters*, October 27, 2023.

6. Rory Carroll, "Nobel Economist Endorses Chávez Regional Bank Plan," *Guardian* (London), October 12, 2007.

7. Not to be confused with the similarly named Centre for Economic Policy Research, a non-partisan European counterpart to the U.S. National Bureau of Economic Research.

8. Center for Economic and Policy Research, "Economists Call on Media to Report 'Overwhelming Evidence' Regarding Venezuelan Election Results," press release, June 7, 2013, https://cepr.net/press-release/economists-call-on-media-to-report-qoverwhelming-evidenceq-regarding-venezuelan-election-results/.

9. CEPR (Washington) researchers argued that the U.S. sanctions greatly amplified Venezuela's downturn. Mark Weisbrot and Jeffrey Sachs, "Economic Sanctions as Collective Punishment: The Case of Venezuela" (Center for Economic and Policy Research, April 2019), https://cepr.net/images/stories/reports/venezuela-sanctions-2019-04.pdf. However, Brookings economists argued that the CEPR paper did not provide a meaningful counterfactual and omitted a number of important factors. They concluded instead that much of the decline in socioeconomic indicators and living standards had occurred long before U.S. sanctions were imposed in August 2017, and were continuing to trend downward in the run-up to the sanctions. Dany Bahar et al., "Impact of the 2017 Sanctions on Venezuela: Revisiting the Evidence," policy brief (Brookings Institution, May 2019).

10. Carmen Reinhart and Kenneth Rogoff, "Venezuela's Spectacular Underperformance," *Project Syndicate*, October 13, 2014.

11. Vanessa Buschschlüter, "Venezuela Crisis: 7.1 Million People Leave Country Since 2015," *BBC*, October 17, 2022.

12. Kenneth Rogoff, "Why Did Trump Accept Venezuela's Money?," *Project Syndicate*, May 4, 2017. (Truth is stranger than fiction.)

13. Anatoly Kurmanaev, Frances Robles, and Julie Turkewitz, "Venezuela's Autocrat Is Declared Winner in Tainted Election," *New York Times*, July 28, 2024.

14. Rudiger Dornbusch and Alejandro Werner, "Stabilization, Reform and No Growth," *Brookings Papers on Economic Activity* 1994, no. 1, 253–314.

15. The current account is the trade balance on goods and services, but it also includes net interest payments and migrant remittances.

16. James Boughton, "Tequila Hangover: The Mexican Peso Crisis and Its Aftermath,"

in *Tearing Down the Walls: The International Monetary Fund 1990–1999* (Washington, D.C.: International Monetary Fund, 2012), chap. 10.

17. Tim Golden, "With Peso's Devaluation, Political Problems Loom," *New York Times*, December 15, 1994; Boughton, "Tequila Hangover," 460.

18. Mark Shields, "A Tale of Two Letters," *Washington Post*, January 14, 1982.

19. Maurice Obstfeld and Kenneth Rogoff, "The Mirage of Fixed Exchange Rates," *Journal of Economic Perspectives* 9, no. 4 (Fall 1995): 73–96.

CHAPTER 13. WHEN EXCHANGE RATE PEGS OUTLIVE THEIR SHELF LIFE

1. Maurice Obstfeld and Kenneth Rogoff, *Foundations of International Macroeconomics* (Cambridge, Mass.: MIT Press: 1996).

2. "Thai Baht to U.S. Dollar Spot Exchange Rate" (series: DEXTHUS), FRED (Federal Reserve Bank of St. Louis).

3. Bijan Aghevli, "Asian Crisis: Causes and Remedies," in *The Asian Financial Crisis: Origins, Implications, and Solutions*, ed. William Hunter, George Kaufman, and Thomas Krueger (Boston: Springer US, 1999): 157–166.

4. Currency conversions and per capita GDP for Indonesia (series: CCUSSP02IDM650N and NYGDPPCAPKDIDN), FRED (Federal Reserve Bank of St. Louis).

5. See Carmen Reinhart and Kenneth Rogoff, *This Time Is Different: Eight Centuries of Financial Folly* (Princeton, N.J.: Princeton University Press, 2009). The chaos surrounding Indonesia's 1966 default is famously the backdrop for Chrisopher Koch's novel *The Year of Living Dangerously* (London: St. Martin's, 1978), and the subsequent 1982 film starring Mel Gibson and Sigourney Weaver.

6. IMF Independent Evaluation Office, *The IMF and Recent Capital Account Crises: Indonesia, Korea, Brazil* (Washington, D.C.: International Monetary Fund, 2003).

7. The 1997–1998 Asian financial crisis occurred well before my time at the IMF.

8. Exchange rates (series: DEXMAUS and FXRATEPHA618NUPN), FRED (Federal Reserve Bank of St. Louis).

9. Western press coverage tends to forget that Hong Kong had long been administered as a colony by the British, who began to introduce democratic reforms only in the mid-1980s in anticipation of returning Hong Kong to China in 1997; it was not a long-standing independent democracy. This issue, and its implications for China's views on Hong Kong, is addressed in Ching Kwan Lee, *Forever Hong Kong: A Global City's Decolonial Struggle* (Cambridge, Mass.: Harvard University Press, forthcoming).

10. "Consumer Price Index for Russian Federation" (series: DDOE01RUA086NWDB), FRED (Federal Reserve Bank of St. Louis).

11. Homi Kharas, Brian Pinto, and Sergei Ulatov, "An Analysis of Russia's 1998 Meltdown: Fundamentals and Market Signals," *Brookings Papers on Economic Activity* 2001, no. 1, 1–68.

12. Brazil's inflation was still 66 percent in 1995 and 16 percent in 1996. Inflation, even in 1996, was far above the rate of exchange rate depreciation being allowed by the Banco Central do Brasil, which averaged only about 10 percent per year during this period. See William Gruben and Sherry Kiser, Brazil: "The First Financial Crisis of 1999," *Southwest Economy* (Federal Reserve Bank of Dallas), March/April 1999, 13–14; Rudiger Dornbusch, "Brazil's Incomplete Stabilization and Reform," *Brookings Papers on Economic Activity* 1997, no. 1, 367–404; Arminio Fraga, "Monetary Policy During the Transition to a Floating Exchange Rate: Brazil's Recent Experience," *Finance & Development* 37, no. 1 (March 2000): 16–18.

13. Gruben and Kiser, "Brazil: The First Financial Crisis of 1999," 13–14.

14. "Brazilian Reals to U.S. Dollar Spot Exchange Rate" (series: DEXBZUS), FRED (Federal Reserve Bank of St. Louis).

15. Juliana Bolzani et al., "Central-Bank Independence Comes to Brazil," *Project Syndicate*, May 21, 2021.

CHAPTER 14. LEBANON AND ARGENTINA

1. It was not the first time Köhler had put me on the spot to explain the IMF's concerns about a country's macroeconomic policies in a small meeting with a highly respected policymaker. He had done the same in a meeting with Fed chair Alan Greenspan.

2. David Schenker, "Lebanon Goes to Paris III: High Stakes in France and Beirut," PolicyWatch No. 1188 (The Washington Institute for Near East Policy, January 2007).

3. The reader should understand that although the IMF is able to lend to countries at rates typically far below what they would pay on their own, it is not strictly speaking an aid agency like the World Bank. Its loans are usually for only a few years and must be paid back.

4. Jeremy Bulow and Kenneth Rogoff, "The Buyback Boondoggle," *Brookings Papers on Economic Activity* 1988, no. 2, 675–698.

5. Douglas Diamond and Philip H. Dybvig, "Bank Runs, Deposit Insurance, and Liquidity," *Journal of Political Economy* 91, no. 3 (June 1983): 401–419.

6. International Monetary Fund, *World Economic Outlook* (December 2001), 54.

7. The transcript for my press conference on December 18, 2001, on *The Interim World Economic Outlook* can be found on the IMF website, www.imf.org/en/News/Articles/2015/09/28/04/54/tr011218. The backdrop and the impact of the press conference are discussed in Gregory Markoff, *Default* (Washington, D.C.: Georgetown University Press, 2024), which primarily explores the ensuing legal battle over Argentine default.

8. Noem, "The Future of Urban Living," accessed May 15, 2024, Noem.com/en-us.

CHAPTER 15. THE TOKYO CONSENSUS

Epigraph: Jon Eaton (1950–2024) was my macroeconomics teaching assistant at Yale. He went on to become one of foremost researchers in international trade and finance. He used the quoted expression when asked why the answer given to a question in a graduate course sometimes seems so strikingly different from the answer given to the same question in an undergraduate course.

1. In 2013 there was a terrific play in London based on Ferguson's moniker, *Chimerica*, by Lucy Kirkwood and co-produced by the Almeida Theatre and the touring company Headlong.

2. Joseph Stiglitz, *Globalization and Its Discontents* (New York: Norton, 2002).

3. "Criticism for the Buenos Aires Consensus," *MercoPress*, November 2, 2003.

4. Carmen Reinhart and Kenneth Rogoff, "The Modern History of Exchange Rate Arrangements: A Reinterpretation," *Quarterly Journal of Economics* 119, no. 1 (February 2004): 1–48. When one considers that roughly half of all advanced-economy international trade today involves intra-firm trade (e.g., Ford Mexico sending parts to Ford USA), it becomes apparent how doubly difficult it is to enforce overly stringent capital controls in an otherwise open economy. For example, a multinational firm can get money into China by having its Chinese plant pay a high price for intermediate parts that it imports from its sister plant in Japan.

5. "Total Reserves Excluding Gold for Japan" (series: TRESEGJPM052N), FRED (Federal Reserve Bank of St. Louis).

6. Total reserves excluding gold for India, Brazil, and South Africa (series: TRESEGINM052N, TRESEGBRM052N, and TRESEGZAM052N), FRED (Federal Reserve Bank of St. Louis).

7. Lorenzo Bini Smaghi, "Reserve Accumulation: The Other Side of the Coin" (speech by ECB Board member to 5th High-Level EMEAP-Eurosystem seminar, Sydney, Australia, February 2010). See also Reza Moghadam (and staff of IMF Strategy, Policy, and Review Dept.), "Reserve Accumulation and International Monetary Stability," IMF Executive Board Document, April 2010.

8. Bank of Japan Act (Act No. 89 of June 18, 1997), www.japaneselawtranslation.go.jp/en/laws/view/3788/en; Rahul Anand, Gee Hee Hong, and Yaroslav Hul, "Achieving the Bank of Japan's Inflation Target," Working Paper No. 2019/229 (International Monetary Fund, November 2019).

9. Parenthetically, aside from meeting Governor Zeti in her office at Bank Negara in Kuala Lumpur, I have on occasion sat next to her at meetings and conferences and watched her draw remarkably artistic mind maps. I believe she once mentioned being exposed to mind mapping from the writings of Tony Buzan. (My chess friend Raymond Keene, the first British player to earn a grand master norm, worked with Buzan on the world mind games, among other projects.)

10. Reinhart and Rogoff, "The Modern History of Exchange Rate Arrangements"; Ethan Ilzetzki, Carmen Reinhart, and Kenneth Rogoff, "Exchange Arrangements Entering the Twenty-First Century: Which Anchor Will Hold?," *Quarterly Journal of Economics* 134, no. 2 (May 2019): 599–646.

11. Reinhart and Rogoff, "The Modern History of Exchange Rate Arrangements." Independently, two prominent Argentinean economists, Eduardo Levy-Yeyati and Federico Sturzenegger, developed a classification that also seemed at odds with the IMF classification. See Eduardo Levy-Yeyati and Federico Sturzenegger, "To Float or to Fix: Evidence on the Impact of Exchange Rate Regimes on Growth," *American Economic Review* 93, no. 4 (September 2003): 1173–1193, as well as Eduardo Levy-Yeyati and Federico Sturzenegger, "Classifying Exchange Rate Regimes: 15 Years Later," CID Working Paper No. 319 (Harvard Center for International Development, June 2016).

12. The suggestion of putting "sand in the wheels" of the global financial system had been proposed by the legendary Keynesian economist James Tobin in the 1980s.

CHAPTER 16. FIXED EXCHANGE RATES REDUX

1. See Michael Dooley, David Folkerts-Landau, and Peter Garber, "The Revived Bretton Woods System," *International Journal of Finance and Economics* 9, no. 4 (October 2004): 307–313; Michael Dooley, David Folkerts-Landau, and Peter Garber, "The U.S. Current Account Deficit and Economic Development: Collateral for a Total Return Swap," Working Paper No. 10727 (National Bureau of Economic Research, September 2004).

2. Ben Bernanke, "The Global Saving Glut and the U.S. Current Account Deficit" (remarks at the Homer Jones Lecture, St. Louis, Mo., April 14, 2005).

3. Dooley, Folkerts-Landau, and Garber did later draw attention to the importance of migration in a later piece, Michael Dooley, David Folkerts-Landau, and Peter Garber, "Direct Investment, Rising Real Wages, and the Absorption of Excess Labor in the Periphery," in *G7 Current Account Imbalances: Sustainability and Adjustment*, ed. Richard H. Clarida (Chicago: University of Chicago Press, 2007), 103–132, though they still stressed other factors contributing to undervaluation as well.

4. Alan Greenspan, remarks on the current account at the Advancing Enterprise 2005 Conference (London, February 4, 2005).

5. A widely acknowledged mistake is the failure to recognize the extent to which globalization exacerbated inequality within the United States and accelerated the trend loss of manufacturing jobs. The United States should have done more to strengthen the social safety net—above all to provide universal basic health insurance, if not necessarily a single-payer system. That said, those who think that trade barriers will restore U.S. manufacturing jobs to what they were five decades ago should recognize that over the long run, automation is a much bigger factor. Just as farming accounted for over 20 percent of U.S. employment in 1930 but accounts for well under 2 percent today, manufacturing, which accounted for 30 percent of employment as recently as 1950, is already down to 8 percent and is likely to continue to decline no matter how large the tariffs that the United States places on China. "All Employees, Manufacturing/All Employees, Total Nonfarm," FRED, series MANEMP (Federal Reserve Bank of St. Louis).

6. The 21st Annual Monetary Conference: The Future of the Euro, sponsored by the

CATO Institute and the *Economist*, Washington, D.C., November 20, 2003. Greenspan's speech is posted on the Federal Reserve's website.

7. Bob Woodward, *Maestro: Greenspan's Fed and the American Boom* (New York: Simon and Schuster, 2001).

8. "Balance of Payments: Current Account: Balance (Revenue Minus Expenditure) for United States" (series: USAB6BLTT02STSAQ), FRED (Federal Reserve Bank of St. Louis).

9. "Current Account Balance (% of GDP)–China," World Bank database.

10. Hélène Rey, "Dilemma Not Trilemma: The Global Financial Cycle and Monetary Policy Independence," in *Global Dimensions of Unconventional Monetary Policy* (2013 Economic Policy Symposium proceedings) (Kansas City, Mo.: Federal Reserve Bank of Kansas City, 2014), 285–333.

11. Suman Basu et al., "A Conceptual Model for the Integrated Policy Framework," *Econometrica* 92 (forthcoming).

12. Yu-chin Chen and Kenneth Rogoff, "Commodity Currencies," *Journal of International Economics* 60, no. 1 (May 2003): 133–160.

13. Silvia Miranda-Agrippino and Hélène Rey, "U.S. Monetary Policy and the Global Financial Cycle," *Review of Economic Studies* 87, no. 6 (November 2020): 2754–2776.

CHAPTER 17. GLOBAL CURRENCIES

1. "Creation of the Bretton Woods System," Federal Reserve History, written November 2013, www.federalreservehistory.org/essays/bretton-woods-created.

2. Barry Eichengreen, *Golden Fetters* (Oxford: Oxford University Press, 1992).

3. See Benn Steil, *The Battle of Bretton Woods: John Maynard Keynes, Harry Dexter White, and the Making of a New World Order* (Princeton, N.J.: Princeton University Press, 2013), and James Boughton, *Harry White and the American Creed: How a Federal Bureaucrat Created the Modern Global Economy (and Failed to Get Credit)* (New Haven, Conn.: Yale University Press, 2021).

4. There does seem to be a commodity currency used at the fringes of the *Star Trek* economy by Ferengi traders. "Latinuum" is an extremely rare and valuable liquid that is unstable unless compressed in comparatively cheap gold plating. Given what we know about earth-bound financial crises, one presumes that absent Federation backing, runs on the Latinuum banking system would likely be a frequent occurrence. The idea is ripe for an economist to submit a script.

5. As governor of the Bank of England, Carney proposed a virtual synthetic currency composed of multiple reserve currencies. See Jason Douglas, "BOE's Carney Floats the Idea of a New, Virtual Reserve Currency," *Wall Street Journal*, August 23, 2019.

6. See Charles Kindleberger, "The Politics of International Money and World Language," *Essays in International Finance* (Princeton IES), no. 61 (August 1967). Other proposals, beyond those mentioned in the text, included those by Robert Roosa and Peter Kenen.

7. Franco Modigliani and Hossein Askari, "The Reform of the International Payments System," *Essays in International Finance* (Princeton IES), no. 89 (September 1971), 15.

8. "Board-Approved SDR Basket Currency Weights at Past Quinquennial Reviews," International Monetary Fund (using 2022 weights).

9. Exchange rates (series: CCUSSP01IFM650N), FRED (Federal Reserve Bank of St. Louis). When the SDR was first created in 1969, it was worth a fractional amount of gold equivalent to one dollar. In 1973, after exchange rates began to float, the SDR morphed into a basket of currencies.

10. Jeff Stein and David Lynch, "Janet Yellen Faces Critical Choice for Global Economy: Poor Nations Rocked by Coronavirus," *Washington Post*, January 19, 2021.

11. Ted Truman, who was the head of the International Finance Division at the Federal Reserve Board in Washington, D.C., and whom I served under in my first job out of graduate school, recently wrote an interesting monograph also arguing in favor of a broader use for the SDR. See Edwin Truman, "Promoting the Special Drawing Right," Working Paper (Mossavar-Rahmani Center for Business and Government, May 2022).

12. "IMF Should Give Poor Countries $300 Billion per Year to Fight Climate Crisis," *Guardian* (London), October 13, 2023.

13. Kenneth Rogoff, "The Sisters at Sixty," *Economist* (print edition), July 22, 2004.

14. Believe it or not, the Russian executive director Aleksei Mozhin was dean of the IMF's executive board when the full-scale invasion of Ukraine began in February 2022. The Russian executive director as of 2024 also represents Syria. See "IMF Directors and Voting Power," International Monetary Fund, accessed March 5, 2024.

15. Kenneth Rogoff and Eduard Brau, "SDR Allocation in the Eighth Basic Period—Basic Considerations," IMF Policy Paper (International Monetary Fund, November 16, 2001).

16. "2021 General SDR Allocation," International Monetary Fund; "IMF to Make $250 Billion SDR Allocation on August 28," International Monetary Fund, August 13, 2009.

17. "IMF Members' Quotas and Voting Power, and IMF Board of Governors," International Monetary Fund, May 12, 2024.

18. See Kris Mitchener and Christoph Trebesch, "Sovereign Debt in the Twenty-First Century," *Journal of Economic Literature* 61, no. 2 (June 2023): 565–623, and Jeremy Bulow, Kenneth Rogoff, and Afonso Bevilaqua, "Official Creditor Seniority and Burden Sharing in the Former Soviet Bloc," *Brookings Papers on Economic Activity* 1992, no. 1, 195–222.

19. Jeremy Bulow and Kenneth Rogoff, "Grants versus Loans for Development Banks," *American Economic Review* 95, no. 2 (May 2005): 393–397.

20. Kenneth Rogoff, "The Case for a World Carbon Bank," *Journal of Policy Modeling* 45, no. 4 (July/August 2023): 693–701.

CHAPTER 18. CRYPTOCURRENCIES AND THE FUTURE OF MONEY

1. Yuval Noah Harari, *Sapiens: A Brief History of Humankind* (New York: Harper Collins, 2015) (translated from original Hebrew edition, 2011). See especially chapter 10, "The Scent of Money." Another beautifully written and important book that does not fall into the same trap is Niall Ferguson, *The Ascent of Money: A Financial History of the World* (New York: Penguin, 2008).

2. For a review of the literature, see Ricardo Lagos, Guillaume Rocheteau, and Randall Wright, "Liquidity: A New Monetarist Perspective," *Journal of Economic Literature* 55, no. 2 (June 2017): 371–440.

3. The point that governments can deflate competitor currencies by simply marginalizing their use is made in Kenneth Rogoff, *The Curse of Cash* (Princeton, N.J.: Princeton University Press, 2016), chaps. 2, 14.

4. For example, the use of cryptographic tokens can potentially allow the securitization of a much broader range of assets than is currently feasible, by reducing legal and transaction fees. In principle, tokenization allows small buyers to own small shares of assets — from art to hedge funds to apartment buildings — where previously the ante was too high. In an earlier era, this is what stock issuance did for companies.

5. Kenneth Rogoff, "Elizabeth Warren's Big Ideas on Big Tech," *Project Syndicate*, April 1, 2019. I was first exposed to Warren's outspoken ideas on regulation when we spoke on a panel together at Harvard's Sanders Theater just after the outbreak of the global financial crisis in September 2008. See Maxwell Child, "Panel Weighs Market Meltdown," *Harvard Crimson*, September 25, 2008.

6. Lina Khan, "Amazon's Antitrust Paradox," *Yale Law Journal* 126, no. 3 (January 2017): 710–805.

7. Steve Lohr, "How the Google Antitrust Ruling May Influence Tech Competition," *New York Times*, August 6, 2024.

8. Rogoff, *The Curse of Cash*.

9. John Carreyrou, *Bad Blood: Secrets and Lies in a Silicon Valley Startup* (New York: Knopf, 2018).

10. "Profile: Sam Bankman-Fried," Forbes, www.forbes.com/profile/sam-bankman-fried.

11. MacKenzie Sigalos, "Jamie Dimon Says He Is Done Talking About Bitcoin: I Don't Care," *CNBC*, January 17, 2024.

12. Ethan Wolf-Mann, "Dogecoin Down Nearly 80% Since Elon Musk SNL Appearance," *Yahoo Finance*, July 20, 2021.

13. See Rogoff, *The Curse of Cash*, chap. 5.

14. "Currency in Circulation: Value," Board of Governors of the Federal Reserve System, www.federalreserve.gov/paymentsystems/coin_currcircvalue.htm. My first paper on the topic, in 1998, looked at the issue in the context of examining the likely demand for soon-to-be issued 500-euro notes. I based my 50 percent estimate for U.S. currency held domes-

tically (versus abroad) on domestic cash holdings in countries with similar financial systems whose currency is not widely used abroad, such as Canada. Kenneth Rogoff, "Blessing or Curse? Foreign and Underground Demand for Euro Notes," *Economic Policy* 13, no. 26 (April 1998): 263–303. The results are updated in my 2016 book, *The Curse of Cash*. More recently, Federal Reserve governor Chris Waller has also suggested 50 percent. See Chris Waller, "The Dollar's International Role" (speech at Climate, Currency and Central Banking conference, University of the Bahamas, February 15, 2024).

15. Rogoff, *The Curse of Cash*, chaps. 5, 6.

16. Edgar Feige, "How Big Is the Irregular Economy?," *Challenge* 22, no. 5 (November/December 1979): 5–13.

17. Francesco Pappada and Kenneth Rogoff, "Rethinking the Informal Economy and the Hugo Effect," *Journal of the European Economic Association* (forthcoming).

18. One might well ask why Europe does not crack down more on tax evasion, but that is easier said than done, both technologically and politically.

19. See, for example, "Feds Announce Seizure of $3.36 Billion in Bitcoin Stolen a Decade Ago from Illegal Silk Road Marketplace," *CNBC*, November 7, 2022.

20. The founders of a popular tumbling site were recently arrested on U.S. soil. See U.S. Attorney's Office, Southern District of New York, "Tornado Cash Founders Charged with Money Laundering and Sanctions Violations," press release, August 23, 2023.

21. Jonathan Wheatley and Adrienne Klasa, "Cryptocurrencies: Developing Countries Provide Fertile Ground," *Financial Times*, September 5, 2021.

22. Clemens Graf von Luckner, Carmen M. Reinhart, and Kenneth S. Rogoff, "Decrypting New Age International Capital Flows," *Journal of Monetary Economics* 138 (September 2023) 104–122.

23. From my correspondence in December 2016 with the late John Heimann, who was the twenty-fourth comptroller of the currency in the United States, serving from 1977 to 1981.

24. Prices from Binance, accessed May 12, 2024, www.binance.com/en/price.

25. There are remarkable parallels between stablecoins and the private moneys of the nineteenth-century free-banking era in the United States. See Gary Gorton et al., "Leverage and Stablecoin Pegs," Working Paper No. 30796 (National Bureau of Economic Research, December 2022).

CHAPTER 19. CENTRAL BANK DIGITAL CURRENCIES

1. Anneke Kosse and Ilaria Mattei, "Making Headway—Results of the 2022 BIS Survey on Central Bank Digital Currencies and Crypto," BIS Papers No. 136 (Bank for International Settlements, July 2023).

2. Federal Reserve Board, *Money and Payments: The U.S. Dollar in the Age of Digital Transformation* (Washington, D.C.: Federal Reserve Board, January 2022).

3. Parenthetically, it should be noted that the U.S. government already offers a way for

retail investors to conveniently save directly with the government. "Treasury Direct" (www.treasurydirect.gov) allows users to directly hold Treasury bills and bonds that pay the same average rate that institutions and wealthy individuals receive, a rate that is usually much higher than ordinary bank accounts pay. As of the end of 2024, one could hold as little as $100 or as much as $20 million in any individual bond issuance. The process of setting up an account does not take long, and subsequent purchases take almost no time at all. Importantly, an account must be linked to a bank account, and Treasury Direct is available only to U.S. citizens. Surprisingly, given its enormous convenience, the use of Treasury Direct is still quite modest; that is most likely because officials are concerned that if they started putting advertisements on buses and subways, Treasury Direct would start pulling too much money out of banks, which could hurt small and medium-size borrowers and lead to the very same kind of disintermediation officials worry about with CBDCs.

4. FDIC, "FDIC Acts to Protect All Depositors of the Former Silicon Valley Bank, Santa Clara, California," press release, March 13, 2023.

5. See John Crawford, Lev Menand, and Morgan Ricks, "FedAccounts: Digital Dollars," *George Washington Law Review* 89, no. 1 (January 2021): 113–172, which also discusses several other options for re-lending CBDC funds.

6. G30 Working Group on Digital Currencies, *Digital Currencies and Stablecoins: Risks, Opportunities and Challenges Ahead* (Washington, D.C.: Group of Thirty, July 2020).

7. Co-sponsors of Singapore's CBDC competition included the IMF, the World Bank, and the United Nations Development Programme, among others.

8. Producing money has long been an extremely high-tech endeavor, a perpetual arms race between government printers and counterfeiters. Most of us know Sir Isaac Newton for his development of calculus and Newtonian physics. In his later years, though, Newton served as the all-important director of the mint in England. Newton's introduction of a new technology for stamping coins with hard-to-replicate notches helped squash a spate of counterfeiting that had been threatening to undermine England's finances. See Kenneth Rogoff, *The Curse of Cash* (Princeton, N.J.: Princeton University Press, 2016), chap. 2.

9. Andrea Baronchelli, Hanna Halaburda, and Alexander Teytelboym, "Central Bank Digital Currencies Risk Becoming a Digital Leviathan," *Nature of Human Behavior* 6, no. 7 (July 2022): 907–909.

CHAPTER 20. PERKS OF CURRENCY DOMINANCE

1. "World Currency Composition of Official Foreign Exchange Reserves," IMF Data (International Monetary Fund), accessed Sept. 17, 2024, https://data.imf.org/regular.aspx?key=41175; "Major Foreign Holders of Treasury Securities," Treasury International Capital (TIC) System (U.S. Department of the Treasury), https://ticdata.treasury.gov/resource-center/data-chart-center/tic/Documents/slt_table5.html.

2. Arvind Krishnamurthy and Annette Vissing-Jorgensen, "The Aggregate Demand for Treasury Debt," *Journal of Political Economy* 120, no. 2 (April 2012): 233–267.

3. The price of a bond is inversely related to the interest rate it pays.

4. The revival of the term in economics owes to Pierre-Olivier Gourinchas and Hélène Rey, "International Financial Adjustment," *Journal of Political Economy* 115, no. 4 (August 2007): 665–703; see also Barry Eichengreen, *Exorbitant Privilege: The Rise and Fall of the Dollar* (New York: Oxford University Press, 2012).

5. Robert Z. Aliber, "The Costs and Benefits of the U.S. Role as Reserve Currency Country," *Quarterly Journal of Economics* 78, no. 3 (August 1964): 442–456. Walter A. Salant, "The Reserve Currency Role of the Dollar: Blessing or Burden to the United States?," *Review of Economics and Statistics* 46, no. 2 (May 1964): 165–172.

6. "Nothing but net," as my Harvard colleague Henry Louis Gates later commented on how Jordan alertly averted a public-relations disaster. Henry Louis Gates, "Net Worth," *New Yorker*, May 25, 1998.

7. Matthew Canzoneri et al., "Key Currency Status: An Exorbitant Privilege and an Extraordinary Risk," *Journal of International Money and Finance* 37 (October 2013): 371–393.

8. One attractive class of explanations is that the public correctly perceives that there is a small risk of catastrophic events (e.g., a pandemic even worse than 2020's) and is willing to pay a significant premium for assets that hold their value in such contingencies. See, for example, Robert Barro, "Rare Disasters, Asset Prices, and Welfare Costs," *American Economic Review* 99, no. 1 (March 2009): 243–264.

9. John Maynard Keynes, *How to Pay for the War: A Radical Plan for the Chancellor of the Exchequer* (London: Macmillan, 1940).

10. Douglass North and Barry Weingast, "Constitutions and Commitment: The Evolution of Institutions Governing Public Choice in Seventeenth-Century England," *Journal of Economic History* 49, no. 4 (December 1989): 803–832.

11. Data source for figure 11: Congressional Budget Office, *The Long-Term Budget Outlook: 2024–2054* (March 2024). The figure shows "net" government debt, which nets out debt owed to other government agencies—for example, the Social Security Administration. The IMF's April 2024 *Fiscal Monitor* projects U.S. gross debt in 2024 to hit 127 percent of GDP and net debt to be only 97 percent (numbers that may have risen before the ink is dry on this book). It is sometimes glibly stated that net debt is the more important number to look at because it ignores money the government owes itself. Unfortunately, for purposes of long-term sustainability, it is cold comfort to know that part of the debt the government owes has been effectively earmarked for the payment of Social Security. Indeed, the fact that the net-debt measure hides these liabilities is precisely the reason that figure 11 jumps up so dramatically going forward. If the intragovernmental debt were netted out by waving a magic wand, the government would still be on the hook for the Social Security payments and would need to find another way to produce the cash. The same is true for most other forms of intragovernmental debt.

12. Zhengyang Jiang, Arvind Krishnamurthy, and Hanno Lustig, "Foreign Safe Asset Demand and the Dollar Exchange Rate," *Journal of Finance* 76, no. 3 (June 2021): 1049–1089.

13. Zefeng Chen et al., "Exorbitant Privilege Gained and Lost: Fiscal Implications," Working Paper No. 30059 (National Bureau of Economic Research, May 2022).

CHAPTER 21. EXORBITANT PRIVILEGE OR TAXATION WITHOUT REPRESENTATION?

1. Data source for figure 12: "Balance on Current Account, NIPA's" (series: NETFI) and "Gross Domestic Product" (series: GDP), FRED (Federal Reserve Bank of St. Louis).

2. Carmen Reinhart and I argued that these massive deficits, along with the concomitant run-ups in housing and equity prices, should have been recognized as signaling that the United States was at high risk of a financial crisis, and indeed the global financial crisis followed a year later. Carmen Reinhart and Kenneth Rogoff, "Is the 2007 U.S. Sub-Prime Financial Crisis So Different? An International Historical Comparison" (paper presented at the American Economic Association meetings, January 2008).

3. Gian Maria Milesi-Ferretti, "The U.S. Is Increasingly a Net Debtor Nation. Should We Worry?," Commentary, *Brookings*, April 14, 2021.

4. Pierre-Olivier Gourinchas and Hélène Rey, "International Financial Adjustment," *Journal of Political Economy* 115, no. 4 (August 2007): 665–703.

5. Data source for figure 13: "U.S. Net International Investment Position" (series: IIPUSNETIA), FRED (Federal Reserve Bank of St. Louis).

6. Bureau of Economic Analysis, "U.S. International Investment Position, 1st Quarter 2024 and Annual Update," press release, June 24, 2024.

7. Andrew Atkeson, Jonathan Heathcoate, and Fabrizio Perri, "The End of Privilege: A Reexamination of the Net Foreign Asset Position of the United States," Working Paper No. 29771 (National Bureau of Economic Research, February 2022 [revised June 2023]).

8. Ricardo Hausmann and Federico Sturzenegger, "The Missing Dark Matter in the Wealth of Nations and Its Implications for Global Imbalances," *Economic Policy* 22, no. 51 (July 2007): 470–518.

9. Ellen McGrattan and Edward Prescott, "Technology Capital and the U.S. Current Account," *American Economic Review* 100, no. 4 (September 2010): 1493–1522.

10. Carol Bertaut et al., "The Global (Mis)Allocation of Capital" (unpublished working paper, Goethe University, December 2023).

11. Charles Kindleberger, "Balance-of-Payments Deficits and the International Market for Liquidity," *Essays in International Finance* (Princeton IES), no. 46 (May 1965).

12. Max Harris, *Monetary War and Peace: London, Washington, Paris and the Tripartite Agreement of 1936* (Cambridge: Cambridge University Press, 2021).

13. Rafael LaPorta et al., "Legal Determinants of External Finance," *Journal of Finance* 52, no.3 (July 1997): 1131–1150.

14. Konrad B. Burchardi, Thomas Chaney, and Tarek A. Hassan, "Migrants, Ancestors,

and Foreign Investments," *Review of Economic Studies* 86, no. 4 (July 2019): 1448–1486. Tarek is a former Ph.D. thesis student of mine.

15. Kenneth Rogoff and Takeshi Tashiro, "Japan's Exorbitant Privilege," *Journal of the Japanese and International Economies* 35 (March 2015): 43–61.

16. There is an older debate going back originally to papers published in 1990 by Mark Gertler and me as well as by Robert Lucas about why, on balance, capital seems to flow from poor countries to rich countries (especially the United States). Lucas's debatable answer, which continues to be very widely cited, argued that there are increasing returns to scale in production (so the more capital a country has, the higher the marginal returns to further investment) and that this factor overrides the fact that wages are so much lower in poor countries. Gertler and I, by contrast, argued that the reason capital flows from south to north traces to the difficulty of enforcing contracts in developing economies. Perhaps both factors are important, with Lucas's increasing-returns argument more important for flows across rich advanced economies (although this was not Lucas's original focus), and contract enforcement more important for poor countries and emerging markets. See Mark Gertler and Kenneth Rogoff, "North–South Lending and Endogenous Domestic Capital Market Inefficiencies," *Journal of Monetary Economics* 26, no. 2 (October 1990): 245–266 (first circulated in 1989 as NBER Working Paper No. 2887); Laura Alfaro, Sebnem Kalemli-Ozcan, and Vadym Volosovych, "Why Doesn't Capital Flow from Rich to Poor Countries? An Empirical Investigation," *Review of Economics and Statistics* 90, no. 2 (May 2008): 347–368; Robert Lucas, "Why Doesn't Capital Flow from Rich to Poor Countries," *American Economic Review* 80, no. 2 (May 1990): 92–96.

CHAPTER 22. SMALL WAYS THE UNITED STATES HELPS COUNTRIES DEAL WITH DOLLAR DOMINANCE

1. David Wessel, "Raghuram Rajan on Global Monetary Policy: A View from Emerging Markets," Commentary, *Brookings*, April 10, 2014.

2. "Bimonthly Meetings," Bank for International Settlements, www.bis.org/about/bimonthly_meetings.htm.

3. Andrea Shalal, "IMF Governors Approve 50% Increase in Lending Resources with No Shareholding Changes," *Reuters*, December 18, 2023.

4. International Monetary Fund, *2023 Global Debt Monitor* (September 2023).

5. "Currency Composition of Official Foreign Exchange Reserves" (COFER), IMF Data (International Monetary Fund).

6. See "Policy Tools," Board of Governors of the Federal Reserve System, www.federalreserve.gov/monetarypolicy/central-bank-liquidity-swaps.htm.

7. Data source for figure 14: "Assets: Central Bank Liquidity Swaps: Central Bank Liquidity Swaps: Wednesday Level" (series: SWPT), FRED (Federal Reserve Bank of St. Louis).

8. "Total Reserves Excluding Gold for Republic of Korea" (series: TRESEGKRM052N), FRED (Federal Reserve Bank of St. Louis).

9. The full list includes the European Central Bank, the Swiss National Bank, the Reserve Bank of Australia, Banco Central do Brasil, the Bank of Canada, Danmarks Nationalbank, the Bank of England, the Bank of Japan, the Bank of Korea, Banco de México, the Reserve Bank of New Zealand, Norges Bank, the Monetary Authority of Singapore, and the Sveriges Riksbank. In March 2020, during the pandemic, the Fed added another facility that was open to a much broader array of central banks and under which the collateral for short-term dollar loans was U.S. Treasury debt. Central banks could use this to deal with very short-term dollar problems without having to sell their Treasury assets and then repurchase them. It clearly involved much less risk for the Fed. Ben Hoffner, "United States: Central Bank Swaps to 14 Countries, 2020" (Yale School of Management Program on Financial Stability Case Study, June 2023).

10. Mark Choi et al., "The Fed's Central Bank Swap Lines and FIMA Repo Facility," in "Policy Actions in Response to the COVID-19 Pandemic," special issue, *Economic Policy Review* (Federal Reserve Bank of New York) 28, no. 1 (June 2022): 93–113.

11. Carmen Reinhart and Kenneth Rogoff, *This Time Is Different: Eight Centuries of Financial Folly* (Princeton, N.J.: Princeton University Press, 2009).

12. Richard Posner, "Economists on the Defensive," *Atlantic*, August 2009.

13. Admittedly, there are many subtleties—for example, the positive effect on dollar liquidity could at least partly offset the higher supply.

14. Saleem Bahaj and Ricardo Reis, "Jumpstarting an International Currency," Staff Working Paper No. 874 (Bank of England, July 2022).

15. For a comprehensive list of the facilities the Fed unleashed during the pandemic, see the collection of articles in "Policy Actions in Response to the COVID-19 Pandemic," special issue, *Economic Policy Review* (Federal Reserve Bank of New York) 28, no. 1 (June 2022).

16. Rohan Kekre and Moritz Lenel, "The High Frequency Effects of Dollar Swap Lines," BFI Working Paper No. 2023-148 (University of Chicago Becker Friedman Institute for Economics, November 2023).

17. Minutes of the Federal Open Market Committee, October 28–29, 2008.

18. Minutes of the Federal Open Market Committee, May 9, 2010 (conference call).

CHAPTER 23. COSTS OF BEING A DOMINANT CURRENCY

1. Matthew Ferranti, "Estimating the Currency Composition of Foreign Exchange Reserves" (Ph.D. dissertation, Harvard University, May 2023). The $2 trillion figure comes from taking China's overall foreign exchange reserves, which are reported to the IMF, and using Ferranti's imputed estimate for the share held in dollars, 60 percent. That is more than twice what the U.S. Treasury reports, likely because some of the Chinese reserves are held by intermediaries offshore. "Major Foreign Holders of Treasury Securities" (table 5), Trea-

sury International Capital (TIC) System (U.S. Department of the Treasury), https://ticdata.treasury.gov/resource-center/data-chart-center/tic/Documents/slt_table5.html.

2. For a theoretical model of the connection between financial and military dominance, see Carolin Pflueger and Pierre Yared, "Global Hegemony and Exorbitant Privilege" (National Bureau of Economic Research Working Paper 32775, August 2024, https://www.nber.org/papers/w32775. July 2024).

3. Chris Clayton, Matteo Maggiori, and Jesse Schreger, "A Framework for Geoeconomics" (mimeo, Columbia University, June 2023). The idea of interconnected bargaining is also suggested in Jeremy Bulow and Kenneth Rogoff, "Cleaning Up Third-World Debt Without Getting Taken to the Cleaners," *Journal of Economic Perspectives* 4, no. 1 ((Winter 1990): 31–42, and in Kenneth Rogoff, "Bargaining and International Policy Cooperation," *American Economic Review* 80, no. 2 (May 1990): 139–142.

4. Data source for figure 15: "Shares of Gross Domestic Product: Government Consumption Expenditures and Gross Investment: Federal: National Defense" (series: A824RE1Q156NBEA), FRED (Federal Reserve Bank of St. Louis).

5. On the one hand, the United States has a volunteer army today versus a conscription army in the late 1960s and early 1970s; factoring in the implicit tax on conscripts would make the decline in defense expenditures appear even steeper. On the other hand, the $140 billion budget for the Department of Veterans Affairs for 2022 is today separate from the Defense Department budget, whereas at one time it was not.

6. SIPRI Military Expenditure Database, https://doi.org/10.55163/CQGC9685.

7. Cédric Pietralunga, "French Military Lacks Ammunition for High-Intensity Conflict," *Le Monde*, February 18, 2023.

8. Mancur Olson and Richard Zeckhauser, "An Economic Theory of Alliances," *Review of Economics and Statistics* 48, no. 3 (August 1966): 266–279.

9. Henry Foy et al., "Emmanuel Macron to Revive Demands for European Defence Bonds," *Financial Times*, March 21, 2024.

10. Chris Miller, *Chip War: The Fight for the World's Most Critical Technology* (New York: Scribner, 2022).

11. Noemie Bisserbe and Stacy Meichtry, "Macron Warns Europe 'Can Die' Without a Stronger Military," *Wall Street Journal*, April 24, 2024; Paul Tucker, "A Message to Economists: Geopolitics Matters, Too," *Financial Times*, April 25, 2024.

12. "A Salute to the U.S. Constitution: Fun Facts You May Not Know About Our Founding Document," Armed Forces Entertainment, September 20, 2020. James Madison addressed the issue in the *Federalist Papers* No. 41: "How could a readiness for war in time of peace be safely prohibited, unless we could prohibit, in like manner, the preparations and establishments of every hostile nation?" The Avalon Project: Documents in Law, History, and Diplomacy.

13. "Real Broad Dollar Index" (series: RTWEXBGS), FRED (Federal Reserve Bank of St. Louis).

14. Pierre-Olivier Gourinchas, Hélène Rey, and Nicolas Govillot, "Exorbitant Privilege and Exorbitant Duty," IMES Discussion Paper Series 10-E-20 (Bank of Japan, 2010).

CHAPTER 24. CENTRAL BANK INDEPENDENCE

1. Kenneth Rogoff, "The Age of Inflation: Easy Money, Hard Choices," *Foreign Affairs*, November/December 2022.

2. The specter of rising political pressures on central banks to inflate is analyzed in Hassan Afrouzi, Marina Halac, Kenneth Rogoff, and Pierre Yared, "Changing Central Bank Pressures and Inflation," *Brookings Papers on Economic Activity* 2024, no.1, 205–241.

3. "Federal Debt: Total Public Debt as Percent of Gross Domestic Product" (series: GFDEGDQ188S), FRED (Federal Reserve Bank of St. Louis).

4. "Market Yield on U.S. Treasury Securities at 10-Year Constant Maturity, Quoted on an Investment Basis" (series: DGS10), FRED (Federal Reserve Bank of St. Louis).

5. The idea that politicians might want to raise spending before elections traces back to classic articles by William Nordhaus and Edward Tufte. William D. Nordhaus, "The Political Business Cycle," *Review of Economic Studies* 42, no. 2 (April 1975): 169–190; Edward Tufte, *Political Control of the Economy* (Princeton, N.J.: Princeton University Press, 1978). There was long the question, however, of why voters could not simply see through this. Anne Sibert and I offered an answer to this puzzle in 1988. We argued that, in reality, it is difficult in the short run for voters to detect the difference between a truly competent government and one that spends excessively through channels that can only be detected with a lag. That creates a dynamic whereby all governments spend excessively before elections, but the competent ones actually overspend by the most, since they get the biggest bang for it. Kenneth Rogoff and Anne Sibert, "Elections and Macroeconomic Policy Cycles," *Review of Economic Studies* 55, no. 1 (January 1988): 1–16. Note the difference between the modern formulation "political budget cycles" and Nordhaus's and Tufte's original thesis of "political business cycles." There is very strong cross-country evidence on the former—that governments spend excessively on visible projects before elections—but the evidence on there being a political business cycle is much weaker.

6. Min Shi and Jakob Svensson, "Political Budget Cycles: Do They Differ Across Countries and Why?," *Journal of Public Economics* 90, nos. 8–9 (September 2006): 1167–1189.

7. Kenneth S. Rogoff, "The Optimal Degree of Commitment to an Intermediate Monetary Target," *Quarterly Journal of Economics* 100, no. 4 (1985): 1169–1189.

8. Finn Kydland and Edward Prescott, "Rules Rather than Discretion: The Inconsistency of Optimal Plans," *Journal of Political Economy* 85, no. 3 (June 1977): 473–492.

9. Carmen Reinhart and Kenneth Rogoff, "Shifting Mandates: The Federal Reserve's First Centennial," *American Economic Review Papers and Proceedings* 103, no. 3 (May 2013): 48–54.

10. A prominent thesis attributed the problem to the "flat Phillips curve." The Phillips curve is named after a British-based economist originally from New Zealand, A. W. Phillips, who in the late 1950s noticed a stable negative relationship between unemployment and inflation in the United Kingdom. When unemployment fell far below its normal equilibrium level, firms would bid up wages, which ultimately led to price inflation, and vice versa. The

correlation worked well in the 1950s and 1960s but started to weaken in the 1970s, eventually almost disappearing. The main explanation posits that as central banks gained anti-inflation credibility, they were better able to engage in countercyclical policy, pushing up inflation when unemployment was high and thereby turning the Phillips curve on its head. Still, reasonable observers are left wondering whether economists ever really understood what was going on.

11. See Ben Bernanke, "Deflation: Making Sure 'It' Doesn't Happen Here" (remarks before the National Economists Club, Washington, D.C., November 21, 2002). More than a decade later, he still argued that helicopter money was a plausible option. See Ben Bernanke, "What Tools Does the Fed Have Left? Part 3: Helicopter Money," Commentary, *Brookings*, April 11, 2016.

12. See, for example, Adair Turner, *Between Debt and the Devil* (Princeton, N.J.: Princeton University Press, 2015), and citations therein.

13. Indeed, with its regulatory hat, the ECB's charter requires it to support European-wide policy.

14. For a thoughtful discussion, see Lars Peter Hansen, "Central Banking Challenges Posed by Uncertain Climate Change and Natural Disasters," *Journal of Monetary Economics* 125 (January 2022): 1–15.

15. Greg Kaplan, Benjamin Moll, and Giovanni Violante, "Monetary Policy According to HANK," *American Economic Review* 108, no. 3 (March 2018): 697–743.

16. Agustín Carstens, "Central Banks and Inequality" (remarks at Bendheim Center for Finance, Princeton University, Princeton, N.J., May 6, 2021).

17. Andrew Restuccia, Nick Timiraos, and Alex Leary, "Trump Allies Draw Up Plans to Blunt the Fed's Independence," *Wall Street Journal*, April 26, 2024; "Trump Signals Interest in Influencing Federal Reserve Decisions If He Regains the White House," *Reuters*, August 8, 2024.

18. To be fair, almost everyone was bamboozled by "quantitative easing," mainly because central banks pushed so hard to insist that it was a big deal. It is basically mumbo jumbo for having the U.S. government use short-term debt to buy up long-term debt it has issued, and thereby shorten the average maturity of debt held by the public. This transaction is smoke and mirrors because the Treasury owns the Federal Reserve in full. A terrific paper, "Fifty Shades of Quantitative Easing," demonstrates the point that although central bank research departments tend to find that quantitative easing "works," outside academic researchers find much weaker effects, if any, with the exception of periods of market dysfunction when the central bank is acting as what economists term "a market-maker of last resort." Brian Fabo et al., "Fifty Shades of Quantitative Easing: Comparing Findings of Central Bankers and Academics," *Journal of Monetary Economics* 120 (May 2021): 1–20.

19. Allan Meltzer, "When Inflation Doves Fly," *Project Syndicate*, August 13, 2013.

20. Allan H. Meltzer, *A History of the Federal Reserve*, vol. 1, *1913–1951* (Chicago: University of Chicago Press, 2004).

21. "Vivek Ramaswamy Takes on the Fed," editorial, *Wall Street Journal*, May 2, 2023.

22. Şebnem Kalemli-Özcan and Filiz Unsal, "Global Transmission of Fed Hikes: The Role of Policy Credibility and Balance Sheets," *Brookings Papers on Economic Activity* 2023, no. 2.

23. The 2012 match with Carlsen ended in a draw, though it is unlikely that result could ever be repeated. The game was written up with detailed notes in many places, including the *New York Times* and *Pravda*; the best notes are those of Lubomir Kavalek, "Magnus Carlsen Storms New York's Chess Scene," *Huffington Post*, September 5, 2012, which also appeared on Chessbase.

24. See, for example, Kenneth Rogoff, "Why Human Chess Survives," *Project Syndicate*, November 18, 2018.

CHAPTER 25. DEBTOR'S EMPIRE

1. A theoretical rationale for financial repression, as a device for improving government no-default credibility at the cost of lower investment, is demonstrated in V. V. Chari, Alessandro Dovis, and Patrick Kehoe, "On the Optimality of Financial Repression," *Journal of Political Economy* 128, no. 2 (February 2020): 710–739.

2. Sebastian Edwards, *American Default: The Untold Story of FDR, the Supreme Court, and the Battle over Gold* (Princeton, N.J.: Princeton University Press, 2018).

3. "Gross Federal Debt as Percent of Gross Domestic Product" (series: GFDGDPA188S), FRED (Federal Reserve Bank of St. Louis).

4. Congressional Budget Office, *The Budget and Economic Outlook: 2024–2034* (February 2024).

5. Ron Suskind, *The Price of Loyalty: George W. Bush, the White House, and the Education of Paul O'Neill* (New York: Simon and Schuster, 2004). I once got a chance to ask Cheney himself. On a commercial flight from Salt Lake City to Wyoming in August 2016 (en route to the Kansas City Federal Reserve's annual "Jackson Hole" conference), I found myself sitting next to a man wearing a large Stetson hat. As one passenger after another walked past and said, "Thank you for your service," I finally turned and incredulously asked, "Are you Dick Cheney?" "Used to be," he quipped. Over the course of the seventy-five-minute flight, we had a fascinating conversation covering topics such as how the U.S. government still had uses for large-denomination paper-currency notes—for example, when it needed to quietly buy off hostile governments in difficult negotiations, which sometimes required hundreds of millions of dollars to be paid under the table. We also discussed the risks of high debt, an area where the former vice president had more nuanced views than he is usually credited with.

6. Olivier Blanchard, "Public Debt and Low Interest Rates," *American Economic Review* 109, no. 4 (April 2019): 1197–1229.

7. Walter Bagehot, *Lombard Street: A Description of the Money Market* (London: Henry S. King, 1871).

8. Data source for figure 16: "General government gross debt (percent of GDP)" and

"Gross domestic product, current prices (U.S. dollars)," International Monetary Fund, *World Economic Outlook* (April 2024).

9. Erica Xuewei Jiang et al., "Monetary Tightening and U.S. Bank Fragility in 2023: Mark-to-Market Losses and Uninsured Depositor Runs?," Working Paper No. 31048 (National Bureau of Economic Research, March 2023).

10. Blanchard emphasized that the fact that the government can tax some of its interest payments reduces the cost. Blanchard, "Public Debt and Low Interest Rates." Overall taxes, of course, are endogenous, so if the government starts collecting more taxes in one area, voters may push back in others.

11. Alvin H. Hansen, "Economic Progress and Declining Population Growth," *American Economic Review* 29, no.1 (March 1939): 1–15.

12. Robert J. Gordon, *The Rise and Fall of American Growth: The U.S. Standard of Living Since the Civil War* (Princeton, N.J.: Princeton University Press, 2016).

13. "Innovation or Stagnation?," Oxford Union Debate, November 16, 2012, www.oxfordmartin.ox.ac.uk/videos/innovation-or-stagnation-oxford-union-debate/. My partner on "team innovation" was the South African technology entrepreneur Mark Shuttleworth.

14. Ben Bernanke is a brilliant economist, and as already intimated, his 1983 paper on the Great Depression richly deserved the Nobel Prize he received in 2022. We have been friends since graduate school, and I had the very good fortune of having the office next to his during my years at Princeton in the 1990s.

15. The Taylor rule, proposed by the economist John B. Taylor, relates the federal funds rate to inflation and economic output. The original Taylor rule had the normal interest rate at 4 percent.

16. Brad DeLong, "Note to Self: I *Still* Fail to Understand Ken Rogoff's Medium-Long Term Macroeconomic Optimism . . . ," Washington Center for Equitable Growth, November 15, 2016, http://equitablegrowth.org/equitablog/note-to-self-i-still-fail-to-understand-ken-rogoffs-medium-long-term-macroeconomic-optimism.

17. As this book has repeatedly emphasized, one must combine the Fed and Treasury balance sheets to understand debt risks, since the Treasury ultimately absorbs all the Fed's profits and losses.

18. Kenneth Rogoff, "America's Looming Debt Decision," *Project Syndicate*, August 8, 2016.

19. Robert Skidelsky, "The Scarecrow of National Debt," *Project Syndicate*, August 24, 2016.

20. My article went on to state: "No one is saying that such a shift is likely or imminent, but the odds aren't as trivial as some might like to believe. For starters, interest rates could spike in the event of a war or some other catastrophic event. Less dramatic but more likely is that the Fed will someday find a way to push up inflation expectations, which, as in most advanced economies, have been drifting inexorably downward. If inflation expectations do start rising, this will push up rates." Rogoff, "America's Looming Debt Decision."

21. Joseph Adinolfi, "Stanley Druckenmiller Criticizes Janet Yellen for Not Locking in Long-Term Interest Rates, Calling It the Biggest Blunder in Treasury History," *Market Watch*, October 30, 2023.

22. "Higher for Longer," *Economist*, November 4, 2023, 16.

23. Łukasz Rachel and Lawrence Summers, "On Secular Stagnation in the Industrialized World," *Brookings Papers on Economic Activity* 2019, no. 1, 1–76.

24. For a discussion of some leading theories on why interest rates might keep trending down, see Kenneth Rogoff, Barbara Rossi, and Paul Schmelzing, "Long-Run Trends in Long-Maturity Real Rates, 1311–2022," *American Economic Review* 114, no. 8 (August 2024): 2271–2307. We found, however, that neither demographics nor productivity pan out as long-term explanations. It is important to note that our paper is the first to look at such long time horizons, so on the one hand, it will likely stimulate significant further research, and on the other, it may not be the last word.

25. Stephanie Kelton, *The Deficit Myth: Modern Monetary Theory and the Birth of the People's Economy* (New York: Public Affairs, 2020).

26. Scott Horsley, "This Economic Theory Could Be Used to Pay for the Green New Deal," *NPR*, July 17, 2019.

27. Doris Geide-Stevenson and Álvaro La Parra-Pérez, "Consensus Among Economists: A Sharpening Picture" (mimeo, Weber State University, 2021). Parenthetically, the shift in polling results among American economists was very similar for the question "the Federal Reserve should focus on a low rate of inflation rather than goals such as employment, economic growth, or asset bubbles." In 2000, 72 percent agreed; in 2021, it was only 38 percent. In some ways, this reversal is even stranger than the answers to the question about who should take the lead in fighting recessions, with many apparently thinking that the Fed should focus more on inequality and climate change instead of inflation.

CHAPTER 26. THE SIREN CALL OF "LOWER FOREVER" INTEREST RATES

1. There is also concern about the vastly deeper inequalities between the roughly 1.1 billion people living in advanced economies and the nearly 7 billion people living in the developing world, but cross-country inequality receives only a small fraction of journal space and research funding.

2. See Kenneth Rogoff, Barbara Rossi, and Paul Schmelzing, "Long-Run Trends in Long-Maturity Real Rates, 1311–2022," *American Economic Review* 114, no. 8 (August 2024): 2271–2307.

3. "Al Gore Warns of One Billion Climate Refugees," *BNN*, January 2, 2024.

4. Full details of the extensive archival sources and data construction algorithms underlying figures 17 and 18 are given in Rogoff, Rossi, and Schmelzing, "Long-Run Trends in Long-Maturity Real Rates, 1311–2022."

5. Julien Acalin and Laurence Ball, "Did the U.S. Really Grow Out of Its World War II

Debt?," Working Paper No. 31577 (National Bureau of Economic Research, August 2023); Yongquan Cao, Vitor Gaspar, and Adrian Peralta-Alva, "Costly Increases in Public Debt When r < g," Working Paper No. 2024/10 (International Monetary Fund, January 2024).

6. Kenneth Rogoff and Paul Schmelzing, "r-g Before and After the Great Wars, 1507–2023," Working Paper No. 33202 (National Bureau of Economic Research, November 2024).

7. For an excellent discussion, see Karen Dynan, "High and Rising Government Debt: Causes and Implications," in *Building a More Resilient U.S. Economy*, ed. Melissa S. Kearney, Justin Schardin, and Luke Pardue (Washington, D.C.: Aspen Institute, 2023), 18–43.

8. Congressional Budget Office, *The Demographic Outlook 2023 to 2053* (January 2023).

9. Charles Goodhart and Manoj Pradhan, *The Great Demographic Reversal: Ageing Societies, Waning Inequality, and an Inflation Revival* (London: Palgrave Macmillan, 2020).

10. Kenneth Rogoff, "Falling Real Interest Rates, Rising Debt: A Free Lunch?," *Journal of Policy Modeling* 42, no 4 (July-August 2020): 778–790.

11. Kenneth Rogoff, "A Prescription for Marxism," *Foreign Policy*, October 22, 2009.

12. Kenneth Rogoff, "The Bank of Japan's Seductive Widow-Maker Trade," *Project Syndicate*, October 5, 2023.

13. Julian Nowogrodzki, "Cash for Catching Scientific Errors," *Nature*, August 19, 2024.

14. Carmen M. Reinhart and Kenneth Rogoff, "Growth in a Time of Debt," *American Economic Review* 100, no 2 (May 2010): 573–578 (and 2013 online errata). Writing in April 2013, Thomas Herndon, Michael Ash, and Robert Pollin (whom the reader will recall from chapter 13 as signing a June 2013 letter arguing that statistical evidence supported the legitimacy of Nicolás Maduro's election in Venezuela), claimed that our 2010 conference paper had multiple errors that led us to conclude that countries with very high debt (over 90 percent of GDP) have historically experienced lower rates of growth than countries with lower debt levels. Thomas Herndon, Michael Ash, and Robert Pollin, "Does High Public Debt Consistently Stifle Economic Growth? A Critique of Reinhart and Rogoff," PERI Working Paper Series No. 322 (University of Massachusetts Amherst, April 2013). In fact, our conference paper did have one error (and only one), though that particular issue happened to be of only minor quantitative significance. Moreover, a much more complete version of the paper—Carmen Reinhart, Vincent Reinhart, and Kenneth Rogoff, "Public Debt Overhangs: Advanced-Economy Episodes Since 1800," *Journal of Economic Perspectives* 26, no. 3 (Summer 2012): 69–86, had no errors and reached the same conclusions, and was published in 2012, a year before their critique. The other "errors" were not errors but reflected different assumptions—assumptions explored in our 2012 paper. Our result that very high debt is associated with lower average future trend growth has now been subject to dozens of further studies, and the weight of the results clearly supports the initial conjecture in our short thought piece. See, for example, Antonio Fata et al., "The Motive to Borrow," in *Sovereign Debt: A Guide for Economists and Practitioners*, ed. S. Ali Abbas, Alex Pienkowski, and Kenneth Rogoff (Oxford: Oxford University Press, 2019), 102–150. Indeed, the correlation we conjectured even comes through in the period of ultra-low interest rates that followed

our study. Greece, Italy, and Japan, the countries with the highest debt of our original sample group, all had dismal growth performances after 2008, when the original data set ended. If real interest rates do indeed revert to trend over the next ten years, the effect will if anything be exacerbated.

15. Importantly, our paper looked at a large group of advanced economies. The group included some poorer countries such as Greece and Portugal, not to mention Italy and Spain, and our results applied to these countries on average as a group, not to any country individually.

16. "Federal Debt: Total Public Debt as Percent of Gross Domestic Product" (series: GFDEGDQ188S), FRED (Federal Reserve Bank of St. Louis).

17. William J. Clinton, *Back to Work: Why We Need Smart Government* (New York: Knopf, 2011), 123–134.

18. Atif Mian and Amir Sufi, *House of Debt: How They (and You) Caused the Great Recession, and How We Can Prevent It from Happening Again* (Chicago: University of Chicago Press, 2014).

19. See Kenneth Rogoff, "Dealing with Monetary Paralysis at the Zero Bound," *Journal of Economic Perspectives* 31, no. 3 (Summer 2017): 47–66.

20. Some critics of our paper noted that the United Kingdom had very high debt in the 1800s, when it still had normal growth. But back then the pound sterling was the dominant currency, which clearly helped; our paper addressed all advanced economies as a group, including periphery advanced economies such as Spain, Portugal, Italy, and Greece. Moreover, the United Kingdom, unlike the United States today, enjoyed large net interest payments (as much as 10 percent of GDP per year) from abroad on its investments. And recall what happened when the United Kingdom gradually lost its dominant-currency status: it defaulted on loans from the U.S. government in 1931 and required recurrent IMF bailout programs after World War II. During these eras, high debt was crippling to growth.

21. See Emmanuel Farhi and Matteo Maggiori, "A Model of the International Monetary System," *Quarterly Journal of Economics* 133, no. 1 (February 2018): 295–355, and Ethan Ilzetzki, Carmen Reinhart, and Kenneth Rogoff, "Exchange Arrangements Entering the Twenty-First Century: Which Anchor Will Hold?," *Quarterly Journal of Economics* 134, no. 2 (May 2019): 599–646, and references therein.

22. Robert Triffin was still teaching when I was an undergraduate at Yale in the 1970s. Unfortunately, as so often happens, I had little idea then what role his research would play later in my life and failed to take Triffin's course. I did take Charles Kindleberger's course when studying later that decade at MIT, but like all the other graduate students, I was mainly absorbed in learning the technical nuances that were essential for publishing in top journals, and did not yet fully appreciate how important his broad-based historical research would turn out to be. Of particular importance was his book *Panics, Manias, and Crashes: A History of Financial Crises* (New York: Basic Books, 1989), as well as his 1960s work on the United States as banker to the world (discussed in chapter 17).

23. Data sources for figure 19: Total Economy Database (The Conference Board) (market rates); Penn World Tables (Groningen Growth and Development Centre) (PPP rates); "Major Foreign Holders of U.S. Treasury Securities," Treasury International Capital (TIC) System (U.S. Department of the Treasury).

24. The point that low interest rates and slow growth in Japan might have spilled over into the United States was made by Gauti Eggertsson, Neil Mehrotra, and Lawrence Summers, "Secular Stagnation in the Open Economy," *American Economic Review* 106, no. 5 (May 2015): 503–507. This, of course, was also the point of Bernanke's "global savings glut" speech and the "Deutsche Bank trio" papers discussed in chapter 16.

25. See "Large U.S. Bank Collapse Ahead, Says Ex-IMF Economist," *Reuters*, August 19, 2008; "More Big U.S. Banks May Fail, Prof Says," *Bloomberg News*, August 19, 2008 (reprinted in the *Denver Post*); Floyd Norris, "Collapsing Banks?," Economix (blog), *New York Times*, August 20, 2008.

26. Norris, "Collapsing Banks?"

ACKNOWLEDGMENTS

This book draws inspiration from my thesis adviser, the late Rudiger Dornbusch, who possessed an extraordinary gift for deconstructing the soft-headed arguments that all too often underlie conventional thinking on international macroeconomic policy issues. I am also deeply grateful to my many different co-authors whose work is featured throughout the book, as well as to several generations of students, who have always forced me to continually reassess the economic theories I am trying to explain to them. And of course, I have been fortunate to have many great colleagues over the years, not only at the leading universities where I have taught but also at the Federal Reserve Board and the International Monetary Fund. Matthew Ferranti, Ethan Ilzetzki, Clemens Graf von Luckner, Andrew Lilley, June Ma, Pierfrancesco Mei, Ulrike Schaede, Allison Schrager, Eric Schmidt, Zoe Weinberg, Chenzi Xu, and Yuanchen Yang all gave very helpful comments on individual draft chapters I sent them or, in some cases, simply on a core idea I was struggling with. June Ma and Sam Ross provided insightful feedback on the book as a whole; Sam Ross also served as my research assistant. Dana Isaacson and Nicole Tateosian helped with checking earlier drafts, while Karen Schoen and Marnie Wiss did copyediting and proofreading for the final draft, Margaret Otzel at Yale University Press oversaw the book's production. Seth Ditchik, the editorial director at Yale University Press,

ACKNOWLEDGMENTS

has once again been a fantastic editor, as he was on two earlier books, *This Time Is Different* and *The Curse of Cash*. Needless to say, all errors in the book, grammatical or analytical, are solely the author's responsibility. Last but certainly not least, I want to thank my wife, Natasha, as well as my two adult children, Gabriel and Juliana, for being a constant source of ideas and inspiration, as well as for keeping me grounded.

INDEX

Acalin, Julien, 277
Alexander the Great, 185
Alibaba, 203
Aliber, Robert, 213, 236
Alipay, 204
AlphaZero, 260
American Economic Association, 55, 271
Americans, The, 19
Argentina, 138, 147–52, 194; Buenos Aires Consensus, 155; default by, 151; financial crisis (2002), 118, 148–52; hyperinflation in, 127, 183; World Economic Outlook Press Conference, 151
artificial intelligence, 259–60, 261
Asian Development Bank, 66
Asian financial crisis (1997–1998), 74, 118, 134–44, 156
Australia, 169, 322 n.9
Austria, 50, 299 n.6
Aziz, Zeti Akhta (Governor, Central Bank of Malaysia), 158–59

"Back in the USSR," 15
Bagehot, Walter: *Lombard Street,* 265
baht (Thailand), 133, 134
Baker, James A. (Treasury Secretary, United States), 30–31, 73
Balassa-Samuelson-Harrod effect, 302 n.12
Ball, Lawrence, 277
Banco Central do Brasil, 142–43, 322 n.9
Banco de México, 142, 232, 322 n.9
bancor, 173
Bankers Trust, 123
Bank for International Settlements (BIS), 77–78, 151; Global Economy Meetings, 230
Bankman-Fried, Samuel, 187–88, 189
Bank Negara Malaysia, 158–59
Bank of Canada, 199, 322 n.9
Bank of England, 124, 199, 215, 232, 251, 252
Bank of Japan, 25–26, 34–35, 39, 157, 158, 232
Bank of Korea, 137, 158, 232

INDEX

banks, 197–98, 201–2; reserves of, 157–58, 257–58. *See also* central banks
Banque de France, 55, 120–21
Barbarians at the Gate, 32
Bear Stearns, 55, 287
Belgium, 44, 50, 54, 58, 299 n.6
Bergson, Abram, 15
Bernanke, Ben (Chair, Federal Reserve Board), 162, 254, 267, 268, 306 n.22, 327 n.14
Bernstein, Edward, 175
Bertaut, Carol, 225
Biden, Joe (President, United States), 8, 216, 281
Big Tech, 186–87, 203
bitcoin, 182, 189, 192–93, 194–95, 197, 257. *See also* cryptocurrencies
Blaine, David, 177
Blanchard, Olivier, 54, 265, 327 n.10
Boughton, James, 131, 132
Brady, Tom, 189
Brazil, 165, 235; Banco do Brasil, 142–43, 232, 322 n.9; Buenos Aires Consensus, 155; currency reserves of, 156; default by, 233; financial crisis (1999), 118, 139, 140–44; hyperinflation in, 127; inflation targeting in, 142–43; real, 140; Real Plan (1994), 140, 144
Bretton Woods system, 4, 45, 118, 119, 174, 213, 226, 282
Brezhnev, Leonid (Premier, Soviet Union), 20
Brookings Institution conference, 131–32, 133
Buffett, Warren, 189
Bulgaria, 46
Bulow, Jeremy, 78
Bundesbank. *See* Deutsche Bundesbank
Burchardi, Konrad, 228
Bush, George H. W. (President, United States), 221
Bush, George W. (President, United States), 216

Calvo, Guillermo, 132; "Fear of Floating," 80–81

Cambridge, Massachusetts, 303 n.2
Canada, 169, 286; Bank of Canada, 118, 199, 322 n.9; military spending by, 49, 237
Canon, 27, 28
Canzoneri, Matthew, 214
capital controls, 155, 157, 194
Cardoso, Fernando Henrique, 142, 143
Carlsen, Magnus, 259, 260, 326 n.23
Carney, Mark, 174
Carter, Jimmy (President, United States), 250, 252
Center for Economic and Policy Research, 129
Central African Economic and Monetary Community, 46–47
central bank digital currencies (CBDC), 199–207, 289, 290; challenges with, 201–3; purposes of, 200
Central Bank of Russia, 139
central banks, 294 n.15; independence of, 51, 121, 142–43, 158, 166, 247–61; political pressures on, 250; swap lines, 231–35. *See also* central bank digital currencies (CBDC); *and specific central banks*
Chaney, Thomas, 228
Chávez, Hugo, 129
Cheney, Dick (Vice President, United States), 264, 326 n.5
chess, xii, 14, 15, 17, 21, 23, 44, 52, 58, 123, 168, 177, 191, 204, 252, 259, 260, 267, 289
Chile, 169, 304 n.3
China, 20, 162–63, 183, 185, 201, 211, 217–18, 285–86; Beidaihe, 88, 89; capital controls in, 71, 84; central control in, 65, 95; China Development Forum, 99; China Development Research Foundation, 93–95; Chinese Executive Leadership Academy Pudong, 87–88; Communist Party in, 83; corruption in, 83; current account surplus, 165; data collection in, 203; debt of, 107; Diaoyutai State Guesthouse, 76, 94; economy of, 7–8, 37, 65–73, 89–90, 94–95,

336

96–109; exchange rate, 159, 289–90; financial crisis, 91–92; forecasting economy of, 74–81; IMF and, 178; infrastructure in, 66–67, 87, 98–99, 105–6; local funding vehicles in, 105, 107; local government financing vehicles (LGFVs), 105; merit-based promotions, 108; migration control in, 72–73, 103, 163; military capacity of, 67, 239; national income of, 86–87; opening of, 68–69; Politburo, 109; Politburo Standing Committee, 109; real estate in, 99–105, 106; taxes in, property, 105, 107; Tianjin, 104; trade surplus, 70, 73, 112; weaponization of dollar reserves, 236. *See also* Hong Kong; People's Bank of China; renminbi (China)

Chinn, Menzie, 84

Civil War, 279

Clinton, Bill (President, United States), 133, 215, 281

Commons, Kim (International Master, Chess), xii

Conference Board, 294 n.16

Connally, John (Treasury Secretary, United States), x, 46

convenience yield, 263

Cooper, Richard, 230

Corbyn, Jeremy, 129

COVID pandemic. *See* pandemic

Crazy Rich Asians, 205

Croatia, 15

Crockett, Andrew (General Manager, Bank for International Settlements), 77–78

CrowdStrike outage, 201

Crypto.com, 189

cryptocurrencies, 182–98, 289, 290; blockchain transactions, 184–85, 186, 193, 196; exchanges, 184–85, 188, 193, 198; fiat currency compared, 182–85; KodakCoin, 28–29; Libra, 200; regulation of, 184, 185, 186, 187; tokens, 316 n.4; tracing transactions, 193, 196; underground economy and, 182, 189–94; value of, 192–93, 195–96; as vehicle currency, 194

currencies: debasement of, 2–3; fiat, 47, 183–84; global, 173–81; history of, 185; paper money, 185; reserve, 176, 213; safe, 156, 242; vehicle, 4, 47, 194. *See also* central bank digital currencies (CBDC); cryptocurrencies; dominant currency; *and specific currencies*

currency board, 148

currency unions, 46–47, 154–55. *See also* European Union

current account, 135, 220, 302 n.10, 309 n.15

Curry, Stephen, 189

Curucu, Stephanie, 225

cybersecurity, 201

Cyprus, 285

Czech Republic, 46

Dai Xianglong (Governor, People's Bank of China), 79

Damon, Matt, 189

Danmarks Nationalbank, 322 n.9

dark-web markets, 193

David, Larry, 188

debt, government, 280; China, 107; and growth, 57, 280, 329 n.14; hidden, 56, 265; Japan, 38–39; safe, 263; United States, 211–12, 215–17, 220–22, 262–72, 274, 278, 279, 290

debt supercycles, 284–85, 286

default, 278–79; by Argentina, 151; by Brazil, 233; by France, 3, 233; by Germany, 233; by Japan, 233; by Mexico, 233; by The Netherlands, 3; by Spain, 3; Trinity, 3; by U. K., 61, 233; by U. S., 264

deflation, 35

de Gaulle, Charles, 213

DeLong, Brad, 268

Democratic Republic of Congo, 127

Deng Xiaoping (President, China), 20, 69

INDEX

Denmark, 46, 47, 322 n.9
Detroit, Michigan, 28
Deutsche Bundesbank, 53, 120, 251, 252
deutsche mark (Germany), 42, 53, 120, 299 n.6
Diamond, Douglas, 150
"Diamond-Dyvig" multiple-equilibrium, 150
digital currencies. *See* central bank digital currencies (CBDC); cryptocurrencies
Dimon, Jamie, 189
disinflation, 254
Dog Day Afternoon, 168
dollar (Hong Kong), 138
dollar (U. S.), 111; as collateral, 211–12; dominance of, xii, 1–2, 4–10, 47, 61, 289; gold standard and, x, 45, 236, 257, 264; high valuation of, 80; large-denomination notes, 190, 195; renminbi decoupling from, 67–68, 110–13. *See also* dominant currency
dominant currency, 284; benefits of having, 211–18; borrowing capacity of, 213–17; costs of being, 236–43; creation of, 1–10; disproportionate losses in downturn, 237; exorbitant privilege of, 4, 212, 219–28; global payments system leverage with, 217; military prowess and, 217–18, 237–41
Dooley, Michael, 161–62
Dornbusch, Rudiger, 54, 91, 119, 131, 132, 298 n.26, 307 n.2
drachma (Greece), 299 n.6
Draghi, Mario (President, ECB), 59, 60; Draghi Report, 51
Druckenmiller, Stanley, 270
Dvorkovich, Arkady (Deputy Prime Minister, Russian Federation), 23, 295 n.15
Dvorkovich, Vladimer (International Chess Arbiter), 23
Dybvig, Philip, 150

Eastern Caribbean Monetary Union, 46–47
Eastman Kodak Company, 28–29, 200–201
Eaton, Jon, 154

Economist, 66, 270
Eichengreen, Barry, 173
emerging markets, 166–70, 258
escudo (Portugal), 299 n.6
euro, 111, 289; challenges of, 43, 49; creation of, 42–43, 45, 46, 53–54, 120–21, 219–20; digital, 203; future of, 291; strengths of, 51–52; success of, 47
Eurodollar, 119–20
European Central Bank, 49, 59–60, 227, 252, 255–56, 322 n.9; digital currency, 199, 203; independence of, 51–52
European Commission, 52; *One Market, One Money,* 44, 54, 300 n.19
European Union, 46, 47, 281; debt crisis (2010–2012), 54, 55–60, 118, 285; deposit insurance in, 49; development of, 120–22; economy of, 7, 44, 49–51; EU bonds, 49; fiscal authority in, 49, 59, 60; military power of, 61, 240–41; NextGenerationEU, 60; technical innovation in, 61; underground economy in, 191–92. *See also* euro; European Central Bank
Evergrande (China), 66
exchange rate, 5, 86; crawling peg, 111, 112, 131; currency board, 148; flexible, 71, 111, 139, 154, 159, 166, 169; floating, 111, 113, 118–19, 120; inflation-adjusted, 224; managed float, 112; volatility of, 119. *See also* fixed exchange rate
exchange rate anchor, 127
exchange stabilization fund, 133

Facebook, 94; Libra cryptocurrency, 200
Faia, Ester, 225
Federal Reserve Bank of New York, 140
Federal Reserve (U. S.), x, 2, 59, 255, 283, 290; bailouts, 55, 140, 265; digital currency, 200, 203, 204; establishment of, 51; impact of actions, 229–33; independence of, 51, 248, 251, 252; interest rate policy,

338

INDEX

169–70, 248; mandate of, 229, 248, 258; quantitative easing, 257; social justice policies and, 247–48, 255–56; swap lines, 231–35
FedNow, 203
Feige, Edgar, 191
Feldstein, Martin (President, National Bureau of Economic Research), 43, 49, 54
Ferguson, Niall, 154, 316 n.1
Ferranti, Matthew, 304 n.4; 322 n.1
fiat currency, 47, 183–84
Finland, 122–23, 299 n.6
Fischer, Bobby (World Chess Champion), 21, 177, 260
Fischer, Stanley (Vice-Chair, Federal Reserve), 132, 134, 152, 303 n.6
Fitzsimmons, Bill, 82
fixed exchange rate, 79, 111; fragility of, 118, 133, 134, 137, 139, 146, 152; inflation control through, 126–27; lure of, 117–25
florin (Netherlands), 1
Folkerts-Landau, David, 161–62
Fraga, Arminio, 142–43
franc (Belgium), 299 n.6
franc (France), 42, 120, 124, 299 n.6
franc (Luxembourg), 299 n.6
franc (Switzerland), 242
France, 44, 45, 54, 226, 281; Banque de France, 55, 120–21; default by (1557), 3; default by (1931), 233; economy of, 50; Golden Room, 55; IMF and, 178; military spending by, 237, 239, 241; National Defense and Armed Forces Committee, 239. *See also* franc (France)
Friedman, Milton, 16, 20, 118–19, 254, 271
FTX, 187–89
Fujiphotofilm, 28, 29

Gagarin, Yuri, 14
Galbraith, James K., 129
Garber, Peter, 161–62
General Motors, 28

General Telephone and Electric, 27
Gensler, Gary (Chair, SEC), 188
Germany, 44, 54, 58, 124, 221, 286; deutsche mark (Germany); Bundeskanzleramt, 57; default by, 233; Detlev Rohwedder Building, 57; economy of, 50; hyperinflation history of, 53, 183; IMF and, 178; military spending by, 237. *See also* Deutsche Bundesbank
Gertler, Mark, 306 n.22, 321 n.16
Ghana, 194
Giavazzi, Francesco, 54
Giscard d'Estaing, Valéry (President, France), 212–13, 219–20
Glaeser, Ed, 99
global currency, 173–81; SDR, 175–80
global financial crisis (2009), xii, 55–56, 178, 231, 232, 234, 242
global financial crisis, predicting, 55, 286
globalization, 313 n.5
Goodhart, Charles, 277
Gopinath, Gita (First Deputy Managing Director, IMF), 76–77, 247
Gordon, Robert J., 267
Gore, Al (Vice-President, United States), 274
Gourinchas, Pierre-Olivier (Chief Economist, IMF), 222, 223, 225, 247, 248
Graf von Luckner, Clemens, 193, 194
Greece, 50; drachma, 299 n.6; financial crisis, 42, 43, 54, 56, 58, 118, 285; underground economy in, 192
Greenblatt, Richard, 259
Greenland, 47
Greenspan, Alan (Chair, Federal Reserve), 163–64, 242–43; on speaking after Greenspan, 164
Griliches, Zvi, 23
guilder (Netherlands), 1, 299 n.6
Guriev, Sergei, 23–24

Hamel, Gary, 27
Hansen, Alvin, 267

INDEX

Harari, Yuval Noah: *Sapiens,* 182, 183
Hariri, Rafic (Prime Minister, Lebanon), 145–47
Harris, Max: *Monetary War and Peace,* 226, 293 n.7, 320 n.12
Hassan, Tarek, 228
Hausmann, Ricardo, 224–25
Heimann, John, 195
Henry VIII (King of England), 2–3
Hezbollah, 147, 194
Holmes, Elizabeth (Theranos), 188
Hong Kong, 31, 37, 97, 138–39, 148, 152, 157, 205, 310 n.9
Hong Kong Monetary Authority, 138, 148
Hope, Bradley: *Billion Dollar Whale,* 205
Horioka, Charles, 54
Hungary, 46
hyperinflation, 20, 53, 126–33, 183
hyryvnia (Ukraine), 195

IBM Deep Blue, 259
Iceland, 56, 285, 301 n.26
Ilzetzki, Ethan, 6, 40, 48, 307 n.4
immigration, 8, 227–28, 274, 278
India, 2, 5, 8, 40, 66, 72, 101, 108, 155, 156, 202, 229
Indonesia, 74, 118, 136, 165
inflation, 2, 35, 126, 158, 253–54, 279; in Europe, 45–46, 120; in Germany, 120; interest rates and, 166, 248, 252, 275–76; in U. S., 46, 119, 253. *See also* hyperinflation
inflation targeting, 142–43, 158
infrastructure: in China, 66–67, 87, 98–99, 105–6; return on investment, 106
insurance, deposit, 49, 241–43
interest rates, x–xi, 144, 249–50, 270; inflation and, 166, 248, 252, 275; lower-forever, 264, 273–88, 290; volatility of, 274, 276
International Monetary Fund, 113, 131, 136, 230–31; Articles of Agreement, 156; board of, 178; China Division, 76; debt forgiveness, 179; establishment of, 177; lending rate, 176; loans from, 9, 56, 139, 143, 148, 150, 152; Research Department, 72; Rogoff employment at, 22, 52, 178; SDR, 175–80; *World Economic Outlook,* 75, 151

Iran, 201
Ireland, 54, 55, 56, 285, 299 n.6
Issing, Otmar (Member of Board and Research Director, ECB), 52–53, 120, 122
Italy, 44, 50, 54, 58, 286; financial crisis, 54, 56, 118, 124; military spending by, 237; underground economy in, 192. *See also* lira (Italy)
Ito, Hiro, 84
Itskhoki, Oleg, 307 n.1

Japan, 156, 211, 221, 239, 286; asset bubble, 34; Bank of Japan Act (1997), 158; currency reserves of, 156, 157; debt of, 38–39, 269, 278; decreasing returns to investment, 36–37; default by, 233; deflation in, 35; economy of, 25–41, 155; financial crisis (1992), 37–38, 66; IMF and, 178; import restrictions by, 28; innovation in, 27–28, 36; Nikkei 225 stock index, 26, 31; Plaza Accord, 30, 73, 157; population of, 36, 38; trade surpluses, 29–30. *See also* Bank of Japan; yen (Japan)
Jen, Gish: *Thank You, Mr. Nixon,* 68–69
Jiang, Zhengyang, 216
Jiang Zemin (President, China), 88–90
Jin, Keyu, 305 n.11
Johnson, Lyndon (President, United States), 250
Johnson, Rob, 123
Jordan, 134
Jordan, Michael, 213
Jorgensen, Annette Vissing, 212

Kasparov, Garry (World Chess Champion), 259, 260, 267–68
Kelton, Stephanie: *Deficit Myth, The,* 270–71

INDEX

Kenen, Peter, 43, 220
Keynes, John Maynard, 124, 173, 174, 214
Khan, Lina (Head, FTC), 187
Khrushchev, Nikita (Premier, Soviet Union), 20
Kindleberger, Charles, 225, 330 n.22
Kirchner, Néstor (President, Argentina), 155
KodakCoin, 28–29
Köhler, Horst (Managing Director, IMF), 143, 146
Koo, Richard, 306 n.22
Korea, 31, 37, 97, 235; financial crisis, 74, 118, 136. *See also* Bank of Korea; won (Korea)
Kosovo, 15
Kosygin, Alexei, 20
Krishnamurthy, Arvind, 212, 216
krona (Sweden), 123
krone (Denmark), 47
Krugman, Paul, 24, 122, 280, 281
Kuwait, 221
Kydland, Finn: "Rules Rather than Discretion," 251

Laffer curve, 22
Lagarde, Christine (President, ECB), 231
Lance Rogoff, Natasha, 21–22, 24, 82, 83, 88, 89, 140, 248; *Muppets in Moscow,* 24;~*Russian Millennials Speak Openly About America,* 24
Larsen, Bent (chess grandmaster), 21, 289
Lebanon, 145–47, 194
Lehman Brothers, 55
Lew, Jack (Treasury Secretary, United States), 270
Lewis, Arthur, 72
Lewis transition, 72
Li Keqiang (Prime Minister, China), 94
Lin, Justin (Chief Economist, World Bank), 87
lira (Italy), 42, 124, 299 n.6
Long-Term Capital Management (LTCM), 139–40
lowflation, 254

Lucas, Robert, 233, 321 n.16
Lula da Silva, Luiz (President, Brazil), 143, 155
Lu Mai, 93
Lustig, Hanno, 216
Luxembourg, 44, 299 n.6

Maastricht treaty, 51–52
Macron, Emmanuel (President, France), 195, 240, 241
Maddison, Angus, 18, 67
Madison, James (President, United States): *Federalist Papers,* 241
Maduro, Nicolás (President, Venezuela), 3, 129
Malaysia, 136–37, 159
Mao Zedong (Chairman, Chinese Communist Party), 69
markka (Finland), 299 n.6
Marshall reconstruction plan, 226
Marx, Karl, 18
Mau, Vladimir, 24
McGrattan, Ellen, 225
McKinnon, Ronald, 111, 112
Meade, James, 121
Meese, Richard, 34
Meltzer, Allan, 257
Merkel, Angela (Chancellor, Germany), 57–58, 59
Mexico, 165, 235; Banco de México, 142, 232, 322 n.9; default by, 233; financial crisis (1994), 118, 130–33
Mian, Atif, 281
middle-income trap, 96–97
Miller, Chris: *Chip Wars,* 61
Miller, G. William (Chair, Federal Reserve Board), 252
Mnuchin, Steven (Treasury Secretary, United States), 270
modern monetary theory, 270, 271, 273, 328 n.25
Modigliani, Franco, 175

INDEX

Mohamad, Mahathir (Prime Minister, Malaysia), 136
Monetary Authority of Singapore, 322 n.9; CBDC contest, 205–7
Montias, J. Michael, 17
Moynihan, Daniel Patrick (U.S. Senator), 15
Mozhin, Aleksei, 315 n.14
Mugabe, Roberto (President, Zimbabwe), 3
Mundell, Robert, 111, 112, 118, 121, 169, 307 n.2
Musk, Elon, 189

National Electronics Corporation, 27
NATO, 239, 240
Netherlands, The, 44, 54, 58, 237; default by (1557), 3; economy of, 50; florin, 1; guilder, 1, 299 n.6
New Keynesianism, 249
Newton, Isaac, 318 n.8
New United Motor Manufacturing, 28
New Zealand, 169, 232
Nigeria, 194
"Nine Million Bicycles," 76
Nixon, Richard (President, United States), 19, 45, 68, 220
Nordhaus, William, 324 n.5
Norges Bank, 322 n.9
Norris, Floyd, 287
North, Douglas, 214
North American Free Trade Agreement (NAFTA), 130, 131
North Korea, 201

Obama, Barack (President, United States), 216, 281, 303 n.6
Obstfeld, Maurice, 43, 124, 133, 141, 220; *Foundations of International Macroeconomics*, 85, 134
Ocasio-Cortez, Alexandria (Member, U.S. House of Representatives), 271
Olson, Mancur, 240
Ortiz, David, 189

Ortiz, Guillermo (Governor, Banco de Mexico), 142
Osaka, Naomi, 189

pandemic, 49, 60, 178, 231, 233, 234, 242, 281
Pappada, Francesco, 191
Paul, Ron (U.S. Senator): *End the Fed*, 257
Pebble Beach Golf Links, 32
Penn World Tables, 96, 294 n.16
People's Bank of China, 79, 83–84, 112; e-CNY, 199, 204; Management of Short-Term Capital Movements and Capital Account Liberalization seminar, 74; renminbi swap lines, 234; seminar presentation at (2005), 82–87
peseta (Spain), 2, 120, 124, 299 n.6
peso (Argentina), 148
peso (Mexico), 131, 133
Phillips, A. W., 324 n.10
Phillips curve, 324 n.10
Plaza Accord, 30, 73, 157
Poland, 17, 46
Pollin, Robert, 129, 329 n.14
Polo, Marco, 183, 185
populism, 274
Porter, Michael: *Competitive Advantage of Nations, The*, 27
Portugal, 50, 54, 56, 299 n.6
pound (Ireland), 299 n.6
pound sterling (U. K.), 1, 3, 47, 61, 119, 330 n.20
Powell, Jay (Chair, Federal Reserve Board), 247, 248
Prahalad, C. K., 27
Prescott, Edward, 225; "Rules Rather than Discretion," 251
purchasing power parity (PPP), 7, 38, 50, 67, 307 n.1
Putin, Vladimir (President, Russian Federation), 22, 24, 118

Queen's Gambit, The, 58, 260

INDEX

Rachel, Lukasz: "Secular Stagnation in the Industrialized World," 270, 275
Rajan, Raghuram (Governor, Reserve Bank of India), 24, 229
Ramaswamy, Vivek, 258
ransomware, 193
Reagan, Ronald (President, United States), 19, 215, 221, 257
real (Brazil), 140, 142
Reinhart, Carmen, 6, 40, 48, 55, 57, 160, 164, 193, 279, 286, 307 n.4; "Fear of Floating," 80–81; *This Time Is Different,* ix, 38, 82, 262, 306 n.22
renminbi (China), 5, 47, 66, 110, 111, 155, 289; artificial valuation of, 70–71, 162–63; bloc, 41; decoupling from dollar, 67–68, 110–13; digital, 203–4; exchange rate, 71, 72, 79, 86, 112, 113
repression, financial, 262–63, 277, 279
Reserve Bank of Australia, 322 n.9
Reserve Bank of New Zealand, 232
reserve currency, 176, 213
reserves, currency, 4, 47, 138, 156–57, 161
Reshevsky, Samuel, 23
Rey, Hélène, 166, 167, 168, 169, 222, 223
Road to Singapore, The, 205
Robinson, David, 74–76, 79, 107
Rochester, New York, 28–29, 69, 104, 201, 227, 296 n.10
Rockefeller Center, 32
Rogoff, Gabriel, 88, 89, 248
Rogoff, Juliana, 88, 89, 90, 248
Romania, 46
Roosevelt, Franklin (President, United States), 264
Rossi, Barbara, 274, 275, 276
Rostow, Walter, 15–16, 19
Roubini, Nouriel, 55, 189
Rubin, Robert (Treasury Secretary, United States), 133
ruble (Russia), 13, 20
rupiah (Indonesia), 136

Russia, 5, 194, 201, 211, 285; chess, adoration of, 21; corruption in, 19, 83; economy of, 22–23; financial crisis (1998), 118, 139; Gaidar Forum presentation (2020), 24; hyperinflation in, 20; IMF and, 178; invasion of Ukraine, 24, 61, 238; media repression in, 23; New Economic School lecture (2006), 23; Russia Forum presentation (2012), 24; sanctions on, 217; Soviet Union economy, 13–21

Sachs, Jeffrey, 126–27, 141, 144
Salant, Walter, 213–14, 236
Salant-Henderson-Krugman model, 122
Samuelson, Paul, 14–15, 19
satoshi, 193
Saudi Arabia, 152, 221
Schaede, Ulrike, 40
Schäuble, Wolfgang (Finance Minister, Germany), 57, 58
schilling (Austria), 299 n.6
Schmelzing, Paul, 274, 275, 276
SDR (special drawing right), 175–80
Sea Hawk, The, 3
secular stagnation, 266–68, 275, 343
Serbia, 15
Shleifer, Andrei, 99, 226
Silicon Valley Bank, 202
Singapore, 31, 37, 97, 159, 205, 235. *See also* Monetary Authority of Singapore
SIX, 3
Skidelsky, Robert, 269
Slick, Grace (singer/songwriter), xii
Solow, Robert, 37
Soros, George, 123, 124, 137, 142, 177
South Africa, 156, 165
South Korea. *See* Korea
Soviet Union: economy of, 13–21
Spain, 3, 54, 237; financial crisis, 54, 55, 118, 124, 285; Trinity Default, 3. *See also* peseta (Spain)
Spassky, Boris (World Chess Champion), 21

INDEX

special drawing right (SDR), 175–80
stablecoins, 196–98
Star Trek, 174: Latinuum currency, 314 n.4
Stiglitz, Joseph, 129, 177, 303 n.6; *Globalization and Its Discontents,* 78
stock exchanges, 299 n.5
Stockholm International Peace Research Institute, 238
Sturzenegger, Federico, 224–25
Sufi, Amir, 281
Summers, Larry (Treasury Secretary, United States), 57–58, 133, 266; "Secular Stagnation in the Industrialized World," 270, 275
Sveriges Riksbank (Sweden), 123–24, 322 n.9
Sweden, 46, 286; Riksbank, 123–24, 322 n.9; financial crisis, 123–24
Swiss National Bank, 322 n.9
Switzerland, 242, 322 n.9

Taiwan, 31, 37
Taylor, John B., 327 n.15
Taylor rule, 327 n.15
tether, 196, 197
Thailand, 133; financial crisis, 74, 118, 134–36
Theranos: Elizabeth Holmes, 188
Thiel, Peter, 267
Tito, Josip Broz (President, Yugoslavia), 15
Tobin, James, 313 n.12
Toyota, 28
Treasury Direct, 318 n.3
Treaty of Rome (1957), 44
Triffin, Robert, 175, 282, 330 n.22
Triffin dilemma, 282–84
Trilemma (Impossible Trinity), 118, 169
Tripartite Agreement (1936), 293 n.7
Truman, Ted, 315 n.11
Trump, Donald (President, United States), 8, 216, 239, 257, 291
Tufte, Edward, 324 n.5
Turkey, 144, 165, 183

Ukraine, 195; invasion of, 24, 61, 238
Ulitsa Sesam, 22, 24, 140–41
underground economy, 182, 189–94, 204–5
United Kingdom (U. K.), 3–4, 9, 47, 204, 237; Brexit, 46; debt of, 330 n.20; default by (1931), 61, 233; financial capital of Europe, 226–27; financial crisis, 9, 124; Glorious Revolution (1688), 214; IMF and, 9, 178; laws of, 226. *See also* Bank of England; pound sterling (U. K.)
United States (U. S.): borrowing capacity of, 213–14; Congressional Budget Office (CBO), 52, 216, 264; Constitutional Convention (1787), 241; debt, federal, 211–12, 215–17, 220–22, 262–72, 274, 278, 279, 290; debt-to-GDP ratio, 216, 249, 280; default by, 264; deficit of current account, 163, 164, 165, 220–21, 277, 279, 281; economy of, 5–7, 8; exchange stabilization fund, 133; financial markets of, 8, 211; Great Inflation, 215; Great Society programs, 250; IMF and, 178, 230–31; immigration to, 8, 227–28, 278; inequality in, 313 n.5; inflation in, 46, 119, 253; Inflation Reduction Act, 8; laws of, 226; military prowess of, 211, 217–18, 237–41; Obamacare, 281; risk, attitude towards, 223–24, 225, 228; sanctions, weaponization using, 217; Securities and Exchange Commission, 188, 204; Social Security, 319 n.11; stimulus package, 281; Treasury bills, 211–12, 263; Treasury Department, 149–50, 270; university system of, 8, 228; Vietnam War, 250. *See also* dollar (U. S.); Federal Reserve (U. S.)
USDC (USD coin), 196

value-added tax (VAT), 191
vehicle currency, 4, 47, 194
Venezuela, 155, 194; hyperinflation in, 3, 128–30, 183
Vietnam, 165

INDEX

Vishny, Robert, 226
Vogel, Ezra: *Japan as Number One: Lessons for America*, 27
Volcker, Paul (Chair, Federal Reserve Board), 229, 249, 250, 251, 275
von der Leyen, Ursula (President, European Commission), 241

Wall Street Journal, 265
Warren, Elizabeth (U.S. Senator), 187
Washington, George (President, United States), 241
Weingast, Barry, 214
Weinstein, Norman, 123
Weitzman, Martin, 17
Werner, Alejandro, 131, 132
West African Economic and Monetary Union, 46–47
White, Harry Dexter, 174
Wolf of Wall Street, The, 205
won (Korea), 112, 113, 136
World Bank, 139, 176, 177, 190
World Trade Organization, 69
Wright, Tom: *Billion Dollar Whale*, 205
Wu Xiaoling, Madame (Vice-Governor, People's Bank of China), 83–84

Xerox, 28, 29
Xi Jinping (President, China), 80, 83, 109

Yam, Joseph (Chief Executive, Hong Kong Monetary Authority), 138
Yang, Yuanchen, 98, 99–100, 102, 104; "Peak China Housing," 66, 100
Yaron, Amir (Governor, Bank of Israel), 247
Yau, Shing-Tung, 82, 88
Yellen, Janet (Treasury Secretary, United States), 177, 270
yen (Japan), 26, 34, 47, 111; appreciation of, 35, 36; floating exchange rate, 112, 113; forced appreciation of, 25, 30, 31–32, 40, 157; as safe currency, 40–41, 242
Yugoslavia, 15

Zeckhauser, Richard, 240
Zedillo, Ernesto (President, Mexico), 132
Zhou Xiaochuan (Governor, People's Bank of China), 84–86, 89–90
Zhu Rongji (Premier, China), 75, 77–79, 98
Zimbabwe, 3, 127, 183
Zipf's law, 103
Zuckerberg, Mark, 94
Zweig, Stefan: "The Royal Game," 52–53